WORSHIP IN ISRAEL

WORSHIP IN ISRAEL

A Cultic History of the Old Testament

by

HANS-JOACHIM KRAUS

Translated by

GEOFFREY BUSWELL

OXFORD

BASIL BLACKWELL

MCMLXVI

FIRST PRINTED IN 1966

PRINTED IN GREAT BRITAIN IN THE CITY OF OXFORD
AT THE ALDEN PRESS

PREFACE

This book, which is now appearing in an English version, was published in Munich by the Chr. Kaiser Verlag in 1962. In outlining the history of worship in the Old Testament I had three main aims in mind:

1. To bring together the references to the worship of Israel within the Old Testament, to consider them from the standpoint of historical criticism and try to evaluate them.
2. To consider the many different investigations into 'Worship in Israel' made by Old Testament scholars, to examine them critically and take account of them in my presentation of the facts.
3. To summarize my own studies on the subject, on which I have been engaged for a good number of years. Where I have set down various more general reflections and theories, I hope these passages will help to encourage discussion among scholars of what are in some cases very complicated problems.

I am grateful to the translator for the care he has taken to bring out my meaning, and to the publishers for making this book available to English readers as a contribution to the further study and teaching of the Old Testament.

Hamburg, February 1965 HANS-JOACHIM KRAUS

CONTENTS

	Page
PREFACE	v
ABBREVIATIONS	x

CHAPTER I.—INTRODUCTION

1. Historical Survey of the Study of Old Testament Worship ... 1
   (*a*) The Symbolism of the Cult 1
   (*b*) Julius Wellhausen 4
   (*c*) The Influence of Archaeological Discoveries on the Study of Old Testament Worship 6
   (*d*) The Results of Form Criticism 10
   (*e*) The Phenomenon of the Cult 14
   (*f*) Trends in Recent Studies of the Cult 16
2. Problems of Approach and Presentation 19
   (*a*) A Phenomenology or History of the Cult? 19
   (*b*) Ancient Eastern Sources 21
   (*c*) The Method of Form Criticism 22
   (*d*) Institutions and Regulations Governing Daily Life 23
   (*e*) The Method of Presentation 24

CHAPTER II.—CULTIC CALENDARS AND REGULATIONS

1. The Cultic Calendars in the Pentateuch 26
   (*a*) Exodus xxiii. 10–19 26
   (*b*) Exodus xxxiv. 18–26 28
   (*c*) Deuteronomy xvi. 1–17 30
   (*d*) Leviticus xxiii. 4–44 32
   (*e*) Numbers xxviii and xxix 35
   (*f*) Aspects of Canaanite Religion 36
   (*g*) Problems Connected with the Calendar 43
2. The Feast of the Passover and of Unleavened Bread 45
   (*a*) The Origin and 'Historicizing' of the Passover Rite 45
   (*b*) The Feast of Unleavened Bread as an Annual Feast in Ancient Israel... 47
   (*c*) The Feast of the Passover and of Unleavened Bread 49
3. The Feast of Weeks 55
   (*a*) The Harvest Festival 56
   (*b*) Post-exilic and Late Jewish Traditions 58
4. The Autumn Festival 61
   (*a*) The Nature Festival 61
   (*b*) The First Day of the Seventh Month 66
   (*c*) The Great Feast of Atonement 68

5. Sabbatical Year and Year of Jubilee ... 70
(*a*) The Meaning of the Institutions ... 70
(*b*) Deuteronomy xxxi. 9–13 ... 74
(*c*) Later Outworkings of the Regulations Concerning the Sabbatical Year ... 75
6. New Moon and Sabbath ... 76
(*a*) The New Moon ... 76
(*b*) The Sabbath ... 78
(*c*) Theories about the Origin of the Sabbath ... 81
(*d*) The Number Seven in Ugarit ... 85
(*e*) The Meaning of the Sabbath Law in the Exilic and Post-exilic Periods ... 87
7. Hanukkah and Purim ... 88
(*a*) Hanukkah ... 88
(*b*) Purim ... 91

CHAPTER III.—THE CULTIC OFFICIALS AND THE SACRIFICIAL SYSTEM

1. The Cultic Officials ... 93
(*a*) The Priests ... 93
(*b*) Prophets ... 101
2. The Sacrificial System ... 112
(*a*) The Gift Offering ... 113
(*b*) The Peace Offering... 118
(*c*) Other Types of Sacrifice ... 121
(*d*) The Significance of the Sacrificial System ... 122

CHAPTER IV.—THE CENTRAL SANCTUARIES OF ISRAEL AND THEIR CULTIC TRADITIONS

1. Ark and Tent ... 125
(*a*) The Ark ... 125
(*b*) The Sacred Tent ... 128
2. Shechem ... 134
(*a*) Canaanite Worship... 134
(*b*) Joshua xxiv ... 136
(*c*) Deuteronomy xxvii... 141
(*d*) The Significance of Shechem in Later Times ... 145
3. Bethel ... 146
(*a*) The Ancient Israelite Sanctuary ... 146
(*b*) The Official Sanctuary of the Northern Kingdom ... 148
4. Gilgal ... 152
(*a*) Gilgal and the Tradition of the Conquest ... 152
(*b*) The Crossing of the Jordan ... 154
(*c*) Jericho ... 159
(*d*) The Worship at Gilgal ... 161

5. Israelite Cultic Centres in the Early Period 165
(*a*) Mount Tabor 165
(*b*) Beersheba 172
(*c*) Mizpah 173
6. Shiloh 173
(*a*) The Worship at Shiloh 173
(*b*) The Fate of the Ark 177

CHAPTER V.—THE CULTIC TRADITIONS OF JERUSALEM

1. The Institution of the Official Cult 179
(*a*) The Election of David 179
(*b*) The Election of Jerusalem... 181
(*c*) The Royal Festival on Mount Zion 183
2. The Ancient Israelite Traditions 188
(*a*) The Divine Law 188
(*b*) The Davidic Covenant and the Sinaitic Covenant 189
3. The Canaanite-Jebusite Cultic Traditions 201
(*a*) The Sacred Mount of God 201
(*b*) The Kingship of God 203
(*c*) A 'Festival of Yahweh's Enthronement'? 205
4. The Festival Cult of Jerusalem 208
(*a*) The Structure of a Festival 208
(*b*) The Individual in the Festival Cult 218
5. Festivals for Special Occasions 222
(*a*) The Enthronement of a King 222
(*b*) Lamentation and Thanksgiving by the People 225
(*c*) The Lament for the Destruction of Jerusalem 226
6. The Post-exilic Cultic Community 229
(*a*) Worship during the Exile 229
(*b*) The Restoration of the Sanctuary 231
(*c*) The Life of the Post-exilic Cultic Community 234

INDEXES 239

LIST OF ABBREVIATIONS

AcOr	*Acta Orientalia*
AJSL	*American Journal of Semitic Languages and Literatures*
ANVAO	*Avhandlinger utgitt av Det Norske Videnkaps-Akademi i Oslo*
AO	*Der Alte Orient*
ARW	*Archiv für Religionswissenschaft*
ATA	Alttestamentliche Abhandlungen
ATANT	Abhandlungen zur Theologie des Alten und Neuen Testaments
ATD	Das Alte Testament Deutsch
BA	*The Biblical Archaeologist*
BASOR	*Bulletin of the American Schools of Oriental Research*
BHT	Beiträge zur historischen Theologie
BJRL	*Bulletin of the John Rylands Library*
BK	Biblischer Kommentar
BWANT	Beiträge zur Wissenschaft vom Alten und Neuen Testament
BZ	*Biblische Zeitschrift*
BZAW	Beihefte zur *Zeitschrift für die alttestamentliche Wissenschaft*
CBQ	*Catholic Biblical Quarterly*
DLZ	*Deutsche Literaturzeitung*
EvTh	*Evangelische Theologie*
FRLANT	Forschungen zur Religion und Literatur des Alten und Neuen Testaments
HAT	Handbuch zum Alten Testament
HK	Handkommentar zum Alten Testament
HUCA	*Hebrew Union College Annual*
IEJ	*Israel Exploration Journal*
JAOS	*Journal of the American Oriental Society*
JBL	*Journal of Biblical Literature*
JDAI	*Jahrbuch des deutschen archäologischen Instituts*
JNES	*Journal of Near Eastern Studies*
JPOS	*Journal of the Palestine Oriental Society*
JTS	*Journal of Theological Studies*
NKZ	*Neue Kirchliche Zeitschrift*
NRT	*Nouvelle Revue Théologique*
Or	*Orientalia*
OTS	*Oudtestamentische Studiën*
PEQ	*Palestine Exploration Quarterly*
PJB	*Palästinajahrbuch des deutschen evangelischen Instituts für Altertumswissenschaft des Heiligen Landes zu Jerusalem*
RB	*Revue Biblique*
RGG	*Die Religion in Geschichte und Gegenwart*
RHPR	*Revue d'Histoire et de Philosophie Religieuses*
SAT	Die Schriften des Alten Testaments in Auswahl
SGK	Schriften der Königsberger gelehrten Gesellschaft
SNVAO	Skrifter utgitt av Det Norske Videnskaps-Akademi i Oslo

LIST OF ABBREVIATIONS

StTh	*Studia Theologica*
ThA	Theologische Arbeiten
ThB	*Theologische Bücherei*
ThLZ	*Theologische Literaturzeitung*
ThR	*Theologische Rundschau*
ThW	*Theologisches Wörterbuch*
ThZ	*Theologische Zeitschrift*
VT	*Vetus Testamentum*
WM	*Wiener Zeitschrift für die Kunde des Morgenlandes*
WMANT	Wissenschaftliche Monographien zum Alten und Neuen Testament
ZAW	*Zeitschrift für die alttestamentliche Wissenschaft*
ZDPV	*Zeitschrift des deutschen Palästina Vereins*
ZKG	*Zeitschrift für Kirchengeschichte*
ZThK	*Zeitschrift für Theologie und Kirche*

CHAPTER ONE

INTRODUCTION

1. Historical Survey of the Study of Old Testament Worship

(a) *The Symbolism of the Cult*

The Christian Church in every age has approached Old Testament worship primarily through the Letter to the Hebrews. In Israel's practice of worship the Church has seen the shadow and outline of that final saving, redemptive work that was accomplished by Jesus Christ. Many allegorizing approaches have been made by interpreters in an attempt to penetrate and understand the mystery of the cultic institutions of the Old Testament, which point beyond themselves to the future. The impulse to do this was provided by passages such as Heb. viii. 5, 6; ix. 11; x. 1, etc.[1]

Even in the Age of Enlightenment, which in many respects broke with the traditional principles of interpretation that prevailed in the Church, there was no essential change in the understanding of Old Testament worship.[2] A rational symbolism took the place of allegory. The new insights provided by the study of history and of comparative religion could not yet be brought to bear on this field of research, although the foundations for these new interpretations were already being laid. There appeared in the first half of the nineteenth century a work in two volumes which shows quite clearly the way that was being taken by the study of Old Testament worship and the goal towards which it was travelling. K. C. W. F. Bähr's *Symbolik des mosaischen Cultus* was published in 1837. This lengthy work shows traces of earlier approaches to the subject and provides us with a convenient and comprehensive summary of them. We can see the rationalistic attempts at interpretation which stamp the whole account, and the ardour of Romantic feeling and sympathy, but also the first traces of the historical, genetic understanding of the phenomenon of the cultic institutions of the Old Testament under the influence of the idealistic theme of development in Hegel's philosophy.

[1] For the history of research into Old Testament worship and the attitude towards it in the Christian Church, see L. Diestel, *Geschichte des Alten Testaments in der christlichen Kirche* (1869).

[2] Cf. H.-J. Kraus, *Geschichte der historisch-kritischen Erforschung des Alten Testaments von der Reformation bis zur Gegenwart* (1956), pp. 70 ff.

The attempt to penetrate the inner relationship between religion and cult by means of the 'insights of reason' can certainly be called rationalist. Bähr examined the way in which the 'religious idea', which belongs to man's mind and thought, finds visible and symbolic expression in worship, for, according to Bähr's conception, the 'religious idea' constantly seeks an external, symbolic expression of that which is inward and spiritual. It is by these basic principles that worship has to be interpreted and understood. Bähr writes: 'It is of the nature of the religious consciousness to express, conserve and manifest itself, and it is this that constitutes the cult. There has never been a religion therefore which was purely and entirely spiritual, but every one has had its cult, i.e. its definite manner of giving external expression to its spirit and its thought. Even the word, the most direct expression of what is inward, is still an external thing, something that we can perceive, and therefore worship, although it belongs to the realm of the word, cannot dispense with externals, and is by its very nature inseparable from them. But as the externals are both the expression and the counterpart of that which is inward and spiritual and give direct expression to the religious idea, they are not merely external, but stand in a definite relationship to the spiritual—in other words, they have the character of a symbol.'[3]

Bähr's conception and evaluation of the manifestations of religious and cultic life is of Romantic origin. Whereas the Age of Enlightenment discovered the many possible connections between the texts of the Old Testament and the religious documents of other nations, Romanticism, which gave rise to the historical and comparative study of religions, pursued a particular goal, that of trying to understand by intuition the 'voice of the peoples' in all its depth and primitive mystery, whilst at the same time bringing out clearly the rich variety. The work of the scholar Joseph Görres, *Mythengeschichte der asiatischen Welt* (1810), to which Bähr frequently refers in his *Symbolik des mosaischen Cultus*, was of far-reaching significance. The religious myths and cults, beneath their various outward manifestations, reveal an original similarity which springs from the unity of nature and the religious consciousness of man. This search for a 'primitive religion' dominated the investigations made under the influence of Romanticism. The specifically theological question arose, however, in connection with the Biblical message of the revelation of God in Israel. Lessing in his treatise *Die Erziehung des Menschengeschlechts* had already made an attempt to fit the Biblical message of revelation as a stage in the 'divine education' into a speculative scheme

[3] *Symbolik des mosaischen Cultus*, I, pp. 23 f.

with the emphasis on the aspect of human development, and Romanticism continued along this line. Historical developments and changes were illustrated by reference to the pattern of human life, to different ages and phases of culture. Thus, for example, the Romantics liked to speak of a 'childhood age' of religious development, or they turned in eager search and expectation to the 'first dawn', the earliest manifestions of life.[4] With this approach Old Testament worship was no longer interpreted allegorically with reference to the future Christ of the New Testament, but was understood rationally as the symbolical expression of an early stage in the development of religious experience. Under the influence of Hegel's philosophy the concept of development then became more and more dominant: from the original context of nature that which is spiritual and unseen emerges with increasing clarity. Theological investigation adopted this approach and began to take account of the 'process of development' and of 'progress', and in this way formed a new picture of the worship of Israel. Bähr could therefore establish first of all that religion and worship in the whole of the ancient world reveal a similarity of idea and of expression, but that the Divine decree and plan of education for the human race conferred upon the people of Israel a special role in the development of religion. The chosen people was destined to be the 'bearer of the Divine revelation', and in its midst the 'true religion' was to be prepared and developed both in the inner consciousness and in the symbolism of worship. But this emergence of the 'true religion' from the sphere of nature did not take place suddenly and without an intermediate stage. God's wise process of education brought about a gradual development, which came to its conclusion and fulfilment in the New Testament. Bähr therefore declares: 'Although the outward form of the Mosaic cult is based on religious conceptions which are common to the whole of antiquity and are part of the general course of development of the human race we have also to take into account the special position of the people of Israel. According to the Divine decree and plan of education this people was meant to become the bearer of the Divine revelations and the mediator of the true religion for the whole human race, and from it light and life was meant to come for all nations (John iv. 22). But just as education can never be a sudden, magical elevation or deliverance from the natural level to a higher level, but must be a gradual development, so the light and life, which was to spread from Israel to the whole world, did not appear straight away in all its fulness and completion, perfectly developed, but was planted in Israel like a seed, which grew gradually and did not

[4] Cf. H.-J. Kraus, op. cit., pp. 103 ff.

emerge in all its power and splendour until the time was "fulfilled".'[5] From this insight into the process of development, which was quite clearly understood as a 'process of education', Bähr comes to this conclusion: 'The externals of the cult became the main starting-point for the communication of religious truth, and the whole cult, which uses such a great number and variety of symbols, was able to serve as a bridge from one stage of knowledge to the next.'[6]

In his detailed studies Bähr brings out the two elements in the cultic institutions in the Old Testament, the natural element and the spiritual, historical element. He attempts to show, e.g., how in the feast of the Passover the natural elements are subordinated to the historical: 'Generally speaking, the feast of the Passover has a two-fold significance, one historical and the other natural. The former is by far the more important, and the latter is completely subordinated.'[7] We see emerging here a view which was to have an increasing influence on the study of worship.

(b) *Julius Wellhausen*

A new phase in the study of Old Testament worship begins with Wellhausen. In Bähr's work we can recognize the first traces of the influence of Hegel's philosophy of history, but the author of the *Prolegomena zur Geschichte Israels* makes full use of the concept of development.[8] The threefold process by which—according to Hegel's scheme—absolute spirit strives to emerge with increasing clarity from the depths of nature is adopted by Wellhausen and applied to the Old Testament, with constant reference to the picture of the religious development of Israel supplied by source analysis. In the *Prolegomena zur Geschichte Israels*—to start from the standpoint which determines the whole work—the problem is set out as follows: to which period is the Old Testament law to be attributed—to the pre-exilic or the post-exilic period?[9] With the aid of the new insights provided by the separation of the sources in the Pentateuch, Wellhausen attempts to arrange historically the legal elements in the Old Testament. This arrangement was intended in its turn to provide the essential basis for the inner link in the development of the religion of Israel. This complicated investigation into literary history, which, however, was carried out with great

[5] *Symbolik des mosaischen Cultus*, I, pp. 26 f.

[6] Ibid., I, p. 27

[7] Ibid., II, p. 627.

[8] J. Wellhausen, *Prolegomena zur Geschichte Israels* (6 ed., 1927) (E.T. *Prolegomena to the History of Ancient Israel*).

[9] Ibid., pp. 2 ff.

perspicuity and a masterly control of method, is divided into three main parts: 'In the first, which lays the foundations, the data relating to sacred archaeology are brought together and arranged in such a way as to show that in the Pentateuch the elements follow upon one another and from one another precisely as the steps of the development demonstrably do in the history.'[10] The author therefore sketches in the first part of the book a history of worship, which first covers the place of worship, then examines the various sacrificial customs, and finally deals with the three great annual festivals. The stages in the development are brought out, corresponding to the successive strata in the Pentateuch. Wellhausen distinguishes three different festival calendars in his examination of the annual festivals: the Jehovistic calendar (JE) in Exod. xxxiv. 18–23 and xxiii. 14–17, the Deuteronomic calendar (D) in Deut. xvi and the Priestly calendar (P) in Num. xxviii and xxix and Lev. xxiii. A careful comparison of these three festival calendars leads to the conclusion that JE, D and P represent three different, consecutive stages in the religious development of Israel.

The first stage can be traced in the Jehovistic calendars (Exod. xxxiv. 18 ff. and xxiii. 14 ff.), the main content of which is agriculture and harvesting.[11] The three annual festivals in the worship of Israel were therefore originally agricultural feasts. According to Wellhausen's interpretation, agriculture was the basis of the earliest religion of Israel. The blessing of the land was the goal of all religious endeavour. In this connection he writes: 'The blessing of the land is here the end of religion, and that quite generally—alike of the false heathenish and of the true Israelitish. It has for its basis no historical acts of salvation, but nature simply, which, however, is regarded only as God's domain and as man's field of labour, and is in no manner itself deified.'[12] Quite apart from the festival calendar Wellhausen has no difficulty in showing how strongly nature influenced the cultic celebrations both in form and content. For example, the vintage festival is described in Judges ix. 27 and xxi. 19–21. There is no mention of saving historical events, but dancing, eating and drinking mark the festal gathering. There can be no doubt concerning the Canaanite origin of such a vintage festival. In fact, all the agricultural festivals were taken over from the native Canaanite inhabitants. The main element in worship, however, is the dutiful thanksgiving which the assembled community offers to the divine Giver for the gifts of the land.

The second stage in the development of worship is represented by Deut. xvi.[13] In the Deuteronomic cultic calendar we see a stronger

[10] Ibid., p. 13. [11] Ibid., pp. 90 ff. [12] Ibid., p. 97. [13] Ibid., pp. 89 ff.

connection made between what were formerly nature festivals and historical events. The position is summed up as follows: 'It is in Deuteronomy that one detects the first very perceptible traces of a historical dress being given to the religion and the worship, but this process is still confined within modest limits.'[14] A process is beginning, the process of the 'denaturalization of the feasts'.[15] The historical tradition is coming to stand in antithesis to the nature background of worship.

It is not until the third stage in the historical development, that represented by the priestly cult laws, that the 'denaturalization' comes to its climax and conclusion. The signs that the process is now completed are: (*a*) the separation of the first-fruits from the actual time of harvest (the first-fruits become simply dutiful offerings to the priests); (*b*) the dating of the festivals according to the days of the month (the festivals are no longer considered as spontaneously following the natural cycle); (*c*) the introduction of two new festivals which, far from being rooted in nature, reflect the religious aims of the priestly authors (these are the New Year festival and the great feast of Atonement).

The history of worship, therefore, can be traced in three phases, and in its progress from one phase to the next it brought about a denaturalization of worship. The final outcome is a hardening of the cultic legislation as regards religious ritual in priestly circles. Within the framework of the particular approach and aim of the *Prolegomena zur Geschichte Israels* this whole process, which leads to the ritual and legal rigidity of religious life in the period after the Exile, is evidence for the late origin of the specifically legal elements in the Pentateuch. It is after the Exile that 'Judaism's religion of the law' develops, and the original nature elements are stifled by the legalist tendencies. Whoever acquaints himself with Wellhausen's outline will not be able to escape the impression that he has both grasped and described a fascinating process of development in its various phases in a most comprehensive and logical manner. The study of this process was made possible on the one hand by the separation of the sources within the Pentateuch, and on the other by the methods of Hegel's philosophy.

(c) *The Influence of Archaeological Discoveries on the Study of Old Testament Worship*

The second half of the nineteenth century was a period of sensational excavations and discoveries. By means of archaeological investigations documents from the ancient East came to light, which brought about a

[14] J. Wellhausen, *Prolegomena zur Geschichte Israels* (6 ed., 1927) (E.T. *Prolegomena to the History of Ancient Israel*). pp. 92 ff.

[15] Ibid., p. 102.

new understanding of worship in the ancient world. Particular attention was given to the texts excavated in Mesopotamia, which gave an impressive picture of Babylonian worship. Whilst Wellhausen, for reasons which it is hard to understand, refused to take these discoveries into account, at the beginning of this century new aspects of Old Testament worship slowly came to the fore. The drawing up of schemes based on the philosophy of history and the construction of a 'process of development' was replaced by the comparative study of religions. Numerous connections between ancient Eastern worship and Old Testament worship were noted.

Paul Volz's *Das Neujahrsfest Jahwes* can be considered as the herald of the new approach.[16] If the New Year festival was the centre of religious and cultic life in ancient Babylon, the question now arose whether a similar celebration took place in Israel at the turn of the year. In the early period in Palestine the new year began in the autumn, but the Old Testament fixes the feast of Tabernacles at this significant time. Volz, however, attempts to trace in the traditions of the autumnal festival in Israel a New Year festival similar to the one in Babylon. He also seeks to show traces in the Old Testament of the cultic customs of the great Marduk festival, and quotes in support later Jewish sources, in particular the Mishnah tractate *Sukka*.[17] He describes this 'New Year Yahweh festival', which he builds up from the sources, as Israel's most important festival, and speaks of a preparatory nocturnal festival, of dancing with torches, decking the altar, prayers for rain and other rites. Guided by the Babylonian texts, he constructs a Yahweh festival from the Old Testament traditions, which is meant to provide new insights into the nature of Israelite worship. This leads him to a definite rejection of Wellhausen's main theories. Volz stresses the historical and spiritual character of the New Year Yahweh festival and rejects as without foundation the idea of a natural and agricultural basis for the Old Testament cult. The great feast day was the 'day of Yahweh', the celebration of the great advent of the God of Israel and a remembrance of the creation of the world.[18]

Paul Volz begins his book by declaring: 'The Israelite-Jewish people reached the climax of their cultic and national life in the pilgrimage feasts, such as the Babylonians held when they went up to the city of their god in honour of their principal deity Marduk, and the Greeks when

[16] This work appeared in 1912, in the 'Sammlung gemeinverständlicher Vorträge und Schriften aus dem Gebiet der Theologie und Religionsgeschichte'.

[17] Cf. the edition by H. Bornhäuser, *Die Mischna*. 'Sukka' (Laubhüttenfest), Text, Übersetzung und Erklärung (1935).

[18] P. Volz, op. cit., p. 15.

the states and the nation assembled for the panegyric festivals. The more nation and religion were merged among the Jews in the course of the centuries, and the more the Temple in Jerusalem became the dominant focal point of the whole religious community of Judaism, the greater the grandeur of the panegyric celebration in Jerusalem became for those who took part in the celebrations on Zion, but also for all religiously minded Jews, who each time experienced afresh the strong feeling of unity and of being exalted above the whole world.'[19] In Volz's opinion, this concentration of the cult at one sanctuary is not to be traced back to Deuteronomy: 'The rite by which worship is concentrated does not derive from Deuteronomy, but is part of the original nature of every ancient religion.'[20] He makes clear his opposition to Wellhausen: 'The original character of the Yahweh festival is not agricultural and material, but historical and spiritual. . . . The autumnal festival is not a harvest festival, but a Yahweh and a New Year festival. And Yahweh was not a harvest deity, but much more a warrior God, which is the complete opposite to an agricultural deity.'[21]

Volz's book was a forerunner. The real breakthrough to a new conception of cultic life from the standpoint of the history of religion and of comparative religion was brought about by the Norwegian Sigmund Mowinckel. Mowinckel did not know Volz's work when he brought out his *Psalmenstudien II: Das Thronbesteigungsfest Jahwäs und der Ursprung der Eschatologie* in 1922, but his findings pointed in the same direction. Here again we see scholarly intuition decisively influenced by the religious and cultic texts from the world of ancient Babylon. On New Year's Day the festival of the enthronement of the god Marduk was celebrated at the cultic centre in Babylon.[22] The statue of the god was carried into the temple in solemn procession and placed on the throne. This central cultic act prompted Mowinckel to look for a corresponding act of worship in the Old Testament, and he interpreted the psalms in which the God of Israel is glorified as King as songs for the 'enthronement of Yahweh'. He translated the formula יהוה מלך (JHWH malak) in Ps. xlvii, xciii, xcvi, xcvii and xcix as 'Yahweh has become King' and explained it as an 'enthronement cry'. This means that the 'New Year Yahweh festival' is seen first and foremost as 'Yahweh's enthronement festival', and the newly discovered festival soon becomes the great magnet which attracts to itself the most varied elements in the Old Testament tradition. Records of a solemn carrying of the Ark to Zion (1 Sam. vi; 1 Kings viii; Ps. cxxxii) are taken to be a description of the procession in which the

[19] P. Volz, op. cit., p. 1. [20] Ibid., p. 23. [21] Ibid., p. 16.
[22] See H. Zimmern, 'Das babylonische Neujahrsfest', *AO*, 25 (1926), p. 3.

divine King is brought to his enthronement. The Old Testament traditions concerning 'creation', 'exodus from Egypt' and 'Sinai' are also associated with the cult of Yahweh's enthronement.[23] Like Volz, Mowinckel sees the New Year festival as the 'Yahweh festival' and as the source of all memories and expectations of deliverance, and even goes so far as to take it to be the origin of Old Testament eschatology. It is impossible to mention all the many themes that Mowinckel connects with this principal festival. What is of greatest importance is the new description of the cult as a 'drama that manifests reality'. This marks the emergence of a new point of view: worship is not the symbolic expression of a religious idea (Bähr), nor the point of development in the process of 'denaturalization', moving from nature to ritual (Wellhausen), nor the historical and spiritual deposit of a panegyric Yahweh festival (Volz), but a sacred event which radiates the forces of the myth in a sacramentally conceived drama and produces a renewal of life and creates a pattern of life which is universally applicable, but at the same time bears upon the concrete historical community. In other words, worship is the decisive agent of religion, it is a dynamic reality. Mowinckel's great achievement is that with his new insights into the phenomenology of religion he overthrew the rationalist approach and that of the idealist philosophy of history.

Mowinckel describes the cult in the following words: 'The cult is not only by its origin, but in all places and at all times, drama. The cult is sacred art. But at the same time it is sacred reality, not merely an acted drama or a play, but a real drama and one that manifests reality, a drama which realizes the dramatic event with real power, a reality from which real forces emanate, in other words it is a sacrament. The cult of primitive man is this, and nothing less. . . . The basic idea is this: that through the dramatic, 'symbolic' presentation, realization and reanimation of the particular event this event is actually and really repeated; it repeats itself, happens all over again and exercises afresh the same mighty, redemptive effect that it exercised for our salvation on the first occasion at the dawn of time or in the far distant past.'[24]

Whilst Volz and Mowinckel were deriving their main theories about Old Testament worship from the world of Mesopotamia and trying to understand the worship of Israel by reference to its environment, other investigations were being made into the phenomenon of 'Semitic

[23] On the 'Sinai event', see esp. S. Mowinckel, *Le Décalogue* (1927).

[24] S. Mowinckel, *Psalmenstudien, II,* p. 21. Cf. also S. Mowinckel, *Religion und Kultus* (1953), pp. 73 ff. On the 'dramatic' character of the enthronement cult, see Mowinckel's *Offersang og sangoffer* (1951), pp. 118 ff. (E.T. *The Psalms in Israel's Worship,* I (1962) pp. 169 ff.).

religion' with its ancient cults and rites. Particular attention was given to the groups and tribes of the Near East before they became settled. Could the Old Testament cult be understood merely by reference to the ancient Eastern agricultural religions, or should not more emphasis be given to the origin of the tribes of Israel in the desert? Was it not also necessary to investigate the particular expression of religion and cult in the region of Palestine and Syria? These were the questions that concerned Old Testament scholars. The first investigations and discoveries provided a wealth of comparative material to be laid alongside the often intricate details of the ancient rites and cults. What predominated in these studies was not some sweeping theory which claimed to settle and explain everything, but a detailed examination which aimed to draw distinctions and bring out the various nuances of the different cults.[25]

(d) *The Results of Form Criticism*

Albrecht Alt summed up the motives and aims of form criticism very strikingly in his essay *Die Ursprünge des israelitischen Rechts*.[26] He wrote: 'It was first of all in other parts of the Old Testament, particularly in its lyrical poetry and epic narratives, that the so-called type or form criticism was developed and applied in the last generation as the appropriate procedure for laying bare the pre-literary origins behind the literary compositions. It is based on the insight that in each separate literary type, so long as it maintains its own character, certain contents are firmly tied to certain forms of expression, and that these characteristic connections were not subsequently and arbitrarily imposed upon the materials by the authors, but that they essentially belonged together right from the early pre-literary days of popular oral development and tradition, because they corresponded to the particular, regularly recurring events and needs of life, from which each of the various categories emerged.'[27]

Form criticism seeks, therefore, first of all to recognize and lay bare the so-called 'types' on the basis of certain characteristic formal features.

[25] The following works are of special importance for studying the primitive aspects of Semitic religion: M. J. Lagrange, *Etudes sur les religions Sémitiques* (2 ed., 1905); J. Wellhausen, *Reste arabischen Heidentums* (2 ed., 1927); W. Robertson Smith, *Lectures on the Religion of the Semites* (3 ed. by S. A. Cook, 1927); W. W. Baudissin, *Adonis und Esmun* (1911); ibid., *KYRIOS*, III (ed. by O. Eissfeldt, 1929).

[26] This work appeared in 1934 in the 'Berichte über die Verhandlungen der Sächsischen Akademie der Wissenschaften zu Leipzig, Phil.-Hist. Klasse' (vol. 86, part 1) and has now been included in the *Kleine Schriften zur Geschichte des Volkes Israel*, I, pp. 278 ff.

[27] *Kleine Schriften*, I, pp. 284 f.

These 'types' have grown out of 'regularly recurring events and needs of life', and have a concrete 'setting in life' with which they are connected by their particular and specific content. This gives rise to a new method in the study of worship. It now becomes possible, with the help of form analysis and definition of lyrical and epic texts to find out the 'regularly recurring event' of a cultic festival or at least of a cultic act. Form criticism therefore takes its place as a further method of scientific elucidation of the cultic life in Old Testament times alongside the attempt to interpret and explain from the historical and critical point of view the information contained in the Old Testament in the form of cultic calendars and regulations (Wellhausen), and the attempt to clarify and understand the worship of Israel with the help of ancient Eastern documents (Volz; Mowinckel; the study of 'Semitic religion').

Hermann Gunkel was the first to apply the method of form criticism consistently in Old Testament research, and was in fact the initiator of this new method of approach.[28] The findings which Gunkel set out in his great commentary on the Psalms[29] and in his *Einleitung in die Psalmen*[30] are particularly valuable from the point of view of worship. Investigation into the 'setting in life' of the separate, clearly distinguished types of Psalms has brought to light a great number of regularly recurring occasions in the worship of Israel.

Form criticism is most valuable of all, however, when not just cultic acts but whole festivals are brought to light as a result of investigating the 'setting in life' of a particular type. Albrecht Alt, in the work to which we have already referred, *Die Ursprünge des israelitischen Rechts* (1934) tried to investigate the 'regularly recurring events and needs of life', out of which the different types of law in the Old Testament developed.

The first group of laws which Alt distinguishes is the casuistic form of law. The separate maxims of this type of law are to be found particularly in the Book of the Covenant (Exod. xx. 22–xxiii. 19) and in Deuteronomy. Its formal characteristic can be seen in the pattern by which a particular case is first laid down in a subordinate clause introduced by 'If' and is followed by a main clause beginning with '. . . then', in which a corresponding legal consequence is proclaimed. In all the maxims of this characteristic group of laws expressed in a casuistic form it is evident that a certain juridical content is bound to a fixed form.

[28] Cf. H. Gunkel, 'Die Grundprobleme der israelitischen Literaturgeschichte (*DLZ*, XXVII (1906)). On the method of form criticism, see H. J. Kraus, *Geschichte der historisch-kritischen Erforschung des Alten Testaments*, pp. 309 ff.

[29] H. Gunkel, *Die Psalmen*, HK, II, 2 (4 ed., 1926).

[30] H. Gunkel/J. Begrich, *Einleitung in die Psalmen* (1933).

These forms are inseparably bound up with the contents from the beginning, which raises the question what was the 'setting in life' of this peculiar type of complex of laws with its detailed legislation for every case. Alt comes to the conclusion that the casuistic laws were employed in the sphere of normal jurisdiction, and that they represent a code of law under the guidance of which jurisdiction was exercised 'in the gate', the place of judgement in ancient Palestine.[31] This category of casuistic law has therefore no connection with worship. It is different, however, when we turn to the group of apodeictically expressed laws, which are characterized as regards form by the style of unconditional demand. The Decalogue, for example, consists of apodeictic laws which make an unlimited claim to be accepted and obeyed, and are therefore not tied to any particular situation. The question concerning the 'setting in life' of this apodeictic law brings to the fore a problem that is extremely significant from the point of view of the history of worship. The question is: what was the place in the life of the community of these regulations which are all similarly set out in short series? One thing is clear, that the apodeictic command is addressed to the life of the community from outside, for it makes an unconditional claim. The law expressed in apodeictic form is divine law, and points directly to the sphere of divine revelation. This particular category therefore requires for its explanation a different situation from that of everyday juridical practice, which was the 'setting in life' of the casuistic type of law. There must have been an occasion when the imperative will of God was declared to the whole community, when a detailed differentiation of the legal requirements could not be made in the particular situation. In this connection Alt points out the significance of the passage Deut. xxvii. 11–26,[32] and suggests that the apodeictic divine law had its 'setting in life' in worship. Deut. xxxi. 9–13 gives further evidence of the cultic significance of the proclamation of the law; this passage even shows that the commandments of the apodeictic law were declared 'at the end of every seven years, in the set time of the year of release, in the feast of tabernacles'.

His studies of the 'setting in life' of the apodeictic law by the method of form criticism led Alt to the conclusion that in ancient Israel on the occasion of the 'year of release' celebrated 'every seven years' there took place a rededication of all the tribes to the will of Yahweh. At this cultic occasion the divine law was again proclaimed. Alt declares: 'Although it may not be usual to express it in this way, the proclamation of the apodeictic law every seven years at the feast of Tabernacles as binding

[31] Op. cit., I, pp. 288 f. [32] Op. cit., I, pp. 313 ff.

upon the whole community really amounts to a regularly repeated renewal of the covenant between Yahweh and Israel. . . . .'[33] This festival of the renewal of the covenant, though the existence of it cannot be directly proved from the Old Testament sources, certainly suggests an important hypothesis for understanding the worship of Israel. Form criticism here presents for the first time a finding that is of far-reaching significance for the whole study of worship in the Old Testament. This time it is not ancient Eastern patterns but the literary traditions of Israel itself that open up for us an important festival that had previously never been recognized.

This 'festival of the renewal of the covenant' dominates the picture of worship presented in Gerhard von Rad's studies in form criticism even more than in Alt's.[34] With a perceptive insight into the passages that are relevant from the point of view of worship, Mowinckel had also shown in his book *Le Décalogue* (1927) that the Sinai pericope in the Old Testament was used in worship and shows everywhere traces of dramatic realization. But Mowinckel laid so much emphasis on his thesis of the overwhelming significance of the festival of Yahweh's enthronement that he could see the cultic realization of the Sinai events only in the framework of this all-embracing enthronement festival. Thus, for example, the Decalogue is assigned to the procession in the so-called 'entrance liturgy' (Ps. xv; xxivA). The consistent method of form criticism is undermined by a general theory and therefore breaks down. Von Rad, on the other hand, shows himself to be a pupil of Gunkel's and starts from the text of the Old Testament without any general presuppositions.

In his essay on 'Das formgeschichtliche Problem des Hexateuch' von Rad presents a form-critical analysis of the Sinai pericope and of Deuteronomy. The Sinai pericope is recognized to be a festival legend,[35] which had already been suggested by Mowinckel. The tradition, which was formerly thought of as being self-contained, had its definite place in the life of the community and played an important part in worship. The following picture emerges in Exod. xix ff. and xxxii ff: in the accounts of the Sinai event there is first and foremost a preparatory (ritual) purification and sanctification. Then the people approach God to the sound of trumpets, Yahweh reveals Himself in an act of theophany in order to declare His will, and finally the community makes its sacrifice

[33] Op. cit., I, p. 328.

[34] G. von Rad, *Das formgeschichtliche Problem des Hexateuch*, BWANT, IV (1938), p. 26, reprinted in *Gesammelte Studien zum Alten Testament* (1958).

[35] *Gesammelte Studien zum Alten Testament*, pp. 28 ff.

and enters into the covenant. All these actions have a distinctly cultic connection, in other words they point to a festival of worship in which the Sinai tradition has its 'setting in life'. The pattern of this 'festival of the renewal of the covenant' can be reconstructed from the festival legend as follows:

1. Exhortation (Exod. xix. 4 ff.), with an historical account of the Sinai events (Exod. xix f.).
2. Proclamation of the law (Decalogue and Book of the Covenant).
3. Promise of blessing (Exod. xxiii. 20 ff.).
4. Ratification of the covenant (Exod. xxiv).

In Ps. l and lxxxi von Rad sees an echo of the sequence of the festival such as can be reconstructed from Exodus. In von Rad's examination Deuteronomy is also seen in a new light. The question that comes to the fore is: how is the form of Deuteronomy with its remarkable sequence of addresses, laws, etc., to be assessed and explained?[36] The book falls naturally into the following main sections:

1. Historical account of the Sinai events and exhortation (Deut. i–xi).
2. Proclamation of the law (Deut. xii–xxvi).
3. Covenant obligations (Deut. xxvi. 16–19).
4. Blessing and curse (Deut. xxvii ff.).

Von Rad comments on these divisions as follows: 'In these four sections we can see again the basis of what was formerly a purely cultic celebration, apparently the festival that is reflected in the J and E traditions of the Sinai pericope in Exod. xix ff.'[37] Deuteronomy, therefore, in form as well as content, stands in the same festival tradition. In this connection we should note the emphatic 'Today' that runs through the message of Deuteronomy. This 'Today' is a sign of the actualization in worship of the Sinai events.

(e) *The Phenomenon of the Cult*

Sigmund Mowinckel's book *Psalmenstudien II* represents an achievement of the greatest importance for the study of religion in that it laid a new foundation for the investigation of worship. In passing this judgement we are thinking less of the discovery of 'Yahweh's enthronement festival' than of his general interpretation of the cult in terms of a 'drama that manifests reality'. It is the merit of Scandinavian scholarship, such as we see it also in Grönbech and Pedersen, that it seeks to

[36] *Gesammelt Studien zum Alten Testament*, pp. 33 ff. [37] Ibid., p. 35.

interpret the phenomenon of the cult in the light of the internal factors of its original dynamic and so showed the inadequacy of the rationalistic and systematizing conceptions. In his book *Israel—Its Life and Culture, III–IV* (1940) Johannes Pedersen gave an impressive account of the way in which religion and cult took shape at the primitive level. The forces of a magical, ritual renewal of life are seen from a new angle. Although the question must be raised whether this phenomenology of primitive religion offers the right presuppositions for a correct explanation of Old Testament worship, there is no doubt whatever that the essential background of Israel's cult is clearly brought out. The objection could be made that in Mowinckel as well as in Pedersen the principles of interpretation of the ancient cults and rites are too uniform, and that they see the manifold reality too much as a uniform phenomenon of primitive life. But the danger of distortion in these two scholars is slight compared with the trends to which we must now turn.

In 1933 there appeared in England a volume of essays under the title *Myth and Ritual*, edited by the Professor of Old Testament Studies in the University of London, S. H. Hooke. The editor himself contributed the first essay on the theme 'The Myth and Ritual Pattern of the Ancient East'. In 1935 a further volume appeared under the title *The Labyrinth*. The decisive note is struck in the introductory essay by S. H. Hooke with the idea of 'pattern'. Those who support Hooke's views seek to show that there is one cultic-mythical scheme which covers the whole of the ancient East and that all the cults in their variety of individual structure can be reduced to this common determining pattern.[38] The aim is to identify from the abundance of cultic phenomena a basic phenomenon which determines all the rites, and so an attempt is made to show that in the varied cultic ceremonies there is an annually recurring renewal of the whole of life, and that a New Year festival, determinative for human life, was thought to effect a change of fortune through the cultic-mythical medium of dying and rising gods. The whole of worship, both in its underlying motives and its forms of expression, is traced back to this universal renewal of life which is concentrated in the New Year celebration, in which the event of 'sacred marriage' also plays a large part. Mowinckel had already drawn attention to the fact that in the ancient cults of the Near East an absolutely decisive significance attaches to the king as the personification of the community over which he rules on the one hand and as the embodiment

[38] For an account and discussion of this trend, see esp. M. Noth, 'Gott, König, Volk im Alten Testament', *ZThK* (1950), pp. 157 ff., reprinted in *Gesammelte Studien zum Alten Testament* (1957), pp. 188 ff.

of the deity on the other. These ideas now found forceful expression in the works published on the theme of the 'Myth and Ritual Pattern'. The king himself, it is claimed, was thought of as ritually effecting the renewal of life in the action of the 'sacred marriage'. Consequently 'divine kingship' was the basis and guarantor of the whole of life. The worship of Israel has to be assigned a place in this complex scheme. 'Pattern' is the key concept in this comprehensive religious and cultic phenomenology, which seeks to prove that underlying all the variations of time and place there are essential similarities among the ancient Eastern cults.

This approach to cultic phenomena which originated with Hooke gave rise to a still more extreme approach in the Uppsala school, which drew also on the ideas of Grönbech, Pedersen and Mowinckel, and gave even greater prominence to the idea of 'divine kingship' and developed it still further. The most significant studies produced by this school are G. Widengren's 'Psalm 110 och det sakrala kungadömet i Israel' published in the *Uppsala Universitets Årsskrift* in 1941 and the book by the Uppsala Old Testament scholar Ivan Engnell, *Studies in Divine Kingship* (1943). The latter book seeks to show that the idea of 'divine kingship' had a central importance with a direct bearing upon life in the worship of the west Semitic region, and is based mainly on an interpretation from the point of view of cultic phenomenology of the recently discovered Ras Shamra texts. The whole inquiry, however, points to a radical reassessment of the Old Testament and a new interpretation of it in the light of the ancient Eastern ideology of the divine king. The Psalms in particular are seen in a new light. It is an important peculiarity of the study of Old Testament worship in Scandinavian and Anglo-Saxon countries that it shows this tendency to lose sight of the distinctions in worship at different times and places behind a unifying and all-embracing phenomenology. An ideological principle is maintained, which displaces the methods of the history of religion, historical criticism and form criticism, and even the recent archaeological discoveries supply further material for those who seek to trace one underlying pattern.

(f) *Trends in Recent Study of the Cult*

In recent decades Mowinckel's radical theories have had a great influence on the study of Old Testament worship, and we frequently find discussions of 'Yahweh's enthronement festival' in commentaries, monographs and articles. Some scholars give unqualified support to Mowinckel's ideas. In his *Die Thronfahrt Jahwes am Fest der Jahres-*

wende im alten Israel Hans Schmidt expresses his agreement with the presuppositions which form the basis of Mowinckel's picture of the New Year festival in Israel.[39] Hermann Gunkel also expresses appreciation of Mowinckel's achievement in reconstructing a cultic festival from the indications in the 'hymns of Yahweh's enthronement': 'To have discovered these traces and to have demonstrated that they provide evidence of a festival will, I believe, still be considered Mowinckel's abiding achievement by scholars in the future, an achievement all the greater because he drew our attention afresh to the link between the Psalms and worship (although of course we were not unaware of this previously)'.[40] At the same time, however, Gunkel sharply criticizes Mowinckel's inadequate preliminary studies in form criticism and condemns the way in which, in contradiction of all exact form analysis, many Psalms are placed together which are connected only by very slender threads of peripheral theme associations. In this connection Gunkel strongly disputes the overwhelming importance of the enthronement festival in the worship of Israel. He suggests there was a festival which arose in Jerusalem under Babylonian influence immediately before the Exile, and was given an eschatological interpretation by Second Isaiah, its traditional material ('the hymns of Yahweh's enthronement') being set down later. According to this theory, the eschatological elements in Ps. xlvii, xciii, xcvi, xcvii and xcix are to be traced back to the influence of the unknown prophet of the Exile (Isa. xl–lv).[41]

Mowinckel's theory concerning 'Yahweh's enthronement festival' is more often rejected than accepted either fully or with reservations. Most commentaries on the Psalms dismiss Mowinkel's suggestions in a few sentences, without detailed examination. Buttenwieser goes so far as to describe the suggested festival as 'an imaginary creation, with no foundation in the facts'.[42] What one often finds is 'just short and occasionally passionate argument' (J. J. Stamm). A more detailed refutation is to be found in the following books: L. I. Pap, *Das israelitische Neujahrsfest* (1933), N. H. Snaith, *The Jewish New Year Festival* (1947), S. Aalen, *Die Begriffe 'Licht' und 'Finsternis' im Alten Testament, im Spätjudentum und im Rabbinismus*, SNVAO, II, Hist.-Filos. Klasse

[39] This work appeared in the 'Sammlung gemeinverständlicher Vorträge und Schriften aus dem Gebiet der Theologie und Religionsgeschichte' (1927).

[40] *Einleitung in die Psalmen*, p. 105.

[41] In contrast to Mowinckel, who interprets the so-called 'Yahweh's enthronement Psalms' in the terms of cultic drama and ascribes to them an actual meaning in the external manifestations of worship, Gunkel considers the essential theme to be 'eschatological'.

[42] Cf. J. J. Stamm, 'Ein Vierteljahrhundert Psalmenforschung', *ThR*, 23/1, pp. 48 ff.

(1951), H.-J. Kraus, *Die Königsherrschaft Gottes im Alten Testament* (1951).

In the studies of worship made by the Old Testament scholars who accept the 'pattern principle' or who belong to the Uppsala school, Mowinckel's arguments about Israel's New Year festival form an essential basis. The blurring of the specific historical outlines of the cult has been carried to such an extent in these circles that Mowinckel himself has had to define his own position more and more over against their endless schematizing. In his more recent publications his aim has been to define more precisely the views put forward in his *Psalmenstudien II* (1922) and so to avoid exaggerated interpretations.[43] The 'historical element' in Old Testament worship is brought out more clearly.[44] On the other hand, as a result of the 'pattern ideology', the historical foundations of Israel's worship disappear more and more. Myth covers the whole field. A typical example can be seen in the essays 'The Rôle of the King in the Jerusalem Cultus' (*The Labyrinth*, 1935), on the theme of 'Divine Kingship', by A. R. Johnson, and *Messias*, *Moses redivivus*, *Menschensohn* (1948) by A. Bentzen.[45] The volume of essays edited by S. H. Hooke, *Myth*, *Ritual and Kingship* (1958), develops the position of the cultic-mythical 'pattern principle' and embraces the most varied realms of the ancient East in one scheme. No note was taken of Martin Noth's critical examination of the methods of the cultic phenomenology school of thought in his essay 'Gott, König, Volk im Alten Testament',[46] and no reference was made to Noth's clear indications of the historical foundations of Israelite kingship, which rule out a mythical interpretation.

At present there is great confusion in the study of Old Testament worship. Many articles are written, but they do not seem to arrive at many conclusions. Principles, schemes and ideological programmes are set out, and various schools of thought express their views. Real conversation has to a large extent ceased. More serious, however, is the fact that the texts of the Old Testament are no longer examined for what they are and in their historical context. Instead, the contents of the Old Testament are illuminated by reference to the cultic institutions

[43] We must mention particularly Mowinckel's publications *Offersang og Sangoffer* (1951) (E.T. *The Psalms in Israel's Worship* (1962)), 'Zum israelitischen Neujahr und zur Deutung der Thronbesteigungspsalmen', *ANVAO*, II, Hist.-Filos. Klasse (1952) and *He That Cometh* (1956).

[44] S. Mowinckel, *Religion und Kultus*, pp. 77 ff.

[45] See also A. R. Johnson, *Sacral Kingship in Ancient Israel* (1955); G. Widengren, *Sakrales Königtum im Alten Testament und im Judentum*; G. W. Ahlström, *Psalm 89—Eine Liturgie aus dem Ritual des leidenden Königs* (1959).

[46] *ZThK*, 47 (1950), pp. 157 ff.

of Israel's neighbours and in the light of general cult-myth theories. Studies which deal with the Biblical texts are almost ignored, and the stream of theories and hypothesis passes them by. All the more noteworthy, therefore, is the objective and detailed account which R. de Vaux gives of the cultic institutions of the Old Testament in his book *Les Institutions de l'Ancien Testament II* (1960) (E. T. *Ancient Israel: Its Life and Institutions*, 1961), in which he seeks to follow through the maze of hypotheses the path that is indicated by the Old Testament sources.

2. Problems of Approach and Presentation

(a) *A Phenomenology or History of the Cult?*

The survey we have made of the history of research into Old Testament worship has shown that the phenomenological approach has increasingly supplanted and excluded the historical approach. This development, however, produced confusing results, especially when the decisive standpoints of the phenomenological approach were drawn from an alien cultic world and from ideological principles which ignore all distinctions. It is surprising to see how such substantial Old Testament texts as the cultic calendars and regulations play either no part at all or only a small part in the writings of Mowinckel, the 'pattern school' and the school of thought associated with Uppsala.[47] These passages reflect the ever-changing history of Israel's worship, which is for the most part ignored. The great value of Wellhausen's work was that he tried to investigate and set out the historical developments on the basis of the cultic documents in the Old Testament. If this great achievement were firmly borne in mind it could point a way for Old Testament scholarship out of the many varied phenomenological theories which generalize and distort. It is true that there are two important points where we can no longer follow Wellhausen. Hegel's philosophy of history with its three stages of development is a system into which the Old Testament texts cannot be pressed. In his *Prolegomena zur Geschichte Israels* Wellhausen was guided by a premiss which is alien and inappropriate from the point

[47] The cultic calendars in the Old Testament receive fuller treatment in the following studies: E. Kutsch, *Das Herbstfest in Israel*, Diss., Mainz (1955); ibid., 'Erwägungen zur Geschichte der Passahfeier und des Massotfestes', *ZThK*, 55, 1 (1958), pp. 1 ff.; ibid., 'Der Kalender des Jubiläenbuches und das Alte und das Neue Testament', *VT*, XI, 1 (1961), pp. 39 ff.; G. Kretschmar, 'Himmelfahrt und Pfingsten', *ZKG*, vol. 65, part III, pp. 209 ff.; E. Auerbach, 'Die Feste im alten Israel', *VT*, VIII, 1 (1958), pp. 1 ff.; 'Neujahrs- und Versöhnungsfest in den biblischen Quellen', *VT*, VIII, 4 (1958), pp. 377 ff.; 'Der Wechsel des Jahres-Anfangs in Juda', *VT*, IX, 2 (1959), pp. 113 ff.; 'Die Umschaltung vom judäischen auf den babylonischen Kalender', *VT*, X, 1 (1960), pp. 69 ff.

of view both of the arrangement of epochs and also of the underlying spiritual principle. In the assessment of source criticism also we can no longer agree with Wellhausen today. The historical division of the sources JE, D and P, which are based on strictly literary considerations, into three different periods now appears questionable as a result of study of the history of tradition. Since the inner life of the sources, the stream of traditions and the various circles to which they belonged have been brought to light, the presuppositions on which the approach from the standpoint of literary history is based have been called in question.[48] The findings resulting from the source criticism undertaken by Wellhausen and his followers are still valid for the most part, but if we are to trace the history of the cult we must in the first place inquire into the historical and geographical origin of the traditions that appear in the sources, into the effect these traditions have and the way they are altered. We have recently come to see more and more clearly, for example, that the Priestly Code (P), which from the literary point of view has to be assigned to a relatively late period, embodies some very old traditional material, which to some extent has retained its archaic character, but has also been modified by changed cultic circumstances.[49] This presents some difficult problems for the study of the cult, which need to be carefully examined. On the one hand we need to look carefully at the blocking of the stream of tradition brought about by the sources at certain times. In the literary reservoir of the 'sources' the traditions as they flow together are given a definite form corresponding to the institutions of worship contemporary with the source. On the other hand, however, we have to give close attention to the elements in the tradition as such, for they often maintain—even in the more recent forms of the sources—their own life and point back to older, even to the oldest, origins. If we do not give equal consideration to source criticism and to the history of tradition, then distortions and mistaken assessments arise which can be very far-reaching in their effect. It is significant that in many circles of Scandinavian research into the cult where a general-

[48] H. Gunkel's commentary on Genesis (HK, I, 1 (5 ed., 1922)) was a pioneering work in this respect. Reference should also be made to H. Gressmann, *Mose und seine Zeit*, FRLANT, N.F., i (1913); M. Noth, *Überlieferungsgeschichliche Studien I, Die sammelnden und bearbeitenden Geschichtswerke im Alten Testament*, Schriften der Königsberger Gelehrten-Gesellschaft (1943); *Überlieferungsgeschichte des Pentateuch* (1948). On the problem of investigation into the history of tradition, cf. H. J. Kraus, 'Zur Geschichte des Überlieferungsbegriffs in der alttestamentlichen Wissenschaft', *EvTh*, 16, 8/9 (1956), pp. 371 ff.

[49] Cf. K. Koch, *Die Priesterschrift von Exodus 25 bis Leviticus 16—Eine überlieferungsgeschichtliche und literarkritische Untersuchung*, FRLANT, 71 (1959), where a fuller bibliography can be found.

izing phenomenology holds sway, an extreme interpretation of tradition has developed which rejects the findings of source criticism and overthrows the basic principles of Old Testament scholarship with a strong bias against Wellhausen and his followers, the reasons for which are not always clear.[50]

(b) *Ancient Eastern Sources*

Sigmund Mowinckel's book *Psalmenstudien II* first presented students of Old Testament worship with great force with the problem to what extent and with what justification the cultic institutions of Israel's neighbours can be used as illuminating parallels or even as basic presuppositions for the understanding of Old Testament worship. Wellhausen had already drawn attention to the fundamental difficulties in setting out the thesis: 'The cult is in reality the ethnic element in the religion of Israel.'[51] Is this view correct or is Heinrich Graetz right when he states: 'Judaism when it emerges in history presents itself as a negation, a negation of paganism.'[52] Nobody can ignore the fact today that the Old Testament is linked by countless threads with the religious and cultic traditions of its neighbours. There is scarcely an idea in the life of worship, scarcely a rite or a gesture, for which a parallel could not be traced in ancient Eastern sources. But what is the nature of this link, this participation in the institutions and spiritual movements of her neighbours? Old Testament scholarship in its researches into the history of religions and into comparative religion at the turn of the century made an attempt to discover the 'characteristic' and 'peculiar' element in the tradition of Israel. With the growth of phenomenology these studies were pushed into the background. Whenever a striking manifestation of cultic life was noted in Babylon, Egypt or Ras Shamra, then the corresponding phenomenon was immediately traced in the Old Testament, regardless of the specific circumstances and background, and set up on an alien foundation. Myth destroys history, and magic replaces a faith in God which was interpreted in Israel in an eminently personal way. There is insufficient discrimination in research and interpretation. The question of the peculiar way in which foreign institutions and traditions were accepted and transformed in Israel is not really faced.

[50] Cf. H. Birkeland, *Zum hebräischen Traditionswesen—Die Komposition der prophetischen Bücher des Alten Testaments* (1938); H. S. Nyberg, *Studien zum Hoseabuche* (1935); I. Engnell, *Gamla Testamentet—en traditionshistorisk inledning*, I (1945).

[51] J. Wellhausen, *Israelitische und jüdische Geschichte* (9 ed., 1958), p. 17. Cf. also p. 32: 'Israelite religion only gradually emerged from paganism; this is the very substance of its history.'

[52] H. Graetz, *Die Konstruktion der jüdischen Geschichte* (1936), p. 10.

If the rudiments of the ancient Eastern cult, a great number of which can be traced in the worship of Israel, are viewed from a foreign standpoint, they appear in a different light from that of their particular Old Testament context. This, however, presents some very complex problems, because the mythical and magical elements derived from her neighbours are not always sufficiently deeply rooted in Israel to attain their proper significance in their new setting. What is most important is that the cult in its original pagan form embodies a desire which undermines the faith of the Old Testament. 'The purpose of the cult in all its practices is to enter into union with the deity and to influence him. This applies in two directions—to win the favour and grace of the deity, and to appease his anger.'[53] The question arises as to what extent this basic pagan motive was able to assert itself in Israel. It was present in latent form, and—as we know from the protest in the message of the prophets—it expressed itself in a most unfortunate way. But these brief indications give only a vague idea of the problems. We need to examine each case in turn, to see which cultic elements Israel adopted from its ancient Eastern neighbours, how it assimilated them and to what extent the external and internal transformation was effected.

(c) *The Method of Form Criticism*

The great importance of this method for the understanding of Old Testament worship has been clearly demonstrated in the work of Gunkel, Alt and von Rad. It has been shown, particularly in connection with the 'setting in life' of the Psalms and the different types of law, that underlying factors in Israel's worship, previously unrecognized, now come into view. It is often possible, on the basis of a newly discovered cultic festival or act of worship, to go on to further highly significant interpretations. Thus, for example, the festival of the renewal of the covenant, which was first studied by Alt, is not merely confirmed in the writings of von Rad, but both its course and its content are comprehensively set out.[54] At the same time, of course, there is the danger of overstepping the limits set by the Old Testament texts. Alt thought it possible—with reference to Deut. xxxi. 9 ff.—that a festival for the renewal of the covenant was held 'every seven years' in Israel,[55] and also suggested that this festival could be connected with the regulations concerning the 'year of release'. These attempts to define a

[53] U. von Wilamowitz, *Der Glaube der Hellenen*, I (1931), p. 35.

[54] G. von Rad, 'Das formgeschichtliche Problem des Hexateuch', *Ges. Stud. zum A.T.*, pp. 28 ff.

[55] A. Alt, *Kleine Schriften*, I, pp. 328 f.

close relationship fall into the background in von Rad. The 'festival of the covenant' takes the place held by 'Yahweh's enthronement festival' in Mowinckel's interpretation of the cult. He suggests that it was celebrated annually and that it exerted its influence constantly in the history of Israel's worship. Artur Weiser goes a step further in his commentary on the Psalms, in taking the 'covenant festival' and the 'covenant ideology' as the heart of all the religious institutions and traditions in the Old Testament.[56] This takes us far beyond the limits of the insights possible by the method of form criticism. Mowinckel's approach exercises a powerful influence on what is discovered by the study of types and leads to an undifferentiated mixing and blending of materials. If we are to follow the method originating with Gunkel we must not make a cultic 'setting in life' discovered as a result of form criticism into an absolutely valid principle for explaining worship, but try to discover carefully what geographical and historical importance this cultic activity possesses.

The 'cultic legend' presents us with special difficulties. Reliable criteria are still lacking in this field—and it is not likely that they will ever emerge. When, for example, it is stated that the Sinai pericope was a 'festival legend', this immediately raises the question what the actual relationship between the epic account and the cultic event was. It is too easy to avoid answering this question by asserting that there was a mutual interaction. Where can one really point to features with a cultic significance in the epic account? Are there any parallels in specifically cultic passages? To what extent and to what degree could traditions which originally had nothing to do with worship be supplied with secondary cultic elements? And on the other hand, what is the part played by the epic tradition, which permeates materials which once belonged to the cult with new aspects? Such are the questions which have to be faced by anyone who attempts an explanation, questions which warn one against the danger of reading too much into passages which reveal some cultic traces.

(d) *Institutions and Regulations Governing Daily Life*

It is often scarcely conceivable how the institutions and regulations of Israel are overlooked or neglected in the study of the history of worship. Without regard to the sociological problems, various studies apply

[56] A. Weiser, *Die Psalmen*, ATD 14/15 (5 ed., 1959), Introduction (E.T. *The Psalms* 1962)); see also ibid., *Das Buch Hiob*, ATD, 13 (1951), *Das Buch des Propheten Jeremia*, ATD, 21 (1955) and, on the question of the connection of the Psalms with the cult, 'Die Darstellung der Theophanie in den Psalmen und im Festkult', *Festschrift A. Bertholet*, (1950), pp. 513 ff. Reprinted in *Glaube und Geschichte* (1961), pp. 303 ff.

either primitive animistic standpoints or the concepts of splendid imperial cults to Israel. The correct basis of study and inquiry, in keeping with the regulations which can be traced in the Old Testament, requires closer consideration. It is necessary to draw careful distinctions. Did the semi-nomadic clans coming from the desert in the process of migration possess the same cult as the groups that had attained a settled way of life?[57] To what extent did the desert background affect the worship of the tribes after they had settled? Martin Noth has examined and described the institution of the 'sacral confederacy of the twelve tribes'.[58] The importance of this sacral institution for the foundation, history and tradition of Old Testament worship can scarcely be overstated, but the question remains, whether older cultic traditions from the desert period or from the pre-amphictyonic groups of tribes still exerted an influence. Out of the confederacy of the twelve tribes there grew the State. What was the effect of this change of form on worship? Which elements from the pre-monarchical period were able to assert and maintain themselves, which new rites and customs were introduced? How were the new elements adopted? The State split into two kingdoms after the death of Solomon. Which of the two kingdoms preserved the ancient traditions of Israel's worship? Do we see new official cults emerging? What happened after the collapse of the Northern Kingdom? Was the Jerusalem cult affected by these events? What significance had the Babylonian exile for the development of the worship of Israel abroad and at home? How did the post-exilic institutions become effective in the politically powerless cultic community in Jerusalem? All these questions refer not only to the historical events, but first and foremost to the institutions and ways of life which prevailed in Israel at the different periods. It would be a foolish simplification to suggest that there was a cult which had no connection with the sociological pattern of the community in the midst of which it fulfilled its function.

(e) *The Method of Presentation*

The account of the history of Old Testament worship which follows starts from the cultic calendars and regulations in the Old Testament. The main Israelite festivals are first examined with reference to these passages from the point of view of their special characteristics, the course they followed and their history. In this way we aim to clarify the historical

[57] A. Alt's *Der Gott der Väter*, BWANT, III, 12 (1929), reprinted in *Kleine Schriften*, I, pp. 1 ff., contains an excellent examination of this question; but see also L. Rost, 'Weidewechsel und altisraelitischer Festkalender', *ZDPV*, 66, pp. 205 ff.

[58] M. Noth, *Das System der Zwölf Stämme Israels*, BWANT, IV, 1 (1930).

context and underlying tradition of the cultic regulations which in the form in which they are set down appear relatively straightforward. This picture of Old Testament worship has to be brought out as distinctly as possible from the available sources and serve as a guide for all the subsequent investigations. But the background of the religious and cultic world of Palestine must be recognizable from the start.

A chapter follows which deals with the cultic officials and the sacrificial system. Only after these preliminary studies can we go on to the two chapters in which an account is given of the cultic traditions at the central sanctuaries of Israel. As regards the section headings here, the important reservation has to be borne in mind that they imply the thesis that has still to be established in detail, viz. that there was at all times in the cultic history of Israel a specially distinguished 'chosen' central sanctuary.[59] The numerous local shrines with their rites and traditions therefore deliberately fall into the background. The complex history of worship before the formation of the confederacy of the twelve tribes, of which we can trace only the main elements, cannot be dealt with in full. The outlines of worship in the post-exilic period, on the other hand, must be set out as fully as possible.

[59] On this point, see esp. M. Noth, *Geschichte Israels* (3 ed., 1956) (E.T. *History of Israel* (1958)).

CHAPTER TWO

CULTIC CALENDARS AND REGULATIONS

1. THE CULTIC CALENDARS IN THE PENTATEUCH

(a) *Exodus xxiii. 10–19*

In the group of cultic calendars in the Pentateuch Exod. xxiii. 10–19 occupies a special position on account both of the literary and traditional context in which it stands and also the peculiar arrangement in which the social and cultic institutions of Israel are presented. After setting out the passage we shall make a literary analysis of it, and finally consider the question of the sources to which the regulations concerning the calendar belong.

'10. And six years thou shalt sow thy land, and shalt gather in the increase thereof: 11. But the seventh year thou shalt let it rest and lie fallow; that the poor of thy people may eat: and what they leave the beast of the field shall eat. In like manner thou shalt deal with thy vineyard, and with thy oliveyard.

12. Six days thou shalt do thy work, and on the seventh day thou shalt rest: that thine ox and thine ass may have rest, and the son of thy handmaid, and the stranger, may be refreshed.

13. And in all things that I have said unto you take ye heed: and make no mention of the name of other gods, neither let it be heard out of thy mouth.

14. Three times thou shalt keep a feast unto me in the year.

15. The feast of unleavened bread shalt thou keep: seven days thou shalt eat unleavened bread, as I commanded thee, at the time appointed in the month Abib (for in it thou camest out from Egypt); and none shall appear before me empty:

16. And the feast of harvest, the firstfruits of thy labours, which thou sowest in the field: and the feast of ingathering, at the end of the year, when thou gatherest in thy labours out of the field.

17. Three times in the year all thy males shall appear before the Lord God.

18. Thou shalt not offer the blood of my sacrifice with leavened bread: neither shall the fat of my feast remain all night until the morning.

19. The first of the firstfruits of thy ground thou shalt bring into the house of the Lord thy God. Thou shalt not seethe a kid in its mother's milk.'

If we consider first the times that have to be observed by the cultic community, two groups of commandments can be distinguished: the rules which refer to times of rest which have to be observed periodically (*vv.* 10–12) and the calendar of feasts proper, which indicates the three great annual festivals (*vv.* 14–17). These commandments are set out in the apodeictic style. What is unusual for the Old Testament is the direct association of the sabbatical year and the sabbath, based on the period of seven common to both times of rest.[1] *Vv.* 14–17, however, present a pattern which is common to all the cultic calendars: feast of Unleavened Bread (and Passover)—feast of Weeks—feast of Ingathering. The sequence follows the agricultural year. It is true that the feast of Ingathering is celebrated 'at the going out of the year', which means in fact the beginning of the year,[2] but it concludes the agricultural year. Both groups of commandments (*vv.* 10–12 and 14–17) stand in a framework of other regulations, the original connection of which it is not easy to see.[3] *V.* 13a looks like a concluding formula of exhortation.[4] *V.* 13b forbids the mention of the names of strange gods in worship, and probably in daily life as well.[5] *Vv.* 18 and 19b probably refer to details of the ritual of the feast of the Passover which is not mentioned in *v.* 15 (in the series of annual festivals).[6] *V.* 19a deals with the offering of the 'first fruits'.[7] In *vv.* 10–19, therefore, a number of regulations from the sacral and cultic spheres are brought together. The two groups in *vv.* 10–12 and 14–17 stand out clearly in this compilation.

The cultic rules in Exod. xxiii. 10–19 are part of the so-called 'Book of the Covenant', a collection of some of the most ancient Israelite laws from the period before the monarchy.[8] It is hard to say for certain

[1] Cf. M. Noth, *Das zweite Buch Mose* (ATD, 5, 1959), pp. 153 f. (E.T. *Exodus* (1962), pp. 190 f.). The regulations concerning the Sabbath are mentioned here in this first section, which deals with the 'Cultic Calendars in the Pentateuch', only because the immediate context in Exod. xxiii. 10–19 requires it.

[2] The translation of בצאת השׁנה in *v.* 16 is disputed. Noth renders the Hebrew phrase correctly as 'at the beginning of the year' (op. cit., E.T., p. 191). This is supported by the idea we find in the Old Testament of the 'going out', i.e., the 'going forth' of the planets (Gen. xix. 23; Ps. xix. 6; Neh. iv. 15).

[3] A. Jepsen rightly points out: 'The arrangement of the following regulations is not altogether clear. To connect *v.* 18 with the feast of the Passover, 19a with the feast of Weeks and 19b with the vintage festival is an expedient for which there is no real proof, for the connection of *v.* 18 with the Passover is possible only in the light of Exod. xxxiv, nor is there evidence of any real link between *v.* 19b and the autumn festival' (*Untersuchungen zum Bundesbuch*, BWANT, III, 5 (1927), p. 50).

[4] This call to obedience 'looks like the end of a collection of laws' (G. Beer/K. Galling, *Exodus*, HAT, I, 3 (1939), p. 119).

[5] Cf. with this verse Exod. xx. 23; xxii. 19.

[6] A new light has been thrown on the prohibition in *v.* 19b by the discoveries at Ras Shamra, and we can now recognize it as an explicit ritual polemic against a cultic practice observed in Syria and Canaan. The Ugaritic text reads: 'The (altar) servers shall seethe a kid in milk seven times on the fire. . . .'

[7] Cf. O. Eissfeldt, *Erstlinge und Zehnten im Alten Testament* (1917); W. Eichrodt, *Theologie des Alten Testaments* (5 ed., 1959), pp. 91 ff. (E.T. *Theology of the Old Testament* (1959), pp. 152 ff.).

[8] Cf. A. Jepsen, op. cit.; O. Eissfeldt, *Einleitung in das Alte Testament* (2 ed., 1956), pp. 252 ff. As far as the time of origin of the Book of the Covenant is concerned, scholars

whether this passage, Exod. xxiii. 10–19 was intended to be a literary supplement to the great complex of laws. The 'house of Yahweh' mentioned in *v.* 19a is not necessarily the Temple in Jerusalem, but could also refer to Shiloh, for example. There is no reason why we should not take the cultic laws in the Book of the Covenant (along with the rules handed down in Exod. xxxiv) to be the most ancient regulations of this kind in the Old Testament.

(b) *Exodus xxxiv. 18–26*

The cultic regulations in Exod. xxxiv. 18–26 should be considered directly after Exod. xxiii. 10–19, for the two passages must have stood 'in some relationship' with one another.[9]

'18. The feast of unleavened bread shalt thou keep. Seven days thou shalt eat unleavened bread, as I commanded thee, at the time appointed in the month Abib: for in the month Abib thou camest out from Egypt.

19. All that openeth the womb is mine; and all thy cattle that is male, the firstlings of ox and sheep.

20. And the firstling of an ass thou shalt redeem with a lamb: and if thou wilt not redeem it, than thou shalt break its neck. All the firstborn of thy sons thou shalt redeem. And none shall appear before me empty.

21. Six days thou shalt work, but on the seventh day thou shalt rest: in plowing time and in harvest thou shalt rest.

22. And thou shalt observe the feast of weeks, even of the firstfruits of wheat harvest, and the feast of ingathering at the year's end.

23. Three times in the year shall all thy males appear before the Lord God, the God of Israel.

24. For I will cast out nations before thee, and enlarge thy borders: neither shall any man desire thy land, when thou goest up to appear before the Lord thy God three times in the year.

25. Thou shalt not offer the blood of my sacrifice with leavened bread; neither shall the sacrifice of the feast of the passover be left unto the morning.

26. The first of the firstfruits of thy ground thou shalt bring unto the house of the Lord thy God. Thou shalt not seethe a kid in its mother's milk.'

[9] O. Eissfeldt, *Einleitung*, p. 254.

---

are tending more and more to accept the view that the body of laws reflects Israel's early struggles with its Canaanite environment. 'As there is no evidence of a king (cf. the tribal princes in Exod. xxii. 27) or of a rigid organization, nor is there any mention of fixed dues, the most likely time of origin seems to be the period between Joshua and Samuel, and most likely of all the period of the formation of the sacral confederacy of the twelve tribes, in other words in the period of the judges before the formation of the state by Saul' (C. Kuhl, *Die Enstehung des Alten Testaments* (1953), p. 107; E. T. *The Old Testament: Its Origins and Composition*, p. 98).

These cultic regulations are found in the context of a larger collection of commandments and laws, which reveal characteristic features of the Yahwistic standpoint. It is not really possible, however, to reconstruct from the series of statutes that have been grouped together a 'Yahwistic decalogue'.[10] Attempts of this kind lead to a forced and artificial arrangement of the material. The connection of certain rules with the apodeictic Divine law of the Decalogue must not mislead us into imposing a pattern on the original Yahwistic collection. Various laws have been brought together in Exod. xxxiv. The fact that the status and significance of the basic Divine law set down on the two tables has been conferred upon these regulations (Exod. xxxiv ff.) affects the general purpose, but not the structure of these traditions of the law. A comparison with Exod. xxiii. 10 shows clearly that the Yahwistic editor, in the part of his compilation that is concerned with worship, is making use of a group of regulations that is to be found in the collection of traditions. In the details of the wording also J (with only slight variations) adopts the traditional material. As far as the details are concerned, the following picture presents itself: the cultic calendar based on the three great annual festivals (cf. Exod. xxiii. 14–17) is set out in Exod. xxxiv. 18–23. As in Exod. xxiii. 17, in Exod. xxxiv. 23 also a summarizing formula concludes the tripartite calendar, but in Exod. xxxiv. 18–23 two further items have been inserted into the regulations for the feast of Unleavened Bread—the rule about the redemption of the firstborn (*vv.* 19, 20a) and the rule in *v.* 21, which gives a special application to *v.* 18.[11] The requirement 'And none shall appear before me empty' (*v.* 20b), on the other hand, is part of the regulations for the feast of Unleavened Bread in Exod. xxiii. 15 as well. The passage in Exod. xxxiv. 25–26 is in harmony in its basic outlines with Exod. xxiii. 18–19, but *v.* 25 now contains a more precise definition of the sacrificial rite with reference to the feast of the Passover. *V.* 24 is an interpolation meant to give encouragement.

If the Yahwistic source is to be ascribed to the period of David or Solomon, then we have in Exod. xxxiv. 18 ff. elements of older cultic traditions from the pre-monarchical period. Traditions, which were drawn upon also in the Book of the Covenant, have been preserved here.

[10] G. Beer constructs a Decalogue as follows: I: *v.* 14; II: *v.* 17; III: *v.* 19a; IV: *v.* 20b; V: *v.* 21; VI: *v.* 23; VII: *v.* 25a; VIII: *v.* 25b; IX: *v.* 26a; X: *v.* 26b (*Exodus*, HAT I, 3, p. 161). The impulse to this kind of reconstruction arises from Goethe's question, 'What was on the tables of the law?' On the problems raised by such reconstructions, see E. Sellin/L. Rost, *Einleitung in das Alte Testament* (9 ed., 1959), p. 52.

[11] The way in which *v.* 21 has been inserted into the details concerning the feast of Unleavened Bread is peculiar, and the second half of the regulation is particularly remarkable (cf. M. Noth, *Exodus*, pp. 263 f.).

The connection between Exod. xxiii. 10 ff. and xxxiv. 18 ff. have therefore to be explained in the light of the history of tradition. The details of the different phraseology will have to be considered and interpreted later. It is worth noting that in the Yahwistic version the sabbath and the sabbatical year are not mentioned, and we shall have to consider this matter also later.

(c) *Deuteronomy xvi. 1–17*

The traditions of the cultic calendar undergo a very decisive adaptation and adjustment in Deuteronomy. We will first consider the passage in Deut. xvi. 1–17.

'1. Observe the month of Abib, and keep the passover unto the Lord thy God: for in the month of Abib the Lord thy God brought thee forth out of Egypt by night. 2. And thou shalt sacrifice the passover unto the Lord thy God, of the flock and the herd, in the place which the Lord shall choose to cause his name to dwell there. 3. Thou shalt eat no leavened bread with it; seven days shalt thou eat unleavened bread therewith, even the bread of affliction; for thou camest forth out of the land of Egypt in haste: that thou mayest remember the day when thou camest forth out of the land of Egypt all the days of thy life. 4. And there shall be no leaven seen with thee in all thy borders seven days; neither shall any of the flesh, which thou sacrificest the first day at even, remain all night until the morning. 5. Thou mayest not sacrifice the passover within any of thy gates, which the Lord thy God giveth thee: 6. But at the place which the Lord thy God shall choose to cause his name to dwell in, there thou shalt sacrifice the passover at even, at the going down of the sun, at the season that thou camest forth out of Egypt. 7. And thou shalt roast and eat it in the place which the Lord thy God shall choose: and thou shalt turn in the morning, and go unto thy tents. 8. Six days thou shalt eat unleavened bread: and on the seventh day shall be a solemn assembly to the Lord thy God; thou shalt do no work therein.

9. Seven weeks shalt thou number unto thee: from the time thou beginnest to put the sickle to the standing corn shalt thou begin to number seven weeks. 10. And thou shalt keep the feast of weeks unto the Lord thy God with a tribute of a freewill offering of thine hand, which thou shalt give, according as the Lord thy God blesseth thee: 11. And thou shalt rejoice before the Lord thy God, thou, and thy son, and thy daughter, and thy manservant, and thy maidservant, and the Levite that is within thy gates, and the stranger, and the fatherless, and the widow, that are in the midst of thee, in the place which the Lord thy God shall choose to cause his name to dwell there. 12. And thou shalt remember that thou wast a bondman in Egypt: and thou shalt observe and do these statutes.

13. Thou shalt keep the feast of tabernacles seven days, after that thou hast gathered in from thy threshing-floor and from thy winepress: 14. And thou

shalt rejoice in thy feast, thou, and thy son, and thy daughter, and thy manservant, and thy maidservant, and the Levite, and the stranger, and the fatherless, and the widow, that are within thy gates. 15. Seven days shalt thou keep a feast unto the Lord thy God in the place which the Lord shall choose: because the Lord thy God shall bless thee in all thine increase, and in all the work of thine hands, and thou shalt be altogether joyful.

16. Three times in a year shall all thy males appear before the Lord thy God in the place which he shall choose; in the feast of unleavened bread, and in the feast of weeks, and in the feast of tabernacles, and they shall not appear before the Lord empty: 17. Every man shall give as he is able, according to the blessing of the Lord thy God which he hath given thee.'

The observance of the three great annual festivals is laid down in this comprehensive cultic calendar. As in Exod. xxiii. 17 and xxxiv. 23, after the three ordinances the main commandment is once again set out as a summary in a concluding formula (*v.* 16). If we start from this concluding formula in Deut. xvi. 16–17, we can see straight away the first problem that the Deuteronomic text presents. *V.* 16, in common with the older cultic calendars such as we find in Exod. xxiii. 14–17 and xxxiv. 18–23, requires for the springtime only a feast of Unleavened Bread. In *vv.* 1–8, on the other hand, there emerges a Passover festival with detailed regulations, of which there was no mention in the older cultic laws or which was indicated with only a few ritual notes in connection with the cultic calendar (cf. Exod. xxiii. 18, 19b; xxxiv. 25, 26b). The Deuteronomic requirements therefore for the first time include the Passover in the cultic regulations of the festival calendar, and link it with the feast of Unleavened Bread. This gives rise to discrepancies, which have to be explained by an analysis of the text. 'A seven-day feast of Unleavened Bread, the last day of which has to be celebrated by a cultic assembly (*v.* 8) cannot be reconciled with the regulation in *v.* 7, according to which one must return to one's home on the morning following the Passover meal. . . .'[12] If we compare the Deuteronomic cultic calendar with the older regulations in Exod. xxiii. 10 ff. and xxxiv. 18 ff. what strikes us particularly, along with many points of detail, is that a strong demand for centralization and an extension of the circle of those who take part in the cult have come to the fore. These are unmistakably the aims of the authors who are responsible for the Deuteronomic conception. We must also not overlook the connections with the cultic reforms of Josiah the King of Judea. But it would be a mistake not to take note of the characteristic features of the theology and tradition of the

[12] Cf. C. Steuernagel, *Das Deuteronomium*, Göttinger Handkommentar zum Alten Testament (2 ed., 1923), p. 112.

Deuteronomists which also point back to the earliest period.[13] The various strata of regulations and concepts in Deut. xvi. 1–17 cannot be fully grasped and adequately explained merely from the standpoint of literary criticism.[14] The first provisional result of our analysis to be noted, therefore, is that the Deuteronomic cultic calendar links the regulation concerning the Passover with the institution of the feast of Unleavened Bread,[15] that the trend towards centralization emerges, and that compared with earlier practices the circle of those who take part in worship is extended. All these points will have to be considered in greater detail later.

(d) *Leviticus xxiii. 4–44*

The regulations concerning the great annual festivals are preceded by a short section (*vv.* 1–3) dealing with the observance of the sabbath. The position occupied by this passage in relation to the cultic calendar is reminiscent of Exod. xxiii. 12, and perhaps indicates a very ancient pattern that has disintegrated in the course of time.[16]

[13] On the problem of the tradition of Deuteronomy, see esp. G. von Rad, *Deuteronomium-Studien* (2 ed., 1948) (E.T. *Studies in Deuteronomy* (1953)) and A. Alt, 'Die Heimat des Deuteronomiums', *Kleine Schriften*, II, pp. 250 ff.

[14] F. Horst makes a careful analysis in *Das Privilegrecht Jahwes*, FRLANT (1930), reprinted in *Gottes Recht* (1961). Horst shows that the section Deut. xvi. 1–17 in its present form is dominated by two overlapping subjects, firstly by the regulation concerning the Passover (linked with the rule concerning the firstborn), and secondly by the definition of the three festivals that have to be observed annually. If we separate the details about the Passover from the connection with the parts concerning the feast of Unleavened Bread, we see that there are two sections (*vv.* 1–3aα and *vv.* 4b–7), which rest on a pre-Deuteronomic foundation not yet affected by the centralization of worship: *vv.* 1a, 3aα, 4b (*Gottes Recht*, pp. 110 f.). Horst ascribes the motive of cultic centralization to edition B, and that of the extension of the circle of cultic participants to edition D. The whole cultic calendar is critically examined from this standpoint, and Horst shows 'that the basic details that are set out in Deut. xvi. 1 ff. concerning the three annual festivals are derived from edition B' (op. cit., p. 123). It is questionable, however, whether we can trace the specific development within the Deuteronomic tradition with such precision. Have we not here the outcome of special redaction of the cultic laws in a particular situation (at the time of Josiah), a redaction which exerted its influence from an early period, no doubt with the intention of influencing the situation?

[15] The question of the relationship between Passover and Unleavened Bread in the pre-Deuteronomic cultic traditions still awaits thorough investigation. But we can note already that the older cultic calendars (Exod. xxiii. 10 ff. and xxxiv. 18 ff.) include rules concerning the Passover rite. Nor should we overlook the JE tradition in Exod. xii.

[16] If we can attempt to set down this scheme, the following order suggests itself: (1) Sabbatical year; (2) Sabbath; (3) The three annual feasts: (*a*) Unleavened Bread, (*b*) feast of Weeks, (*c*) autumn festival. It is surprising, however, that the regulations about the sabbatical year follow separate courses both in Deuteronomy (xv. 1 ff.) and also in the Holiness Code (Lev. xxv. 1 ff.) and that they are expanded by the addition of humane instructions. The sabbath law, however, has a definite place in the Decalogue: Exod. xx. 8 ff. and Deut. v. 12 ff.

Instead of setting out in full the section Lev. xxiii. 4–44 we will make a detailed survey of its structure and contents. When we analyse the passage we see the following picture:

Vv. 4–8. This section first lays down that the feast of the Passover should be held on the fourteenth day of the first month. The Passover element therefore appears independently (as in Deut. xvi. 1 ff.) alongside or before the feast of Unleavened Bread. The latter feast follows the Passover and begins on the fifteenth day of the first month, it lasts a full week and is begun and ended with great days of celebration. During the week burnt offerings are to be presented.

Vv. 9–14. The dues, sacrifices and rites of this double festival that takes place in the first month are described.

Vv. 15–22. The second feast of the year—corresponding to the arrangement of the cultic calendar—is the feast of Weeks. This section first deals with how to reckon the time at which this feast should take place (*vv.* 15 and 16). Seven weeks or fifty days must be counted 'from the morrow after the sabbath' (i.e. presumably from the first day of the feast of Unleavened Bread). Once again the festival week is opened and closed with two great solemn assemblies. The dues, sacrifices and rites which are to be offered during the feast of Weeks are enumerated in detail. The section then concludes with the demand: 'And when ye reap the harvest of your land, thou shalt not wholly reap the corners of thy field, neither shalt thou gather the gleaning of thy harvest: thou shalt leave them for the poor, and for the stranger: I am the Lord your God'. (*v.* 22).

The feast of Ingathering is now divided into three parts:

Vv. 23–25. On the first day of the seventh month a great festival is to be held, which is begun by a characteristic 'blowing of trumpets'. No work may be done, and burnt offerings have to be presented to Yahweh.

Vv. 26–32. On the tenth day of the seventh month the great Day of Atonement is to be observed; the emphasis again is on a festival in the course of which sacrifices have to be offered. Above all, the solemn assembly is marked by a sacred fast and a ceremony of atonement.

Vv. 33–43. On the fifteenth day of the seventh month the festival week of the feast of Tabernacles begins, opened and closed by great feast days. Sacrifices, dues and rites are commanded and set out. The concluding passage, *vv.* 40–43, is particularly significant: 'And ye shall take you on the first day the fruit of goodly trees, branches of palm trees, and boughs of thick trees, and willows of the brook; and ye shall rejoice before the Lord your God seven days. And ye shall keep it a feast unto the Lord seven days in the year: it is a statute for ever in your generations: ye shall keep it in the seventh month. Ye shall dwell in booths seven days: all that are homeborn in Israel shall dwell in booths: That your generations may know that I made the children of Israel to dwell in booths, when I brought them out of the land of Egypt: I am the Lord your God.'

The final words in *v.* 44 are: 'And Moses declared unto the children of Israel the set feasts of the Lord.'

Lev. xxiii is part of the Holiness Code and in certain places clearly shows the marks of the cultic traditions of the Old Testament that are preserved in this body of laws.[17] Whether we place this Holiness Code in the immediate pre-exilic or early exilic period—the signs of this late period are unmistakable—we can see in H (as in Deuteronomy) older traditions of a quite definite circle of tradition.[18] We shall consider this more closely later.

Lev. xxiii provides the occasion for us to consider the question of the different categories in the cultic calendars and regulations. We must first distinguish between 'calendars' and 'rituals'.[19] The calendars fix מועדי יהוה (*v.* 44): the time, duration and names of the feasts which have to be celebrated ליהוה. The rituals lay down the course of the cultic assemblies and deal with the dues and sacrifices that have to be offered, with the ceremonial and the finer points of procedure. Both the categories, the calendars and the rituals, are part of the Torah, which is declared to the people by an authorized spokesman or by the priests.[20] The short form of the cultic calendars has been preserved best of all in Exod. xxiii. 14–17. Ritual regulations have been loosely attached to this very old traditional material (Exod. xxiii. 18 ff.), and in the course of time rituals came to be included more and more with the calendars in the process of instructing the people. We have already seen a good example of this in Deut. xvi. 1 ff. But in Lev. xxiii we can see very clearly the way in which in *vv.* 9–14 the ritual proper follows the regulations about the calendar in *vv.* 4–8, although these verses are of course also interspersed with ritual rules. In the regulations about the feast of Weeks and the feast of Ingathering in Lev. xxiii. 15 ff. we can see that the calendar and the ritual have now merged into an indissoluble

[17] On the 'Holiness Code', see H. Reventlow, 'Das Heiligkeitsgesetz', *WM*, vol. 6 (1961).

[18] Cf. H. Reventlow, op. cit., pp. 103 ff.

[19] On this distinction drawn by form criticism, see R. Rendtorff, *Die Gesetze in der Priesterschrift*, FRLANT (1954).

[20] See H. Reventlow, op. cit., pp. 24 ff.

unity. To distinguish between the two categories at any rate makes it possible to examine the traditional material in both the calendars and the rituals and to recognize the theological and the practical purpose behind the cultic teaching.

We must take particular note of the fact that for the first time in Lev. xxiii we see the division of the feast of Ingathering into three separate cultic observances. The instructions for celebrating the feast of Tabernacles, together with the meaning of the feast, in *vv.* 40–43 also require further examination.

(e) *Numbers xxviii and xxix*

As in the case of Lev. xxiii, we shall give a summary of the structure and contents of Num. xxviii and xxix:

xxviii. 1–8. This section deals with the daily sacrifices. The different offerings are laid down.

xxviii. 9–10. The offerings and sacrifices of the sabbath are described. This makes clear what is required over and above the daily sacrifices.

xxviii. 11–15. Special offerings and sacrifices are stipulated for the first day of each month for the 'new moon'.

xxviii. 16–25. The feast of the Passover is to be held on the fourteenth day of the first month, and the week's feast of Unleavened Bread follows. This week is opened and closed with great solemn assemblies. Rites, sacrifices and offerings are carefully laid down.

xxviii. 26–31. In *v.* 26 the feast of Weeks is called the 'day of the first fruits'. It begins with a great celebration. The sacrifices and offerings are set out in detail.

xxix. 1–6. A solemn assembly is to be held on the first day of the seventh month. It is the 'day of blowing of trumpets', of sacrifice and acts of atonement

xxix. 7–11. A great assembly has to be held also on the tenth day of the seventh month. It is primarily a day of atoning sacrifices.

xxix. 12–39. Detailed regulations concerning the festival week of the feast of Tabernacles, which begins on the fifteenth day of the seventh month. The offerings and sacrifices for each separate day are carefully set out. A great number of ritual requirements are stipulated.

The cultic institutions in Num. xxviii and xxix are part of the Priestly Code. The fixing of these laws should probably be ascribed to the exilic period.[21] Even from the summary we have given we can see that all the regulations are characterized by a great growth of ritual. The

[21] O. Eissfeldt, *Einleitung in das Alte Testament*, pp. 243 ff.

calendar references merely provide the occasion for detailed ritual requirements. This predominance of the ritual element is in keeping with the teaching of the priestly circles in which the body of laws originated.

(f) *Aspects of Canaanite Religion*

When the groups which were to come together in Palestine around 1200 B.C. to form the confederacy of the twelve tribes of Israel left the desert behind them and entered the cultivated land, they encountered the agricultural religion of the native Canaanite population. The agrarian cult which was practised in the country was as colourful and varied as the native inhabitants themselves. The Old Testament provides in a number of passages an insight into the local religious and cultic traditions of the Canaanite shrines which the Israelites discovered, and reveals a great number of the most varied spirits, rites and customs.[22] Early strata of tradition tell of the encounter of the patriarchs of Israel with the cults they found in Palestine, and it was through this encounter with the religious practices of the native inhabitants of Canaan, both in the minor cults and also at the great central sanctuaries, that Israel sought and found its own path of cultic development. There is no element in the cultic tradition of the Old Testament which is not in some way connected with the world of Canaanite religion.[23] The worship of Israel did not fall down complete from Heaven, but arose out of a keen struggle with the powerful religious forms and practices of the country. Its distinctive features developed as a result of sifting, transforming and adopting what they found there on arrival. For this reason it is necessary, in an outline of Old Testament worship, to uncover and recognize the background and the foundations against which the peculiar and characteristic features in Old Testament worship stand out. For an investigation into the history of worship it is therefore necessary constantly to trace the historical and religious connections. The proper way to make such an investigation would no doubt be to make a thorough exegetical examination of those passages in the Old Testament which are relevant to our theme and the aims we have in view. Only by the exegesis of each separate passage could we explore the great variety of detail in the religious and cultic life of Canaan and bring out its significance for the growth and formation of Israel's worship.

[22] H. Gunkel, *Genesis* (5 ed., 1922, HK ed. by W. Nowack, I, 1). A. Alt, 'Der Gott der Väter', *Kleine Schriften*, I, pp. 1 ff.

[23] Noth therefore declares in his article 'Von der Knechtsgestalt des Alten Testaments', *EvTh*, 5/6, (1946), p. 302, that the 'human and historical dependence of the Word contained in the Old Testament is real and complete'.

A systematic summary or 'compendium of Canaanite religion' preliminary to our specific study of the Old Testament can only give the outlines of the various relationships in the history of religion. We can give only a sketch of the great variety of different Canaanite traditions connected with places and sanctuaries, of rites and institutions and customs. Unfortunately, in recent scholarly research into the background of Old Testament worship the attempt to survey the richly varied world of Canaanite religion in 'patterns', and to sum up the basic outlines of the historical developments and local varieties and so to present 'the phenomenon' has led to far-reaching distortions of the facts.[24] This simplifying, systematizing phenomenology can certainly bring to light the main streams and movements which determine religious and cultic life, but it overlooks the infinitely rich ramifications, the peculiarities and the historical and local varieties of 'religious circumstances'. If, for example, we wanted to describe the nature of human existence and stated 'Man is born, gets married and dies', we have no doubt mentioned the main data, but we have not given even an approximate description of the peculiarities in the life story of different human groups or of individuals. The same applies to the study of religion. If we place in the foreground the phenomena 'life and death' or 'sacred marriage', etc., then we are certainly stating some of the main themes, but we are overlooking the great variety in the manifestations of worship at different times and places. It is true that the schematizing studies of certain groups in our day do not proceed in such a generalizing and simplifying manner as our example might suggest, but they do tend towards a very questionable generalization. In particular, they are inclined to force elements that are peculiar and unique into an overall pattern.

We cannot, of course, avoid prefacing our own study of the Old Testament with a few basic remarks about Canaanite religion, but these preliminary indications are not to be taken as the outlines of a scheme which will serve as the key to interpretation and a yardstick for the subsequent studies both of Canaan and of Israel. We simply wish to indicate, by reference to certain extra-Biblical texts from the Canaanite-Syrian world, the larger sphere to which belong the cults and institutions of the nature religion of Palestine, which we shall be examining later in greater detail.

[24] Cf. the two composite volumes edited by S. H. Hooke, *Myth and Ritual* (1933) and *Myth, Ritual and Kingship* (1958), and also the following: S. H. Hooke, *The Origins of Early Semitic Ritual* (Schweich Lectures, 1935); I. Engnell, *Studies in Divine Kingship in the Ancient Near East* (1943); ibid., 'The Text II K from Ras Shamra', *Horae Soederblomianae*, I (1944); G. Widengren, *Sakrales Königtum im Alten Testament und im Judentum* (1955), and other studies which will be referred to later.

The subtropical climate with its seasonal rhythm of succeeding summer drought and winter rain gives an unmistakable stamp to Canaanite worship, bound as it is to the natural cycle. The forces which man encounters in these regions confront him in the natural order. We might first give a preliminary survey and description of this realm, but we cannot undertake this without serious hesitation. Even if the climatic conditions we have mentioned had for the most part a great influence in the Syrian-Canaanite region, we must not overlook the fact that 'for its limited size the country combines the greatest differences and contrasts in geography and also in climate'.[25] These simple observations are therefore of very great significance for the difficult task of drawing distinctions, which we can never lose sight of. Only if we keep this task constantly in mind dare we attempt to make a preliminary survey of the whole field.

An important document concerning early Palestinian agriculture was found at Gezer, a farming calendar inscribed on a small limestone tablet, probably belonging according to its script to the period about 1000 B.C.[26] The rhythm of the months that are important for the farmer's work is set out in a series. The calendar begins with October, the month at the beginning of the year that is so important in the ancient Canaanite division of the year:

> 'A month for gathering
> a month for sowing
> a month for the later sowing
> a month for gathering the flax
> a month for the barley harvest
> a month for harvesting the other crops
> a month for pruning the vines
> a month for the fruit harvest.'

This calendar marks the natural order of the year, but all the sowing and harvesting is a celebration, a religious event. The farmer in his work confronts the forces of nature, interferes with their realm and must take account of this fact in his conduct and all his activity. To the view that all life is sacred no action is 'profane' and no step is 'a matter of course'. Time after time it was necessary to bring beneficial forces into play and to check and resist the influences of harmful powers. The calendar indicates the times and places at which the encounter with these forces

[25] M. Noth, *History of Israel*, p. 9.

[26] M. Lidzbarski, *Handbuch der nordsemitischen Epigraphik* (1898), p. 442, line 6; ibid., *Ephemeris für semitische Epigraphik*, III (1915), pp. 36 ff.; K. Galling, *Biblisches Reallexikon* (1937), Supp., pp. 185 f.

takes place, and mentions the beneficent parts of the year. The year is not divided by quantitative units of time, but is marked by qualitative agricultural celebrations springing from the rhythm of nature.

Whereas the agricultural calendar from Gezer shows a series of tasks to be performed throughout the year and a sequence of periods of special potency, the texts discovered at Ras Shamra reveal a twofold division of the year, imposed upon the sequence of the months. The conditions of a sub-tropical climate split the year into two seasons: the summer drought and the winter rains. Each period represents a sphere of power. In winter Baal, the god of the rain and of blessing, rules. Man attributes the fruits of the field and the gifts of the land to his activity (Hos. ii. 10), but Baal's throne is not secure. When the summer drought begins, then the cry of terror breaks out: 'Baal is dead! *Woe* to the people of Dagân's Son. *Woe* to the multitudes *of* Baal!'[27] The god Mot comes to the fore and establishes the rule of death and drought in the land. Here we see the two powers confronting one another—the power of good fortune and the power of disaster, to which we have already referred. The time when Baal regains the mastery is greeted with rejoicing, and the good news is proclaimed: 'For Aliyn Baal is alive, For the Prince, Lord of Earth, exists.'[28] The 'Lord of the Plowed *Furrows*' now appears.[29] The lightning flashes, the thunder rolls and the clouds open. Baal has triumphed over Mot:

> 'Môt calls from his throat
> The Beloved meditates in his inwards:
> "I alone am he who will rule over the gods
> Yea command gods and men
> Even domin[ate] the multitudes of the earth." '[30]

This dualism of Baal and Mot is characteristic of the conflicts between the powers which the myth discerns behind the seasonal rhythm and which come to a head in the cultic drama.[31] Every cultic action is by its very nature a drama.[32] The good power is attracted and brought into

[27] C. H. Gordon, *Ugaritic Literature*, Scripta Pontifici Biblici, 98 (1949); ibid., *Ugaritic Manual*, Analecta Orientalia, 35 (1955). See J. Aistleitner, *Die mythologischen und kultischen Texte aus Ras Schamra* (1959), I AB I, 6 (trans. C. H. Gordon, *Ugaritic Literature*, p. 42).

[28] C. H. Gordon, op. cit., p. 46.

[29] Ibid.

[30] Ibid., pp. 36 f.

[31] A. S. Kapelrud, *Baal in the Ras Shamra Texts* (1952).

[32] 'The cult is not only originally, but everywhere and at all times, a drama. Cult is sacred art, but it is at the same time sacred reality. Not merely an acted drama, a play, but a real drama which creates reality, a drama which realizes the dramatic event with real force and from which real forces radiate—in other words, a sacrament' (S.

play, and the evil power is repelled and banished. The cultic community is brought into a natural course of events which transcends it but which at the same time carries it along from year to year, in which the gods and the powers are at work. 'A *dromenon*, then, always depends on some deed that is superior to man: it is always "re-done" or "pre-done", and in *this* sense cult action is "representative action." '[33] The great cultic drama, however, as has often been correctly pointed out, was probably celebrated at the turn of the year, in the autumn. It is at this time that the rainy period, the rule of Baal the god of blessing, begins. The resurrection and enthronement of this deity is the real climax of all the religious and cultic life. And we can assume that the pattern of the Baal-Mot cult of Ras Shamra, certain features of which we have just outlined, was, if not determinative, at least characteristic in some form in a great variety of modifications and idiosyncracies for the Syrian-Canaanite region.[34] We can only present this picture tentatively and with caution, for if anyone looks carefully into the texts from Ras Shamra which are known to us, he will certainly soon discover that the evidence we have assembled on the Baal-Mot theme represents only a small part of the cultic mythology of ancient Ugarit. Baal, for example (to quote a further but again only small section of the Ras Shamra texts), fights not only with Mot, but also with the sea god Yam.[35] This theme in the cultic drama reminds us of the particular situation of ancient Ugarit by the sea, and the spiritual intercourse which this outstanding city culture of Syria could have with the religious traditions of Egypt and Mesopotamia. Here we can see straight away the special features of a cultic tradition which arose under specific geographical and historical conditions. Other themes in the Ras Shamra texts confirm this view.[36] It could be asked what right one has to call special attention to the Baal-Mot theme in its simplest manifestations. The answer can only be given by reference to the fact that in the conflicts of the two powers there are reflected in a clear and

[33] G. van der Leeuw, *Phänomenologie der Religion* (1933), p. 350 (E.T. *Religion in Essence and Manifestation* (1938), p. 373).

[34] For the significance of the Ras Shamra texts, cf. J. Friedrich, 'Ras-Schamra—Ein Überblick über Funde und Forschungen', *AO*, 33, 1/2 (1934); C. F. A. Schaeffer, *Ugaritica*, (I), II, III, *Mission des Ras Shamra*, III, V, VIII, Bibliothèque archéologique et historique, XXXI, XLVII, LXIV (Paris, 1939, 1949, 1956); T. H. Gaster, *Thespis. Ritual, Myth and Drama in the Ancient Near East* (1950); W. Schmidt, *Königtum Gottes in Ugarit und Israel*, BZAW 80 (1961).

[35] See esp. Aistleitner, op. cit., III AB A.

[36] Ibid., BH II 43–46.

Mowinckel, *Psalmenstudien, II: Das Thronbesteigungsfest Jahwäs und der Ursprung der Eschatologie* (1921), p. 21). Cf. also Mowinckel's *Religion und Kultus*, (1953), pp. 73 ff.

convincing way the underlying religious realities which come out in the rhythmic succession of summer drought and winter rains. The dramatic event of the enthronement of Baal in the mythological texts also throws light on the decisive cultic celebrations corresponding to the transfer of power, in which at a significant moment nature religion is caught up into the supernatural event, but at the same time sets it in motion by representative action.

We can see in many religions the attempt to incorporate the annual festival cycle in a longer period. As examples we might quote the ancient Egyptian Sed festival, the ninefold and threefold periods which we find in Greece and the Roman *lustrum* and *saeculum*. The Ras Shamra texts also contain traces of such longer periods. Whilst we are considering these periods of time in this introductory part of our study we will turn to a final, longer passage. In the section BH II, 43–45 we read:

> 'Seven years the god is abundant [ ]
> Even eight cycles, until [ ].'[37]

Alongside this we should set the passage ID 38–48:

> 'Thereupon Daniel, Man of Rp', imprecates:
> "Clouds in the *heat* of *evil*
> *The early rains*
> Clouds that rain on the summer fruit
> Dew that falls on the grapes!
> Seven years may Baal fail
> Eight, the Rider of Clouds!
> Without dew
> Without rain
> Without *surging* of the Two Deeps
> Without the goodness of Baal's voice!"
> As she tears the garb of Daniel, Man of Rp',
> The garment of the Hero, Ma[n] of Hr[nmy]. . . .'
>
> (C. H. Gordon, op. cit., pp. 94 f.)

We can see clearly from these two passages that the period of seven years was a superimposed, longer period of time which had to be observed as regards the rule of the gods.[38] It would, of course, be possible to question whether these seven years of drought had any significance as a period, and to suppose that an exceptional drought lasting for years

[37] Ibid., I D 38–48 (trans. C. H. Gordon, op. cit., p. 55). The period of seven years is mentioned also in D 176–180, where the reference is to the period of mourning for *Aqht*, which is brought to an end in the seventh year by *Dnl*. See also III K III 22.

[38] C. H. Gordon, *Ugaritic Literature*, pp. 3 ff.; ibid., 'Sabbatical Year or Seasonal Pattern? Reflections on a New Book', *Or*, N.S. 22 (1955), pp. 79–81.

once provided the occasion for marking out this longer period with a symbolic number. In this case the cultic mythology would reflect this particular occurrence. But we should note how consistently in the Ras Shamra texts 'seven years' is mentioned several times. The religious thought of the ancient world is far more complex than the rational conception of modern thought can suggest. Behind every manifestation of power there are deeper, more basic realities. The series of annual celebrations which we can see in the agricultural calendar from Gezer falls within the sphere of the two seasons and their gods. These two seasons in turn are over-arched by a higher division into periods.[39] One could speak of a hierarchy of these spheres of power, but the idea of a structure with logical gradations would be misleading, because the links in the chain leading up to an astral mythology are interlocked in a magical complexity. The times of continuous drought, therefore, are basically not a historical vicissitude, but the effects of a higher ordering of periods, upon which myth and cult seek to act with divination and ritual. It would be a fundamental mistake to transform the number '7' into a unit of time which could be reckoned mathematically. Here again time is not to be assessed quantitatively, but can be understood only as a complete unit of power. It is not necessary here to speculate about the symbolical significance of the number '7', for it is not the formal general symbolic value that determines the nature of the period of time, but its actual content of power as it confronts man. If the two texts we have quoted seem to suggest some reservation in the passage 'seven years . . . eight years . . .' as regards the extent of the event, we should not take this to be a vague reference to time (in the sense of the modern attitude to time), but rather an indication of the fact that the intensity of the manifestation of power can exceed what can well be contained within the system of periods. We can tell how sharply defined the idea of a seven-year period is from the fact that the Old Testament also mentions 'seven fat' and 'seven lean years' in Gen. xli. 1 ff. This legendary motif no doubt signifies in the narrative context of the Joseph stories some exceptional experience that befell Egypt, but against the background of the Ras Shamra texts we can see the wider context to which it clearly belongs. Periods of great continual drought proclaim the powerful emergence of a period superimposed upon the 'normal rhythm of nature'. We can see here the underlying power of an all-

[39] The alternatives suggested in the discussion between A. S. Kapelrud (*Baal in the Ras Shamra Texts*, 1952) and C. H. Gordon, 'period of seven years or annual cultic activity', does not really take into account the complexity of the religious thought of the ancient world.

embracing reality which threatens the very basis of life. Even the natural catastrophe has its place in a higher ordering. But 'ordering' does not mean that everything can now be understood and adjusted and controlled. The rhythms and periods—as we have just indicated—always radiate direful effects. The transitions from one period to another are laden with danger and fear, and sacrifices and rites impinge upon this fatal realm. But against this background the festal joy has its special significance, for it celebrates the breakthrough to a renewal of life, the liberation from the spell of evil powers.

(g) *Problems Connected with the Calendar*

In ancient times the dates in the calendar were based primarily upon agricultural factors. Seed-time and harvest determined man's relationship to time. Another important landmark was provided, however, by observations concerning the flood waters, both in Mesopotamia and also in Egypt. But men looked for signs by which times could be fixed not only on the earth but also in the heavens. In Mesopotamia even in the earliest period the moon was thought of as 'Lord of the calendar'.[40] Priestly sciences studied the cycles and calculated the lunar months, and from time to time the differences from the solar year were made up by an intercalary month (*dirigû*).[41] The stars were studied with the aid of gauging instruments.[42] In Egypt observations of Sirius were decisive for fixing the cultic calendar: 'Sirius, after the lapse of 365 days during which it cannot be seen, becomes visible again as a bright star for the first time before sunrise (heliacal rising) and the regularity of its appearance, which occurred about the beginning of the flooding of the Nile, the time of which always varied, led the Egyptians to think of the rise of Sirius, which could be calculated in advance, as the New Year's day in the calendar and as the "bringer of the floods". This is how the 365-day Egyptian year, reckoned by observation of the stars and based on the Nile floods, arose.'[43] These astronomical definitions were important, as there were variations in the rhythm of nature. Above all, the State had a great interest in making the fixing of the calendar through priestly science the basis of a cult, the appointed times of which could be accurately laid down. The Egyptian New Year feasts were the 'beginnings of the division of time into periods'.[44] Official processions

[40] H. Schmökel, *Das Land Sumer*, Urban-Bücher, 13, p. 130.

[41] B. Meissner, *Babylonien und Assyrien*, II (1925), pp. 395 ff.

[42] Ibid., p. 401.

[43] E. Otto, *Ägypten—Der Weg des Pharaonenreiches* (1953), p. 39.

[44] Cf. H. Bonnet, *Reallexikon der ägyptischen Religionsgeschichte* (1952), p. 186; also G. Roeder, *Kulte, Orakel und Naturverehrung im alten Ägypten* (1960), p. 158. In

were held in honour of the gods. In the Old Testament the earliest indications of time refer mostly to seed-time and harvest (cf. Joshua iii. 15). The barley harvest (2 Sam. xxi. 9; Ruth i. 22) and the corn harvest (Gen. xxx. 14; Judges xv. 1; 1 Sam. xii. 17) are the main occasions by which dates are reckoned. Nature is the great calendar.[45] In the early period worship also follows the pattern of this natural calendar (cf. Gen. viii. 22). As amongst their Canaanite-Syrian neighbours, the principal festival observed by the Israelites comes in autumn. When the fruits are ready for harvesting, before the first rain falls, is the time of the turn of the year. But in ancient Israel also astronomical observations help to fix the times exactly.[46] The stars indicate the times (Gen. i. 14) and the moon in particular serves to fix the calendar (Ps. civ. 19; Ecclus. xliii. 7). It was probably the task of the priests to calculate the appointed times for worship.[47] The State, however, exercised also in Israel a final regulating function in respect of the times of the festivals. 'The Israelites based their reckoning of time on the lunar-solar calendar, according to which the months are fixed by the cycle of the moon and the year by the sun. The difference between 12 months = 354 days and the 365¼ days of the solar year is made up by an intercalary month.'[48] In this way the year measured by time grew gradually out of the year based on the rhythm of nature.

The transfer of the turn of the year from autumn to spring presents a special problem in the Old Testament. In the early period the year began in autumn. Later the conquering powers of Babylon imposed their chronology, with the beginning of the year in the spring, on their subject states.[49] The month Abib, in which the cultic calendar places the feast of Unleavened Bread, becomes the first month of the year (cf., in particular, Exod. xii. 2), whereas the month Etanim, which was once the period of the turn of the year and the autumn festival, is reckoned as the seventh month. When did this change in the calendar

[45] G. Dalman, *Arbeit und Sitte in Pälastina*, I (Jahreslauf und Tageslauf), pp. 1 ff.

[46] Ibid., pp. 9 ff.

[47] 'The beginning of the dry season and the wet season in Palestine is subject to considerable variations' (G. Dalman, op. cit., p. 36).

[48] E. Kutsch, *Das Herbstfest in Israel*, Diss., Mainz (1955), p. 58.

[49] The Babylonian year began with the spring equinox at Nisan. 'But the seventh month *tischrîtu*, which began at the time of the autumn equinox, is also referred to in the texts of the Sargonide period as the beginning of the year (the name *tischrîtu* in fact means "beginning"), but it is doubtful whether this was ever observed in practice' (B. Meissner, *Babylonien und Assyrien*, II, p. 396).

---

ancient Sumeria great festivals were celebrated when 'a new year appeared in the sky'; cf. A. Falkenstein/W. von Soden, *Sumerische und akkadische Hymnen und Gebete* (1953), p. 168.

take place? Probably by the end of the eighth century,[50] but certainly by the time of the subjection of Judah under Babylonian supremacy. We can now see emerging alongside each other a secular calendar and a sacral calendar. Whilst the year officially begins with the 'first month' in spring, the cultic community in Jerusalem celebrates the turn of the year according to tradition in autumn—in the 'seventh month.'

2. The Feast of the Passover and of Unleavened Bread.

The regulation about the feast that has to be celebrated in spring occupies the first place in the cultic calendar in the Old Testament. The pre-Deuteronomic traditions refer only to the feast of Unleavened Bread as a pilgrimage feast that is held in the spring. It is not until Deut. xvi. 1–18 that we meet a feast of the Passover and of Unleavened Bread in the cultic calendars, which is celebrated from now on in the central sanctuary (Lev. xxiii. 4 ff.; Ezek. xlv. 21 ff.; Num. xxviii. 16 ff.). The Passover rite is nevertheless very old and points back to nomadic or semi-nomadic conditions of life.

(a) *The Origin and 'Historicizing' of the Passover Rite*

The designation פסח for the rite observed in the springtime is found in the pre-Deuteronomic tradition in Exod. xii. 21 f. and xxxiv. 25—i.e. in the Yahwistic source.[51] It is not certain how the meaning of this old designation should be understood. There are four possible interpretations which have to be considered: (1) The root פסח according to 1 Kings xviii. 21 contains the idea of 'hopping' or 'limping', which suggests that פסח described a special cultic dance. Against this, however, we have to set the fact 'that there is no evidence of a חגג although the festival is called חג in Exod. xii. 14; xxiii. 18; xxxiv. 25; Ezek. xlv. 21, 23, suggesting that the feast is linked with the house, which one cannot leave before daybreak'.[52] (2) The attempt has sometimes been made to connect the root פסח with the Akkadian word *pašāḫu*, and to deduce from this the ritual act of 'appeasing' and 'assuaging' the deity. But this suggestion also gives rise to difficulties, for the liturgical views

[50] Cf. E. Kutsch, op. cit., p. 68: 'Under Assyrian influence there emerges at the end of the eighth century alongside this system another system whose year begins in spring.' The months are first numbered counting from the spring, and under Babylonian influence are later given names.

[51] It is generally recognized by scholars who adopt the criteria of source analysis that the passages Exod. xii. 21–23, 29–34, 37–39 belong to J. We have already considered Exod. xxxiv. 25.

[52] B. Stade, *Biblische Theologie des Alten Testaments* (1905), p. 174.

and actions that prevailed in Mesopotamia cannot simply be transferred to the nomadic or semi-nomadic sphere. (3) B. Couroyer in his article 'L'origine égyptienne du mot "Pâque"' (*RB*, 62 (1955), pp. 481 ff.) attempted to trace the Egyptian origin of the concept פסח but his theory also is questionable, because it brings together two dissimilar sociological spheres. (4) The most reasonable interpretation, therefore, seems to be to take פסח, in the light of Exod. xii. 23, as a concept signifying the 'merciful passing over' of a destructive power. This would make 'Passover' a rite which effects this 'merciful passing over'. But this explanation can only be a tentative one, for it is impossible to say with any certainty what the ancient ideas and customs were. The earliest actions in the Passover rite have to be deduced from the Yahwistic traditions. We can see clearly the communal setting in which the celebration takes place, that of the clan, the camp community. Every family has to sacrifice one young animal from the flock (Exod. xii. 21).[53] The doors (originally the entrances to the tent) are smeared with the blood of the sacrificial animal (Exod. xii. 22). This apotropaic rite is meant to protect man and beast against demonic influences and attacks. Then the camp community breaks up in haste (Exod. xii. 33). Leonhard Rost in his article 'Weidewechsel and altisraelitischer Festkalender' points out that this breaking up signifies a specific situation in the life of nomadic shepherds.[54] In the spring the semi-nomads—in keeping with the rhythm of the seasonal migration—leave the desert region and move into the cultivated parts. This transition was begun at a definite time (probably on a night of the full moon in spring). The Passover ritual should therefore be considered as an 'observance to secure protection' in the night immediately before the start of the migration.[55] The prohibition of leaven which is laid down in the Old Testament cultic

[53] It is possible that the rite laid down in Exod. xxiii. 19b and xxxiv. 26b should be connected with the celebration of the Passover. The contrast to the agricultural practice that can be traced at Ugarit could be of nomadic origin.

[54] L. Rost, 'Weidewechsel und altisraelitischer Festkalender', *ZDPV*, 66 (1943), pp. 205 ff. Reprinted in *Das kleine Credo und andere Studien zum AT* (1965), p. 101 ff.

[55] Ibid., p. 211. G. Dalman makes the interesting point that even in the quite recent past similar rites were observed among the Beduins. If these rites belong to the context of an autumn festival, then they are of the greatest significance. 'The *Rašaide* Beduins kill a sacrificial victim (*fidu*). . . . They kill the animal in the camp and smear with blood a point between the eyes of the young children, three lines to the right and to the left on the camels' humps, and also all the three tent poles that are inside. Then they go, the men firing off their guns and the women in their finery, to Moses' grave, kiss it and say "Lord Moses, we beseech thee to protect us from evil, from the evil of villains, spare our cattle, spare our children, punish our enemies and save us from evil befalling our white camels".' (Cf. *Arbeit und Sitte in Palästina*, VI: Zeltleben, Vieh- und Milchwirtschaft, Jagd, Fischfang, p. 374.)

laws essentially for the feast of Unleavened Bread no doubt played a part also in the Passover rite (Exod. xii. 34; xxxiv. 25; xxiii. 18). It is possible that the semi-nomads adopted this custom from the Canaanite inhabitants (see below). The prohibition of leaven is explained by the speed of the departure, which made it impossible for the dough to be leavened (Exod. xii. 39).

In Israel the Passover rite was taken over and 'historicized' at an early stage. The demonic element was excluded and Yahweh came to occupy the centre of the event (Exod. xii. 23). In particular, the annual 'exodus' from the desert was regarded in the light of new presuppositions under the influence of the historical traditions concerning the 'exodus from Egypt'. The feast of the Passover acquired a connotation connected with redemptive history. This 'historicizing' is already assumed by J (Exod. xii. 21 ff.). But immediately questions arise. Where and how was the Passover rite observed in ancient Israel? Can we assume that in the earliest period, immediately after the conquest, the families celebrated the 'historicized' feast?[56] Was the situation of the community that dwelt in tents transferred to the community when it came to live in houses? What was the relationship then between the Passover rite and the feast of Unleavened Bread? Did they observe the Passover in the family circle and then go on pilgrimage to the sanctuary and celebrate Unleavened Bread there? There are many problems here which can only be clarified when we have considered more fully the cultic calendars and the local traditions.

(b) *The Feast of Unleavened Bread as an Annual Feast in Ancient Israel*

Whereas the Passover rite had its origin in the semi-nomadic sphere, the feast of Unleavened Bread belonged to the agricultural sphere. The observances are from different backgrounds. In the story of Cain and Abel the shepherd's worship is very clearly contrasted with that of the farmer.[57] We must again begin by considering the name of the festival. It is called חג המצות (Exod. xxiii. 15; xxxiv. 18). מצות, flat unleavened bread cakes, are to be eaten (Exod. xxiii. 15; xxxiv. 18). In Joshua v. 11 מקצות וקלוי are referred to in ancient terminology. מצות (Akkadian *kalû*)

[56] J. Pedersen examined the Passover legends that have come down to us in the Old Testament in his article 'Passahfest und Passahlegende', *ZAW*, 52 (1934), pp. 161 ff. Unfortunately he does not go fully into the sociological questions. Pedersen starts from the general concept of 'primitive cultic practice' and brings out the dramatic and legendary element very clearly, but the historical development of the festival remains vague.

[57] Cf. J. Wellhausen, *Prolegomena*, E.T., p. 89.

means the fresh roasted grains. The original meaning of the rite seems to have been as follows. The farmers assembled at the sanctuaries in the cultivated land at the time of the barley harvest in order to enjoy the first new corn and the fresh loaves in a devout observance. Nothing leavened was permitted, for the new crop could not be mixed with the produce of the past year. Offerings to the deity, sacrifices and thanksgiving ceremonies were probably linked with this rite.[58] Wellhausen's words can be applied to this pre-Israelite agricultural festival: 'The blessing of the land is here the end of religion. . . . It has for its basis no historical acts of salvation, but nature simply, which, however, is regarded only as God's domain and as man's field of labour, and is in no manner itself deified. . . . In accordance with this, worship consists simply of the thanksgiving due for the gifts of the soil, the vassalage payable to the superior who has given the land and its fruits.'[59] Unleavened Bread was originally a Canaanite agricultural festival, which began at the time of the barley harvest, probably immediately after the spring equinox, and lasted seven days.[60]

Israel adopted the feast of Unleavened Bread from the native Canaanite population. In three respects we can see how the agrarian rite is modified and reshaped: (1) The whole celebration is directed towards Yahweh. The ליהוה of Exod. xxiii. 14 which refers the cultic actions to the God of Israel is characteristic. The harvest thanksgiving is for him alone. But whilst the festival is drawn from Baal religion, the cultic actions exclude the nature myth. W. Eichrodt has therefore correctly drawn attention to the fact that the rituals connected with the Old Testament feast of Unleavened Bread contain no lament about the dying of the vegetation.[61] (2) The festival is centralized.[62] The men have to

[58] There is no concrete evidence for Engnell's assertion that the Israelite feast of the Passover and of Unleavened Bread was in its original form a Canaanite New Year festival, and that Passover was a southern and Unleavened Bread a northern type of this cult. It is incomprehensible how, when everything is determined by the idea of a 'pattern', all the actual evidence becomes blurred. If it suits one's purpose, it is assumed that in Canaan, where the turn of the year was celebrated in autumn, there was also (corresponding to the ancient Eastern calendar) a New Year festival in the spring. Cf. I. Engnell, 'Paesah-Maṣṣōt, a Hebrew Annual Festival of the Ancient Near East Pattern', *Proceedings of the 7th Congress for the History of Religion*, ed. by C. J. Bleeker (1951), pp. 111 ff.

[59] J. Wellhausen, op. cit., p. 97.

[60] E. Kutsch has rightly raised the question whether the seven-day festival week was an element taken over from the Canaanites. This question has an important bearing on the problem of the origins of the sabbath, and will be considered when we turn to this subject. See E. Kutsch, 'Erwägungen zur Geschichte der Passahfeier und des Massotfestes', *ZThK* (1958), pp. 1 ff.

[61] W. Eichrodt, *Theology of the Old Testament*, I, p. 121.

[62] See chapter 3, section 1, below.

appear 'before the face of the Lord God' (cf. Exod. xxiii. 17; xxxiv. 24), and in Exod. xxiii. 19 'the house of the Lord' is mentioned. The existence of a central sanctuary has certainly to be presupposed for the cultic calendars in Exod. xxiii and xxxiv. (3) Attempts were made to 'historicize' the feast of Unleavened Bread as well as the Passover.[63] This can be seen most clearly in Joshua v. 11, where the 'first' corn becomes the 'first corn of the children of Israel as they enter and conquer Canaan'.

The place occupied by the feast of Unleavened Bread in the cultic calendar in the series of three annual festivals clearly shows that it was a pilgrimage festival which was celebrated every year in the (central) sanctuary. The two passages Exod. xxiii. 15 and xxxiv. 18 ff. point to the period before the monarchy. For the monarchical period 1 Kings ix. 25 (2 Chron. viii. 13) testifies to the status and importance of the spring festival.

(c) *The Feast of the Passover and of Unleavened Bread*[64]

Deut. xvi. 16 f. sums up the regulations concerning the festivals as follows:

'Three times in a year shall all thy males appear before the Lord thy God in the place which he shall choose; in the feast of unleavened bread, and in the feast of weeks, and in the feast of tabernacles. . . .'

[63] We must not overlook the fact that both in Exod. xxiii. 15 and also in Exod. xxxiv. 18 it is stated in the cultic calendar that Israel 'came out from Egypt' in the month Abib. The time of the festival is therefore determined by the remembrance of an historical event.

[64] Bibliography dealing with the feast of the Passover and Unleavened Bread: J. Müller, *Kritischer Versuch über den Ursprung und die geschichtliche Entwicklung des Passah-Mazzothfestes* (1883); G. Beer, *Pesachim* (*Die Mischna*. Text, Übersetzung und ausführliche Erklärung, II, 3 (1912)); N. M. Nicolsky, 'Pascha im Kult des jerusalemischen Tempels', *ZAW* (1927), pp. 171 ff.; F. Horst, *Das Privilegrecht Jahwes*, FRLANT (1930), *Gottes Recht*, pp. 17 ff.; J. Jeremias, 'Die Passahfeier der Samaritaner und ihre Bedeutung für das Verständnis der alttestamentlichen Passahüberlieferung', BZAW, 59 (1932); J. Pedersen, 'Passahfest und Passahlegende', *ZAW*, 52 (1934), pp. 161 ff.; L. Rost, 'Weidewechsel und altisraelitischer Kultkalender', *ZDPV*, 66 (1943), pp. 205 ff., reprinted in *Das kleine Credo und andere Studien zum AT* (1965), pp. 101 ff.; S. Mowinckel, 'Die vermeintliche "Passahlegende" ', *StTh*, 5 (1951), pp. 66 ff.; H. J. Kraus, 'Gilgal—Ein Beitrag zur Kultgeschichte Israels', *VT*, I (1951), pp. 181 ff.; ibid., 'Zur Geschichte des Passah-Massot-Festes im Alten Testament', *EvTh*, 18 (1958), pp. 47 ff.; I. Engnell, '*Paesah-Massot* and the Problem of "Patternism" ', *Orientalia Suecana*, I (1952), pp. 39 ff.; H. Haag, 'Ursprung und Sinn der alttestamentlichen Paschafeier', *Luzerner theologische Studien*, I (1954), pp. 17 ff.; B. Couroyer, 'L'origine égyptienne du mot "Pâque" ', *RB*, 62 (1955), pp. 481 ff.; E. Kutsch, 'Erwägungen zur Geschichte der Passahfeier und des Massotfestes', *ZThK*, 55 (1958), pp. 47 ff.; ibid., 'Feste und Feiern in Israel', *RGG* (3 ed.), II, pp. 910 ff.; E. L. Ehrlich, *Die Kultsymbolik im Alten Testament und im nachbiblischen Judentum*, Symbolik der Religionen, III (1959), pp. 65 ff.; R. de Vaux, *Les Institutions de l'Ancien Testament*, II (1960), pp. 385 ff. (E.T. *Ancient Israel: Its Life and Institutions* (1961), pp. 484 ff.).

In this list we can see clearly the marks of the Deuteronomic adaptation and phraseology (centralization and extension of the circle of those who participate in the cult), and it seems surprising that in contrast to Deut. xvi. 1–8 there is no mention of the feast of the Passover. The Deuteronomist is evidently following in this final summary the traditional arrangement, which includes only the feast of Unleavened Bread among the pilgrimage festivals for the spring. There is therefore a special purpose behind the inclusion of the Passover among the spring festivals (Deut. xvi. 1 ff.). A rite which hitherto has been observed in each locality as a family festival is now to be transferred to the sanctuary in Jerusalem as part of the thoroughgoing centralization of all worship (cf. Deut. xvi. 5 f.). It was an old custom for the three great annual festivals to be celebrated at the cultic centre.[65] But the feast of the Passover, as a result of its ancient connection with the clan, continued its separate existence apart from the sanctuary. 'In Deut. xvi. 1–8 we see the process whereby Deuteronomy (as the "Book of the Law" which was the basis of Josiah's reform [2 Kings xxii f.]) seeks to elevate the Passover, which the Israelites previously celebrated at home, into a pilgrimage festival and at the same time—in order to preserve the traditional number of three pilgrimage festivals—to put it in place of the feast of Unleavened Bread, which was also observed in the spring, "in the month of Abib" or "in the first month".'[66] In 2 Kings xxiii. 21 ff. we learn how the Deuteronomic law was adopted and observed in the practice of worship in the period of Josiah. But this account makes a special point which cannot be overlooked: 'And the king commanded all the people, saying, keep the passover unto the Lord your God, as it is written in this book of the covenant. Surely there was not kept such a passover from the days of the judges that judged Israel, nor in all the days of the kings of Israel, nor of the kings of Judah; but in the eighteenth year of King Josiah was this passover kept to the Lord in Jerusalem.' This passage is meant to make it quite clear that when we think of the feast of the Passover as a pilgrimage and sanctuary feast we are not to think of it as an absolute innovation, but as the reintroduction of an old custom from the period before the monarchy. The tendency has been to

[65] P. Volz had already pointed out in *Das Neujahrsfest Jahwes* (1912) that centralization was not a late development, but a tendency present in Old Testament worship from the beginning (p. 9 and esp. p. 23). Noth's studies have since shown quite clearly that Israel as a sacral tribal federation had a central sanctuary even in the period before the monarchy, upon which all cultic activity was concentrated (*Das System der Zwölf Stämme Israels*). For further comments, see chapter 3, section 1, below.

[66] E. Kutsch, 'Erwägungen zur Geschichte der Passahfeier und des Massotfestes', *ZThK*, 55 (1958), p. 12.

consider this reference to a cultic tradition of the period of the judges as without historical foundation and to see it as the claim of a conservative movement conscious of tradition. But if we ask whether there is any evidence in the Old Testament traditions from the period of the judges of a Passover which 'all Israel' celebrated, we are confronted by Joshua v. 10 ff., which refers to a feast of the Passover and of Unleavened Bread which was celebrated by 'all Israel' at Gilgal. As this passage raises very complicated questions concerning the history of various traditions and problems of literary criticism, the full significance of which can only be understood in the context of the local cultic traditions at the sanctuary of Gilgal, the question of the ancient Israelite feast of the Passover and of Unleavened Bread in the time of the judges will have to be considered later. We shall see that the information contained in 2 Kings xxiii. 22 is reliable (cf. p. 163).

There can be no doubt, however, that the measure carried out by Josiah to include the Passover in the pilgrimage and sanctuary festival of the spring meant a revolutionary change for the monarchical period. The account in 2 Chron. xxx seems to suggest otherwise, for in this chapter of the Chronicler's record we are told that after the fall of the northern kingdom King Hezekiah sent out an invitation to all Israel to celebrate the Passover in Jerusalem. Is this account in keeping with the facts or was the Chronicler, writing apparently in the third century B.C., trying to point the moral for his own time?[67] The problem facing this later period was the relationship of the sanctuary in Jerusalem to the cultic community of the Samaritans. In order to answer the question we have posed we need to examine the attitude adopted by the Chronicler to the traditions that had come down to him, in particular his attitude to the 'Deuteronomic history'. Martin Noth points out 'that the Chronicler takes up a fundamentally positive attitude towards the sources that were available to him: he made them the basis of his record not only as regards content but essentially also as regards the actual wording, even where he followed them to a greater degree than we now know was desirable, but believing that he used them only in the light of what he considered to be the correct interpretation of the sources'.[68] What should be our attitude towards 2 Chron. xxx? A comparison with the 'Deuteronomic history' shows that the latter provides no basis for the account given in 2 Chron. xxx. And it is hardly possible to accept the suggestion that there was a 'separate tradition' from which the author might have drawn. It is probably a free addition

[67] See E. Kutsch, op. cit., pp. 22 f.

[68] M. Noth, *Überlieferungsgeschichtliche Studien*, I (1943), p. 166.

made by the Chronicler. Noth describes these 'additions' as follows: 'What really gives the historical narrative of the Chronicler its different aspect are the additions, which . . . depend only to a very small degree on the use of another ancient source in the monarchical period, but have been almost entirely contributed by the Chronicler from his own material. . . . With these additions he could believe he was interpreting his sources objectively, without altering their wording, whilst he added to this or that statement that seemed important to him in the sources and so considerably expanded the historical account or introduced new features by combining various elements from the sources. By doing this and by formulating the additions from the standpoint of his own day he introduced into his account of history those anachronisms which so much disfigure the historical account based on ancient traditions.'[69] This description of the 'additions' fits 2 Chron. xxx exactly. The Chronicler, in connection with the 'covenant' newly made by Hezekiah, has projected into his historical account the parallel events of Josiah's period, in particular the celebration of the Passover. In this way he was able to deliver a message to his own day which could be particularly effective in view of the analogy of the events. Hezekiah calls the northern Israelites to return. 'But a return to Yahweh means a return to the Temple in Jerusalem—that is the essence of this call, which of course in the eyes of the Chronicler applies as well to the Samaritans of his own time.'[70] According to the narrative in 2 Chron. xxx. 10 f. Hezekiah's messengers who carried the invitation to the Passover in Jerusalem are supposed to have been scorned. The reception given to the royal message in the northern kingdom reflects what was the experience with Samaria time after time in the period of the Chronicler: Jerusalem's claim to be the only true Yahweh sanctuary is ridiculed and mocked by the majority (*v.* 10).[71] The account in 2 Chron. xxx has therefore to be understood in the light of the situation prevailing in the third century B.C., and we shall have to consider this aspect of it again later. The information given in 2 Kings xxiii. 22 is therefore substantiated: 'in all the days of the kings of Israel nor of the kings of Judah' no feast of the Passover for the whole of Israel, such as Josiah reintroduced, was celebrated.

The connection between the feast of the Passover and the feast of Unleavened Bread which is made in Deut. xvi. 1–8 forms the basis for the festival calendar in the Holiness Code.[72] On the fourteenth day of the first month the Passover is celebrated and on the fifteenth the festival

[69] M. Noth, *Überlieferungsgeschichtliche Studien*, I (1943), p. 166.
[70] W. Rudolph, *Chronikbücher*, HAT, I, 22 (1955), p. 300.
[71] Ibid., p. 300.
[72] Cf. H. Reventlow, *Das Heiligkeitsgesetz* (1961), pp. 111 f.

week of Unleavened Bread begins (Lev. xxiii. 4 ff.). The inclusion of this week within two 'feast days' which are called מקרא קדש is to be noted.[73] The ritual laid down becomes more extensive and more detailed, and the sacrificial actions and customs concerning the offerings stand out in greater detail. But the ancient prescription ליהוה is still asserted (*v.* 6). The emphasis on this aspect is all the more important as there is no suggestion in Lev. xxiii. 4–14 of any basis in redemptive history for the feast of the Passover and of Unleavened Bread. Whereas the cultic calendars in Exod. xxiii and xxxiv and Deut. xvi at least suggested that the spring festival was connected with the exodus from Egypt, in Lev. xxiii. 4–14 there is no trace of this suggestion. In the cultic calendar of the Holiness Code it is rather the feast of Tabernacles that is thought of as a memorial celebration which represents the event of the exodus (cf. Lev. xxiii. 43).

The observance of a feast of the Passover and of Unleavened Bread at the sanctuary in Jerusalem is also prescribed in Ezek. xlv. 21 ff.: 'In the first month, in the fourteenth day of the month, ye shall have the passover, a feast of seven days; unleavened bread shall be eaten. And upon that day shall the prince prepare for himself and for all the people of the land a bullock for a sin offering. And the seven days of the feast he shall prepare a burnt offering to the Lord, seven bullocks and seven rams without blemish daily the seven days: and a he-goat daily for a sin offering. And he shall prepare a meal offering, an ephah for a bullock, and an ephah for a ram, and an hin of oil to an ephah.'

This cultic calendar belongs to 'Ezekiel's outline of a constitution'.[74] The spring festival is now simply described as פסח (*v.* 21). The rites connected with the feast of Unleavened Bread are merely part of the great feast of the Passover, and it is noticeable that in the cultic calendar in Ezek. xlv. 21 ff. only an autumn festival is added, and that the feast of Weeks is missing. The ritual in *v.* 22 applies exclusively to the prince, who, as the cultic mediator, is the dominant figure in the sacral ordinances and is responsible for the sacrifices.

The Priestly Code considerably develops in Num. xxviii the ritual aspect of the cultic traditions that are laid down in the Deuteronomic law and expanded in Lev. xxiii. 4 ff. and Ezek. xlv. 21 ff. More and more distinctions are made in the regulations about sacrifices and the stipulations concerning the offerings. But we can recognize even in Exod. xii the work of priestly circles, which gave a new form to the traditions that had been handed down. Traditions concerning the Passover and

[73] For the meaning of מקרא see E. Kutsch, מקרא, *ZAW*, 65 (1953), pp. 247 ff.

[74] Cf. H. Gese, *Der Verfassungsentwurf des Ezechiel*, BHT, 25 (1957), pp. 80 ff.

traditions concerning the feast of Unleavened Bread were amalgamated.[75] It is explicitly laid down that 'the whole assembly of the congregation of Israel' (Exod. xii. 6) should celebrate the festival; in other words all the cultic regulations point to the feast of the Passover and of Unleavened Bread as it was celebrated after the Exile. We can tell from the account in Ezra vi. 19 ff., however, how much the Passover element dominated in this period:

'And the children of the captivity kept the passover upon the fourteenth day of the first month. For the priests and the Levites had purified themselves together; all of them were pure: and they killed the passover for all the children of the captivity, and for their brethren the priests, and for themselves. And the children of Israel, which were come again out of the captivity, and all such as had separated themselves unto them from the filthiness of the heathen of the land, to seek the Lord, the God of Israel, did eat, And kept the feast of unleavened bread seven days with joy: for the Lord had made them joyful, and had turned the heart of the king of Assyria unto them, to strengthen their hands in the work of the house of God, the God of Israel.'

In the period after the Exile[76] the feast of the Passover and of Unleavened Bread had the status and dignity of the principal feast of the cultic community in Jerusalem. The measures adopted by king Josiah (2 Kings xxiii. 21 ff.) were decisive for this development, and their significance became more and more evident in the period that followed. But it is possible that the marked predominance of the spring festival was influenced by the arrangement of the Babylonian calendar, in which the year began in spring (cf. Exod. xii. 2). Particularly by contrast with the great New Year festivals with which the exiles became acquainted abroad, the tradition of the feast of the Passover and of Unleavened Bread seems to have grown in importance. This development can be seen also in the north in the period after the Exile. We do not know when the cultic community at Gerizim was formed. The first definite evidence of its existence is in 2 Macc. vi. 2.[77] But we shall not go far wrong if we presuppose the fact of the 'Samaritan schism' as early as the third century B.C. The feast of the Passover on Mount Gerizim had an outstanding importance, the effect of which can still be seen today.[78] The cultic community in Jerusalem, which had its

[75] See G. Beer/K. Galling, *Exodus*, pp. 61 f.

[76] It is hardly conceivable that there is a reference here to Assyria, which had fallen long ago; the reference is probably to the Persian king. For a discussion of the problems raised by the passage, see W. Rudolph, *Esra und Nehemia*, HAT, I (1949), p. 64.

[77] Cf. M. Noth, *History of Israel*, pp. 355 ff.

[78] J. Jeremias has made a special study of the Samaritan Passover. See *Die Passahfeier der Samaritaner und ihre Bedeutung für die alttestamentliche Passahüberlieferung* (1932).

main support in Galilee, had to answer the claim of the Samaritan cult. Traces of the controversy can be seen in the Chronicler's historical record, particularly in 2 Chron. xxx, the account we have just been considering. We can see from this account that the attempt was repeatedly made from Jerusalem to extend an invitation in the Samaritan region to the 'true central sanctuary of Israel'. These approaches and invitations had no success. Whatever grounds they put forward in history and tradition for Jerusalem's sacral right of election, all their efforts were in vain. We are told in 2 Chron. xxx. 2: 'For the king had taken counsel, and his princes, and all the congregation in Jerusalem, to keep the passover in the second month.' Has this remark any significance for the cultic practices at the time of the Chronicler?[79] If we take note of the context (*v.* 3) we see that the change of time is based on a definite sacral arrangement. In Num. ix. 9–13 the concession is made that men who could not present themselves at the usual time of the festival because of serious uncleanness could celebrate the Passover on the fourteenth day of the second month. This sacral regulation was obviously resorted to in the controversy with the Samaritan cultic community in order to give all those who took part in the festival on Mount Gerizim in the first month an opportunity to visit the sanctuary in Jerusalem as well. King Jeroboam had followed a similar procedure at the foundation of the northern kingdom. He had to reckon with the fact that the members of the northern kingdom, following traditional practice, still visited the central sanctuary in Jerusalem for the feast of Tabernacles 'in the seventh month', even after the division of the kingdom. So in order to establish the new official cult at Bethel, the king laid down a feast of Tabernacles for the northern kingdom 'in the eighth month' (cf. 1 Kings xii. 32).

The cultic calendars give a vivid picture of the history and development of the feast of the Passover and of Unleavened Bread, but there are various details that cannot be properly grasped until we have given an adequate account of the local cultic traditions of the central sanctuaries of Israel.

3. The Feast of Weeks

The Old Testament has not bequeathed to us any traditions about the second great annual festival in the cultic calendar, the feast of Weeks.[80]

[79] On this point, see E. Kutsch, op. cit., pp. 22 ff.

[80] Bibliography dealing with the feast of Weeks: H. Grimme, *Das israelitische Pfingstfest und der Plejadenkult: Studien zur Geschichte und Kultur des Altertums*, I, 1 (1907); G. Dalman, *Arbeit und Sitte in Palästina*, I, 2 (1928); E. Brögelmann, 'Pfingsten

Apart from the rules set out in the calendars we can discover practically nothing about the pre-exilic period, but the material from the post-exilic and late Jewish periods, which in recent times has been thoroughly investigated and has thrown fresh light on the primitive Christian Pentecost, presents a series of complicated questions.[81]

(a) *The Harvest Festival*

In the oldest Israelite cultic calendar the second annual festival is called חג הקציר (Exod. xxiii. 16). This title clearly indicates that it was the cult connected with the harvest, in particular with the summer wheat harvest. The other festival calendars in the Old Testament give the proper designation חג שבעת (Exod. xxxiv. 22; Deut. xvi. 10, 16) or שבעתיכם (Num. xxviii. 26). From the revelations contained in the calendars it is clear that we are to assume that it was a one-day festival which was later extended to a whole week (Num. xxviii. 24).[82] But when was the festival celebrated? The name חג הקציר (Exod. xxiii. 16) is evidence of the connection with the wheat harvest that is gathered in summer. More significant, however, is the term חג שבעת, which is to be traced back to a characteristic process of reckoning. According to Lev. xxiii. 15 'seven weeks' should be counted—'from the morrow after the sabbath, from the day that ye brought the sheaf of the wave offering'. In Deut. xvi. 9 it is 'seven weeks . . . from the time thou beginnest to put the sickle to the standing corn'. This reckoning means that the barley harvest and the wheat harvest are linked by a seven-week period, or that starting from the feast of Unleavened Bread 'seven weeks' or 'fifty days' (Lev. xxiii. 16) have to be counted. According to this, the feast of Weeks was originally the festival which concluded a special period of seven weeks.[83] Hence the title 'feast of Weeks' or, to be exact, 'feast of

[81] The studies of E. Kutsch and G. Kretschmar in particular have drawn attention to the cultic problems of the post-exilic and late Jewish period.

[82] But even in Num. xxviii. 26 ff. a trace of the traditional arrangement of the one-day festival can be seen, when the יום הבכורים is mentioned in *v.* 26.

[83] 'We cannot exclude the possibility that in the reckoning of the seven weeks the number seven had the effect of making the working week with its day of rest appear to be multiplied by seven in the harvest period, connected with the fact that one can fix for the barley and wheat harvest, which is all that we are concerned with here, a period of nearly two months,' (G. Dalman, op. cit., I, 2, p. 462).

---

in Altisrael', *Monatsschrift für Gottesdienst und kirchliche Kunst*, 44 (1939), pp. 119 ff.; K. H. Rengstorf, 'Christliches und jüdisches Pfingstfest', *Monatsschrift für Gottesdienst und kirchliche Kunst*, 45 (1940), pp. 75 ff.; E. Lohse, *ThW*, VI, pp. 44 ff.; G. Kretschmar, 'Himmelfahrt und Pfingsten', *ZKG*, 65 (1955), pp 209 ff ; E. Kutsch, *Das Herbstfest in Israel*, Diss., Mainz (1955); ibid., 'Der Kalender des Jubiläumsbuches und das Alte und Neue Testament', *VT*, XI (1961), pp. 39 ff.; R. de Vaux, *Ancient Israel: Its Life and Institutions*, pp. 493 ff.

(seven) Weeks'. The customs and rites connected with this feast were originally concerned exclusively with the harvest. בכורים (Exod. xxiii. 16) or בכורי קציר חטים (Exod. xxxiv. 22) are offered; a מנחה חדשה, a new meal offering, stands at the centre of it (Lev. xxiii. 16; Num. xxviii. 26). Harvest jubilation and festal joy are the keynotes of the celebration. There is no doubt that the Israelites adopted the feast of Weeks from the native Canaanite population, which means that the whole period of the 'seven weeks' was taken over by the Old Testament cultic regulations. We cannot now discover the original meaning of this 'seven-week period'. The hypothesis first put forward by H. Grimme, that it was connected with the seven Pleiades, has not been substantiated.[84] There is little evidence to help us in the Canaanite environment, but we must not ignore the fact that the 'period of seven' was an important element in the Ugaritic cultic tradition.[85] In the Old Testament appropriation of what was originally the Canaanite harvest festival, two main trends are to be noted: (1) The emphasis on the fact that all the customs and rites are to be observed ליהוה (Deut. xvi. 10; Lev. xxiii. 16; Num. xxviii. 26). (2) The centralization of the cult at the 'sanctuary of Yahweh' at which the great pilgrimage festivals took place. On the other hand it is noticeable that there is no evidence of any attempt to 'historicize' the feast of Weeks, and that it is therefore not rooted in redemptive history. Only in Deut. xvi. 12 do we find the statement: 'And thou shalt remember that thou wast a bondman in Egypt.' But this exhortation is quite incidental; it is in keeping with the message of Deuteronomy, and has no vital significance for the festival.

There is one fact that we know about the history of the feast of Weeks before the Exile, for in 1 Kings ix. 25 (2 Chron. viii. 13), we are told that the three great annual festivals were celebrated in Solomon's Temple. This is the first evidence we have of the clear emergence of the sacrificial cult in the context of the feast of Weeks which is to be seen in the later cultic calendar. In the cultic practice of the Temple the pilgrimage festivals become primarily sacrificial celebrations. It appears, however, that the feast of Weeks never had a great significance in the period before the Exile. The reason cannot have been simply that the

[84] Grimme suggests that the seven-week-long festival was originally a feast rooted in astral mythology, in which the Pleiades were venerated as gods, and that Israel adopted this cult and transformed it in a monotheistic direction (*Das israelitische Pfingstfest und der Plejadenkult*).

[85] The problem of these periods will have to be considered in greater detail when we turn to the sabbath and the sabbatical year, but even at this stage we can see that this 'period of seven' must have been of great importance in pre-Israelite worship. In connection with the sabbath and the sabbatical year we shall also need to take into account the Ras Shamra texts.

new interpretation of the cult in the light of redemptive history and based on the specifically Old Testament traditions was not yet established. In the cultic section of 'Ezekiel's constitutional outline' the feast of Weeks is missing completely (Ezek. xlv. 21 ff.), and this can only be interpreted as a deliberate omission. The probability is that this festival which was entirely rooted in agrarian rites always provided entry for alien Canaanite fertility customs which threatened to undermine and destroy the worship of Israel which was offered ליהוה.

(b) *Post-exilic and Late Jewish Traditions*

According to the Assyrian-Babylonian calendar the time of the feast of Weeks was in the 'third month'. This date plays no part in the cultic regulations in the Old Testament, because the traditional reckoning of the time of the festival was dependent on the 'seven-week scheme'. Nevertheless the date of the 'third month' should be noted, for in two places in Old Testament tradition this 'third month' is specifically mentioned, in Exod. xix. 1 and 2 Chron. xv. 10–14. Both passages are to be ascribed to the post-exilic period. Exod. xix. 1, according to the findings of literary criticism, belongs to the Priestly Code, and 2 Chron. xv. 10–14 is a section of the Chronicler's historical record. This brings to our notice some important traditions in the post-exilic period.[86] The Sinai pericope in the Pentateuch begins at Exod. xix. 1 with the following words: 'In the third month after the children of Israel were gone forth out of the land of Egypt, the same day came they into the wilderness of Sinai.' The aim of the Priestly Code here is quite plain—by giving this date to connect the Sinai event with the period of the feast of Weeks. What is the reason for this linking of the two dates? Mowinckel and von Rad have shown that the Sinai pericope, with its main elements of the proclamation of the law and the ratification of the covenant, was the festival legend of a great cultic celebration.[87] The events on Sinai were ceremonially re-presented in the cult. The views of the two writers diverge when they come to defining and explaining the underlying festival. Mowinckel had in mind 'Yahweh's enthronement festival', and von Rad the feast of Tabernacles. Both views are based on quite definite presuppositions and theories, which we shall have to consider later in detail in another connection. However, the intention of Exod. xix. 1 is quite plain—to connect the Sinai event with the feast of Weeks. How

[86] E. Kutsch was the first to point out the significance of the two passages Exod. xix. 1 and 2 Chron. xv. 10 ff. for the history of Israel's worship (*Das Herbstfest in Israel*, Diss., Mainz (1955), pp. 152 ff.).

[87] S. Mowinckel, *Le Décalogue* (1927); G. von Rad, *Das formgeschichtliche Problem des Hexateuch*, BWANT, IV, 26 (1938). *Ges. Stud. zum AT*, pp. 9 ff.

are we to interpret this suggested connection? Is it based on an older tradition and, if so, to which period does it belong? What cultic practice does it presuppose? In answering these questions we must bear in mind that nowhere in the Priestly Code, neither in the legal nor in the narrative sections, are there any parallels to this connection that is suggested in Exod. xix. 1. It is therefore necessary to look more carefully at the other passage in which the 'third month' is mentioned.

In 2 Chron. xv. 10–14 we find the following account:

> 'So they gathered themselves together at Jerusalem in the third month, in the fifteenth year of the reign of Asa. And they sacrificed unto the Lord in that day, of the spoil which they had brought, seven hundred oxen and seven thousand sheep. And they entered into the covenant to seek the Lord, the God of their fathers, with all their heart and with all their soul; And that whosoever would not seek the Lord, the God of Israel, should be put to death, whether small or great, whether man or woman. And they sware unto the Lord with a loud voice, and with shouting, and with trumpets, and with cornets.'

In this account the Chronicler has freely expanded and developed the traditions he found in the 'Deuteronomic history'. By combining traditions he has made the thorough purification of the cult, which is reported in 1 Kings xv. 12, into a solemn renewal of the covenant. In this procedure the events connected with King Josiah's reformation (2 Kings xxiii. 1 ff.) doubtless provided the model for the Chronicler. If Josiah's purification of the cult was of the nature of a solemn pledging of the community and a renewal of the relationship between God and the people, then this cultic event could be transposed into the period of Asa as well. The remarkable thing, however, is that the Chronicler dates this solemn event by referring to the 'third month' and in this way establishes a connection with the feast of Weeks.[88] Neither the traditions in 1 Kings xv. 9 ff. nor the combinations with 2 Kings xxiii. 1 ff. provide any support for this particular time. The Chronicler evidently must have had in mind a cultic practice of his own time. We can therefore assume that in the third century B.C. the solemn renewal of the covenant with God was part of the feast of Weeks, and this is confirmed by late traditions in the Book of Jubilees, where the main feast of the year is declared to be the 'feast of the renewal of the covenant' or of the 'promises made upon oath' (to Yahweh). This main feast is the feast of

[88] In the Targum the ceremony observed by Asa is therefore applied to the feast of Weeks. On this point, see G. von Rad, 'Die levitische Predigt in den Büchern der Chronik', *Festschrift O. Procksch* (1934), pp. 113–24, reprinted in *Ges. Stud. zum AT*, pp. 248 ff.; W. Rudolph, *Chronikbücher*, HAT, I, 21, pp. 245 f.

Weeks.[89] The Book of Jubilees interprets חג שבעות, the feast of Weeks, as 'feast of oaths' (שבע). So we read in Jub. vi. 21: '(And do thou command the children of Israel to observe this festival . . .). For it is the feast of weeks and the feast of first fruits: this feast is twofold and of a double nature.' Here we see alongside the agricultural element of the offering of the first fruits the basic event in the Old Testament story of salvation—the covenant. The statement in 2 Chron. xv. 10 and the cultic tradition in the Book of Jubilees point without any doubt to a solemn event that has become the essential content of the feast of Weeks—the renewal of the covenant.[90]

Against this background we can now see the significance of Exod. xix. 1. The dating of the Sinai event in the 'third month' is connected with a phase in the cultic history of the Old Testament, in which the feast of Weeks represented in worship the events on Sinai. But to which period is this significant new development in connection with the feast of the 'third month' to be attributed? E. Kutsch suggests that the feast of Weeks was given this new interpretation in respect of 'law and covenant' after the destruction of Solomon's Temple.[91] According to this, the date in the Priestly Code in Exod. xix. 1 would have to be interpreted as a *terminus a quo*. But is this explanation correct? It is quite clear from Neh. viii that in the time of Ezra the solemn pledging of the cultic community to the law was an act of worship forming part of the feast of Tabernacles. There is also no evidence anywhere in the Priestly Code to show that the dating in Exod. xix. 1 has a counterpart or the slightest support in the cultic traditions of this source. We have therefore to be careful in evaluating and interpreting Exod. xix. 1. It is even questionable whether this verse is part of the Priestly Code.[92] It is not until the

[89] Cf. G. Kretschmar, *Himmelfahrt und Pfingsten*, pp. 226 ff.; E. Kutsch, *Der Kalender des Jubiläenbuches*, pp. 43 f.

[90] G. Kretschmar emphasizes the fact 'that as far as the calendar is concerned the Book of Jubilees does not reflect any isolated individual opinion, but represents the view of a definite circle, where it was read and it exerted its influence. The Jewish sect with which we have become acquainted through the discovery of some of its writings in the Qumran caves by the Dead Sea must have belonged to this circle' (*Himmelfahrt und Pfingsten*, pp. 227 f.); see also the suggestions made by H. H. Rowley, *The Zadokite Fragments and the Dead Sea Scrolls* (1952), pp. 82 f.; the 'form of covenant' in the Book of Jubilees has been examined by K. Baltzer, *Das Bundesformular*, WMANT, No. 4 (1960), pp. 142 ff.

[91] E. Kutsch, *Das Herbstfest in Israel*, pp. 152 ff.

[92] We are not disputing the fact that the dates in the Priestly narrative can be traced back to P. The scheme of these dates is so deeply rooted in these texts that we cannot describe them as secondary. But it is still questionable whether such strange and loosely interpolated dating such as the one we find in Exod. xix. 1 has to be considered as part of the Priestly Code.

Chronicler's history that we have any evidence that the act of ratifying the covenant, which is testified later in the Book of Jubilees, actually set the pattern for the feast of Weeks. If we take note of the observations made in Neh. viii, we have to allow for the fourth century at the earliest as the time for the new form of the feast of Weeks as the *terminus a quo*. Exod. xix. 1 could then be taken to be an editorial interpolation. In any case it is impossible to take the cultic act of the solemn ratification of the covenant as an older, pre-exilic tradition of the feast of Weeks. The background factors and causes of the changes in the history of the cult in the post-exilic period are unknown to us. It might be that the controversies with the Samaritan schism played a part, but it is also conceivable that old traditions of the cultic ratification of the covenant were given new life by a movement of renewal and influenced the feast of Weeks which hitherto had no connection with redemptive history. Other aspects of this movement of renewal could be traced in the institutions of the Qumran sect.[93]

4. The Autumn Festival

(a) *The Nature Festival*

The third of the three great annual festivals is called חג האסף in the oldest cultic calendars (Exod. xxiii. 16; xxxiv. 22) and this name proves straight away that the feast which took place in the autumn was also originally linked with the processes of nature.[94] The 'feast of Ingathering' was to be celebrated 'after that thou hast gathered in from thy threshing-floor and from thy winepress' (Deut. xvi. 13). The

[93] We cannot say for certain whether the liturgy of the feast of the renewal of the covenant at Qumran was part of the feast of Weeks, as E. Kutsch suggests, as there is no definite evidence.

[94] Bibliography dealing with the feast of Tabernacles: P. Volz, *Das Neujahrsfest Jahwes* (1912); S. Mowinckel, 'Das Thronbesteigungsfest Jahwäs und der Ursprung der Eschatologie', *Psalmenstudien*, II (1922); ibid., *Le Décalogue* (1927); ibid., *He That Cometh* (1956); J. A. Wensinck, 'Arabic New Year and the Feast of Tabernacles', *Verhandlungen d. kön. Akad. v. Wetenskap, Letterkunde*, N.R. XXV, 2 (1925), pp. 1 ff.; H. Schmidt, *Die Thronfahrt Jahwes am Fest der Jahreswende im alten Israel* (1927); I. Pap, *Das israelitische Neujahrsfest* (1933); S. H. Hooke, *Myth and Ritual* (1933); ibid., *Myth, Ritual and Kingship* (1958); A. Alt, 'Zelte und Hütten', *Festschrift F. Nötscher* (1950), pp. 16 ff., *Kl. Schriften*, III, pp. 241 ff.; H. Bornhäuser, *Sukka*, Die Mischna, II, 6 (1935); N. H. Snaith, *The Jewish New Year Festival* (1947); H. J. Kraus, 'Die Königsherrschaft Gottes im Alten Testament', loc. cit.; E. Kutsch, *Das Herbstfest in Israel*, Diss., Mainz (1955); R. Rendtorff, 'Der Kultus im alten Israel', *Jahrbuch für Liturgik und Hymnologie*, 2 (1956), pp. 1 ff.; E. L. Ehrlich, *Die Kultsymbolik im Alten Testament und im nachbiblischen Judentum*, Symbolik der Religionen, III (1959), pp. 53 ff.; R. de Vaux, *Ancient Israel: Its Life and Institutions* (1961), pp. 495 ff.

Deuteronomic calendar here clearly envisages the harvest time in the autumn months of September and October as the period in which the festival falls. The fixing of the time might once have been linked with the fact that at this time work on the threshing floor and in the winepress had to be finished because the start of the rain or the heavier dew made it impossible to leave the corn, the fruits and the grapes any longer in the open.[95] In Lev. xxiii. 39 also the date is determined by the gathering in of the produce of the fields: באספכם את־תבואת הארץ. Thanksgiving for the harvest and festive joy were the keynotes of the festival (Deut. xvi. 14; Lev. xxiii. 40). The customs of the originally agricultural celebration can be clearly seen in Judges xxi. 19: there was celebration and dancing in the vineyards (Judges xxi. 21), and the feast lasted seven days (Deut. xvi. 15; Lev. xxiii. 41).

Difficulties arise, however, when we try to determine the exact time when the festival was held. Whereas in the earliest period it was simply the serious situation as regards the harvest that determined when the festival should start, at a quite early stage it became necessary to fix the date more accurately. We have to consider the possibility whether—as in the spring—the equinox or a particular full moon played a part. More significant, however, is the fact that the turn of the year coincided with the time of the autumn festival. In Exod. xxxiv. 22 this division of time is called תְקוּפַת הַשָּׁנָה. But we must note straight away that in the oldest cultic calendars there is no trace of a New Year festival coming into prominence in connection with the autumn festival.[96] It seems far more likely that the חַג הָאָסִף was primarily the end of the year and the close of the agricultural year.[97] It is true that the time given in Exod. xxiii. 16 really means the 'beginning of the year', but we must note that the verse goes on to refer to the time of the harvest.[98] The position of the autumn festival in the series of pilgrimage festivals also makes it clear that חַג הָאָסִף concludes the cultic celebrations of the year.[99] The autumn ripening and harvesting are a sign of the end, of overflowing abundance and the fulfilment of all that the earth yields. The association of קֵץ and קַיִץ in the prophecy of Amos (viii. 1 ff.) is

[95] Cf. G. Dalman, *Arbeit und Sitte in Palästina*, I, 2, p. 121.

[96] Cf. also E. Auerbach, 'Neujahrs- und Versöhnungsfest in den biblischen Quellen', *VT*, VIII (1958), pp. 337 ff.

[97] See F. Horst, 'Das Privilegrecht Jahwes', *Gottes Recht* (1961), p. 123.

[98] Cf. G. B. Gray, *Sacrifice in the Old Testament* (1925), pp. 300 f., and S. Mowinckel, *Zum israelitischen Neujahr und zur Deutung der Thronbesteigungspsalmen* (1952), pp. 10 ff.

[99] The placing of the autumn festival at the end of the annual festivals cannot be traced back to the changing of the calendar, the effect of which was not felt until the eighth century at the earliest, under Mesopotamian influence.

not merely a play on words, but a profoundly significant suggestion of the primitive experience of autumn, which the prophet now transposes into history.

In the cultic calendar in Deut. xvi and Lev. xxiii the autumn festival is referred to by the term חג הסכות which we meet frequently in the Old Testament (Deut. xvi. 13; Lev. xxiii. 34, 42 f.; Deut. xxxi. 10; Zech. xiv. 16, 18 f.; Ezra iii. 4; Neh. viii. 14 f.; 2 Chron. viii. 13). The customs underlying this terminology will have to be considered in detail later. The first fact we must note is that in Israel the feast of harvest and of Tabernacles which was obviously taken over from the native Canaanite inhabitants was given a new form and purpose by the Yahweh faith. It became חג ליהוה (Lev. xxiii. 41; Num. xxix. 12), a festival which concerned only the God of Israel. The autumn festival, as we shall see later, was in the pre-exilic period simply 'the feast of Yahweh' (חַג־יהוה Lev. xxiii. 39; Hos. ix. 5; Judges xxi. 19). It emerged from the series of annual festivals as the principal festival. Just as the celebrations in the spring and the summer, the autumn cultic assembly was also held at the central sanctuary. 'All Israel' came together in order to celebrate the great feast.

What was the part played by the 'tabernacles' (סכות) by which the feast got the name of 'feast of tabernacles' (חג־הסכות)? In attempting to answer this question the picture of the Bacchus cult has often been conjured up and it has been assumed that the autumn agricultural celebrations took place in vine bowers and specially prepared booths in the fields and vineyards. Judges xxi. 19 f. might seem to give support to this idea, and in any case it would seem reasonable to assume that there was an ancient custom rooted in the agricultural world of Canaan. But the statements made in the Old Testament are more important than these general suppositions. There are two passages that give us further details about the preparation of the booths, Lev. xxiii. 40–43 and Neh. viii. 15 ff. The instructions given in Lev. xxiii. 40 ff. are of special importance because at the same time a historical explanation is given of the ritual for the autumnal festival:

> 'And ye shall take you on the first day the fruit of goodly trees, branches of palm trees, and boughs of thick trees, and willows of the brook; and ye shall rejoice before the Lord your God seven days. And ye shall keep it a feast unto the Lord seven days in the year: it is a statute for ever in your generations: ye shall keep it in the seventh month. Ye shall dwell in booths seven days; all that are homeborn in Israel shall dwell in booths: That your generations may know that I made the children of Israel to dwell in booths, when I brought them out of the land of Egypt: I am the Lord your God.'

These instructions bear the clear marks of a harvest festival such as was celebrated in Canaan. The booths were made of thick branches of trees and decorated with various fruits. Those who took part in the festival entered a sphere of harvest rejoicing and abundance and they celebrated the festival for seven days. But the 'historicizing' explanation in Lev. xxiii. 43 is very strange. 'If this temporary dwelling in booths during the feast was thought of as a repetition commanded by Yahweh of the way of life which he laid down for the forefathers of the people during their journey through the wilderness after the exodus from Egypt, then this historicizing interpretation of the custom contained an anachronism; for the rest of Israelite tradition concerning that period assumes quite unanimously, and of course correctly, that the tribes under Moses' leadership lived in "tents", not in "booths".'[100] This anachronism cannot be explained by declaring that 'at an earlier period the booths seem to have been tents made of cloth'.[101] The problem is more complex than this. Obviously the aim of the regulation laid down in Lev. xxiii. 40 ff. is to explain and justify the practice of dwelling in booths which was observed in Canaan by reference to the fact that at an earlier period, during the exodus from Egypt, Israel dwelt in tents. What is the significance of this? Is the reference to the exodus from Egypt merely part of the cultic calendar's tendency to 'historicize', which had no real effect upon the way in which the feast of Tabernacles was actually celebrated, or was the autumn festival mainly characterized by the fact that it represented the saving event of the exodus from Egypt? We have also to go on and ask the question whether, when we read in Hos. xii. 10 of a feast that was celebrated 'in tents', we have to assume that in an earlier period the feast of Tabernacles was observed as a tent festival. This last question brings us up against a problem which cannot be solved merely in the context of the cultic calendar. In order to deal with this problem we have to examine in detail the sociological and cultic situation of ancient Israel, a task to which we shall turn later. Nevertheless, we can already say for certain that the cultic calendar contains indications that point to an earlier period, which cannot be explained away by the view that they are simply an 'anachronism'.

In Neh. viii. 14 ff. also we can see the effect of this tendency to refer to older cultic customs. This passage is probably based on Lev. xxiii. 40 ff., and reads as follows:

'And they found written in the law, how that the Lord had commanded by Moses, that the children of Israel should dwell in booths in the feast of the

[100] A. Alt. 'Zelte und Hütten', *Kleine Schriften*, III, pp. 241 f.

[101] As P. Volz states, *Das Neujahrsfest Jahwes*, p. 20.

seventh month: And that they should publish and proclaim in all their cities, and in Jerusalem, saying, Go forth unto the mount, and fetch olive branches, and branches of wild olive, and myrtle branches, and branches of thick trees, to make booths, as it is written. So the people went forth, and brought them, and made themselves booths, every one upon the roof of his house, and in their courts, and in the courts of the house of God, and in the broad place of the water gate, and in the broad place of the gate of Ephraim. And all the congregation of them that were come again out of the captivity made booths, and dwelt in booths: for since the days of Jeshua the son of Nun unto that day had not the children of Israel done so. And there was very great gladness'.

At the end of this passage there is the surprising statement that 'since the days of Jeshua' Israel had not celebrated the feast of Tabernacles in the manner in which it was performed in the time of Ezra.[102] We can interpret this statement only as a combination of Lev. xxiii. 43 and 2 Kings xxiii. 22. The celebration as directed by Ezra is meant to follow the cultic law which points back to the earliest period (Lev. xxiii. 40 ff.) and observe a feast 'in the original form'. But what is this 'original form'? Certainly not the practical aspect of preparing booths of branches and dwelling in them. חג-הסכות was no doubt always observed in this way. Then is it merely the archaizing tendency to point back to ancient traditions which Neh. viii. 15 ff. has taken over from Lev. xxiii. 40 ff.? In this case the cult at the time of Ezra would have to be seen as a revival of ancient Israelite festival traditions, but this does not explain what exactly as far as content is concerned the resumption of the ancient cultic traditions involved. Here again we come to a point where we can go no further, until we have gone beyond the formal and institutional aspect of the cultic awareness of tradition to a fuller understanding of the background.

None of the three great annual festivals in Israel was as complex in its history and its tradition as the autumn festival. We can see this even from a brief survey of the passages which deal explicitly with this festival. Deut. xxxi. 10 speaks of a celebration which came 'every seven years' at the time of the feast of Tabernacles. In 1 Kings viii. 1 ff. acts of worship are mentioned which will have to be considered when we come to examine the local Jerusalem traditions. In the time of Solomon the autumn festival, celebrated in the Temple and accompanied by sacrifices (1 Kings ix. 25), was the main festival of the year. According to 1 Kings xii. 32 f., in the northern kingdom Jeroboam made a corresponding festival in Bethel the basis of the official cult. The people assembled on

[102] On Neh. viii. 14 ff., cf. W. Rudolph, *Esra und Nehemia*, HAT, I, 20 (1949), pp. 144 ff.

Zion year by year for a great feast of rejoicing (Isa. xxix. 1; xxx. 29).[103] Sacrificial offerings are the keynote of the festival in the cultic regulations in Ezek. xlv. 25. Zech. xiv. 16 ff. reflects characteristic traditions of the feast of Tabernacles. Before we can bring out the full meaning of the customs which are reflected in these passages, we shall have to examine the cultic traditions of the central Israelite sanctuaries from the standpoint of form criticism and the history of tradition.

(b) *The First Day of the Seventh Month*

In Lev. xxiii. 23 ff. we find two factors which represent a break and a new development in the history of the autumn festival. First we should note the date. The whole autumn cult is appointed for the 'seventh month', and the days are carefully defined. But then we see for the first time the division into three acts of worship of what was formerly a self-contained festival lasting seven days. On the first day of the seventh month a great feast is held, but it is not given any specific name. On the tenth day the יום הכפרים (Lev. xxiii. 27) follows, and on the fifteenth day the seven-day feast of Tabernacles begins (Lev. xxiii. 33 ff.). The festival calendar in Num. xxix follows this order. If we base our consideration of the history of worship in the light of these changes in the later cultic calendars on the fact that the Deuteronomic law (Deut. xvi) shows no trace of this threefold division of the autumn festival, then we must assume that it was introduced about 600 B.C.

The information we have about the celebration on the first day of the seventh month is very sparse. As we have already pointed out, Lev. xxiii does not even give a name for the day. In Num. xxix. 1 the description יום תרועה, which refers to the custom of 'blowing the trumpet', does not give us much information. The feast day is marked by the sound of trumpets (Lev. xxiii. 24; Num. xxix. 1 f.). As on the 'sabbath', strict rest must be observed (Lev. xxiii. 24 f.; Num. xxix. 1), and sacrifices are required. The actual contents of the festival cannot be deduced from the cultic calendars. We get a somewhat clearer idea from the cultic regulation in Ezek. xlv. 20, where it is laid down that on the first day of the seventh month 'so shall ye make atonement for the house'; in other words, a ritual cleansing of the sanctuary is to take place.[104] It is doubtful whether we can draw any conclusions about the contents of the feast on the first day of the seventh month from Neh. viii. 2, for the 'reading of the law' which Ezra performs could be an exceptional action, and in any case it is continued until the feast of

[103] Cf. B. Duhm, *Das Buch Jesaja* (3 ed., 1922), ad. loc.
[104] See H. Gese, *Der Verfassungsentwurf des Ezechiel*, pp. 76 ff.

Tabernacles on the fifteenth day of the seventh month (Neh. viii. 18). We have to conclude, therefore, that the picture we gain from the relevant Old Testament passages is incomplete and indistinct.

Some students of Old Testament worship have often stated with great confidence that the celebration on the first day of the seventh month was a New Year festival.[105] This idea springs mostly from the fact that everywhere in the worship of the ancient East there was such a celebration at the turn of the year and that in the Old Testament calendar the New Year's Day was part of the feast of Tabernacles in the earlier period. Some scholars have tried to show that this feast day emerged from the hitherto self-contained feast week, and the obvious thing was to suggest that changes in the calendar, as for example the complete adoption of the Babylonian calendar which reckoned by months and days, were the cause of this development. If the year began according to the Babylonian reckoning of time on the first day of the first month in the spring, then it might have been the aim of the Israelites to set over against this 'secular' beginning of the year a religious New Year festival derived from the autumn feast week. But these theories come up against great difficulties. Neither the older regulations concerning the autumn festival nor the cultic traditions in the Old Testament which presuppose the feast day on the first day of the seventh month make it possible to prove that there was a New Year festival in Israel.[106] As we have already seen, the feast of Tabernacles concludes the agricultural year, and although the 'turn of the year' is mentioned in Exod. xxxiv. 22, there is no trace in the Old Testament of an act of worship to celebrate the beginning of the year. It is true that the seventh month represented the turn of the year. This can be seen particularly in Ezek. xl. 1, where we find the month called ראש השנה.[107] But was the first day of the seventh month really New Year's Day? We must not forget that both in the cultic calendars in Lev. xxiii and Num. xxix and also in Ezek. xlv. 20 ff. the feast on the first day of the seventh month is an act of worship in preparation for the main festival

[105] P. Fiebig, *Rosch ha-schana*, Die Mischna, II, 8 (1914); S. Mowinckel, *Psalmenstudien*, II (1922); P. Volz, *Das Neujahrsfest Jahwes* (1912).

[106] E. Auerbach expounds the view that 'the ancient Israelite calendar has no New Year festival' (*VT*, III (1958), p. 337).

[107] That the dating ראש השנה refers not to a day (e.g. the tenth day of the seventh month), but to a month, is proved for one thing by the Septuagint (where the translation is 'in the first month') and also by the normal sequence of dates in Ezekiel: year—month—day. Cf. G. Fohrer/K. Galling, *Ezechiel*, HAT, I, 13, ad. loc. The view that ראש השנה refers to the first day of the new year is held by, among others, S. Mowinckel, *Zum israelitischen Neujahr und zur Deutung der Thronbesteigungspsalmen* (1952), p. 27.

proper which begins on the fifteenth day. The feast on the tenth day, the Day of Atonement, which we have still to consider, has the same preparatory character. If a cleansing of the Temple is laid down in Ezek. xlv. 20 for the first day of the seventh month, this ceremony (as also the corresponding rite on the first day of the first month) can refer only to the principal feast that follows. The first day of the month is the 'new moon', when the moon-month phase begins. It seems reasonable to assume that on the first day of the seventh month the festival month is begun and announced with the 'blowing of trumpets' (cf. Ps. lxxxi. 3). If we examine the contents of the feasts on the first and tenth days of which we have evidence in the cultic calendars, it becomes plain that the preparatory acts of atonement and cleansing are related to the main seven-day festival which begins on the fifteenth day. In the cultic instructions for the 'Day of Atonement' in particular we can see that rites which originally belonged to the self-contained week of the autumn festival were fixed for a particular day and appointed to be observed in advance of the main festival.

(c) *The Great Feast of Atonement*

The festival which is held on the tenth day of the seventh month is called יום הכפרים in Lev. xxiii. 27.[108] Complete rest as on the 'sabbath' is required (Lev. xxiii. 28; Num. xxix. 7), and like all the other feasts, the 'day of atonement' is marked in Lev. xxiii and Num. xxviii and xxix by sacrifices and offerings. But in its ritual more sharply defined rules are laid down. A 'fast' must be observed (Lev. xxiii. 27, 29, 32; Num. xxix. 7), and 'atoning sacrifices' are at the centre. This last rite is particularly characteristic of the feast, and indicates a ritual such as has come down to us in Lev. xvi.

From the point of view of literary criticism and the history of tradition Lev. xvi presents a number of difficult problems.[109] Various rituals from different situations and different periods have been merged. Three cultic acts can, however, be clearly distinguished: the expiation for the tent sanctuary (Lev. xvi. 2 ff.), the act of expiation for the Ark and the altar (*vv.* 11 ff.) and the expiation for the cultic community (*vv.* 21 f.).

[108] Bibliography dealing with the Day of Atonement: J. Meinhold, *Joma*, Die Mischna, II, 5 (1913); S. Landersdorfer, *Studien zum biblischen Versöhnungstag*, ATA, 10, 1 (1924); M. Löhr, 'Das Ritual von Lev. 16', SGK, 2, 1 (1925); T. Vriezen, 'The Term Hizza: Lustration and Consecration', *OTS*, 7 (1950), pp. 201 ff.; R. de Vaux, *Ancient Israel: Its Life and Institutions* (1961), pp. 507 ff.

[109] For a discussion of these problems, see M. Löhr, op. cit.; R. Rendtorff, *Die Gesetze in der Priesterschrift*, FRLANT (1954—of fundamental importance for the study of the 'ritual' from the standpoint of form criticism); K. Koch, *Die Priesterschrift von Exod. 25 bis Lev. 16*, FRLANT (1959), pp. 92 ff.

Whilst this last cultic procedure refers to the people and can be used in a variety of situations and historical forms, the first two customs indicate traditions which we must examine more closely. The ceremonial of expiation for the tent sanctuary certainly goes back in its original form to very ancient traditions which were linked with the 'sacred tent', the 'tent of meeting' (אהל מועד). In the course of time rituals from the Temple sanctuary found their way into these cultic traditions, and the merging is so complete that it is difficult to separate the more ancient material from the more recent.[110] However, where the Ark and the altar are mentioned we clearly have ritual elements which presuppose the existence of the Temple sanctuary, and it is not hard to recognize the archaic nature of the oldest regulations in Lev. xvi where the desert setting has left its mark on the ritual practices. The goat on which the sins are 'laid' and to which they are transferred is driven into the wilderness (Lev. xvi. 10, 21 f.): this presupposes that the cultic community has pitched camp in the wilderness (Lev. xvi. 26). Here we meet for the second time within the 'Holiness Code' a reminder of the desert (cf. Lev. xxiii. 40 ff.). This time it is even assumed in the cultic traditions that the community observed the fast of expiation in an encampment. The different strata and traditions in Lev. xvi show, however, that under changed circumstances this feast of expiation was also celebrated in the area of the Temple. We can therefore conclude that the special 'Day of Atonement' that is laid down for the first time in Lev. xxiii. 26 ff. was part of the autumn festival from the earliest period and points back even as far as the desert period.[111] We shall have to consider more closely later what is meant by 'desert period'. What seems to have happened is that the act of expiating the sanctuary, which is part of the ritual in Lev. xvi, was fixed for the first day of the seventh month (cf. Ezek. xlv. 20), whilst the expiation of the cultic community, which was accompanied by a great 'fast', became the main content of the 'Day of

[110] For the details, see K. Koch, op. cit., pp. 92 ff.

[111] The purification of the sanctuary was originally a purely priestly ceremony, but because of its importance it came to be performed openly before the whole cultic community at a quite early stage. W. Eichrodt comments: 'It is extremely significant for any study of the laws relating to festivals in the Old Testament that the Day of Atonement should have been brought out of its isolation as a purely priestly ceremony in this way. The majority of the religions of the great civilizations were concerned to develop mystery rites, mediating a special way of redemption not available to the mass of mankind and conferring on the central object of the religion the character of an impenetrable secret. So little is this tendency observable in Israel, that on the contrary even rites which might seem to have been specifically designed for such a purpose are deliberately incorporated into the cultic activity of the whole congregation and brought into the broad daylight of public participation' (*Theology of the Old Testament*, I, pp. 130 f.).

Atonement' (cf. Lev. xxiii. 28 f.; Num. xxix. 7 ff.). We might go so far as to see in the fixing of the two preparatory feast days an increased enforcement of the ritual handed down in Lev. xvi, but it is also possible to see it as a radical revival of acts of worship which had tended to fall into the background in the week of the autumn festival because of the preponderance of customs connected with the harvest. The fact that the tenth day of the seventh month is not mentioned in Ezek. xlv. 20 ff. and is no longer referred to in Neh. viii. 1 ff. and 2 Chron. vii. 7–10 could be accounted for by the fact that the ceremonies of expiation were concentrated more on the first day—without, of course, the tenth day being abandoned.

5. Sabbatical Year and Year of Jubilee

(a) *The Meaning of the Institutions*

The oldest rule about the sabbatical year is found in Exod. xxiii. 10, 11, linked in a remarkable way with the exhortation to observe the sabbath every week. Just as on every seventh day absolute rest must prevail in the dwellings of the people, so in the seventh year the land must rest and be left undisturbed. What grows wild in this fallow year is to be given to the poor. The verb שמט is significant, meaning 'to release' or 'to renounce'. The sabbatical year, which in all the regulations bears the stamp of the שבת, is consequently called שמטה. The question which immediately arises, of course, is whether this fallow year 'every seven years' is to be included among the cultic activities of Israel, or whether it is not rather a purely agricultural, economic institution. G. Beer states in his commentary: 'The purpose of the period of rest is to increase productivity',[112] but he also believes that it contains a religious-cultic element, in that the 'rest' is meant to secure for the ground the favour and power of the vegetation spirits.[113] O. Procksch tries to form some idea of the area included in such a fallowing period. He considers it impossible that the whole land was abandoned for a year: 'The fallow affected only a seventh of the arable land at any given time; a fallow year for the whole land was impossible in view of the limited agricultural economy, and was not carried out until a late period.'[114] In Procksch's view, the institution shows 'the ethos of the Israelite as it affects the economic sphere'.[115] A. Jepsen, who thinks that

[112] G. Beer, *Exodus*, HAT, I, 3 (1939), p. 119.
[113] Ibid.
[114] O. Procksch, *Theologie des Alten Testaments* (1950), p. 112.
[115] Ibid.

the humane considerations are more important than the cultic, is of similar opinion.[116] Noth, on the other hand, declares: 'Thus its original "rest" is to be given back to the land, undisturbed by the hand of man (cf. Lev. xxv. 4).'[117] The institution should be interpreted from the point of view of *restitutio in integrum*. These views diverge considerably, and we must certainly ask ourselves to what extent the sabbatical year might originally have been a Canaanite institution, and at what point the specifically Old Testament attitude becomes evident. When we read in Lev. xxv. 2 that the land should keep a 'sabbath' ליהוה, in view of this emphasis on the connection with the God of Israel we have to ask whether the שׁמטה in Canaan was not originally connected with other powers. G. Beer is possibly on the right lines when he suggests that the favour and power of the vegetation spirits was meant to be secured by means of the 'rest' of the land. If this religious-cultic aim comes to the fore, the economic aspect of an increase in productiveness would have to be subordinated to the sacral aspects. Rational and economic aims in the ancient world had a pan-sacral foundation. We must also ask ourselves whether Procksch is not also correct when he assumes that the fallow was only partially carried out. We can well imagine that in the Canaanite agricultural religion certain sections of the land were periodically 'consecrated' by a sacral fallow and that an increase of power was procured by means of the vegetation spirits.

These customs, however, which were possibly observed in Canaan, do not explain the rules laid down in Israel according to which 'every seven years' the whole land must be left untouched for a year. Nor do they explain the special relationship that Israel was expected to adopt in regard to the land. We have therefore to bear in mind the fact that the Israelite tribes emerged from the nomadic sphere, and think especially of the period in which as they emerged from the desert they were slowly adapting themselves to the cultivation of the land. A. Alt therefore rightly states on the question of the Old Testament sabbatical year: 'The introduction of this institution in my opinion is conceivable only at a time when the Israelite tribes have not yet completely left behind the semi-nomadic existence of their earliest period and have taken up agriculture but not yet made it the centre of their economy.'[118] But can we speak of an 'introduction', of the growth of the institution of the sabbatical year rooted in the semi-nomadic surroundings? Should we not rather assume that the religious-cultic institution of the sacral

[116] A. Jepsen, *Untersuchungen zum Bundesbuch*, BWANT, III, 5 (1927), p. 47.
[117] M. Noth, *Exodus* (1962), p. 190.
[118] A. Alt, *Kleine Schriften*, I, pp. 327 f.

fallow which they found in Canaan was given a new stamp by the Israelites by the fact that it was performed exclusively ליהוה as a new complex covering space and time. This would mean that the Canaanite practice that was adopted was influenced by both the nomadic and the Yahwistic elements, and that the nomadic aspect would be represented by the still relatively loose connection with the soil, which would help to explain the complete rest 'every seven years', and the Yahwistic aspect by the attempt 'to acknowledge God's sovereignty over the ground and soil . . . by a complete cessation of cultivation'.[119] The two elements, however, the nomadic and the Yahwistic, were indissolubly joined in Israel's early period. If these suggestions are correct, they throw much light on the cult of the שׁמטה. The sacral fallow observed 'every seven years' is seen on each occasion as a new beginning of life on the land, free from all the harm and corruption arising from ownership. Sociological studies have shown that down to quite recent times the fresh allocation by lot of the plots of land was customary among the semi-nomads,[120] and in the Old Testament also there is evidence of the institution of the sacral lot by means of which a portion of land was allocated to the tribes from time to time.[121] It is therefore reasonable to assume 'that originally a fresh distribution of the separate plots of land was made every sabbatical year to those within the tribe or clan who were entitled to a share'.[122]

The regulations concerning the sabbatical year in Lev. xxv. 1 ff. are not essentially different from the picture we find in Exod. xxiii. 10, 11.[123] Here again the law is stamped with the idea of the sabbath.[124] The individual commandments are more detailed and—as in Exod. xxiii. 11 —lay stress on the social aspect (Lev. xxv. 6 f.). The Deuteronomic law in Deut. xv. 1 ff., however, introduces a new note. The rules no longer refer to the sacral period of rest, but to a general release from debts in trade and business affairs to be carried out 'every seven years'. 'The sabbatical year, which had a social emphasis even before Deuteronomy, now loses its agricultural basis completely and is thought of purely in social terms', states von Rad.[125] The ancient sacral fallow with its

[119] A. Alt, *Kleine Schriften*, I, p. 150. See also H. Wildberger, 'Israel und sein Land', *EvTh*, 8/9 (1956), pp. 411 ff.

[120] A. Musil, *Arabia Petraea*, III (1908), pp. 293 f.

[121] Cf. Num. xxvi. 55; xxxv. 54; xxxiv. 13; xxxvi. 2; Joshua xiv. 2; xvi–xx.

[122] A. Alt, *Kleine Schriften*, I, p. 150.

[123] For the details, see H. Reventlow, *Das Heiligkeitsgesetz*, WMANT, No. 6 (1961), pp. 123 ff.

[124] A. Jepsen, op. cit., p. 47.

[125] G. von Rad, *Das Gottesvolk im Deuteronomium*, BWANT, III, 11 (1929), p. 30.

renunciation of the land already contained, of course, an abandonment of all claims for debts and everything that would disrupt the life of the community, but by the time of Deuteronomy we have arrived at a situation where Israel is no longer in a position to achieve a total and absolute fallow. The tribes were so firmly rooted in agriculture that the ancient regulations had become Utopian, and the social application by which the Deuteronomic law now connects the שמטה with matters concerning property and debt is therefore all the more remarkable. It is quite evident that the early laws concerned with the soil presuppose a way of life which had a meaning in Israel only in the early period immediately after the occupation of Canaan.

The Holiness Code preserves, in connection with the instructions concerning the שמטה which has to take place 'every seven years', a strange regulation concerning the observance of a 'year of jubilee' that is meant to be observed after forty-nine years (Lev. xxv. 8 ff.).[126] The way in which this year is reckoned is similar to the way in which the feast of Weeks is fixed. Whereas seven weeks have to be counted (from the feast of the Passover and Unleavened Bread) for determining the second of the great Yahweh feasts, the time of the year of Jubilee is arrived at by adding up seven sabbatical years. As in the Deuteronomic law concerning the שמטה the agricultural regulations fall into the background in Lev. xxv. 8 ff. but in *v.* 11 it is laid down that sowing and reaping should be omitted. This festival year, which is announced by the blowing of trumpets, is meant to bring about, in particular, the release of slaves and the remission of all heavy material debts.

Scholars are not agreed upon the meaning of this institution of the year of Jubilee. Whilst some see a great significance in the regulations, from the point of view of the history of worship, others doubt whether the rules ever had any real validity in the life of the community. The very way in which the date is reckoned, by multiplying the sabbatical year by itself, suggests that the year of Jubilee is a theory, or perhaps an actual attempt to rescue the decaying institution of the sabbatical year by a שמטה carefully preserved at least to some degree.[127] It is quite certain that the sabbatical year and the year of Jubilee cannot be understood apart from one another.[128] The regulations for the year of

[126] On the year of Jubilee, see A. Jirku, 'Das israelitische Jobeljahr', *Festschrift Seeberg* (1929), pp. 169 ff.; H. Schmidt, *Das Bodenrecht im Verfassungsentwurf des Esra* (1932); R. North, *Sociology of the Biblical Jubilee* (1954); H. Reventlow, *Das Heiligkeitsgesetz* (1961), pp. 123 ff.

[127] Cf. A. Alt, *Kleine Schriften*, I, p. 328, note 1.

[128] A. Jirku's suggestions, which separate the sabbatical year from the year of Jubilee, are questionable.

Jubilee reflect the rules for the שמטה that is to take place 'every seven years'.[129] However, if we do not wish to consider Lev. xxv. 8 ff. simply as a theory or even as a fiction, it is possible to think of it as an attempt at restoration which was effective for the time being but could no longer be carried out to the full. The following passages could be quoted as evidence of such a limited revival of ancient regulations in the period immediately before the Exile: Jer. xxxiv. 8, 15, 17; Ezek. xlvi. 17 and Isa. lxi. 1.

(b) *Deuteronomy xxxi. 9–13*

Among the regulations concerning the שמטה Deut. xxxi. 9 ff. occupies a special place. In recent times this passage has been thoroughly examined and analysed.

> 'And Moses wrote this law, and delivered it unto the priests the sons of Levi, which bare the ark of the covenant of the Lord, and unto all the elders of Israel. And Moses commanded them, saying, At the end of every seven years, in the set time of the year of release, in the feast of tabernacles, when all Israel is come to appear before the Lord thy God in the place where he shall choose, thou shalt read his law before all Israel in their hearing. Assemble the people, the men and the women and the little ones, and thy stranger that is within thy gates, that they may hear, and they may learn, and fear the Lord your God, and observe to do all the words of this law; And that their children, which have not known, may hear, and learn to fear the Lord your God, as long as ye live in the land whither ye go over Jordan to possess it.'

The characteristic themes and expressions of the Deuteronomic message are unmistakable in this passage. What is of great significance, however, is the fact that the feast of Tabernacles in the שמטה year is marked by a proclamation of the Torah that takes place before the whole cultic community. C. Steuernagel could still write in his commentary on Deuteronomy: 'It is conceivable, but cannot be proved, that the requirement of a regular reading of the Law is linked with a practice already in existence (possibly introduced by Josiah). In later Judaism it led to the introduction of the feast of rejoicing in the law following the feast of Tabernacles and to the reading section by section of the whole Pentateuch on the sabbaths'.[130] More recent studies in form criticism have shown

[129] One can even use the details concerning the year of Jubilee in order to reconstruct the contents of the sabbatical year (cf. A. Alt, loc. cit.).

[130] C. Steuernagel, *Das Deuteronomium*, HK, I, 3 (2 ed., 1923), p. 161. Steuernagel tries to trace the sources underlying the passage Deut. xxxi. 9 ff., and the section is attributed to the strata D^{2}c. In other words, Deut. xxxi. 9–13 belongs to the later additions to the basic material of the body of laws. The period of Josiah is therefore out of the question. Nevertheless, Steuernagel does mention the time indicated in the

more and more clearly, however, that the Deuteronomic law in Deut. xxxi. 9 ff. is based upon an older custom. Alt in particular, in his form-critical investigations into ancient Israelite law, has shown that the apodeictic divine law was proclaimed in a sacral act in the cultic community of the early period,[131] and it is here that the שמטה plays a large part. It is, however, very surprising that in Deuteronomy, which is to be ascribed to the seventh century, the proclamation of the Torah is linked with such an ancient institution as that of the sabbatical year. A practice which had been introduced in the time of Josiah would hardly have inserted the promulgation of the law into an institution which had long fallen into disuse and had been interpreted in a social sense in Deut. xv. 1 ff. But more significant than these considerations are the studies in form criticism that we have mentioned, which point back to the earliest times. Alt has shown in his investigation that there was linked with the sacral fallow and the suspension of all legal obligations and debts in ancient Israel not only a fresh proclamation of the law, but also a fresh commitment of the people to the will of God, equivalent to the renewal of the covenant between Yahweh and his people.[132] According to this, the שמטה would attain an outstanding and all-embracing significance as the occasion when the relationship of God and His people was completely renewed and each time put on the firm basis of a new beginning. The effects upon the history of worship and the developments of this institution will have to be considered later from a different angle and in other connections.

(c) *Later Outworkings of the Regulations Concerning the Sabbatical Year*

We have seen that the שמטה in its complete and exclusive form could be valid only for a period in which Israel had not yet any firm connection with the soil and was not yet established in Canaan. Both the Deuteronomic law (Deut. xv. 1 ff.) and also the regulations about the year of Jubilee (Lev. xxv. 8 ff.) show that in later times the attempt was made by relegating the agricultural obligations to the background to give new validity to the old stipulations. We can see time after time that both

[131] A. Alt, *Kleine Schriften*, I, pp. 327 ff.
[132] Ibid., p. 328.

---

quotation. The findings of Noth's *Überlieferungsgechichtliche Studien*, I, point in the same direction, but Noth separates Deut. xxxi from the complex of the Deuteronomic tradition of law and links it with the Deuteronomistic tradition of history. Deut. xxxi. 9–13 is a passage which belongs to the 'secondary framework elements of the Deuteronomic law' (Noth, op. cit., p. 87). It is therefore obvious, as far as the literary presuppositions are concerned, that it is not possible to envisage an earlier period of origin before Josiah for the cultic regulations set out in Deut. xxxi.

Deuteronomy and also the Holiness Code attempt to revive the cultic traditions of the early period and give them fresh validity under changed circumstances. These trends are without doubt historically connected with the renaissance of Israel in the time of Josiah.

The days were already approaching, however, when Israel would lose its land and be carried away into exile. It is a remarkable fact that in Lev. xxvi. 34 ff. the historical event of the loss of the land is accounted for by the decline of the שׁמטה:

> 'Then shall the land enjoy her sabbaths, as long as it lieth desolate, and ye be in your enemies' land; even then shall the land rest, and enjoy her sabbaths. As long as it lieth desolate it shall have rest; even the rest which it had not in your sabbaths, when ye dwelt upon it.'

This explanation confirms first of all that the שׁמטה had in practice not been observed in Israel for a long time.[133] Since the time that Israel 'found rest' and settled in the land, the sabbatical year had no longer been held. For this reason the loss of the land brought about by the deportation is to be thought of as a 'sabbath' of great historical significance and effect which makes up for the cultic neglect of the past. The prophet Jeremiah also speaks of the exile from this standpoint:

> 'And thou, even of thyself, shalt discontinue (שׁמט) from thine heritage, that I gave thee; and I will cause thee to serve thine enemies in the land which thou knowest not: for ye have kindled a fire in mine anger which shall burn for ever' (Jer. xvii. 4).

In connection with this announcement of judgement the question arises whether the period of the Exile, lasting 'seventy years', prophesied in Jer. xxv. 11, was not deliberately adopted from the period laid down for the שׁמטה and was meant to present the challenge to the people as forcefully as possible. In any case this is the way in which the Chronicler interprets Jeremiah's prophecy of judgement when he states in 2 Chron. xxxvi. 21:

> 'To fulfil the word of the Lord by the mouth of Jeremiah, until the land had enjoyed her sabbaths: for as long as she lay desolate she kept sabbath, to fulfil threescore and ten years.'

6. New Moon and Sabbath

(a) *The New Moon*

The new moon (חדשׁ) is first mentioned in the Old Testament as a feast day in 1 Sam. xx. 5 ff. and 18 ff. We learn that a solemn sacrificial

[133] Cf. J. Wellhausen, *Prolegomena*, pp. 119 f.

meal was held at the court of Saul in which all the members of the family had to take part. But cultic regulations for the day of the new moon are not found in the Old Testament until relatively late, therefore the passage Ezek. xlvi. 1 ff. has to be ascribed to the exilic period. Its ritual prescriptions refer exclusively to the Temple sanctuary and lay down offerings of produce as well as sacrifices (Ezek. xlvi. 6 f.). Similar regulations are to be found also in Num. x. 10 and xxviii. 11 ff. We can see already from these passages that there was a development which led from a celebration instituted within the family circle to a rite observed in the Temple. Several passages bring 'new moon and sabbath' into the closest association in the period between these two extremes, e.g. Amos viii. 5; Hos. ii. 13; 2 Kings iv. 23; Isa. iv. 13; lxvi. 23. The customs on the day of the new moon which we can discern from these passages need closer examination.

'He appointed the moon for seasons' (Ps. civ. 19). The first day on which the moon becomes visible again is חדש. As early as the ancient Sumerian epoch in connection with the lunar arrangement of the calendar the day of new light (*ud-sar*) was celebrated in worship.[134] In the ancient Babylonian period the 'day in the month on which the moon rises' was celebrated,[135] and in the Ugaritic texts too the *ym ḥdṯ* is mentioned[136]—'the day on which the moon is renewed'.[137] The division of time is based on the synodical month which lasts from new moon to new moon and covers 29 days, 12 hours, 44 minutes and 3 seconds. Intercalations, the application of which is unknown in detail, make up the difference between the lunar year and the solar year. חדש, however, is the decisive time, the day on which the beginning of the month was solemnly celebrated.

As we have already pointed out, the day of the new moon was celebrated in Israel with a sacrificial meal in the family (1 Sam. xx. 5 ff., 18 ff.). There is no evidence of any connection between this feast day and the central sanctuary in the early period. The older calendars contain no reference to חדש. We gather from Amos viii. 5 that on the new moon trade and business was suspended. In Hosea ii. 13 חדש is marked by joy, even by ecstasy, and the prophet includes the feast day

[134] Cf. B. Meissner, *Babylonien und Assyrien*, II (1925), p. 92, and in particular A. Falkenstein/W. von Soden, *Sumerische und akkadische Hymnen und Gebete* (1953), pp. 91, 148, 189.

[135] B. Meissner, op. cit., p. 92.

[136] C. H. Gordon, *Ugaritic Handbook*, Analecta Orientalia, 25 (1947), II, Texts in Transliteration, p. 130, Text: 3 48.

[137] J. Aistleitner, *Die mythologischen und kultischen Texte aus Ras Schamra* (1959), p. 74, Text III D I 9.

quite openly among the ימי הבעלים. In this connection, G. Boström has suggested that in Canaanite religion חדש was a festival of the *hieros gamos*.[138] Sacrificial rites on the feast of the new moon are mentioned in Isa. i. 13. One might even assume from this passage that the cult took place in the area of the Temple, and the context supports this assumption. There are, in fact, Old Testament passages which show quite plainly that the feast of the חדש was held in the Temple sanctuary. The regulations in Ezek. xlvi. 6 f. and Num. x. 10 and xxviii. 11 ff. have already been mentioned. On the day of the new moon the cultic community assembled in the Temple for sacrifices and offerings. The feast day was announced by the blowing of trumpets (Ps. lxxxi. 3; Num. x. 10). In Ezekiel's outline of a cultic constitution the prince has the task of offering the sacrifice (Ezek. xlv. 17). These regulations, which in their essence go back to the period of the exile, mould the cult of the post-exilic period. At the new moon the people come to the Temple to worship Yahweh (Isa. lxvi. 23). The strict observance of the feast is laid down in Neh. x. 34, 1 Chron. xxiii. 31 and 2 Chron. ii. 3.

To sum up the development we have outlined, we can state that a feast that was celebrated every month in the religion of the ancient East was introduced first of all into the families of Israel. There was a very real danger, however, that together with the sacrifices fertility rites and rites connected with astrology might find their way into the Israelite way of life (cf. Hos. ii. 13). Subsequently the Temple sanctuary more and more drew the חדש cult to itself and 'centralized' it by means of rules and rituals.

(b) *The Sabbath*

In some of the very early legal stipulations in the Old Testament there is already the tradition of a sabbath law.[139] The regulations in the

[138] G. Boström, *Proverbiastudien* (1935), pp. 135 f.

[139] Bibliography dealing with the sabbath law: J Meinhold, *Sabbath und Woche im Alten Testament* (1905); J. Hehn, *Siebenzahl und Sabbat*, Leipziger semitische Studien, II, 5 (1907); J. Meinhold, 'Die Entstehung des Sabbats', *ZAW*, 29 (1909), pp. 81 ff.; ibid., 'Zur Sabbatfrage', *ZAW*, 36 (1916), pp. 108 ff ; H. Webster, 'Rest Days—A Sociological Study', *University Studies of the University of Nebraska*, XI (1911); T. J. Meek, 'The Sabbath in the Old Testament', *JBL*, 33 (1914), pp. 201 ff.; B. D. Eerdmans, 'Der Sabbat', *Festschrift K. Marti* (1925), pp. 79 ff.; K. Budde, 'The Sabbath and the Week', *JTS*, 30 (1929), pp. 1 ff.; J. Meinhold/K. Budde, 'Zur Sabbathfrage', *ZAW*, 48 (1930), pp. 121 ff.; W. W. Cannon, 'The Weekly Sabbath', *ZAW*, 49 (1931), pp. 325 ff.; E. J. Kraeling, 'The Present Status of the Sabbath Question', *AJSL*, 49 (1932/3), pp. 218 ff.; S. Langdon, *Babylonian Menologies and the Semitic Calendars* (1935); H. Cazelles, *Études sur le Code de L'Alliance* (1946), pp. 92 ff.; N. H. Tur-Sinai, 'Sabbat und Woche', *Bibliotheca Orientalis*, VIII (1951), pp. 14 ff.; H. H. Rowley, 'Moses and the Decalogue', *BJRL*, 34 (1951/2), pp. 81 ff., reprinted

J passage in Exod. xxxiv. 21 and in the Book of the Covenant (Exod. xxiii. 12) lay down that after a six-day working week the שבת is to be held on the 'seventh day'. On this day no work is to be done in the house or in the field, not even at the time of ploughing and of harvest (Exod. xxxiv. 21). The שבת is a day of rest for man and beast (cf. ינוח in Exod. xxiii. 12). Besides the familiar name שבת we meet later the term שבת שבתון (Lev. xxiii. 3), which has obviously to be interpreted as an intensive form. The sabbath law is firmly established in the Decalogue (Exod. xx. 8 ff.; Deut. v. 12 ff.), but the theological explanations are different. Exod. xx. 8 ff. refers to the seventh day of the creation, but Deut. v. 12 ff. to the sojourn in Egypt.[140] Both the explanations are secondary, but they show how the Old Testament tradition attempted to anchor the sabbath in the fundamental mighty acts of Yahweh.

We must examine once again the passages in the Old Testament where 'new moon and sabbath' are mentioned together. We find here a reflection of the basic regulations, but also traces of different customs. Amos viii. 5 shows that the sabbath rest applied to trade and business. The influence of Canaanite nature religion can be seen in Hos. ii. 13. 2 Kings iv. 23 reveals what the significance of the sabbath was in Israel. An extremely important place is given to the sabbath in the prophecy of Ezekiel and in the Priestly Code, but these later developments will have to be considered in a separate section. As far as the early period and the pre-exilic period are concerned, the first fact we have to establish is that the sabbath was not really a feast. There is no indication of a ritual that might have set the pattern for the day. The seventh day of the week was merely a day of rest. It would certainly be a mistake to link the name שבת in its original sense with the verb שבת, for in Babylon there was an important day which was called *šabattu* or *šapattu* and which might well have influenced the Old Testament term. But there is no question that in Israel the שבת was interpreted in the sense of 'day of rest', 'day of ceasing from work' (Exod. xxxiv. 21). It is of decisive importance for the understanding of this sabbath day in the Old Testament

[140] For a detailed discussion, see E. Jenni, op. cit., pp. 15 ff.

---

in *Men of God* (1963), pp. 1 ff.; G. J. Botterweck, 'Der Sabbat im Alten Testament', *Theologische Quartalschrift* 134 (1954), pp. 134 ff., 448 ff.; T. H. Gaster, 'Le jour du repos', *Evidences*, 43 (1954), pp. 43 ff.; C. R. North, 'The Derivation of Sabbath', *Biblica*, 36 (1955), pp. 182 ff.; E. Jenni, *Die theologische Begründung des Sabbatgebotes im Alten Testament* (1956); E. L. Ehrlich, *Kultsymbolik im Alten Testament und im nachbiblischen Judentum* (1959), pp. 77 ff.; E. Vogt, 'Hat "*sabbāt*" im Alten Testament den Sinn von "Woche"?', *Biblica*, 40 (1959), pp. 1008 ff.; R. de Vaux, *Ancient Israel: Its Life and Institutions*, pp. 475 ff.

that it should be observed ליהוה (Exod. xx. 10; Lev. xxiii. 3). The seventh day was characterized not just by rest as such, but by the connection of the rest with Yahweh. What is the meaning of this connection? It may be possible to draw the conclusion from the close link between the sabbatical year and the sabbath day in Exod. xxiii. 10 ff. that just as the sacral fallow proclaimed the fact that the earth belonged to Yahweh, so the sabbath was a sign of Yahweh's lordship over man's time. But this explanation should not be interpreted in an abstract sense. On the seventh day man gives back to Yahweh a 'normal day' kept free from all dissipation, and so acknowledges God's 'rightful claim' to every day.[141] Although the people may not always have been aware of this meaning—the sabbath was constantly interpreted in other senses (cf. Hos. ii. 13)—this was the meaning intended by the reference ליהוה in the commandments. This intention can be seen later in the fact that the 'observance' aspect (שמר) of the sabbath develops more and more into the 'holy' aspect (קדש). The day preserved ליהוה becomes the 'holy time' that belongs exclusively to Yahweh—but this development takes us on to the exilic period.

Like the new moon, the sabbath also had originally no connection with the holy place, for the simple reason that it was not a feast day. Therefore it is all the more significant that the observance of this seventh day which was not marked by any act of worship—in contrast to the new moon celebrations which were marked by ritual practices—was laid down by regulations even at an early period. Exod. xxiii. 12, as part of the Book of the Covenant, points to the pre-monarchical period,[142] and Exod. xxxiv. 21, which belongs to J, is no doubt also a traditional element from the same period.[143] But the insertion of the sabbath law into the Decalogue shows clearly that the actual observance of the day of rest could not be controlled by the legal and cultic authorities. As has often been noted, the apodeictic clauses of the Decalogue penetrate to hidden realms which could be scrutinized only in the rarest cases by the law and legal actions; they touched upon man's innermost motives and brought them under the sovereignty of Yahweh.[144]

[141] Cf. G. von Rad, *Theologie des Alten Testaments*, I (1957), p. 25, note 2 (E.T. *Old Testament Theology*, I (1962), p. 16, note 3).

[142] Cf. C. Kuhl, *Die Entstehung des Alten Testaments*, p. 107.

[143] On the question of sources, see G. Beer/K. Galling, *Exodus*, HAT, I, 3 (1939), pp. 163 ff.

[144] The fact that the individual clauses of the Decalogue begin with the words of command 'Thou shalt (not) . . .' should not be taken to imply that this turn of phrase is primarily a threatening command, presented to men as a command that cannot be fulfilled; but we should note that the unconditional negative present in the Hebrew (לא with the Imperfect) points to the fact that the requirement is a command of a

Gradually, however, the central sanctuary attracted the sabbath to itself and imposed cultic regulations upon it in the process of growth from שמר to קדש. We can see the first traces of this development even in the pre-exilic period, for the שבת certainly brought to the Temple a stream of visitors from the immediate neighbourhood (cf. 2 Kings xi. 5 ff. and probably also Isa. i. 13).

(c) *Theories about the Origin of the Sabbath*

The story of the origin and development of the sabbath law in the Old Testament is extremely complicated, and it is almost impossible to throw any adequate light upon it. There are, however, a number of theories and hypotheses to be considered.[145]

Studies on the Babylonian-Assyrian calendar have given rise to certain questionable theories. In the Hammurabi dynasty the days of the new moon and full moon were celebrated on the first and fifteenth day of the month, and the day of the full moon, the fifteenth day of the month, was called *šapattu* or *šabattu*. Therefore, as 'new moon and sabbath' are found as 'doubles' in certain passages in the Old Testament, the conclusion was drawn that the Old Testament שבת—like the Babylonian *šabattu*—must originally have been a day of the full moon. But there is no support in the Old Testament for this hypothesis, apart from the admittedly remarkable similarity of the names. Even for the sabbath laws of Israel which point back to the pre-monarchical period the sabbath is the 'seventh day' that has to be observed periodically. The passages which have to be ascribed to a later period, and which mention 'new moon and sabbath' together cannot be explained without reference to these older regulations.

Another possibility for clarifying the origin of the sabbath presented itself with reference to the Babylonian texts which indicated 'a sort of seven-day week'.[147] In the divisions of the month in the Babylonian

[145] See the comprehensive surveys in E. J. Kraeling, 'The Present Status of the Sabbath Question', *AJSL*, 49 (1932/3), pp. 218 ff., and J. J. Stamm, *Der Dekalog im Lichte der neueren Forschung* (1958), pp. 39 ff.

[146] K. Marti, *Geschichte der israelitischen Religion* (5 ed., 1907), p. 54. On the Babylonian 'day of the full moon', cf. B. Landsberger, *Der kultische Kalender der Babylonier und Assyrer* (1915), pp. 99 f.

[147] B. Meissner, *Babylonien und Assyrien*, II, p. 396.

---

unique ruler, whose words 'do not return unto him void' (Isa. lv. 11). The commandment 'Thou shalt have none other gods beside me' is an effective, dynamic word that directly assumes its own fulfilment, and could therefore be best translated 'Thou wilt have none other gods beside me', taken not in the sense of a promise (as H. F. Kohlbrügge suggests), but in the sense of an effectual, present fulfilment of what is commanded.

calendars the first day is followed by the seventh day (*sibûtu*), the fifteenth day (*šabattu*), the twenty-first day and finally the twenty-eighth day (*bubbulu* = black moon). But if we examine these divisions within the lunar month, we meet with difficulties when we translate them to the Old Testament context. The arrangement of the week concluding with the sabbath does not fit the calendrical system. In particular, as has often been pointed out, the arrangement laid down in the sabbath laws of the Old Testament is applied independently of the phases of the moon.[148] This hypothesis suggesting that the Old Testament sabbath was derived from the phases of the moon has always found it hard to show how the transition was made in the development of the institution.[149]

At this point we have to consider another theory, which disregards the lunar month and assumes that there was a system of weeks entirely independent of the phases of the moon which run through the whole year. It has been pointed out, for example, that there were market days which were held periodically and were made into feast days[150] and reference has been made to the *nundinae* of the Romans and other regularly recurring fixed times. But no evidence has yet been found that there were such market days among Israel's neighbours. Indeed, we have to ask ourselves whether this assumption of a week, independent of the phases of the moon, which ran through the whole year is not on the wrong lines entirely. What really is the meaning of an 'independent arrangement of weeks'? There must be a fixed point at some particular time in order to provide a norm for the division into periods. Are we to assume that this normative fixed point was set at the turn of the year, or at some other imaginary position? Does not this suppose a principle that was without foundation in real life? Was the week concluding with the sabbath really derived from the unit of the lunar month regulated by the fixed point of the new moon? Is the week in Israel independent of the lunar month? Doubts arise as soon as we consider the Old Testament cultic calendar in Lev. xxiii.[151] Even in Deuteronomy a feast week of seven days is presupposed for the feast of Unleavened Bread and the feast of

[148] 'The distinctive nature of the sabbath, from the standpoint of the history of religion, is based not so much on the way in which it is different from the other days of the week, but rather in the fact that it is independent of any periodically recurring events in nature. Even in the earliest period, as Exod. xxxiv. 21 and xxiii. 12 show, the sabbath is independent of the lunar revolution and of the phases of the moon' (E. Jenni, *Die theologische Begründung des Sabbatgebotes*, p. 11).

[149] See E. Jenni, op. cit., p. 12.

[150] H. Webster, op. cit., pp. 50 ff.; E. Jenni, op. cit., pp. 12 f.

[151] E. Kutsch pointed out the connections between the cultic week and the sabbath once again in his article 'Erwägungen zur Geschichte der Passafeier und des Massotfestes', *ZThK*, 55, 1 (1958), pp. 25 ff.

Tabernacles (Deut. xvi. 3, 15). Are we to believe that this feast week, which was linked in earlier times with a date derived from a nature context and from astronomical associations, prevailed over a week which was independent of this connection? This question becomes more significant when we examine the cultic calendar in Lev. xxiii. The following picture presents itself:

Feast of Passover and Unleavened Bread:
- Fourteenth day of first month: Passover (Lev. xxiii. 5).
- Fifteenth day of first month: Day of rest at the beginning of the feast of Unleavened Bread (xxiii. 7).
- Twenty-second day of first month: Day of rest at the end of the feast of Unleavened Bread (xxiii. 8).

Autumn festival:
- First day of seventh month: Day of rest (xxiii. 25).
- Tenth day of seventh month: Day of rest on the occasion of the Day of Atonement (xxiii. 28).
- Fifteenth day of seventh month: Day of rest at the beginning of the feast of Tabernacles (xxiii. 34 f.).
- Twenty-third day of seventh month: Day of rest at the end of the feast of Tabernacles (xxiii. 36).

From the point of view of literary history, Lev. xxiii contains the first cultic calendar dated exactly according to month and day. Can we draw any conclusions from these dates concerning the relationship between the feast week and the reckoning of periods by weeks? What we notice first of all is that in the passages listed above the name שבת does not appear; there is just a general command that work should cease.[152] We must also note that in connection with the autumn festival an arrangement based on seven days is upset by the fact that a day of rest is appointed for both the tenth and the twenty-third days of the seventh month (the feast of Tabernacles is meant to last eight days). But if we disregard these two occasions and attribute their appointment to the particular sequence of the autumn festival, then the first, fifteenth and twenty-second days stand out as fixed days of rest in an interrupted sequence

[152] Lev. xxiii. 15 is instructive, as it speaks of a שבת which is meant to be identical with the first day of the feast of Unleavened Bread. The manner of expression is circumstantial, but in reckoning the feast of Weeks it starts from the fifteenth day of the first month. But if in this reckoning 'seven weeks' are counted from the fifteenth day of the first month, then it is quite clear that it was the festival week that inaugurated the system of weeks for the period that followed. On the textual problems, see E. Vogt, 'Hat "šabbāt" im Alten Testament den Sinn von "Woche"?', *Biblica*, 40 (1959), pp. 1008 ff.

of seven. Are we to believe that this arrangement of the two festival months cut across a week derived from the lunar month? This seems hardly possible. It seems much more reasonable to put the fixed point from which the arrangement of the week concluding with the sabbath begins at the day of the new moon or the full moon in spring and autumn. The following picture would then emerge: in the earliest period a festival week (Unleavened Bread) was linked with the fixed date of the feast of the Passover, which became the pattern for and the origin of the division into periods of weeks until the next gathering for the feast in the autumn. The feast of Tabernacles then began afresh and with its festival week inaugurated the sequence of weeks for the next half year. In the calendar in the Holiness Code this sequence which is rooted in the two festivals is exactly dated according to the days. The fact that the week of the feast of Tabernacles is lengthened by one day can hardly be connected with intercalary measures. Unfortunately we know nothing about intercalation in the Israelite calendar. Most of the explanations of this problem rest on unproved assumptions, which often adduce a forced interpretation of Ezek. xl. 1. It is not until the Mishnah that we have evidence of an intercalary month (*Megilla*, I, 4, and *Eduyoth*, VII, 7).

We can set out the origin of the sabbath as follows. The twofold division of the month of which there is evidence in Babylon, which fixed the 'day of new light' as the first day of the month and the *šabattu* as the fifteenth day, had undoubtedly a decisive importance for all cults based on the lunar calendar. Among these cultural influences radiating from the region of Babylon the idea of the *šabattu* certainly played its part. But then a system of reckoning was introduced into this arrangement of the calendar which was based on the number seven. The sabbath laws of the Old Testament are influenced by this seven pattern and no longer call the fifteenth day of the month a שׁבת, but the days of rest which are to be held after periods of six days. The sequence of weeks, however, is always dependent on the original model of the festival weeks fixed on the occasion of the two main feasts in the spring and the autumn. The fifteenth day of the first month and the fifteenth day of the seventh month are the points of reference for the institution of the sabbath.[153] But the question arises, what is the origin of this system

[153] If the fifteenth day of the first month and the fifteenth day of the seventh month are as it were the model for the שׁבת in the time of festival which inaugurates the periods, then it would be conceivable that the name *šabbattu* used in Babylon exercised its decisive influence at this point. As far as the Sabbath laws in the Old Testament are concerned, the suggestions about the basis of the period of the week in the arrangement of the feast open up new perspectives. The Sabbath laws have their 'setting in life'

of 'seven'? This question can be answered only in a larger context, for we have already met a variety of institutions based on 'seven': 'seven years' (sabbatical year), 'seven weeks' (the period between the feast of Unleavened Bread and the feast of Weeks), and 'seven days' (the week concluding with the sabbath). Are we to assume—as is often stated in a superficial symbolical interpretation—that Israel introduced the 'sacred number' into the calendar?

(d) *The Number Seven in Ugarit*

The texts discovered at Ras Shamra, the ancient Ugarit, have in various respects greatly increased our understanding of Syrian-Canaanite religion and culture, and numerous links with the Old Testament have been brought to light. Ideas, customs, rites, cults and mythical elements have come to be seen differently in the light of the Ugaritic texts. We can avail ourselves of the same evidence to help us to interpret the significance of the number seven. We have already indicated in another connection that there was a division into periods of 'seven years' (pp. 41 ff). We must now point out again that the Ras Shamra texts speak of two periods qualitatively quite different but equal in length. There is a seven-year period of fertility and life during which Baal reigns,[154] and a seven-year period of infertility, of lamentation and death.[155] The number 'seven' indicates periods of nature mythology which cannot be explained by reference to the so-called 'number saying'. Perhaps there

[154] We find the following passage in I AB V:

'Môt *is vanquished*
Reaches earth.
[*Baal returns*] to the throne of his kingship
[*Dagân's Son*] to the seat of his sovereignty.
From [days] to months
From months to years
[Lo] in the seventh year
And the god Môt [*addresses himself*] to Aliyn Baal.
He lifts his voice
And shouts:
"Because of thee, O Baal, I have experienced humiliation . . ." '
(C. H. Gordon, op. cit., p. 47).

[155] The period of destruction is described in BH II. One passage reads:

'Seven years the god is abundant [ ]
Even eight cycles, until [ ].'
(C. H. Gordon, op. cit., p. 55).

Cf. also I D 40 ff. and I D 176 ff.

---

in the normative cultic week, which determines how the 'seventh day' is to be reckoned in the half-year that follows. The system of weeks runs its course through the months independently of all the phases of the moon, beginning with the festival week—on to another festival.

are astrological ideas connected with the Pleiades (believed to be made up of seven stars) in the background. In any case the period of 'seven years' is thought of as specially significant in content, a unit of time of great potency and fateful in its meaning. The natural year is similarly overarched by more far-reaching events. It seems very likely that at the boundary between the infertile and the fertile periods there were acts of worship which sought to influence the forces of fate. We cannot know for certain whether the sacral fallow that was observed in Canaan played any part in this connection, but it is possible that it did. Israel, however, gave a completely new interpretation to the 'sabbatical year', the outward form of which is related to the seven-year period, and replaced the fate-ridden nature religion by a cultic confession of the will of God disclosed in the covenant and of the fact that the land belongs to Yahweh.

The same is true of the way in which the days are reckoned. A quantitative, self-contained sequence of seven days was known in the Syrian-Canaanite sphere, but we do not find it anywhere as a unit in the calendar, and certainly not with a concluding sabbath. Nevertheless, we should bear in mind those passages in which a fixed sequence of 'seven days' is mentioned. We know from the Old Testament that the rite of mourning lasted for 'seven days' (Job ii. 13), and the Ugaritic texts also mention this fixed period of mourning.[156] But this 'week of mourning' has possibly little bearing on our problem. More striking is the Old Testament rite—obviously belonging to the sphere of worship—according to which the Ark was carried round the city of Jericho for six days, until on the seventh day, after seven circuits, the walls fell down (Josh. vi. 6 ff.). There are parallels to this story in the Ugaritic texts. On six days a particular rite is performed, so that on the seventh day the desired outcome follows.[157] Magical ideas prevail in this sequence of seven days. We read, for example, in the passage II AB VI:

'Fire is set on the house
  Flame on the palace.
Behold a day and a second
  The fire eats into the house
    The flame into the palace.
  A third, a fourth day
    The fire eats into the house
      The flame into the palace.
  A fifth, a sixth day
    The fire eats into the house

[156] Cf. II D I 6 ff.
[157] Cf. II AB VI 22 ff.; III Rp B 21 ff.; I K 106 ff., 114 ff.

The flame in[to the pala]ce.
Behold, on the seve[nth] d[ay]
The fire departs from the house
The flame from the palace.'[158]

This is probably the description of an act of consecration and cleansing, and the goal of the rite is reached on the seventh day. Other passages reveal similar procedures which always last 'seven days' and come to their conclusion and fulfilment on the last day. These facts suggest that the festival week was known in Ugarit as well, and we have to assume in fact that Israel found in Canaan not only a fixed cultic occasion that took place at harvest-time but also the festival week as a pattern for the spring and the autumn. The feast of Unleavened Bread and the feast of Tabernacles are to last 'seven days' (Deut. xvi. 3, 13). But if the festival week was already in existence, then it is only a short step to the assumption that the origin of the seven-day week was the festival week, which was carried over either by the Canaanite inhabitants or first by Israel in a periodic sequence from the cultic festival and from the cultic week to the reckoning of time as a whole. It is not impossible, but at the moment cannot be proved, that the Israelites found this institution of the week and together with it the Sabbath already in existence in Canaan. In any case the statement that the שבת is to be observed ליהוה (Exod. xx. 10; Lev. xxiii. 3) suggests that a traditional institution was taken over by the Yahweh faith.

(e) *The Meaning of the Sabbath Law in the Exilic and Post-exilic Periods*

During the exile in Babylon the exiles were far from the holy places at which worship was offered in Palestine. With the loss of the holy place the 'holy time' became more important. Furthermore, the observance of the sabbath became a confessional act of great importance in a foreign land where different time systems prevailed. We notice for the first time in the prophecy of Ezekiel the outstanding importance that came to be attached to the sabbath law in the period of the Exile.[159] The שבת becomes a sign of the covenant between Yahweh and his people (Ezek. xx. 12). This character of a confession and sign of the covenant which is now attributed to the sabbath can be clearly seen when Ezekiel declares in the name of Yahweh: 'And hallow my sabbaths; and they shall be a sign between me and you, that ye may know that I am the Lord your God' (xx. 20). The sabbath is not merely to be 'observed' (שמר)

[158] Trans. C. H. Gordon, op. cit., pp. 34 f.
[159] On Ezek. xx. 12, cf. W. Zimmerli, *Ezechiel*, BK, 13, pp. 445 f.

and 'hallowed' (קדש). Any desecration is vehemently opposed (Ezek. xx. 13, 16, 21; xxii. 8; xxiii. 38).

Ezekiel's outline of a cultic constitution places the sabbath completely within the Temple cult (Ezek. xlvi. 1 ff.).[160] The prince is to offer sacrifices and gifts. The day of rest has not only become a 'holy day' which has to be thought of as a sign of the covenant and affirmed as a confessional act, but it has also developed into a day of sacrifice which has to be celebrated in the Temple sanctuary. In later passages from the post-exilic period we can see the way in which the community is called to worship Yahweh at the cultic centre (Isa. lxvi. 23). Every kind of activity is strictly forbidden (Isa. lvi. 2, 4, 6; lviii. 13).

We must place the Priestly Code in the closest association with Ezekiel, for the priestly laws also see in the sabbath primarily the sign of the covenant. Among the many regulations concerning, and references to, the sabbath Exod. xxxi. 12–17 is of particular importance.[161] Any kind of work is forbidden on the שבת with the utmost stringency. He who transgresses the sabbath law is to be put to death. As in Exod. xx. 8 ff., the theological explanation of this law refers to the rest with which God concluded and crowned the work of the creation on the seventh day (Gen. ii. 2 f.). All the laws concerning the sabbath in the Priestly Code are marked by the greatest strictness of observance, but the unconditional nature of the obedience that is required is in keeping with the generosity of God's saving grace. It would lead us too far afield to trace the effects of Ezekiel's message and of the law contained in the Priestly Code upon the post-exilic period. We must be content with indicating the beginnings of the new developments.

7. Hanukkah and Purim

These two festivals of the Jewish cultic community belong to a relatively late period, and we shall give an outline of them to conclude this chapter.

(a) *Hanukkah*

The name *hanukkah* which became customary means 'dedication',[162]

[160] Cf. H. Gese, *Der Verfassungsentwurf des Ezechiel*, BHT, 25 (1957), pp. 75 ff.

[161] On this passage, see K. Koch, *Die Priesterschrift*, pp. 37 f.

[162] Bibliography of the feast of Hanukkah: H. Höpfl, 'Das Chanukafest', *Biblica*, 3 (1922), pp. 165 ff.; O. S. Rankin, *The Origins of the Festival of Hanukkah* (1930); E. Bickermann, 'Ein jüdischer Brief vom Jahre 124 v. Chr.', *ZAW*, 32 (1933), pp. 233 ff.; O. S. Rankin, 'The Festival of Hanukkah', *The Labyrinth* (1935), pp. 159 ff.; F. M. Abel, 'La fête des la *Hanoukkah*', *RB*, 53 (1946), pp. 538 ff.; J. Morgenstern,

and wherever the feast was celebrated in the Jewish communities the outstanding event of the Maccabean period was recalled. At the command of the Seleucid king Antiochus IV Epiphanes, the Temple in Jerusalem was plundered in the year 168 B.C. and desecrated by the offering of sacrifices to Zeus Olympius (1 Macc. i. 20 ff.). It was not until 165 B.C. that the Maccabeans succeeded in taking Jerusalem and restoring the Temple worship.[163] We read in 1 Macc. iv. 52 ff.:

'And they rose up early in the morning, on the five and twentieth day of the ninth month, which is the month Chislev, in the hundred and forty and eighth year, and offered sacrifice according to the law upon the new altar of burnt offerings which they had made. At what time and on what day the Gentiles had profaned it, even on that day was it dedicated afresh, with songs and harps and lutes, and with cymbals. And all the people fell upon their faces, and worshipped, and gave praise unto heaven which had given them good success. And they kept the dedication of the altar eight days, and offered burnt offerings with gladness, and sacrificed a sacrifice of deliverance and praise. And they decked the forefront of the temple with crowns of gold and small shields, and dedicated afresh the gates and the priests' chambers, and made doors for them. And there was exceeding great gladness among the people, and the reproach of the Gentiles was turned away. And Judas and his brethren and the whole congregation of Israel ordained, that the days of the dedication of the altar should be kept in their seasons from year to year by the space of eight days, from the five and twentieth day of the month Chislev, with gladness of joy.'

The feast of the Hanukkah refers to an historical event. The explanation of the time of the feast given in 1 Macc. iv. 54 is that the community chose the date for the dedication of the Temple exactly to the day and the month at the time when years before the sanctuary was destroyed by the Seleucids (cf. also 2 Macc. x. 5). The twenty-fifth day of the ninth month (Kislev) is, however, also the day of the winter solstice, which raises the question whether Antiochus IV Epiphanes in his destructive measures in Jerusalem fixed the sacrifice for Zeus Olympius on the day of the winter solstice. If the date was fixed in this way this would explain why the act of the dedication of the Temple, which had come to be a cultic festival, became so definitely linked with the twenty-fifth day of the ninth month. The Old Testament traditions and those

[163] For the historical events, see M. Noth, *History of Israel*, pp. 368 ff.

'The Chanukkah Festival and the Calendar of Ancient Israel', *HUCA*, 20 (1947), pp. 1 ff.; ibid. (1948), pp. 365 ff.; T. H. Gaster, *Festivals of the Jewish Year* (2 ed., 1955); R. de Vaux, *Ancient Israel: Its Life and Institutions*, pp. 510 ff.

of late Judaism provide no explanation of this particular time. The Maccabean record, however, does give an account of the rites which characterized the cultic festival that had been brought into being. The Temple and altar were consecrated, and the rekindling of the sacred altar fire seems to have been at the centre of this ceremony. The festal joy was expressed in liturgical music, which accompanied the adorning and festooning of the Temple chambers. The offering of sacrifice could be started again, and the feast lasted eight days. At a quite early period Hanukkah became a feast of light.[164] This feature may have been connected with the winter solstice, but might have been thought of primarily with reference to the rekindling of the altar fire and of the lamps of the seven-branched candlestick. We are told in 1 Macc. iv. 50: 'And they burned incense upon the altar, and they lighted the lamps, that were upon the candlestick, and they gave light in the temple.'

The custom referred to in 2 Macc. x. 7 in connection with the feast of the dedication of the Temple has given rise to some far-reaching questions. We are told in this passage that during the days of the feast boughs festooned with ivy and fine branches were carried around, and Kittel has drawn the conclusion from this practice that there were connections between Hanukkah and the feast of Dionysus.[165] It is unlikely that this is the case, for the Maccabean record makes it quite clear that rites from the feast of Tabernacles have been carried over into the feast of the Hanukkah (cf. 2 Macc. i. 9; x. 6).[166] We should therefore look first of all to Lev. xxiii. 40 ff. and Neh. viii. 15 ff. rather than to a feast of Dionysus. The character of the feast of lights is also best explained by reference to the feast of Tabernacles.[167] The main question we have to ask, however, is whether the central act of the dedication of the Temple was once part of the feast of Tabernacles. We could interpret the event described in 1 Kings viii, which came at the time of the autumn festival, as a 'dedication of the Temple' and assume that this dedication was a permanent cultic act belonging to the feast of Tabernacles (cf. 2 Chron. vii. 7 ff.). Ps. xxx is described by the liturgical heading in *v.* 1 as שִׁיר־חֲנֻכַּת הַבַּיִת. This description indicates a ceremonial event that could not have taken place only on one occasion even in the period before the Maccabean rising. However, the cultic traditions of the feast of Tabernacles will throw further light on this matter (pp. 185 ff.).

[164] Josephus points out that the light symbolizes the Divine grace (*Ant.* 12, 7. 7).

[165] R. Kittel, *Die hellenistischen Mysterienreligionen und das Alte Testament* (1924), p. 81.

[166] Cf. J. Morgenstern, op. cit., also R. de Vaux, op. cit., pp. 511 ff. ('the Hanukkah and the feast of Tents').

[167] See P. Volz, *Das Neujahrsfest Jahwes*, pp. 26 ff.

(b) *Purim*

The Hebrew word פּוּר, which gave the feast its name, is to be found in Esther iii. 7. It can be elucidated by the Akkadian concept *puru*, for *puru* means the 'lot' cast on New Year's Day and פּוּר means 'lot'. The basis and origin of the feast of Purim is made clear in the Book of Esther.[168] In the form of an 'historical novel' this book introduces us to the life of the Jewish diaspora, some members of which had achieved distinguished positions in the Persian kingdom and won influence at the court in the royal capital of Susa. Serious danger suddenly befell this diaspora community, but by a miraculous dispensation the evil was averted and turned into a mighty triumph. It is pointless to look for an 'historical kernel' for the story.[169] The Book of Esther reveals the background circumstances of the Jewish groups in the Persian kingdom, but its main purpose is to give a typical account of the sufferings and victory of Judaism. The gigantic proportions of certain aspects of the story related in the Book of Esther can only be explained by a critical examination of the materials and main themes. The literary study of this book has shown more and more clearly that mythological complexes underlie the narrative. It seems indisputable that the name 'Esther' must be connected with 'Ishtar', and 'Mordecai' with 'Marduk'. The attempts to trace an Elamite power behind the name 'Vashti' are more doubtful. In other words, Jewish tradition took over mythological materials and gave them a historicizing interpretation as a means of depicting actual circumstances and giving a vivid picture of the fate of the Jewish people as it expressed itself in suffering and victory. But these more general interpretations cannot ignore the fact that behind the story in the Book of Esther there stands an historical experience, however much it may have been modified.

In any case the Jews of the eastern dispersion celebrated on the day of Purim their safe delivery from a mortal danger and their miraculous victory over all destructive attacks. The feast was held in Susa on the fifteenth day of the twelfth month, and in the provinces of the Persian

[168] Bibliography on the feast of Purim: H. Gunkel, *Esther*, Religionsgeschichtliche Volksbücher II, 19/20 (1916); N. S. Doniach, *Purim, or the Feast of Esther* (1933); J. Lewy, 'The Feast of the 14th Day of Adar', *HUCA*, 14 (1939), pp. 127 ff.; V. Christian, 'Zur Herkunft des Purim-Festes', *Festschrift F. Nötscher* (1950), pp. 33 ff.; J. Lewy, 'Old Assyrian *puru'um* and *purum*', *Revue Hittite et Asianique*, V (1939), pp. 117 ff.; A. Bea, 'De origine vocis *pûr*', *Biblica*, 21 (1940), pp. 198 ff.; T. H. Gaster, *Purim and Hanukkah in Custom and Tradition*' (1950); H. Ringgren, 'Esther and Purim', *Svensk Exegetisk Årsbok*, 20 (1955), pp. 5 ff.; E. L. Ehrlich, *Kultsymbolik im Alten Testament und im nachbiblischen Judentum* (1959), pp. 75 ff.; R. de Vaux, *Ancient Israel: Its Life and Institutions*, pp. 514 ff.

[169] Cf. H. Gunkel, *Esther*, pp. 54 ff.

empire on the fourteenth day. There are traces of the feast in Palestine about 100 B.C., but it could go back earlier in this area too (cf. 2 Macc. xv. 36). There is an indication of what the ritual was in Esther ix. 19. Purim is a joyful feast marked by banquets and by gifts, but the day of rejoicing was preceded by three days of lamentation and fasting. It is therefore going too far to call it a 'popular festival' of a 'purely secular character'.[170] By the use of mythological materials and customs Jewish tradition succeeded in depicting in a typical story the fate of the Jews scattered in the pagan world. Although the name of the God of Israel is not mentioned at all in the Book of Esther, we must remember that the suffering and victory of the Jews is not merely a secular political fact but the mark of the life of God's elect in a foreign land.

[170] Cf. H. Gunkel, *Esther*, pp. 80 f.

CHAPTER THREE

THE CULTIC OFFICIALS AND THE SACRIFICIAL SYSTEM

1. The Cultic Officials

(a) *The Priests*

In the early period the performance of cultic and ritual actions was not the privilege of the priests.[1] It was the *pater familias* who killed the Passover sacrifice when it was celebrated in the family and the clan. Whether in the sphere of the tent and the house or of the sanctuary, free men always had the right to offer sacrifice (Judges vi. 19; xiii. 19 ff.; 1 Sam. i. 2 ff; xiv. 34). Elkanah offered sacrifice although a priest was present (1 Sam. ii. 13). The task of 'blessing' the sacrifice (1 Sam. ix. 13) fell to the cultic officials of the sanctuary, but we can assume that the עלה laid upon the altar was subject to the ritual privilege of the priests in the sacred realm.

A priest could be 'appointed' for a period or for good. Anyone who managed to erect a sanctuary for the family or clan appointed a qualified man for the cult by 'filling his hand' (Judges xvii. 5).[2] This procedure of call and appointment was of course followed also by the individual tribes and the larger groups. The priests were chosen from recognized groups and families.[3] Physical wholeness and ritual purity were the conditions for sacral service (Lev. xxi. 1 ff.; Ezek. xliv. 15 ff.). The priesthood was hereditary (Judges xviii. 30; 1 Sam. ii. 12; xxii. 11, etc.) and was represented by highly respected families, whose members of an age to perform the cult had conferred upon them the title 'father' (אב, Judges xvii. 10). There is no evidence in the literary sources of any

[1] On the history of the priesthood and the general questions it raises, see: W. W. Baudissin, *Die Geschichte des alttestamentlichen Priestertums* (1889); A. van Hoonacker, *Le sacerdoce lévitique dans la loi et dans l'histoire des Hébreux* (1889); G. B. Gray, *Sacrifice in the Old Testament. Its Theory and Practice* (1925), pp. 179–270; W. Eichrodt, *Theology of the Old Testament*, I (1961), p. 392 ff.; M. Noth, 'Amt und Berufung im Alten Testament', *Bonner Akademische Reden*, 19 (1958), now in *Gesammelte Studien zum Alten Testament*[2], pp. 309 ff.; R. de Vaux, *Ancient Israel: Its Life and Institutions*, pp. 345 ff.

[2] Cf. M. Noth, op. cit., pp. 6 ff. Noth draws attention particularly to the connections between the custom of 'hand-filling' and corresponding installation rites in the Mari texts, which mean that 'we must assume that there were historical connections between the ruling class in Mari and the beginnings of Israel, which must have been quite considerable' (p. 8).

[3] Judges xviii. 19 names as the employers of priests בית, שבט and משפחה.

consecration of priests in the earlier period, but the rite indicated in Num. viii. 7 might have been the customary one in this period.[4]

The priests of the central sanctuary of Israel, to whose support the cultic community of the whole confederacy of the twelve tribes had to contribute, were held in particular respect. These priestly families were considered 'chosen' (1 Sam. ii. 28; Ps. cv. 26, etc.), and their great privileges were based on Yahweh's appointment. The God of Israel made a 'covenant' with them in order to preserve 'for all time' an immediate relationship of trust and a special position that could not be challenged (Num. xxv. 10 ff.; Jer. xxxiii. 21). In the early period this highly privileged priestly office was the special right of the Levites, who were depicted particularly by the Deuteronomic or Deuteronomistic tradition as the 'ministers before the ark', as the bearers and guardians of the most sacred cultic object (Deut. x. 8; xviii. 7). They officiated at the great central sanctuaries, at Shechem (Deut. xxvii. 14; Joshua viii. 33), Gilgal (Joshua iii. 3 ff.) and at Jerusalem (in the time of David, 2 Sam. xv. 24). But who were these 'Levites'?[5]

The attempt to answer this question leads us into an extremely complicated story of origins and developments. Ancient sources of Old Testament tradition contain the unquestionable tradition that 'Levi' was one of the twelve tribes. He is named as one of the sons of Jacob in Gen. xxix. 34 and is put immediately next to Simeon (Gen. xxxiv. 25). In 'Jacob's blessing and prophecy' about his twelve sons (tribes) Levi again appears in connection with Simeon. Both are under a 'curse' (Gen. xlix. 5 ff.). We can see here clearly the subsequent dispersion which broke up and scattered the two groups and which points back into the early history of the tribal confederacy.[6] From all these observations (of which we have given only an indication here) scholars have repeatedly drawn the conclusion concerning the Levites filling the priestly office that after the dissolution of the 'secular' confederacy Levi

[4] The expiation with the מי חטאת indicates the antiquity of this consecration rite. Cf. B. Stade, *Biblische Theologie des Alten Testaments*, I (1905), p. 127.

[5] On the problem of the Levites, see: H. Grimme, 'Der südarabische Levitismus und sein Verhältnis zum Levitismus in Israel', *Museon*, 37 (1924), pp. 169 ff.; K. Möhlenbrink, 'Die levitischen Überlieferungen des Alten Testaments', *ZAW*, 52 (1934), pp. 184 ff.; L. Waterman, 'Some Determining Factors on the Northward Progress of Levi', *JAOS*, 57, (1937), pp. 375 ff.; T. J. Meek, 'Moses and the Levites', *AJSL*, 54 (1939), pp. 113 ff.; H. H. Rowley, 'Early Levite History and the Question of the Exodus', *JNES*, 3 (1944), pp. 73 ff.; M. Greenberg, 'A New Approach to the History of the Israelite Priesthood', *JAOS*, 70 (1950), pp. 41 ff.; G. E. Wright, 'The Levites in Deuteronomy', *VT*, 4 (1954), pp. 325 ff.; M. Noth, 'Remarks on the Sixth Volume of Mari Texts', *Journal of Semitic Studies*, I (1956), p. 327; R. de Vaux, *Ancient Israel: Its Life and Institutions*, pp. 358 ff.

[6] M. Noth, *History of Israel*, pp. 70 f., 75 ff.

became a group of cultic officials, but this idea is contradicted by the remarkable fact that in Judges xvii. 7 ff. the word לוי has an appellative meaning and is used as though referring to a profession. The designation of the priest as לוא in the Minoan scripts is a significant parallel. M. Noth therefore raises the question, 'Should we not simply trace the transformation of the secular tribe of Levi into a "priestly tribe" to the "accidental" similarity of the name לוי to this appellative לוי?'[7] In fact there is no early tradition in the Old Testament which provides conclusive evidence of such a 'transformation' or transition. The attempt to compromise between the two views by assuming that the family of Levi was a 'priestly family' even before it was dispersed is impossible if for no other reason than that in the earlier traditions the confederacy appears as a completely secular grouping and brought upon itself a curse which deprived it of all honour on account of its acts of violence.[8] This same distinction between the 'tribe of Levi' and the (Levitical) priests can be seen very clearly in Deut. xxvii. 12 ff., where in keeping with the ancient system of the twelve tribes, the tribe of לוי comes next to Simeon in the grouping of the whole confederacy. But then the הלוים, the priests, speak before the twelve tribes and proclaim the Divine law (Deut. xxvii. 14). We cannot make a detailed study here of the 'problem of the Levites', but we can already say that there is plenty of evidence that the assumption that there was a connection between the tribe of Levi and the priests (הלוים) is based on insufficient evidence.

This, however, leads on to the question of the relationship between the official titles לוי and כהן. In interpreting the term כהן it is important to remember that it is related to the Arabic *kâhin*, which means 'prophet' or 'seer', but this semantic relationship would probably not tell us much if we had not come to know of the Canaanite term *kâhinu* (Ugaritic *khn*) through the documents from Ugarit.[9] In Ugaritic the *khn* is the cultic official in the sanctuary in a general sense. The charismatic gift of 'prophecy' and of 'seeing', which is so predominant in the Arabic use, was apparently only one of the many functions of the priest—but probably the most significant when we remember that the delivery of the oracle was one of the main features of the sacral activity of the Old Testament כהן as well. The Canaanite-Ugaritic uses of the word *khn* suggest that we can take כהן to be a customary name for the priest in Canaan. So we find in the Old Testament that the priests of Dagon

[7] M. Noth, *Überlieferungsgeschichte des Pentateuch* (1948), p. 197, note 503.

[8] Cf. Gen. xlix, 5 ff.

[9] C. H. Gordon lists in the 'Comprehensive Glossary' under number 958 the passages in the Ugaritic texts where *khn* is found. See *Ugaritic Handbook*, III (1947).

are called כהנים (1 Sam. v. 5; vi. 2), and the 'priests of the high places' which held sway in the country are also called כהן (1 Kings xii. 32; 2 Kings xxiii. 9). On the other hand, there is no evidence of the term לוי in Syria and Palestine outside the Old Testament. The לוא of the Minoan scripts of *el-ᶜola* points to south-west Arabia. This raises the question whether לוי in the Old Testament might have been an ancient designation for the priest, the origin of which goes back to the nomadic or semi-nomadic sphere. Exod. xxxii in particular, which ascribes to the Levites the true service of Yahweh (*vv.* 26 ff.) seems to presuppose disagreements with a priesthood which adhered to Canaanite practices (*vv.* 1 ff.). To whatever historical context we may attribute Exod. xxxii[10] the Levites are designated as the proper priests of Yahweh, whose duty it is to wage constant battle against every Canaanite cultic practice.

In 'the Blessing of Moses', which is 'certainly pre-exilic and also certainly earlier than the collapse of the northern kingdom',[11] the priestly service 'of Levi' is laid down as follows (Deut. xxxiii. 8–11):

> 'And of Levi he said,
> Thy Thummim and thy Urim are with thy godly one,
> Whom thou didst prove at Massah,
> With whom thou didst strive at the waters of Meribah;
> Who said of his father, and of his mother, I have not seen him;
> Neither did he acknowledge his brethren,
> Nor knew he his own children:
> For they have observed thy word,
> And keep thy covenant.
> They shall teach Jacob thy judgements,
> And Israel thy law:
> They shall put incense before,
> And whole burnt offering upon thine altar.
> Bless, Lord, his substance
> And accept the work of his hands:
> Smite through the loins of them that rise up against him,
> And of them that hate him, that they rise not again.'

To begin with, we must leave open the question as to what connections the Levites had with the cultic centre of Kadesh which is often mentioned when this passage is discussed.[12] In any case the fact that the priesthood originated in the desert period is seen clearly in this passage. Whether the deliberate separation and isolation of Levi from its genealogical context has the secondary purpose of bringing about a separation of the

[10] Cf. S. Lehming, 'Versuch zu Ex. 32', *VT*, X (1960), pp. 16 ff.
[11] O. Eissfeldt, *Einleitung in das Alte Testament* (2 ed., 1956), p. 272.
[12] Cf. E. Meyer, *Die Israeliten und ihre Nachbarstämme* (1906).

priestly group from the secular tribe of Levi cannot be decided for certain. However, the context into which the Levi passage is placed in Deut. xxxiii suggests that in Israelite tradition at one time an original link was seen between the (priestly) לוים and the tribe of Levi. The similarity of the names would inevitably suggest such an association. Deut. xxxiii. 8–11, however, is exclusively concerned with the priests. Their service receives the blessing of Moses' prayer, and they are thought of as the 'Mosaic priesthood'. Their work consists of administering the sacred lot 'Urim and Thummim' and in teaching the divine law.[13] The offering of sacrifice is only mentioned at the end. It is obvious that the Levites had the task in the first place of giving guidance and instruction. There is evidence of this function also in Deuteronomy, which contains a preponderance of Levitical traditions and is linked with the oldest institutions of Israel's central sanctuaries, and indeed in many respects provides valuable information about worship in the early period.[14] In Deut. xxvii. 14 ff. the Levites appear as the proclaimers of the apodeictic divine law before the community of Israel. Their task is to expound the תורה to the people of God (Deut. xxxi. 9), and as the priesthood 'authorized by Moses' they are the guardians of the תורה (Deut. xvii. 18). In legal disputes they have to pass the decisive sentence (Deut. xvii. 8 ff.; xxi. 5). They perform their ministry before the ark of the covenant God (Deut. x. 8), proclaim the ברית to Israel (Deut. xxvii. 9), and by their knowledge and authority in matters of sacral medicine decide who shall be admitted to the Yahweh community and can exclude anyone from taking part in worship (Deut. xxiii 1 ff.). Deuteronomy confirms that the sacrificial cult plays a surprisingly small part in the ministry of the Levites. They are in the first place priests of the divine law.

In the time of David the Levites still occupied a privileged position in the worship of Israel within the central sanctuary.[15] They are mentioned in 2 Sam. xv. 24 as the bearers of the Ark, but even during the time of

[13] On the 'Urim and Thummim', see R. Press, 'Das Ordal im Alten Testament', *ZAW*, 51 (1933), pp. 227 ff.; A. Jirku, 'Die Mimation in den nordsemitischen Sprachen und einige Bezeichnungen der altisraelitischen Mantik', *Biblica*, 34 (1953), pp. 78 ff.; R. de Vaux, *Ancient Israel: Its Life and Institutions*, p. 352.

[14] For the evaluation and elucidation of the Deuteronomic tradition, see G. von Rad, *Deuteronomium-Studien* (2 ed., 1948) (E.T. *Studies in Deuteronomy* (1953)).

[15] It is difficult to say where the sons of Eli belong. It is assumed that the 'family of Eli' was also of Levitical origin, but we still have to ask whether the priesthood which was bound to the sacrifices of the Temple sanctuary which is so prominent in the traditions (cf. 1 Sam. ii. 27 ff.) does not represent the Canaanite type of the כהן. It is possible that the emergence of the sacral institution of the Temple in Israel brought about important changes as regards the cultic officials.

David the high priest Zadok comes to the fore (2 Sam. viii. 17; xv. 24; xx. 25). With the deposition and banishment of Abiathar by Solomon the Levitical element in Jerusalem seems to have been excluded (1 Kings ii. 26). The Zadokites become the privileged priests of the Temple sanctuary. But who is this Zadok? He has no family name and could be described as a 'homo novus'.[16] Was the priestly family of the Zadokites perhaps Jebusite in origin? Was Zadok (like Melchizedek—see Gen. xiv. 18 ff.) the priest-king of pre-Israelite Jerusalem?[17] It is certain that the Zadokites stood in a quite different way from the Levites, who in the course of time were forced to assimilate, in a close connection with the sacral institutions and traditions of a Temple worship influenced by the Canaanite cult, but it is hardly possible to think of them as foreign officials. Here again the problems are very complicated and can lead only to suppositions. A subsequent approval is accorded to the Zadokites in 1 Sam. ii. 35, and it cannot be questioned that the priesthood derived from Zadok enjoyed an absolute prerogative at the Jerusalem sanctuary before the Exile and had charge of worship at the altar (Ezek. xl. 46).

What happened to the Levites? In the official cult of northern Israel at the sanctuary of Bethel newly founded by Jeroboam the king deliberately excluded the Levites (1 Kings xii. 31). כהנים were appointed who were familiar with the ritual of a Canaanite sanctuary and whose duty it was to offer worship before the calf image. The official sanctuaries with their varied worship accordingly empowered officials who could adapt themselves to the new sphere and who in particular took over the dominant sacrificial cult as their main function. The Levites, however, were scattered throughout the country, living in towns and villages as גרים and had the support of the conservative, land-owning classes, the עם־הארץ.[18] It would be a mistake to identify these לוים who lived in the country towns with the כהנים of the unofficial sanctuaries and the cults of the high places who were active everywhere. The Levites, however, did not maintain their position only in the country towns, but also at the ancient Yahweh sanctuaries, particularly at Shechem and Gilgal.[19]

[16] G. von Rad, *Old Testament Theology*, I, p. 249.

[17] See H. H. Rowley, 'Melchizedek and Zadok', *Festschrift Bertholet* (1950), pp. 461 ff.

[18] On the connection of the Levites and the עם־הארץ, see G. von Rad, *Studies in Deuteronomy*, pp. 66 ff. On the עם־הארץ, see E. Würthwein, *Der am ha-arez im Alten Testament*, BWANT, IV, 17 (1936).

[19] In Deut. xxvii the traditions point clearly to Shechem. Gilgal is mentioned in Deut. xi. 30. More recent studies have therefore shown more and more clearly that the Levitical traditions in Deuteronomy are derived from northern Israel. Cf. G. von Rad, op. cit., p. 68; A. Alt, 'Die Heimat des Deuteronomiums', *Kleine Schriften*, II (1953), pp. 250 ff.

Through the common activity of the לוים and the עם־הארץ the Levites again came to the fore in the time of Josiah,[20] and Deuteronomy gives proof of this movement. Under the impetus of the great revival of ancient Israelite traditions the Levites made good their claim to the service of the Ark and in the sphere of the central sanctuary at Jerusalem. To what extent Josiah met these demands we do not know. According to 2 Kings xxiii. 8, 'all the priests out of the cities of Judah' were supposed to take part in the thorough purification and centralization of the cult commanded by the Deuteronomic law. Only the 'priests of the high places' who had taken part in the nature rites were excluded (2 Kings xxiii. 9). Ezekiel's plan for the Temple, however, assumes that Levites had shared in the prerogatives of the Zadokites and that they also possessed the highest priestly privilege of קרב (Ezek. xl. 46; xliii. 19; xliv. 15). It is peculiar that in these passages the Levites appear to be included in the priesthood of the Zadokites.[21] An attempt had evidently been made to reconcile the two competing claims in order to prevent the emergence of two groups parallel to one another or even in opposition to one another.[22]

The Priestly Code breaks up this union again. It represents the claim to special privileges of the hereditary Temple priesthood, which is traced back to Aaron as the original priest. The sons of Aaron are the only legitimate officials, and only they can 'approach' Yahweh.[23] The place of the Levites is outside the sanctuary (Num. iii–iv.), for they are subject to the sons of Aaron and occupy the position of a *clerus minor*. In Chronicles the Levites finally appear in subordinate functions as doorkeepers (1 Chron. xxvi. 1 ff.) and singers (1 Chron. xxv). This whole development is extraordinarily complicated and the decisive turning-points in it cannot be properly clarified. In particular we cannot answer the question as to how it came about that the Aaronic

[20] In Jer. xxxiii. 21 the ancient privilege of the Levites is sanctioned by reference to Yahweh's 'covenant' with Levi. It is remarkable that this priestly privilege is directly linked with that 'covenant' which Yahweh made with David. Does this passage refer to the fact that in the time of David the Levites possessed the priestly privilege in Jerusalem?

[21] בן in Ezek. xliv. 15 indicates both the derivation and also the group to which they belong. Cf. G. Fohrer/K. Galling, *Ezechiel*, HAT, I, 13 (1955), p. 249.

[22] On Zadok and the Zadokites, cf. T. J. Meek, 'Aaron and the Sadocides', *AJSL*, 45 (1928/9), pp. 149 ff.; E. Auerbach, 'Die Herkunft der Sadokiden', *ZAW*, 49 (1931), pp. 327 ff.; A. Bentzen, *Studier over det Zadokidiske Praestekabs historie* (1931); ibid., 'Zur Geschichte der Sadokiden', *ZAW*, 51 (1933), pp. 173 ff.; K. Budde, 'Die Herkunft Sadok's', *ZAW*, 52 (1934), pp. 42 ff.; H. H. Rowley, 'Zadok and Nehushtan', *JBL*, 58 (1939), pp. 113 ff.; ibid., 'Melchizidek and the Sadocides', *Festschrift Bertholet* (1950), pp. 461 ff.

[23] T. J. Meek, op. cit., pp. 149 ff.

traditions in the priesthood suddenly come to have such great importance. What is the origin of these traditions? In what relation do they stand to the statements about the Zadokites who ruled in Jerusalem in the pre-exilic period?

The ministry of the priest controlled and regulated in Israel's cult the whole relationship of the Yahweh community with its God. An extensive expert knowledge (דעת) was handed down from generation to generation in the families of the officials.[24] Rites and regulations, skills in the medical and biological, legal and ethical fields were conveyed by tradition. Clear guidance (תורה) was expected from the priest in all sacral and ethical matters.[25] He had to guard the holiness of the Yahweh community and determine what was 'clean and unclean'. He had to determine by declaratory formulae who could enter the sanctuary as צדיק.[26] In difficult decisions a choice was made by the sacral technique of casting lots.[27] The community at worship or the individual making a petition expected from the priest the word of God, the 'oracle'.[28] It is in this connection that charismatic faculties are assumed. The cultic official had to perform the ministry of intercession before Yahweh, for he was able to 'approach' the God of Israel.[29] In involved legal disputes the Israelite visited the sanctuary in order to learn the divine judgement from the priest.[30] It was his task to carry out correctly the ceremony of abjuration and of the 'ordeal' which determined life or death.[31] He had to be familiar with all the details of the divine law and instruct the cultic community. There were many rites and regulations of sacrifice, and the priest determined whether the offering was accept-

[24] Cf. J. Begrich, *Die priesterliche Thora*, BZAW, 66 (1936), pp. 84 f., reprinted in *Ges. Stud. zum AT* (1964), pp. 232 ff.; R. Rendtorff, *Die Gesetze in der Priesterschrift* (1954), pp. 34 f., 66 f., 77; G. von Rad, *Old Testament Theology*, I, p. 247.

[25] Priesthood and the giving of תורה are intimately connected in the Old Testament. The worshipper takes the first step by asking questions, as we can see, for example, from Hag. ii. 11 ff. On the subject of 'priest and תורה', see Hos. iv. 1 f., 6; Zeph. iii. 4; Mic. iii. 11; Jer. ii. 8; xviii. 18; Ezek. vii. 26.

[26] Cf. G. von Rad, *Old Testament Theology*, I, p. 247, where a fuller bibliography is given.

[27] Cf. R. de Vaux, *Ancient Israel: Its Life and Institutions*, pp. 352 f.

[28] See F. Küchler, 'Das priesterliche Orakel in Israel und Juda', *Abhandlungen zur semitischen Religionskunde und Sprachwissenschaft: Festschrift Baudissin* (1918), pp. 285 ff.; J. Begrich, 'Das priesterliche Heilsorakel', *ZAW*, 52 (1934), pp. 81 ff., reprinted in *Ges. Stud. zum AT* (1964), pp. 217 ff.

[29] Cf. F. Hesse, *Die Fürbitte im Alten Testament*, Diss., Erlangen (1952), pp. 108 ff.

[30] The section Deut. xvii. 8–13 should be particularly noted in this connection.

[31] Cf. R. Press, 'Das Ordal im Alten Testament', *ZAW*, 51 (1933), pp. 227 ff. Num. v. 12 ff., a passage which points back to a very early period, brings out clearly the priest's functions in the ritual. On the renunciation (*abiuratio*) in the realm of sacral law, see F. Horst, 'Der Eid im Alten Testament', *Gottes Recht* (1961), pp. 295 ff.

able or not.[32] The layman prepared the sacrifice, but it was the cultic official who presented it and proclaimed the 'law of sacrifice'. Just as he could impose the curse and decree exclusion from the Yahweh community, so also he was responsible for the ceremony of blessing.[33] Everything in the cultic sphere was supervised, regulated and carried out by him.

(b) *Prophets*

In the period of Old Testament study which was dominated by J. Wellhausen and his school it was customary to consider the popular cult influenced by nature and the prophetic ethos as two entities sharply distinguished from one another. In the view of many scholars prophecy with its ethical emphasis fought and conquered the nature worship, but at the same time forced it into a ritual fossilization governed by strict laws. This familiar picture was abruptly destroyed when in the third volume of his *Psalmenstudien* S. Mowinckel demonstrated the phenomenon of cultic prophecy in the Old Testament and so brought to light an institution of outstanding importance rooted in the worship of Israel.[34] Studies by G. von Rad[35] and A. R. Johnson[36] have made further investigations into this institution and have set out in greater detail the position of the cultic prophet in the sacral life of the community. E. Würthwein in particular has given his attention to the relationship between the cultic officials and the 'free prophets'.[37] It can no longer be doubted that the cultic prophets played an important rôle in Israel, but when we come to define exactly and differentiate their functions and official connections we must do so more carefully than has often been done in the past.

We do not know how the wandering ecstatic groups of which we read in 1 Sam. x. 5 ff. and 1 Sam. xix. 19 ff. were connected with the

[32] On the question of these declarations, see R. Rendtorff, *Die Gesetze in der Priesterschrift*, pp. 74 f.; E. Würthwein, *ThLZ* (1947), pp. 147 f.

[33] The priest had to 'put' the blessing upon the congregation in the name of Yahweh (Num. vi. 22 ff.).

[34] S. Mowinckel, *Psalmenstudien, III: Kultprophetie und prophetische Psalmen* (1923).

[35] G. von Rad, 'Die falschen Propheten', *ZAW*, 51 (1933), pp. 109 ff.

[36] A. R. Johnson, *The Cultic Prophet in Ancient Israel* (1944). Cf. also A. Haldar, *Associations of Cult Prophets among the Ancient Semites* (1945); N. W. Porteous, 'Prophet and Priest in Israel', *Expository Times*, 62 (1950/1), pp. 4 ff.; O. Plöger, 'Prophet und Priester', *ZAW*, 63 (1951), pp. 157 ff.; A. C. Welch, *Prophet and Priest in Old Israel* (1953); H. H. Rowley, 'Ritual and the Hebrew Prophets', *Myth, Ritual and Kingship*, ed. S. H. Hooke (1958), pp. 236 ff.

[37] E. Würthwein, 'Der Ursprung der prophetischen Gerichtsrede', *ZThK*, 44 (1952), pp. 1 ff.

cult. Presumably they were free bands which roamed throughout the country, transporting themselves into a state of ecstasy with the aid of musical instruments and babbling their messages in a state of orgiastic possession. The influence of the ecstatic element in the nature cults is unmistakable. It has been pointed out that there is a parallel in the story of Wen Amun,[38] and we might also mention the prophets of Baal who appeared on Carmel (1 Kings xviii. 21). In Israel these 'prophets' were detested and were rejected as 'crazy fools' (Hosea ix. 7). However, the ecstatic element always remained in nebiism, although restrained by the predominance of the דבר which was expected from a נביא. The derivation of the word נביא cannot be stated for certain. If it is connected with the Akkadian *nabû* = 'to call' it would be reasonable to take נביא in the sense of the 'caller'.[39] As the cultic prophet also—as we shall now be showing—is called נביא these observations on the ecstatic element and on the connection of prophecy with word and call are not without significance.

In the narratives about the prophets in 1 and 2 Kings נביאים appear at various points who belong to the important cultic centres of Israel. Ahijah belongs to the sanctuary of Shiloh (1 Kings xi. 29), and 1 Kings xiii. 11 ff. tells of a prophet at Bethel. The picture of these sanctuary prophets becomes clear in the stories of Elijah and Elisha, where we see that important men of God were surrounded by schools of prophets (בני־הנביאים, 2 Kings ii. 3 ff.). The groups of prophets were domiciled at the time-honoured Yahweh sanctuaries of Gilgal and Bethel, but it seems that Elijah and Elisha as the authoritative leaders of several groups of prophets went from one cultic centre to another (2 Kings ii. 1 ff.). The stories about these two men of God that have come down to us undoubtedly originated in the circles of the בני־הנביאים.[40] They show that ancient Israelite traditions, the themes of which point back to the time of Moses, were kept alive in the prophetic groups. It therefore seems reasonable to assume that there was a common link of tradition

[38] In the story of Wen-Amun we read: 'Now while he was making offering to his gods, the god seized one of his youths and made him possessed. And he said to him: "Bring up [the] god! Bring the messenger who is carrying him! Amon is the one who sent him out! He is the one who made him come!" And while the possessed (youth) was having his frenzy on this night, I had (already) found a ship headed for Egypt and had loaded everything that I had into it' (D. Winton Thomas, *Documents From Old Testament Times* (1958), p. 26).

[39] W. F. Albright gives a different explanation. He points out that in the Code of Hammurabi the verbal adjective *nabi'* means 'called', and that according to this נביא would have the meaning of 'one who has been called'. See *From the Stone Age to Christianity* (1946), pp. 232, 332.

[40] Cf. G. Fohrer, *Elia*, *ATANT*, 31 (1957), pp. 42 ff.

between the Levites who controlled the ancient Yahweh sanctuaries and these בני־הנביאים who surrounded Elijah and Elisha. H. W. Wolff has shown in an interesting study that the prophet Hosea who emerged in northern Israel should be seen as belonging to this Levitical-nebiistic tradition.[41] They were mainly groups who stood in opposition to the official cult of northern Israel. This means that these sanctuary prophets had no wealthy patron, and were therefore dependent on the gifts of the worshippers who were loyal to Yahweh, but in Judah in any case they had the support of the עם־הארץ as an influential, conservative group among the people. If even Elijah wandered about the country in great need, how must the schools of the prophets have fared! Elisha erected a house for himself 'by the Jordan' and evidently lived by the gifts given him for his prophetic ministry (2 Kings vi. 1 ff.).

The prophets who were employed as cultic officials at the official sanctuary had a quite different mode of life. Nathan held an influential position at the court in Jerusalem (1 Kings i. 8). He confronted his king as 'God's messenger' and delivered to him Yahweh's sayings and instructions (2 Sam. vii. 4 ff.).[42] It was possible for David to be severely brought to account by Nathan (2 Sam. xii. 1 ff.). In this early example of a prophet at the king's court we should note his character as a messenger. Later the essential function of a court prophet is that he discerns and communicates Yahweh's reply when he is consulted by the king. It is not clear whether David asked for a word from God from a prophet before his campaigns (2 Sam. ii. 1; v. 19, 23, etc.), but we can assume that this was the case. The situation is quite clear, however, in 1 Kings xxii. Before the general campaign Jehoshaphat, the king of Judah, commanded the northern Israelite ruler: 'Inquire, I pray thee, at the word of the Lord today' (1 Kings xxii. 5), whereupon Ahab gathered together four hundred נביאים who were to make known the 'word of the Lord'. We cannot imagine that this great number of prophets was constantly in the service of the king and was maintained by him. These נביאים probably received a gift for services they actually rendered (Micah iii. 5), and only a narrower circle can be considered as 'officials'. The cult required—as we shall show later—not only priestly functions, but also charismatic mediators who had to exercise their functions on certain occasions.

[41] H. W. Wolff, 'Hoseas geistige Heimat', *ThLZ*, 81 (1956), pp. 83 ff., reprinted in *Ges. Stud. zum AT*, ThB, 22 (1964), pp. 232 ff.

[42] On the figure of the 'messenger of God' and his emergence in Israel and Mari, see M. Noth, 'Geschichte und Gotteswort im Alten Testament', *Gesammelte Studien zum Alten Testament* (1957), pp. 230 ff.

In the time of Isaiah 'priests and prophets' were cultic officials in the Temple referred to in direct connection with one another (Isa. xxviii. 7 ff; xxix. 10), and Micah opposed certain נביאים who proclaimed שלום and communicated visions in the service of the State (Micah iii. 5 ff.). In the prophecy of Jeremiah we see these שלום prophets in a clearer light. They cry 'Peace, peace' (Jer. vi. 14) and comfort the people with the message 'Ye shall not see the sword' (xiv. 13). Together with the priests they have supervisory functions in the Temple sanctuary (xxvi. 7 ff.), and their outstanding spokesman performs the symbolic actions of his prophetic message of salvation within the Temple, in the presence of the priests and all the people (Jer. xxviii. 1 ff.). G. von Rad was the first to show plainly how misleading it is to describe as 'false prophets' these נביאים who appear in the cultic sphere.[43] These cultic prophets had their definite place in the covenant and salvation tradition of Israel. When we consider the evidence carefully we cannot avoid 'placing the office and message of our Shalom prophets in direct relation with an authoritative doctrine of salvation'.[44] With their charismatic gift and their message they guarded the 'redemptive vocation' of the people and tried to avert all obstacles and disturbances in the שלום sphere by virtue of their prophetic office. Their teaching was directed to a happy future, which was promised to Israel under the election and blessing of Yahweh. Religious faith and a message for the nation were merged to form a powerful complex of the שלום ideology in the circle of the cultic prophets who exercised their ministry at the official sanctuary. This was a basic element in the influence of the cultic prophet, but we must now consider his particular functions. The heart of his ministry was of course the דבר—the word of God—which was delivered not only when he was consulted, but also had its part to play when the complaints of the cultic community and the petitions of the individual were brought before Yahweh. It is not entirely clear what the relationship was between priestly commission and prophetic charismatic gift in the matter of the word of God and of oracles. In describing the priestly ministry we noted that the priest had the task of delivering the 'oracle' (p. 97). It is not likely that this function was restricted to the methods of sacral technique. The best example of a 'priestly oracle of deliverance' is the word of Eli, who declared in answer to Hannah's lament: 'Go in peace: and the God of Israel grant thy petition that thou hast asked of him' (1 Sam. i. 17). It is possible that such oracles were nothing but the expression in words

[43] G. von Rad, 'Die falschen Propheten', *ZAW*, 51 (1933), pp. 109 ff.; cf. also G. Quell, *Wahre und falsche Propheten* (1952).

[44] G. von Rad, op. cit., p. 117.

of a technical sacral lot. However, we should not underestimate the charismatic powers that were expected of a priest in connection with the oracle.[45] In any case the cultic prophet had a broader and more embracing sphere of activity in this field. He had the power of discovering through dream, through vision and audition, what fate awaited the community and the individual. His activity was directed to the goal of שׁלום and was meant to remove any obstacles that occurred in the actual events in the life of the nation and the everyday world. The cultic prophets therefore emerged primarily as intercessors (Gen. xx. 7; 1 Sam. vii. 5; xii. 23). In all questions of military undertakings their services were invoked (1 Kings xx. 13 ff.; xxii. 5 ff.).

Having sketched this outline picture of the sanctuary prophets and the נביאים who officiated in the official cult, we must now ask the question whether this picture has given an adequate indication of this institution of a prophetic ministry rooted in the cult. Who exactly are the prominent individuals, whom we have already met to some extent? Who is Elijah? Who is Ahijah of Shiloh? Who is the איש האלהים of whom we read in 1 Kings xiii. 11 ff.? And finally, who is Samuel, of whom we are told in 1 Sam. iii. 20—at the end of an account of a prophetic call—that he, the man of God who held authority at Shiloh, was known and acknowledged in all Israel as a נביא ליהוה? Can we simply include these outstanding men of God in the same category as the many cultic prophets?[46] There is a very remarkable word of God recorded in Num. xii. 6–8:

'And he said, Hear now my words: if there be a prophet among you, I the Lord will make myself known unto him in a vision, I will speak with him in a dream. My servant Moses is not so; he is faithful in all mine house: With him will I speak mouth to mouth, even manifestly, and not in dark speeches; and the form of the Lord shall he behold: wherefore then were ye not afraid to speak against my servant, against Moses?'

This saying, which comes from an ancient source,[47] contrasts the prophets who receive the revelations through dreams and visions, with 'thy servant Moses'. He had special access to Yahweh, which we might describe as 'direct communion'.[48] He saw 'the form of the

[45] Cf. J. Begrich, 'Das priesterliche Heilsorakel', *ZAW*, 52 (1934), pp. 81 ff., *Ges. Stud.*, pp. 217 ff.

[46] On this matter, see also H. J. Kraus, *Die prophetische Verkündigung des Rechts in Israel*, Theol. Stud. 51 (1957).

[47] O. Eissfeldt considers Num. xii. 6–8 to be a part of the 'oldest narrative thread' in source L. See *Einleitung in das Alte Testament*^{3}, p. 258. Noth thinks it belongs to source J (*Überlieferungsgeschichte des Pentateuch*, p. 34).

[48] Cf. Exod. xxxiii. 11 and Deut. xxxiv. 10 with Num. xii. 8.

Lord' and received the word of the Lord directly. Is this saying in Num. xii. 6–8 only an historical reminiscence, merely a subsequent confirmation of the great authority that Yahweh conferred upon Moses? We must not forget that this contrast is not as unique as it appears at first. The prophet Jeremiah declares in his great attack upon the שלום prophets that dreams are the dark source of their 'revelations' (xxiii. 26 ff.), but Jeremiah himself knows on the other hand that he received his commission direct from Yahweh. His sharp attack comes to its climax in the question 'For who hath stood in the council of the Lord, that he should perceive and hear his word? who hath marked my word, and heard it?' (xxiii. 18). סוד יהוה (cf. *v.* 22) is the 'heavenly council' such as is described in Job i. 6 ff. and ii. 1 ff. He who stands 'in the council of the Lord' sees 'the form of the Lord', and is very near to him. Jeremiah sees the difference between his mission and that of the שלום prophets in the fact that he has received his message direct from Yahweh —he does not say this, but it is clearly meant—whereas the נביאים have received their message from dreams. There is a similar contrast drawn in 1 Kings xxii. After the four hundred prophets called together by the king have promised a successful outcome to the military adventure, Micaiah the son of Imlah appears and gives a warning of disaster. His message, which entirely rejects the message of hope delivered by the prophets, is based on a vision in which Micaiah saw Yahweh 'sitting on his throne and all the host of heaven standing by him on his right hand and on his left' (1 Kings xxii. 19). The prophet of disaster saw 'the form of the Lord'. Through 'direct communion' the lying spirit in the messages of hope was unmasked. These two examples, taken from two quite different periods and contexts, show that the contrast in Num. xii. 6–8 is more than a reminiscence or retrospective confirmation of Moses. We shall therefore have to look into the question whether there was alongside the cultic prophets or amongst them an outstanding individual who was authorized in a special way.

We can begin by trying to answer this question in the light of Deut. xviii. 15 ff. It is Moses who is speaking:

> 'The Lord thy God will raise up unto thee a prophet from the midst of thee, of thy brethren, like unto me; unto him ye shall hearken; According to all that thou desiredst of the Lord thy God in Horeb in the day of the assembly, saying, Let me not hear again the voice of the Lord my God, neither let me see this great fire any more, that I die not. And the Lord said unto me, They have well said that which they have spoken. I will raise them up a prophet from among their brethren, like unto thee; and I will put my words in his mouth, and he shall speak unto them all that I shall command him.'

From the point of view of the translation it is important in the first place to note what C. Steuernagel states in his commentary on Deuteronomy: 'The Messianic interpretation of *v.* 15 (Acts iii. 22; vii. 37) is based on a failure to note the context, according to which it is not a question of a single, ideal prophet of the last days, but of a number of prophets who will gradually take the place of Moses. . . .'[49] יקים in *v.* 15 and אקים in *v.* 18 should be translated in a distributive sense ('from time to time'). We should also note in interpreting Deut. xviii. 15 ff. that the passage dealing with נביא in the structure of Deuteronomy stands in the closest relation to the 'regulations of office'. It therefore seems reasonable to see in this passage an important statement concerning the prophetic office.[50] M. Noth questions this interpretation: 'It is questionable whether at this point there is a definite reality in the background of the Deuteronomic law, or whether the law-giver has not attempted as a matter of ideology to include the fact of prophecy within the pattern of an office.'[51] This question cannot be decided in the light of Deut. xviii. 15 ff. alone, but the passage is best understood as the exact expression of an act of inauguration such as is described in Exod. xx. 18 ff. Deut. xviii. 15 ff. is not merely related in a general sense to the 'phenomenon of prophecy', but to the Sinai tradition. What we have is not the outline of an 'ideological pattern' but an event, reported as part of the tradition of the revelation of the divine law, given concrete expression in the form of a decree and a promise. These factors are often overlooked and this 'ideology' of the prophet, which is extremely strange for the Deuteronomist, is taken for granted. If Form Criticism has shown that Deuteronomy as a whole is rooted in the Sinai tradition,[52] then we must note a reference back to this tradition immanent in the passage Deut. xviii. 15 ff. The question that arises is how does Deuteronomy interpret the account to which it refers (as though to 'Scriptural evidence')? Is there merely a loose association or are some essential elements and trends taken over in the strange decree and promise concerning the נביא?

[49] C. Steuernagel, *Das Deuteronomium*, p. 121.

[50] It is established 'that the work of the prophet is not so much that of proclaimer of the future, but rather that of mediator of the claim of Yahweh' (C. Steuernagel, op. cit., p. 121). In his essay 'Die falschen Propheten', von Rad declares with reference to Deut. xviii. 15 ff: 'The very promise concerning "a prophet from the midst of thee, of thy brethren", indicates something institutional, a kind of succession of prophets. He then goes on to describe the נביא as follows: 'He is in the first place a mediator, a fixed court of appeal between God and people' (p. 113).

[51] M. Noth, 'Amt und Berufung im Alten Testament', p. 25, note 46.

[52] Cf. G. von Rad, *Das formgeschichtliche Problem des Hexateuch* (1938), pp. 23 ff., reprinted in *Ges. Stud. zum AT*, pp. 33 ff.

Exod. xx. 18 ff. belongs to the context of the Sinai tradition and follows directly upon the proclamation of the Ten Commandments:

'And all the people saw the thunderings, and the lightnings, and the voice of the trumpet, and the mountain smoking: and when the people saw it, they trembled, and stood afar off. And they said unto Moses, Speak thou with us, and we will hear: but let not God speak with us, lest we die. And Moses said unto the people, Fear not: for God is come to prove you, and that his fear may be before you, that ye sin not. And the people stood afar off, and Moses drew near unto the thick darkness where God was.'

What really happens in this passage? The people are not in a position to bear the presence of Yahweh that is made known by thunder, lightning and smoke. They can no longer hear the mighty voice of God who proclaimed the commandments (Exod. xx. 1–17), therefore Moses has to act as mediator, approach Yahweh and deliver the word of God to the people. What is the meaning of this account? Is it meant to be a historical description of 'the appointment of Moses as mediator of the covenant'?[53] What is the purpose of the narrative, and what is its significance? Since it was recognized that the Sinai pericope was meant to be used as the festival legend for a feast of the renewal of the covenant and the proclamation of the divine law, a new dimension has been opened up for passages such as Exod. xx. 18 ff.[54] The question that immediately presents itself is: who is the 'Moses' who could see the form of the Lord at the cultic realization of the Sinai event (cf. Num. xii. 8), who received the word of God in a unique 'direct communion' and delivered it to the assembled community? In its specific form of 'apodeictic law' the Decalogue is the word of God, in which Yahweh speaks in the first person (Exod. xx. 1). Who was authorized to proclaim this דבר in the cult and to apply it to new situations? Was it 'the' cultic prophets? Exod. xx. 19 ff. ascribes the high office of mediator to Moses alone, and Deut. xviii. 15 ff. takes up this point and declares that this 'Mosaic prophetic office' of the mediator, into whose mouth Yahweh himself will put his words, is to last 'forever'. Yahweh will constantly 'raise up' from Israel men who will take the place of Moses and officiate as authorized prophets and mediators in the cult of the renewal of the covenant and the fresh proclamation of the divine law. When we bear in mind that Deuteronomy—as we have already noted—draws on the cultic elements of the

[53] G. Beer/K. Galling, *Exodus*, p. 104.

[54] S. Mowinckel was the first to point out the cultic background of the Sinai pericope (*Le Décalogue* (1927), pp. 114 ff.). G. von Rad has subsequently interpreted the 'Sinai tradition as a festival legend' (*Das formgeschichtliche Problem des Hexateuch* (1938), pp. 18 ff.).

Sinai tradition, then the significance of the context and background of the passages Exod. xx. 19 ff. and Deut. xviii. 15 ff. can hardly be overestimated. We must also note that both in the Sinai tradition of the book of Exodus and also in Deuteronomy the picture given of Moses as the mediator between Yahweh and his people has such a cultic stamp and is so consistently set out that we can state without any hesitation that in this respect the traditions were confronted by a sacral institution —a 'Moses' figure who was not merely historically unique.[55] Is it not a characteristically modern way of thinking to attempt to interpret the numerous speeches by Moses in the Pentateuch by reference to a later manipulation? It is suggested that this or that tradition, this or that author, set out their schemes 'under the authority of Moses' and that they 'ascribed to Moses' their own—later—words and speeches, but are these suggestions feasible if there stood behind all these speeches of Moses the institution of the office of prophet and mediator endowed with the highest authority? This puts everything in a different light. In particular the speeches of Moses in Deuteronomy would be seen to be not a fiction or a surreptitious authorization, as has often been stated, but the proclamation of the 'Mosaic prophetic office' which is based on the evidence of the decree in Deut. xviii. 15 ff., and which took the place of Moses himself.

But how are we to explain the puzzling convergence of office and charismatic gift in Deut. xviii. 15 ff.? This is the real problem of this institution which looks like an 'ideology'. An office implies continuity, and even succession, whereas the charismatic gift cannot be bequeathed, therefore in Deut. xviii. 15 ff. the institution and the charismatic gift are closely interwoven. The strangeness of the idea of an immediate connection between office and charismatic gift must not be allowed to mislead us into imputing a Utopian conception to the text. The call of Samuel related in 1 Sam. iii might help to clarify the problem. A boy was consecrated to the service of Yahweh at the central sanctuary at Shiloh (1 Sam. i. 28), but one day Samuel received a revelation from Yahweh (1 Sam. iii. 1 ff.) which happened at the place of the divine presence, the Ark (1 Sam. iii. 3). After this event the prophet, endowed with the charismatic gift, was recognized and acknowledged in the whole of Israel as the נביא ליהוה (1 Sam. iii. 20). Other strata of the Samuel tradition depict the prophet as the interceding mediator between Yahweh and his

[55] The Deuteronomic introduction to the Decalogue is characteristic of the picture of Moses in the Sinai tradition: 'The Lord spake with you face to face in the mount out of the midst of the fire. (I stood between the Lord and you at that time, to show you the word of the Lord: for ye were afraid because of the fire, and went not up into the mount) . . . ' (Deut. v. 4 f.).

people (1 Sam. vii. 5 ff.) and as the administrator of justice (1 Sam. vii. 15 f.). Samuel occupies a prominent, central office in Israel. These stories give at least some indication of how the relation between charismatic gift and office might have been conceived. Among the youths who had been 'dedicated' to Yahweh it was expected at the main cultic centre that one would be endowed with the charismatic gift. It was possible there could be a time when the revelations of Yahweh were rare (1 Sam. iii. 1), when there was no direct call from the place of the immediate divine presence. Then they waited for the event through an incubation oracle (1 Sam. iii. 1). When the call came the high priest was the first to be told. We can only suppose what was the further course of events up to the installation in office. Presumably the prophet first had to give an account of himself by fulfilling a divine oracle delivered by him. In this connection Deut. xviii. 20 ff. appears in a new light when directly linked with the decree concerning the 'Mosaic prophetic office'. Samuel himself had first to submit the message received at the Ark to this test. We then read in 1 Sam. iii. 19: 'And Samuel grew, and the Lord was with him, and did let none of his words fall to the ground.' The fulfilment of the prophetic message gives all Israel the assurance that Samuel is a נביא ליהוה. Presumably the proof of fulfilment was already decisive for entrance upon the central office which included all the functions of mediation and direction laid down in the divine law concerning intercession and sacrifice which were required as between Yahweh and his people. It is a mistake to separate the various functions carried out by Samuel by attributing them to different literary strata and to interpret them as tendentious insertions made by interested circles who wanted to 'rediscover' in Samuel their own special ministerial duties. Although the tasks of the Levites stretched from oracles through the declaration of the divine law to the offering of sacrifices (Deut. xxxiii. 8 ff.), how much more extensive must the cultic responsibilities of the authorized mediator have been. These observations on the Samuel tradition, however, can be nothing more than an attempt to clarify a little the puzzling convergence of charismatic gift and office in the central prophetic office. We have to allow for accretions to and overlapping of the various elements in the tradition.

Although it is difficult to prove from Deut. xviii. 15 ff. that there was a succession in the office of the prophetic mediator, we must at least raise the question whether there are traces in the Old Testament of a continuity in Mosaic prophecy. There are two instances that throw light on this matter. We are told in 2 Kings ii. 9 ff. that Elijah transferred to Elisha the charismatic gift of the רוח, so that Elisha takes the place of the great prophet. This spiritual transference was evidently an act of charismatic appointment which had its place in the matter of succession.[56] The other example comes at the end of Deuteronomy (xxxiv. 9). Moses passes on his רוח charisma to Joshua by the laying on of hands. Although this passage may belong to a later literary source (P), it nevertheless points to a fact which is presupposed in the tradition as a whole—that Joshua is Moses' successor. It is significant, e.g., that the Deuteronomist first chapter of Joshua starts its account of 'Joshua's speech' by stating 'the Lord spake unto Joshua' (i. 1). Moses' successor is presented as a prophet who communicates to the people the personal word of the Lord. These two examples again give only an indication of how the connection is to be understood, but we can say that there is no evidence of an office completely determined by the charismatic gift. There were times when few appointments were made (1 Sam. iii. 1).

If finally we examine the evidence of the Psalms, we find the reality of the prophet's office as mediator confirmed. Ps. l depicts the cultic realization of the ratification of the covenant and the promulgation of the divine law.[57] A prophetic voice is heard in *vv.* 7 ff. calling the cultic community to true worship and fresh obedience. In Ps. xcv. 8 ff. also we can recognize the message of a prophet. In Ps. lxxxi. 5b, 10b the prophetic speaker points to the time of his inspiration:

> 'I heard a language that I knew not:
> Open thy mouth wide, and I will fill it.'

Then we hear in the message of the prophet as he appears in the act of worship the exhortations which spring from the first commandment of the Decalogue:

> 'Hear, O my people, and I will testify unto thee:
> O Israel, if thou wouldest hearken unto me!
> There shall no strange god be in thee;
> Neither shalt thou worship any strange god.
> I am the Lord thy God,
> which brought thee up out of the land of Egypt.'

In these passages from the Psalms we see the mediator and speaker who is referred to in Exod. xx. 19 ff. He proclaims the word of the Lord to

[56] We should also refer to the connections between the prophecy of Hosea and Deut. xviii. 15 ff. With reference to the passage in Deuteronomy H. W. Wolff states: 'Here Moses is spoken of as a prophet, as in Hosea, but nowhere else', and continues, 'There is also proclaimed here a succession of true prophets "like Moses", with which again the only comparison is Hosea's way of speaking of the prophets' ('Hoseas geistige Heimat', p. 94).

[57] Cf. H.-J. Kraus, *Psalmen*, BK 15 (1960), pp. 370 ff. On Ps. lxxxi, cf. pp. 561 ff.

the worshipping community and is the 'Moses' in the realization of the Sinai event in worship.

2. The Sacrificial System

In Amos v. 25 and Jer. vii. 22 the prophets declare that Yahweh did not require of his people either burnt offerings or sacrifices in the wilderness. This points to a time when it was simply the Divine law that determined the relationship between God and his people. But do the statements of the prophets Amos and Jeremiah really correspond to the facts, or should they perhaps be taken as tendentious statements? In any case it is certain that the Passover sacrifice has to be attributed to the desert period. Apart from that, we must certainly assume that sacrifices were offered in a nomadic or semi-nomadic cult.[58] Both prophets, however, are obviously alluding to definite ancient Israelite traditions which gave precedence to the divine law over the sacrificial cult. These traditions no doubt contrasted the fact that groups within later Israel received the law in the desert with the fact that the sacrificial cult was such a powerful influence in Canaan. We might recall in this connection the passage about Levi in Deut. xxxiii. 8 ff., where the divine law is to the fore and sacrifices are mentioned only secondarily. Prophets like Amos and Jeremiah belong with their message to this stream of tradition. They raise their voice in protest and complaint against the sacrificial cult of Canaan which follows its own laws and has inundated the worship of the Yahweh community.[59] However, it would be rash and one-sided to allow ourselves to be guided in our consideration and evaluation of sacrifice in Israel by the ancient Levitical and prophetic traditions. The adaptation of the tribes of Israel to the rites and customs

[58] Bibliography dealing with the history of sacrifice: G. B. Gray, *Sacrifice in the Old Testament, Its Theory and Practice* (1925); A. Wendel, *Das Opfer in der altisraelitischen Religion* (1927); A. Bertholet, 'Zum Verständnis des alttestamentlichen Opfergedankens', *JBL*, 49 (1930), pp. 218 ff.; W. O. E. Oesterley, *Sacrifices in Ancient Israel* (1937); A. Metzinger, 'Die Substitutionstheorie und das altisraelitische Opfer', *Biblica*, 21 (1940), pp. 159 ff., 247 ff., 353 ff.; J. E. Coleran, 'Origins of the Old Testament Sacrifice', *CBQ*, 2 (1940), pp. 130 ff.; R. Dussaud, *Les origines cananéenes du sacrifice israélite* (1941); H. Wheeler Robinson, 'Hebrew Sacrifice and Prophetic Symbolism', *JTS*, 43 (1942), pp. 129 ff.; J. Gray, 'Cultic Affinities between Israel and Ras Shamra', *ZAW*, 62 (1949/50), pp. 207 ff.; H. H. Rowley, 'The Meaning of Sacrifice in the Old Testament', *BJRL*, 33 (1950/1), pp. 74 ff.; W. B. Stevenson, 'Hebrew '*olah* and *zebach* Sacrifices', *Festschrift Bertholet* (1950), pp. 488 ff.

[59] On the Canaanite sacrificial cult, see: T. H. Gaster, 'The Service of the Sanctuary. A Study of Hebrew Survivals', *Mélanges Syriens offerts à R. Dussaud*, II (1939), pp. 577 ff.; R. Dussaud, *Les découvertes de Ras Shamra et l'Ancien Testament* (2 ed., 1941); D. M. L. Urie, 'Sacrifice among the West Semites', *PEQ* (1949), pp. 67 ff.; J. Gray, *The Legacy of Canaan*, Supplements to *Vetus Testamentum*, V, (1957).

of Canaan brought about extensive assimilation of the existing cultic traditions. We know today that there is scarcely a sacrificial concept or practice in the Old Testament that was not taken over from the Canaanite inhabitants. The Ras Shamra texts in particular have brought the connections to light.[60] Old Testament sacrifice—as has often been stated—was the 'ethnic element' in the religion of Israel.[61] We must therefore give special attention to the regulations and specific setting of the rites that were adopted from the new environment. Even in the stories of the patriarchs we can see Canaanite customs influencing the cult. The holy place is where the sacrifice must be offered, and it became a numinous place by means of a theophany. The originator of the cult erects an altar and performs the cult at the consecrated place.[62] The individual can offer sacrifice, but also the family and the tribe, and larger groups can also perform the service, but it is mainly the tribal confederacy that assembles at the central sanctuary. The Old Testament contains numerous references to the sacrificial practices performed in different circles. The Priestly Code records the rituals and various regulations concerning an expert priestly knowledge (דעת) that directs and supervises the complicated apparatus of offerings.[63] We must now arrange these sacrificial traditions into categories and give an account of them.

(a) *The Gift Offering*

The earliest and original expression of sacrifice is that of giving. A 'gift' is left at a holy place or ceremonially delivered. This מנחה in its original form included bloody and unbloody offerings (Gen. iv. 4 f.) and was characterized by a basic conception described by G. van der Leeuw in the following terms: 'The word *dare* means to place oneself in relation to, and then to participate in, a second person by means of an object, which however is not actually an "object" at all, but a part of one's own self.'[64] 'The gift is powerful: it has binding force.'[65] 'We both give and receive, and it is quite impossible to say who is actually donor and who recipient.'[66] Such a communication as takes place in the act of giving can arise spontaneously and voluntarily, but it can also come about as a result of definite causes or of fulfilling one's obligations. In the gift

[60] Cf. J. Gray, 'Cultic Affinities between Israel and Ras Shamra', *ZAW*, 62 (1949/50), pp. 207 ff.

[61] Cf. L. Koehler, *Old Testament Theology* (E.T. 1957), p. 181.

[62] Cf. A. Alt, 'Der Gott der Väter', *Kleine Schriften*, I, pp. 19 ff.

[63] See R. Rendtorff, *Die Gesetze in der Priesterschrift* (1954).

[64] G. van der Leeuw, *Religion in Essence and Manifestation* (1938), p. 351.

[65] Ibid., p. 352.

[66] Ibid., pp. 353 f.

offering a powerful intention is directed from the giver to the one to whom the gift is offered. The deity is meant to receive homage, gratitude and reverence in the gift, but the original conception of feeding the spirit is in the background. The Ugaritic texts show us what significance this supply of power had in Canaanite religion. As an example we can quote from passage I AB 1. The god Baal has died (*bᶜl mt*). In the vegetation cult this event is of very great significance. Funerary sacrifices are offered to the dead Baal, wild cattle, oxen, sheep, deer and goats—seven of each kind. They are killed (*ṭbḫ*) 'as food for Puissant Baal' (*kgmn aliyan bᶜl*).[67] The sacrificial offerings are meant to give life and power to the dead god. There was a danger that this primitive pagan idea of feeding the god should influence the Yahweh community with the adoption of the cultic institutions in Israel, but we can see very clearly in the Old Testament how this idea of giving life to the god is precluded. In Ps. l. 9 ff. we hear the word of the Lord which was conveyed through a prophet in worship:

'I will take no bullock out of thy house,
nor he-goats out of thy folds.
For every beast of the forest is mine,
And the cattle upon a thousand hills.
I know all the fowls of the mountains:
And the wild beasts of the field are mine.
If I were hungry, I would not tell thee:
For the world is mine, and the fulness thereof.
Will I eat the flesh of bulls,
Or drink the blood of goats?
Offer unto God the sacrifice of thanksgiving;
and pay thy vows unto the Most High.'

Even if this reproof has to be attributed to a relatively late period it still clearly shows the conceptions of sacrifice that are determinative for the Old Testament. Yahweh is no vegetation deity, and he requires neither food nor supply of energy. The sacrificial offerings are thought of exclusively in terms of gratitude, of homage and of reverence. The *communio* that takes place in the act of giving is not magical, but personal. The element of homage, which is to be found also in Canaanite sacrifice, dominates the מנחה in the Old Testament.[68]

In the early Old Testament traditions the מנחה includes bloody and

[67] See J. Aistleitner, *Die mythologischen und kultischen Texte aus Ras Schamra* (1959), p. 18.

[68] Cf. KRT, 69 ff. (Pritchard, *Ancient Near Eastern Texts*, pp. 143 f.). The worshipper has to present a sacrificial offering on a tower, and pay homage to Baal (*šrd bᶜl*).

unbloody sacrifices, and they are essentially כליל—a 'whole burnt offering' (1 Sam. vii. 9). Gideon prepares a meal for Yahweh that includes unleavened cakes and flesh, which is then offered as a whole by burning (Judges vi. 18 ff.—cf. also xiii. 19 f.). The offering is presented to God at a holy place, under a terebinth (Judges vi. 19) or on an altar (Judges xiii. 19 f.). It should be noted that in both these episodes the sacrifice is directly linked with a theophany. The one who offers the sacrifice pays homage to the *deus praesens*, submits himself to him and demonstrates his complete devotion.

In the subsequent course of the history of worship, however, the idea of מנחה becomes narrower and narrower, and no longer includes the whole sacrificial meal with the bloody and unbloody offerings. מנחה comes to mean merely the vegetable offering, and can include grain, fruits, oil and wine, but the flesh offering is excluded. Thus the 'oblation' laid down in the ritual instructions in the Priestly Code consists essentially of flour and oil (Lev. ii. 1 ff.; vi. 7 ff.; x. 12, etc.). The ancient rite, however, which we saw in Judges is preserved, for the מנחה is presented to Yahweh 'by fire' (Lev. ii. 2; vi. 8, etc.) and is dedicated to God on the altar. It is a token of homage, but petitions can also be accompanied by a gift offering. In Jer. xiv. 12 there is an allusion to a 'fast' in the course of which 'food offerings' are brought before Yahweh, and the king brings gift offerings in order to beseech the granting of his requests in the most intimate communion with his god (Ps. xx. 3 f.). At times of great distress too, when a vow is made, the מנחה plays an important part (Gen. xxviii. 16 ff.; Judges xi. 30; 2 Sam. xv. 7 ff.).

Whilst the מנחה comes to stand more and more for the vegetable offering, the animal offering is referred to as the עלה. This custom also was adopted by Israel from its Canaanite environment.[69] The sacrificial animal is burnt on the altar, and the smoke is meant to rise to the god on his heavenly throne as a 'sweet savour' (Gen. viii. 20 f.; Exod. xxix. 18). Again, the ריח ניחוח, the smell of the sacrifice that ascends, is a token of the homage and reverence of the worshipper. The עלה is in the first place a gift, an offering to God. Parallels in the Ugaritic texts show, for example, that at the end of a lament reverence is shown to the deity by a burnt offering and smoke. Keret 'offered a sacrifice up to the gods in heaven' (*dbḥ ilm yšᶜly dgṯ bšmym*).[70] The verb *ᶜly*, which characterizes the rite, is significant. Another example shows clearly that the עלה can also accompany the petitions of the worshippers. A

[69] There are a number of examples in the Ugaritic texts of the root *ᶜly* used as a sacrificial term. Cf. C. H. Gordon, *Ugaritic Handbook*, III, No. 1585.

[70] See Aistleitner, op. cit., p. 81.

sacrificial hymn has been found which was sung on the occasion of the presentation of the burnt offering, and came to its climax with the cry 'Arise, El' (*nṣbt il*).[71] Whether it is offered in homage or petition, the עלה always underlines particularly the distance between the one who offers the sacrifice and the deity who reigns in heaven. The same is true of the Old Testament. Burnt offerings give honour to Yahweh in his power and give him homage (Judges xi. 31; 1 Sam. vi. 14). In the Temple worship עלות are presented especially at the great annual festivals (1 Kings ix. 25). The petitions of the community are presented at the burnt offerings (Jer. xiv. 12). The king, in particular, comes before Yahweh with a great number of animal offerings in order to exercise his privilege of making petitions (1 Kings iii. 4; Ps. xx. 4 f.). In the ritual instructions in the Priestly Code the different kinds of offering are finally laid down in fully detailed regulations (Lev. i. 1 ff.; viii. 18 ff.; xiv. 10 ff., etc.). In this connection we are told which animals are acceptable for sacrifice—oxen, sheep, goats and birds, but animals that are hunted are excluded. The sacrificial animals have to be clean and without blemish.

In Micah vi. 6–7 the correct sacrificial offering acceptable to Yahweh is set out in the form of a series of questions concerning the Torah. The questions are as follows:

> 'Wherewith shall I come before the Lord, and bow myself before the high God? shall I come before him with burnt offerings, with calves of a year old? Will the Lord be pleased with thousands of rams, or with ten thousands of rivers of oil? shall I give my firstborn for my transgression, the fruit of my body for the sin of my soul?'

In this series of questions the food offerings and burnt offerings which were required by the rules referred to above are proffered by one who is ready to make sacrifices, but what is remarkable is the purpose behind the gifts, which we have not met before. We have already pointed out that the offerings—voluntary or obligatory—express homage, gratitude and petition on the basis of the striving for communion. What is new is the connection of the offerings with the idea of atonement. This extremely important aspect is often overlooked in explanations of the מנחה and the עלה. It was J. Pedersen's great achievement that he emphatically pointed out that every sacrifice contains the germ of 'the idea of atonement'—even when the gift aspect seems to be very much to the fore.[72]

[71] See Aistleitner, op. cit., p. 108.

[72] 'Whatever the view taken of sacrifice, it always contained germs of what developed into the idea of atonement. The worshipper purified himself and was sanctified by the sacrifice, he presented a gift of the God, he partook of a meal with the God; in all cases a new peace was created for him through the sacrifice, a renewal of harmony.

If we go back to the basic presupposition, that every offering seeks communication with the one to whom the gift is offered (G. van der Leeuw), the decisive thing about this relationship is that it is serene and untroubled. He who approaches Yahweh with his gifts and 'comes before him', 'gives for his transgression' and makes his offering 'for his soul' (Micah vi. 7). As on this occasion even human sacrifice is mentioned as the highest requirement, this fact gives us an opportunity to deal at least briefly with this important theme.

In Exod. xxxiv. 19 an ancient Yahweh law, which was certainly taken over from the Canaanite inhabitants, lays down that 'All that openeth the womb is mine; and all thy cattle that is male, the firstlings of ox and sheep'.[73] This commandment belongs to the larger context of the ראשית dedication. Every 'firstling' of the fertile field or the fertile creature according to the primitive Canaanite conception belongs to the powers of fertility, the Baalim, and the claim of the gods was acknowledged by the dedication of the 'firstlings'. By this return to the proper 'owner' man subjected himself in gratitude to the spirit world and, in hope of a further increase in the power of fertility, offered the most precious gift—the sacrifice of the male firstborn. In Israel these ראשית dedications were referred to Yahweh (ליהוה), and thus took upon themselves a different character. They were presented as signs of gratitude and of dependence on the Lord of the land. Faith in the god of salvation and of history who gave the 'promised land' to his people (Deut. xxvi. 1–11) took the place of the natural and mythical connection with the numinous powers of fertility. The magical influencing of these powers was eliminated by the personal reference to Yahweh. All the gifts and sacrifices of the firstfruits from field and flock became an act of homage and an acknowledgment of Yahweh's claim, and were an expression of gratitude and dependence, but human sacrifice was soon excluded from the dedications and offerings. This decisive rejection of the Canaanite cultic practices was less a process of gradual growth towards a more humane and ethical outlook than something based on the covenant

[73] On the question of human sacrifice, see especially: O. Eissfeldt, '*Molk*' *als Opferbegriff im Punischen und Hebräischen und das Ende des Gottes Moloch* (1935); A. George, 'Le sacrifice d'Abraham', *Études de Critique et d'Histoire Religieuses* (*Mélanges Vaganay*) (1948), pp. 99 ff.; E. Dhorme, 'Le dieu Baal et le dieu Moloch dans la tradition biblique', *Anatolian Studies*, VI (1956), pp. 57 ff.; J. Hoftijzer, 'Eine Notiz zum punischen Kinderopfer', *VT*, 8 (1958), pp. 288 ff.

But man could only be in harmony with God when he was "whole". The sacrifice removed whatever was wasting away this integrity, what was called sin. This was brought about by man being sanctified while at the same time God was induced to be lenient towards him.' J. Pedersen, *Israel. Its Life and Culture*, III–IV (1940), p. 359).

relationship with its personal foundation and on the claim made upon human life by the divine law. The 'redemption' of the human firstborn by an animal sacrifice was therefore laid down. The story of Isaac's sacrifice (Gen. xxii) is an ancient document of this cultic development. Abraham presents a ram as a burnt offering תחת בנו 'in the stead of his son' (xxii. 13).[74] Although the frightful custom of the pagan inhabitants, which was practised in the neighbourhood of Jerusalem in the valley of Hinnom, was occasionally adopted by the Israelites in times of decadence, the horror expressed by the declarations within the Old Testament and the condemnation of this gruesome cult can be clearly seen everywhere.

(b) *The Peace Offering*

The זבח, the peace offering, is a quite different type of sacrifice from the 'gift' offering. Whereas in the עלה the whole animal is burned, in the זבח only the uneatable and unclean parts of the body are consumed by fire. The peace offering is eaten by a community which can consist of the family (1 Sam. i. 4, 21), the clan, the tribe, a group of pilgrims or a larger circle of the tribal confederacy. The idea and expectation that the meal eaten together will create *communio* is basic to this sacrifice. He who eats with another person becomes united with him and proclaims that they are closely bound together. The most valuable parts of the animal that has been killed, the portions of fat, are solemnly offered to God, and only when the fat has been completely burned up can the meal begin (1 Sam. ii. 15), for now God himself shares the food. The *communio* therefore is twofold, the communion among themselves of those who eat together, and the communion of these same people with the *deus praesens*. In the earliest period all killing was a sacrifice. As meat was very rarely eaten in everyday life, the solemn meal which was held at a holy place came to be special and exceptional. It was marked by joy and by the presence of God. 1 Sam. ii. 13 ff. gives us an insight into what happened at the holy place. The pilgrims have brought the sacrificial animals with them, killed them at the cultic centre and cooked them in large cauldrons. Then the people sit down together and celebrate the sacrificial meal with devotion and joy. We must not overlook the fact that the זבח also was thought of as having atoning effects (1 Sam. iii. 14). Whenever the participants experienced fellowship with Yahweh, the sacrifice was primarily thought of as an atoning and cleansing event. As the peace offering can also be called שלם in the Old Testament, it seems most reasonable—in spite of contradictory conceptions—to

[74] Cf. H. Gunkel, *Genesis*, pp. 236 ff.

interpret this concept in the sense of a realm of 'salvation' or of 'welfare', which is established by means of the meal.[75] In Ugaritic *šlmm* are observances which minister 'salvation' and 'peace' and through which a state of dissension can be overcome.[76] In the Amarna Letters *šlm* is the main purpose and content of treaties and covenants.[77] These usages remind us of the fact that in important passages of the Old Testament זבח as well as שלם belongs to the sphere of the ברית and effects the *communio* between God and his people. What was pointed out in connection with the gift offering is also true of the peace offering—that the decisive factor is not magical influences, but a personal communication which is achieved in the ברית.

As we examine the connection between Old Testament sacrifice and the ברית we must consider first the phrase כרת ברית. We are told in a very early tradition that Abraham divided the sacrificial animals (Gen. xv. 9 ff.), that a sacrificial omen was seen (*v.* 11) and that the patriarch (evidently between the portions of the sacrifice) waited in a deep sleep for a theophany, for an encounter with the divine partner of the covenant (*v.* 12). This sacrificial ceremony, of which there are traces also in Jer. xxxiv. 18, has no original connection either with the gift offering or with the peace offering. It is a very ancient rite on which light has been thrown by historical parallels in the Mari texts.[78] The partners in the covenant are surrounded by the sacrificial animals which have been cut up in the sacral act but which are considered as a unity. Their fellowship is sealed by the sacrifice and at the same time—in case there is a possible separation in the future—is marked by the bloody omen of a judgement which is meant to be suggested by the killing and dismembering displayed in the rite (cf. 1 Sam. xi. 7).

[75] The passages Exod. xxiv. 5 and 1 Sam. xi. 15 have often been taken as suggesting that a distinction can be made between זבח and שלם and that we can distinguish two types of sacrifice. L. Koehler, for example, interprets שלם as 'final sacrifice' on the evidence of 1 Kings viii. 63 f., but there is no real foundation for the view (*Old Testament Theology*, p. 188). Both the concepts זבח and שלם signify in the Old Testament the sacrificial meal. The Septuagint translates שלם in 1 Kings viii. 63 as θυσία εἰρηνική. See B. Stade, *Biblische Theologie des Alten Testaments*, I, p. 162.

[76] Cf. C. H. Gordon, *Ugaritic Handbook*, III, No. 1949, where *šlmm* is translated as 'peace offerings'.

[77] When a treaty or alliance is concluded, the invitation is: 'Let us make peace with one another!' (*ù ni-pu-uš sal-ma bi-ri-nu*). Cf. J. A. Knudtzon, *Die El-Amarna Tafeln*, Vorderasiatische Bibliothek 2 (1915), 570/1.

[78] Cf. M. Noth, 'Das alttestamentliche Bundesschliessen im Lichte eines Mari-Textes', *Gesammelte Studien zum A.T.* (1957), pp. 142 ff. Noth shows that the common derivation of the concept ברית from ברה ('to eat') on the basis of Gen. xxxi. 54 and Exod. xxiv. 11 is not really tenable. It seems far more likely that the preposition *birīt* ('between') was used adverbially and even as a noun, in which case *birīt* would mean 'something between', 'a mediation'.

We must place alongside this archaic rite of the ברית, which is preserved in the phrase כרת ברית, the 'covenant sacrifice' which was essentially the climax and conclusion of the sacral act of ratifying a covenant. In the Sinai tradition of the Book of Exodus (xxiv. 9 ff.) the following description is given:

> 'Then went up Moses, and Aaron, Nadab and Abihu, and seventy of the elders of Israel: And they saw the God of Israel; and there was under his feet as it were a paved work of sapphire stone, and as it were the very heaven for clearness. And upon the nobles of the children of Israel he laid not his hand: and they beheld God, and did eat and drink.'

This passage describes a 'covenant meal' that was observed on Sinai at the conclusion of the delivery of the law and the ratification of the covenant. The tradition should probably be ascribed to JE, as it gives the picture of a sacral meal, a זבח or a שלם. The God of Israel manifests his presence and his fellowship with those who offer sacrifice by a theophany. It is clear from Ps. l. 5 that such a 'covenant meal' was a definite part of the cultic renewal of the ברית. We do not know what the details of the rite were. We cannot now say, for example, what part was played by the sprinkling of blood in the sacral act of ratifying a covenant (cf. Exod. xxiv. 6). All we can be certain about is that the fellowship between Yahweh and his people which was preserved by the covenant found its direct and concrete expression in worship in the זבח, by means of which the *communio* between the partners to the covenant was established.

In the Old Testament, however, זבח or שלם are mostly referred to in other, constantly changing, connections. Peace offerings were made on solemn occasions of various kinds: in gratitude for a great victory or for the election of a king (1 Sam. xi. 13 ff.), before a war (1 Sam. x. 8; xiii. 9), at cultic festivals (Exod. xxxii. 6, 8; 1 Kings viii. 63 f.; ix. 25; Amos iv. 4) and at thanksgivings (Ps. cvii. 22). In Deuteronomy in particular זבח is marked by gladness and rejoicing (Deut. xii. 7; xxvii. 7). A constant feature of the peace offering is that it was celebrated in the presence and before the face of Yahweh (לפני יהוה). We must finally mention the fact that the communal meal served as the solemn conclusion to the bearing of the Ark into the holy place (2 Sam. vi. 17). A similar 'feast of solemn entry' is mentioned in the Ugaritic texts.[79]

With the suspension of sacral killing as a result of the Deuteronomic

[79] ᶜ*dbt bhth* in II AB 6, 38 (cf. Aistleitner, op. cit., pp. 44 f.) means to 'prepare an entrance feast'. It was a feast of the gods, at which 'the gods ate and drank' (*lhm sty ilm*). See also A. Falkenstein/W. von Soden, *Sumerische und akkadische Hymnen und Gebete* (1953), p. 181.

law the זבח fell into the background. The centralization of the cult made the killing of animals at a near-by 'holy place' no longer possible, but secular killing was permitted (Deut. xii. 4 ff.). There was a decline in the status and dignity of sacrifice, and the later rituals therefore had strictly to exclude the זבח.

(c) *Other Types of Sacrifice*

The different aims behind the various sacrifices, in particular the gift offering, established in the cultic traditions of the Old Testament a number of conceptions which we can enumerate and explain only briefly. The thank offering, for example, was called תודה. Praise and confession accompanied the presentation of the gifts. In contrast to the מנחה (Lev. ii. 11) it was permitted to offer things that had been leavened (Amos iv. 5). The תודה had its special place in the festivals of thanksgiving, in which the community, or a single member of it, praised Yahweh for deliverance from great distress (Ps. cvii. 22). The gift offering was linked with a peace offering in which the relatives of someone who had been delivered received back into the community the one who had been banished to the sphere of שׁאול. The one who had been banished could satisfy his hunger in the *communio* with Yahweh and receive the meal as the token of life (Ps. xxii. 27; xxiii. 5, etc.).

Another concept which is frequently mentioned, particularly in the Priestly Code, is חטאת, the 'sin offering'. The name itself clearly reveals the specific purpose of this kind of sacrifice. It is meant to 'absolve' either a sphere of life or a person by means of the offering which takes the form of a gift offering. Holy places are reconsecrated by means of a חטאת (Exod. xxix. 15, 26 f.; xxx. 1 ff.; Lev. xvi. 16), but it is by special blood rites that the consecration and cleansing is achieved. Thus, for example, the altar is smeared with the blood of the חטאת (Lev. iv. 25, 30). Much more important is the cleansing of people by the 'sin offering'. Here again we must note that a person who has been consecrated is cleansed again by a חטאת when his holiness has been defiled by some happening (Num. vi. 10 f.). This resanctification is the decisive aspect, in keeping with the attitude to sacrifice in the Priestly Code, in which the חטאת has a predominant function. The holiness of the worshippers, which has been defiled by unintentional lapses, is restored by a 'sin offering' (Lev. iv. 27 ff.; Num. xv. 27 ff.).

In close association with the 'sin offering' we find the 'guilt offering' (אשם) in the priestly traditions and definitions of sacrifice.[80] This

[80] Cf. J. Gray, 'Cultic Affinities between Israel and Ras Shamra', *ZAW*, 62 (1949/50), pp. 207 ff.

sacrifice is concerned with atonement for definite offences or defilements. A 'misappropriation' can be blotted out by an אשם (Lev. v. 14 ff.); what is meant here is an encroachment upon the consecrated realm of the cult. Anyone who had been delivered from leprosy or any other defilement had to offer an אשם sacrifice (Lev. xiv. 14 ff.; xix. 20 ff.; Num. vi. 12).

Although the Priestly Code draws various distinctions in these sacrificial concepts חטאת and אשם which correspond to the ideas concerning sacrifice and holiness that prevail in it, we must not overlook the fact that the emphasis on the absolving and atoning nature of the sacral offering is the development of a basic idea which was always inherent in sacrifice. In this connection we must mention Lev. xvi. The ritual of the Day of Atonement, which contains some very early traditions, is stamped with the idea of absolving and atoning. The sacred realm must be 'whole'. Material things and people have to be cleansed and sanctified by a sacrificial rite at the place of the divine presence. The sacrificial animal is driven out into the wilderness after the guilt and defilement have been ritually laid upon it (Lev. xvi. 10).

(d) *The Significance of the Sacrificial System*

If we approach the sacrificial cult of the Old Testament from the standpoint of the history of religions we cannot avoid emphasizing the ethnic aspect.[81] In fact, as far as names, forms and rites are concerned, there is no sacrifice in Israel for which a pagan origin could not be traced. The cultic traditions and institutions of the Old Testament all participate in the religious life that surrounds them, but it is important not to lose sight of the fact that all the borrowed elements and ideas are referred to Yahweh, the God of Israel. This reference does not have a merely nominal effect in that, for example, the name יהוה now describes the law-giver who lays down the rules concerning sacrifice and the recipient of the offerings. Nor does it merely have the effect of bringing about a new regulation of sacrifice. The great achievement of the Old Testament is the inclusion of the whole sacrificial system within the saving events and the fact of the ברית. The God who has confronted his people and still repeatedly confronts them in revelation and manifestation of himself with the call אני יהוה influences every aspect of the cult. This means most of all that the magical idea of sacrifice is broken down. The personal majesty of Yahweh gives a new direction to the magical powers set in motion by the offerings, and even when the 'sacred realm' is the real goal of the rites and sacral undertakings the personal God

[81] This is what L. Koehler does (*Old Testament Theology*, p. 181).

stands at the centre of this 'realm'. It is true that the 'magical efficacy' of sacrifice cast its spell upon the Israelites time after time. When the prophets raise their voice against the sacrificial cult they do so in the name of the God who has made known his will and who seeks to save his people from the influence of magical manipulations. The call to justice and righteousness and obedience is meant to restore the personal encounter of God and man based on the ברית. It would be a mistake, however, to make the prophetic message the motive for underlining the ethnic character of the Old Testament sacrificial system and for making a sweeping condemnation. A sounder view is 'that Yahweh created in the sacrificial cult too an institution which opened up for Israel a constant way of living intercourse with Him' (G. von Rad). The cultic community seeks fellowship with Yahweh in the sacral institutions for the purpose of atonement, in other words in the assurance that all the things that interrupt and destroy the relationship between God and his people must be removed by the sign of blood. By ritually protecting the holiness of the 'chosen place' and surrounding it with ceremonial forms man bears witness to his reverence before the presence and reality of the *deus praesens*. The 'gift offerings' are marked by a desire for cleansing, by homage, adoration and submission. With the sacrificial offerings petition and thankfulness ascend to heaven. The offerings are the visible and tangible expression of sentiments and words; they are the sacrament of the inward living relationship with Yahweh and belong to a 'realm of silence and mystery'[82] which is at the farthest remove from that of ecstatic manifestations.

L. Koehler has described the cult as an 'act of self-help', or even of 'self-redemption' by man,[83] but this view is hardly adequate even for pagan worship. Even in Canaanite religion man knows that he is primarily a being overwhelmed by the manifestation and activity of the deity. Sacrifices are a reaction completely determined by the actions of the spirits, which take place in a magical sphere in which the powers and their worshippers are bound to one another. Man may live on the gifts of the gods, but on the other hand the gods exist by the food and the oblations offered by their worshippers. The stream of life would cease to flow if this magical circle did not function. To speak of 'man's self-redemption' is to introduce an alien idealistic conception into the account of ancient religious beliefs. The aim in the Old Testament is to set man free from the spell of nature and magic, to break his bondage and establish with the ברית created by Yahweh a relationship with God

[82] G. von Rad, *Old Testament Theology*, I, p. 260.
[83] Op. cit., p. 171.

resting on completely new presuppositions. Even in the vegetation cult sacrifice was rooted in an indissoluble relationship between the spirit and the worshipper, and this was particularly true of Old Testament worship. The one who offers sacrifice does not raise himself by virtue of his longing for redemption, the initiative in his sacral activity does not lie with him. The truth is rather that he already stands in a relationship in which the cultic institutions, as a law emanating from Yahweh, initiate and determine all that he performs. In the ברית he meets a Lord whom he 'serves' (עבד) in all his cultic activity. Worship in the Old Testament is עבדה, and whenever man aspires in any way to 'bestow power' upon Yahweh, to affect him or influence him by means of cultic institutions the עבדה is destroyed. It is on this point that the prophets raise their voice as witnesses of the authority of God.

The sacrificial system in the Old Testament, however, is—as we have already seen—not merely a sphere of silence. It shows us the praying and worshipping community, from the expressions of joy at the זבח to the expressions of homage, thanksgiving and petition at the מנחה and the עלה (Ps. v. 3; xxvii. 6; liv. 8; lvi. 13). And the prayers do not remain unanswered. The studies in form criticism of recent decades have shown more and more clearly that there are formulae and expressions in the cultic traditions of the Old Testament in which the priest declares God's pleasure at the offerings.[84] The practice of inspecting the sacrificial victim and of drawing oracles from it which was customary in the Babylonian world and was deeply rooted in the ancient Eastern cult was of very little significance in Israel. Instead, there was a whole series of 'declaratory formulae' by means of which the priest pronounced an authoritative judgement on the sacrificial animal and the sacrificial action. 'Thus, only the addition of the divine word made the material observance what it was meant to be, a real saving event between Jahweh and his people.'[85] This completes the circle which, by means of the ברית, embraces the congregation that is summoned by the cultic regulations and confirmed by the gracious will of God and its sacrificial system.

[84] Cf. esp. G. von Rad, op. cit., I, p. 261, and the bibliography given there.
[85] Ibid., p. 262.

CHAPTER FOUR

THE CENTRAL SANCTUARIES OF ISRAEL AND THEIR CULTIC TRADITIONS

1. Ark and Tent

(a) *The Ark*

If we examine carefully the oldest traditions dealing with the Ark in the Old Testament we could conclude that it was the portable shrine of the community as early as the 'desert period'. The sayings in Num. x. 35 f. clearly suggest the situation of a wandering group in which Yahweh is present as leader and guardian, and in Joshua iii–v also the Ark is mentioned as the shrine of the tribes that enter Palestine. The picture changes, however, after the occupation. In his *History of Israel* Noth states: 'Among the established tribes in Palestine the Ark was no longer a real travelling shrine but, though it had as yet no permanent resting place, it was set up in one place for a more or less prolonged period and this place then formed the central place of worship, the geographical centre of the ancient Israelite amphictyony.'[1]

There are two strata in the Old Testament statements about the significance of the Ark. The later Priestly Code contains descriptions which interpret this sacred cult object as serving the purpose of a box for preserving the tables of the law (Exod. xxv. 21; xxxvii. 6). The Deuteronomic and Deuteronomistic tradition also takes the Ark to be a container for the tables of the Torah (Deut. x. 1 ff.; 1 Kings viii. 9). Ancient traditions from Shiloh and Jerusalem, on the other hand, depict Israel's central holy of holies as an empty throne of God, above which Yahweh is invisibly present (1 Sam. iv. 4; 2 Sam. vi. 2; 2 Kings

[1] M. Noth, *History of Israel* (1960), p. 91. Bibliography dealing with the Ark: H. Gressmann, *Die Lade Jahves und das Allerheiligste des salomonischen Tempels* (1920); H. G. May, 'The Ark—A Miniature Temple', *AJSL*, 52 (1935/6), pp. 215 ff.; O. Eissfeldt, 'Lade und Stierbild', *ZAW*, 57 (1940/1), pp. 190 ff.; J. Morgenstern, 'The Ark, the Ephod and the "Tent of Meeting"', *HUCA*, 17 (1942/3), pp. 153 ff.; 18 (1943/4), pp. 1 ff.; A. Bentzen, 'The Cultic Use of the Story of the Ark in Samuel', *JBL*, 57 (1948), pp. 37 ff.; M. Haran, 'The Ark of the Covenant and the Cherubs', *Eretz-Israel*, 5 (1958), pp. 83 ff.; G. von Rad, 'Zelt und Lade', *NKZ*, 42 (1931), pp. 476 ff., reprinted in *Ges. Stud. zum AT*, pp. 109 ff.; M. Haran, 'The Ark and the Cherubim. Their Symbolic Significance in Biblical Ritual', *IEJ*, 9 (1959), pp. 30 ff.; D. W. Gooding, *The Account of the Tabernacle.* Translation and Textual Problems of the Greek Exodus (1959); L. Rost, 'Die Wohnstätte des Zeugnisses', *Festschrift F. Baumgärtel* (1959), pp. 158 ff.; R. de Vaux, *Ancient Israel: Its Life and Institutions* (1962), pp. 297 ff.

xix. 15; Jer. iii. 16 f.).[2] The older tradition describing the distinctive character of the Ark can be traced in the texts of the Priestly Code and of the Deuteronomic-Deuteronomistic circles, for the meaning of the word ארון points to a box-like construction or a container (cf. Gen. v. 26). It was probably the addition of the cherubim to the Ark that gave it its throne-like character.[3] The significant phrase יהוה צבאות ישב הכרבים (1 Sam. iv. 4; 2 Sam. vi. 2; cf. also 2 Kings xix. 15) gives support to this idea of Yahweh enthroned above the sacred cult object. But even in the 'Ark sayings' (Num. x. 35 ff.) the presence of Yahweh above the shrine is assumed, and in Joshua iii–v too we could take the *praesentia Dei* as the decisive factor in the Ark tradition. The problems are very complicated and it is hardly possible to distinguish the various phases in the understanding of this central cultic object. If the Priestly Code shows the Ark as part of the desert sanctuary (cf. Exod. xl. 3, etc.), then this certainly reveals a secondary attempt to associate the two, which can be clearly seen if we make a critical analysis of the priestly cultic traditions.[4]

It is made quite clear in the Old Testament tradition that the Ark and its resting place form the cultic centre for the ancient Israelite tribal confederacy,[5] and the references to the locating of the sacred object in the Temple at Jerusalem are quite plain.[6] When David brought the Ark to Zion the place that had been won from the Jebusites and was destined to be the capital became a 'chosen' sanctuary, the place where Yahweh is present (2 Sam. vi.). Solomon built the Temple for the holy object, and the Ark finds its place in the holy of holies from which the light is excluded (1 Kings viii). The great importance of the Ark in the elevation of Jerusalem to be the main cultic centre, however, would be quite inconceivable if the sacred object had not already been the centre of Israelite worship in the pre-monarchical period. The 'Ark stories' in 1 and 2 Samuel make it quite plain that at the close of the period of the judges Shiloh was the central Israelite sanctuary.[7] 'Yahweh's throne'

[2] Cf. J. Meinhold, *Die Lade Jahves* (1900); M. Dibelius, *Die Lade Jahves* (1906).

[3] See H. Schmidt, 'Kerubenthron und Lade', *Eucharisterion*, I (1923), pp. 120 ff., who, however, goes too far when he suggests that the descriptions of the throne chariot in Ezek. i are a reconstruction of the throne of the cherubim.

[4] Cf G. von Rad, 'Zelt und Lade', *NKZ*, 42 (1931), pp. 476 ff., *Ges. Stud.*, pp. 109 ff.

[5] Cf. M. Noth, *History of Israel*, pp. 90 ff.

[6] Noth's comments in his essay 'Jerusalem und die israelitische Tradition' (*Gesammelte Studien zum A.T.* (1956), pp. 172 ff.) are particularly significant for the history of worship.

[7] On the 'Ark narrative', see L. Rost, *Die Überlieferung von der Thronnachfolge Davids*, BWANT, III, 6 (1926), pp. 4 ff., *Das kleine Credo . . .*, pp. 119 ff.

was situated in a temple (1 Sam. iii. 3), and if we go back to still earlier stages in the cultic history of the tribal confederacy we find Gilgal (Joshua iii–v) and Bethel (Judges xx. 26 f.) as Israel's 'chosen cultic centres'. When finally we find Shechem also mentioned as a station of the Ark in Joshua viii. 33, this statement is no doubt to be attributed to a later interpolation,[8] but at the same time it embodies something that has to be assumed in the earliest history of the ancient Israelite amphictyony, indeed in its very beginnings: namely, that Shechem was the first central sanctuary of the tribal confederacy (Joshua xxiv).[9] The stations of the Ark can therefore be clearly set out: Shechem—Bethel—Gilgal—Shiloh—Jerusalem. The question immediately arises, however, whether there were possibly other holy places in the period of the judges which were marked out as Israelite cultic centres by the setting up of the Ark. J. Dus recently made the suggestion that in the early period it was the custom for the Ark to be transported from one place to another and that the sacred object was set up every seven years at a different place to the accompaniment of a quite definite ritual.[10] But these are suppositions which put a great strain upon the evidence. We do not know which cultic centres have to be considered along with the main sanctuaries we have just mentioned, but we could try to discover in making a close examination of the main local cultic traditions whether the place in question had a central function for Israel as a whole.

Recent research, especially the studies of Alt and Noth, has shown the premisses concerning the history of worship adopted in the Wellhausen period to have been mistaken. Wellhausen could still declare with certainty with reference to the pre-monarchical period: 'A strict centralization is inconceivable for that period, no less in the sphere of worship than in any other.'[11] We know today that the Israelite tribal confederacy possessed right from the beginning the institution of a central sanctuary as the basis of its cultic life.[12] Therefore, if we wish to investigate and give an account of the history of worship in Israel, we must give our attention to the traditions of these sanctuaries. This is not, of course, to deny the fact that there were in the tribal confederacy numerous other sanctuaries—cultic centres at the numinous sites in Palestine, clan and tribal sanctuaries or places that had been venerated

[8] Cf. M. Noth, *Das Buch Josua*, HAT, I, 7 (2 ed., 1953), pp. 45 f.

[9] M. Noth, *History of Israel*, p. 91.

[10] J. Dus, 'Der Brauch der Ladewanderung im alten Israel', *ThZ Basel*, 17 (1961), pp. 1 ff.

[11] J. Wellhausen, *Prolegomena*, p. 19.

[12] M. Noth, op. cit., pp. 91 ff.

from time immemorial. King Josiah's reformation in the second half of the seventh century showed clearly what a large number of cultic centres could assert their claims, but it was the 'chosen place' that was decisive for Israel's cultic life, the place to which the tribes went on pilgrimage and at which the great annual feasts of the amphictyony were celebrated.

(b) *The Sacred Tent*

From the point of view of literary history, the earliest piece of information in the Pentateuchal sources concerning the 'sacred Tent' is to be found in the Yahwistic passage, Exod. xxxiii. 7–11:

> 'Now Moses used to take the tent and to pitch it without the camp, afar off from the camp; and he called it, The tent of meeting. And it came to pass, that every one which sought the Lord went out unto the tent of meeting, which was without the camp. And it came to pass, when Moses went out unto the Tent, that all the people rose up, and stood, every man at his tent door, and looked after Moses, until he was gone into the Tent. And it came to pass, when Moses entered into the Tent, the pillar of cloud descended, and stood at the door of the Tent: and the Lord spake with Moses. And all the people saw the pillar of cloud stand at the door of the Tent: and all the people rose up and worshipped, every man at his tent door. And the Lord spake unto Moses face to face, as a man speaketh unto his friend. And he turned again into the camp: but his minister Joshua, the son of Nun, a young man, departed not out of the Tent.'

The Yahwistic tradition is giving an account here of the Tent sanctuary which was the real cultic centre for the people of God in the 'desert period'. The Ark is not mentioned; the 'tent of meeting' was a sanctuary in its own right and in no sense—as the secondary constructions of the Priestly Code suggest—a shelter for the Ark. In the Tent Moses 'met' the God who appeared in his כבוד and received his דבר . This holy place was the cultic centre for a great encampment, in which 'all the people' lived in tents. We are given an impressive picture of an arrangement in which a quite large desert confederacy is assembled, drawn up facing a typical sanctuary of the nomadic world.

The idea of this arrangement of the camp and of the sacred Tent that emerges in the Priestly Code is far more precise and comprehensive than the description in Exod. xxxiii. 7 ff. In his essay on 'Die Lagervorstellung der priesterlichen Erzählung' A. Kuschke has examined the traditions in the Priestly Code,[13] and has tried to investigate the details. The priestly conceptions are extremely vivid and definite: the 'tent of

[13] A. Kuschke, 'Die Lagervorstellung der priesterlichen Erzählung', *ZAW*, 62 (1951), pp. 74 ff.

meeting' is the dominant centre of the whole camp (Num. ii. 17; iii. 38, etc.), around which there is an inner circle containing the tents of the Levites, of Moses the man of God and 'Aaron and his sons', and then in the outer circle there are the groups of tents of all the people arranged according to tribes.[14] In contrast to the Yahwistic account, therefore, the Priestly Code does not envisage the Tent sanctuary outside the camp, but in the centre of the encampment. In view of these Yahwistic and priestly traditions concerning the Tent sanctuary and the arrangement of the Israelite camp in the desert the question that arises straight away is that of the significance of these traditions. In the Wellhausen period it was accepted that all the ideas about the tabernacle and the community of Israel assembled in the camp were basically simply the projection of later cultic institutions into the desert period.[15] It was held that priestly circles wanted to suggest that the Temple cult was already foreshadowed in the desert, in order to give their cultic institutions and practices a high status and in particular to ascribe a Mosaic origin to them. This view is derived from certain observations which are still unquestionably valid today. The Priestly Code did in fact project into the early period institutions and rites which should certainly be assigned to a later period, but the sweeping description of the ideas about the Tent and the camp as 'late constructions by the priestly circles' or as 'the projection of later institutions into the early period' has been corrected by studies of the history of tradition. It has been recognized that the traditions of the אהל מועד cannot be dismissed as a 'construction' but that they are of an earlier date. So, e.g., von Rad states that 'this Kabod-Moed conception is in no wise a new creation of the Priestly Document, but only the reintroduction, in the interests of greater spirituality, of a very old sacral tradition.'[16] Ideas concerning the origin and development of this conception, however, are still quite uncertain. If we assume that the 'tent of meeting' played a part in the early history of Israelite worship then the question immediately arises what the relationship could possibly have been between the Tent sanctuary and the Ark as the central cult object of the tribal confederacy. Von Rad makes the suggestion: 'Is it not possible that the Tent, which was obviously foreign to the Shechem amphictyony, belonged originally to the South, perhaps as the sanctuary of the old amphictyony of the six tribes in or near Hebron?'[17] But these suggestions concerning the history of tradition

[14] Ibid., pp. 79 f.

[15] See esp. J. Wellhausen, *Prolegomena*, pp. 351 ff.

[16] G. von Rad, *Studies in Deuteronomy* (1953), p. 40.

[17] Ibid., p. 43. J. Hempel also suggests that there were Hebronite elements in the traditions of the Priestly Code (*Althebräische Literatur und ihr hellenistisch-jüdisches Nachleben*, Handbuch der Literaturwissenschaft (1930), pp. 152 f.).

disregard for the most part the arrangement of the camp which is closely linked in tradition with the Tent sanctuary. The failure of scholars to clarify this matter prompted A. Kuschke to make his study of the conception of the camp in the Priestly narrative. The result of his examination is to confirm the great antiquity of the tradition of the Tent sanctuary, but to conclude that the arrangement of the camp is a construction of the Priestly Code.[18] Is this explanation correct, and does it really take account of the nomadic atmosphere which is certainly still very vivid in the traditions in the narrative concerning the Tent sanctuary and in that concerning the Tent community encamped in the desert?

We must begin by asking a few basic questions. The first question is whether Israel succumbed completely straight after entering Palestine to the cultic traditions of Canaan. Did the tribes as they emerged from their semi-nomadic state adopt the nature cults of the Canaanite inhabitants without any transitional period? Alt has frequently pointed out that in the early period the Israelites did not completely abandon their semi-nomadic habits but kept their distance from the ways of life of the inhabitants who had long been settled in the land.[19] Drawing lots for the plots of land which was done at fixed intervals clearly reveals sociological circumstances which are in sharp contrast to those of the Canaanite inhabitants. Can we in fact consider it possible that the tribal confederacy which affirmed in its basic confessions the fact that it was descended from the desert, adopted unintentionally in the whole of its worship the institutions and customs of the cultivated land to which it had come? It is certain that individual groups occupied the local Canaanite sanctuaries as they settled in the land and adopted the established institutions and traditions of these places. The stories of the patriarchs are an eloquent witness to this process.[20] But did this process of adoption and assimilation influence the central cult right from the beginning? Did Israel—the Israel that saw itself as originating in the desert not merely from the sociological standpoint but also from that of redemptive history—deny its origins?

These questions lead first to the supposition that in the early period when the occupation was not yet complete the tribal confederacy celebrated its great festivals in the desert and assembled in a camp around the nomadic sanctuary of a אהל מועד. There are certain factors which lend support to this suggestion, and we will now consider them one by one.

[18] A. Kuschke, op. cit., pp. 102 f. [19] A. Alt, *Kleine Schriften*, I, pp. 150, 327 f.
[20] Cf. H. Gunkel, *Genesis*, pp. lvi. ff.

1. Recent sociological studies of the nomadic and semi-nomadic way of life among the Arabs have brought to light the important fact that certain patterns of behaviour have preserved their characteristic forms for thousands of years. These studies are of decisive importance for understanding the way in which Israel arose and developed. Valuable conclusions have been drawn, for example, from observation of the changes of pasture among the semi-nomads concerning the immigration and settlement of the Israelite groups as they emerged from the desert.[21] Observations of this kind should be considered first because they bring to light phenomena which are typical of the inhabitants of the country in which Israel once lived who themselves originated in the desert. In the *Palästina Jahrbuch* for 1925 Alt gave the following account of his experiences on an excursion: 'Our main objective was the great Muslim autumn festival at the sanctuary of *nebi rubin* (Ruben) on the inner edge of the strip of land to the north of *jebna*. Unfortunately we found that the festival, which lasts a whole month, had not yet reached its climax; the townspeople of *jafa*, *lid* and *er-ramle* had already arrived in great numbers, but the peasants were still missing. Nevertheless the camp of tents spread out on the sand dunes all round the sanctuary was an instructive sight. . . .'[22] This account gives a striking example of a tent festival for which the worshippers come on pilgrimage from all the towns around in order to observe the autumn festival in camp for a whole month, far away from their everyday affairs.[23]

2. There are indications of this kind of tent festival in the Old Testament as well. The clearest indication is in the prophecy in Hos. xii. 9, which must of course be seen in the context of Hosea's whole message. For the prophet the desert period was the real time of Israel's salvation (Hos. ix. 10; xi. 1), and the decay and ruin of Israel's worship and of her whole life began at the moment when the people succumbed to the spell of the fertility religion (ix. 10). Baal took the place of Yahweh (ii. 7) and the heathen cults drew Israel away from her intimate fellowship with Yahweh. The breaking of the covenant and the worship of idols are the marks of the period in which Hosea lives, but the prophet proclaims to the backsliding people the way of judgement and salvation —a return to the desert. Far from the spell of nature worship Yahweh will address His people afresh and speak intimately to them (ii. 16).

[21] M. von Oppenheim, *Die Beduinen*, I (1939), II (1943), III (1952).

[22] A. Alt, 'Das Institut im Jahre 1924' (report), *PJB*, 21 (1925), pp. 14 ff.

[23] The worshippers whose tent festival Alt describes are of course not semi-nomads, but elements of a population that is now firmly settled in Palestine. This makes the fact that even at this stage when they were firmly settled they still went out from town and country at the time of the festival all the more significant.

Then in xii. 9 we read: 'But I am the Lord thy God from the land of Egypt; I will yet again make thee to dwell in tents, as in the days of the solemn feast.' מועד is 'the feast'. In ix. 5 יום מועד (synonymous with יום חג יהוה) has without doubt the meaning of 'feast day'. The prophet is therefore clearly referring to a cultic tradition which tells of a tent festival which was held in the desert (cf. Hos. ii. 16).[24] In this connection there is a passage from the cultic calendar in the Holiness Code which also appears in a new light, a passage which we have already considered earlier—Lev. xxiii. 39–44 (see pp. 63 f. above). In this passage the ceremonial custom of erecting booths of leaves and of living in these temporary shelters was explained by the fact that Israel lived 'in booths' during the exodus from Egypt. Alt makes the point that the historicizing interpretation of the feast of Tabernacles in Lev. xxiii. 42 f. obviously contains an anachronism, as the rest of Israelite tradition quite unanimously and correctly assumes that the tribes under Moses' leadership dwelt in tents, not in booths.[25] What are we to make of this 'anachronism'? Is it simply a very remarkable example of 'historicizing', or was there a tent festival behind the feast of Tabernacles at an early period of worship? Hos. xii. 10 throws a new light on the peculiar cultic tradition of the Holiness Code. The assumption that a nomadic tent festival was observed at an early period appears quite possible.

3. The clearest evidence is provided by the traditions of J and P. The cultic character of the arrangement of the camp and of the rites centred upon the tent sanctuary is so firmly rooted in the traditions from the very beginning that to assume that this basic character is a secondary construction is not feasible.[26] Both in the Yahwistic writings and in the Priestly Code the decisive attitudes expressed in the descriptions presuppose the desert situation and present an institution which belongs to the nomadic sphere. This essential connection can also be seen in another cultic tradition—in the ritual of the great feast of Atonement (Lev. xvi). The oldest stratum of the cultic traditions present in Lev. xvi belongs to the world of the desert. Aaron has to place two goats at the entrance to the sacred Tent as a sin offering and

[24] P. Volz also refers to Hos. xii. 10 in *Das Neujahrsfest Jahwes*, but he thinks that this passage is concerned with the feast of Tabernacles. 'In the early period the huts seem to have been tents made of cloth; but in later times the custom grew up of making huts out of branches of trees . . .' (p. 20). This view is hardly in keeping with Hosea's condemnation of Canaanite worship.

[25] A. Alt, 'Zelte und Hütten', *Kleine Schriften*, III, pp. 241 f.

[26] A. Kuschke also points out in connection with the conception of the camp in the Priestly Code: 'how striking the dominant rôle is that all the cultic officials play in this camp' (op. cit., p. 79).

cast lots upon both the animals. One goat is meant for Yahweh, the other for Azazel, a demon of the desert. Then we read: 'But the goat, on which the lot fell for Azazel, shall be set alive before the Lord, to make atonement for him, to send him away for Azazel into the wilderness' (Lev. xvi. 10). This rite certainly requires us to assume the desert situation for the community taking part in this festival. The setting of the camp is quite plain in Lev. xvi. 26; indeed, Lev. xvi. makes it clear that the 'tent of meeting' that was erected in the desert stands at the centre of the cultic activities.

If we can agree that all these suppositions and observations point to a cultic sphere which can in fact be assumed, then the question that immediately arises is how such a tent festival with the אהל מועד as its centre, can be fitted into the history of Israel's worship. The Priestly Code clearly represents the view that in the arrangement of the camp all the twelve tribes of Israel were assembled. The 'tent of meeting' has the status and significance of a central sanctuary in the cultic community. Are these ideas mere invention? We can trace in the details of the plan surprisingly clear regulations and groupings, which in their basic elements could hardly be a free invention of the priestly circles. How would it have been possible for a later period to give such a consistent and detailed account of the amphictyonic arrangement? Here we have a system which, like the ancient כבוד tradition and the אהל מועד conception, came down to the priests through tradition. But if we accept the view that the amphictyonic worship of the early period was held in the desert, then the problem that immediately presents itself is that of the connection between this institution and the observances of the tribal confederacy characterized by the central shrine of the Ark at the Canaanite cultic centres. We cannot expect to find any definite indication of the solution of this problem in the Old Testament sources. We can therefore raise only a few questions which, however, on the basis of the full examination of the problem that we have already made, have a significance that should not be underestimated.

Is it not conceivable that in the early period Israel celebrated its central cult outside Canaan, withdrew to the desert for its great festivals and assembled there encamped in tents around the Tent sanctuary?[27] It is immaterial whether the 'tent of meeting' was outside (J) or inside (P) the camp. Is it not possible that this cult might have existed prior to the 'assembly at Shechem' described in Joshua xxiv, or that it played its part alongside the Shechem amphictyony? It is wrong as a matter of

[27] Num. xxiv. 1 f. tells how Balaam 'set his face toward the wilderness' and saw Israel 'dwelling according to their tribes'.

principle to locate the sacred Tent in Canaan, for it is of the essence of this cultic institution that it is not tied to any place, but that it 'travels' (Isa. xxxiii. 20). The traditions in the Book of Numbers give us valuable information in this respect. The camp of tents has no fixed place, it is broken up time after time, travels on and settles in a different place. Can we not say that from the standpoint of the history of tradition the so-called 'itineraries' belong to this movement of the camp?[28] Should we not assume that the traditions concerning places and journeyings which point to the region of Moab and to the southern desert belonged originally to the camp tradition or were attracted by it?

One thing, however, is certain: that this tent cult belonging to the semi-nomadic sphere could not maintain itself for long. The camp arrangement no doubt changed its function and influenced the assembling of the twelve tribes at the central sanctuaries of Shechem, Bethel, Gilgal, Shiloh and Jerusalem. In this way the sacred Tent lost its proper function, but it was still treated with respect as a venerable relic at the main cultic centres of the tribal confederacy.[29] Tradition, however, preserved a lively memory of the ancient institution, as we can see not only in the fact that the Temple at Jerusalem could be described as a 'tent',[30] but also in the attempt at harmonizing undertaken by the process of tradition in the bringing together of the Ark and the Tent.[31]

2. Shechem

(a) *Canaanite Worship*

The town of Shechem (*tell balata*) in the period before the immigration of the Israelite tribes was the most powerful city state in central Palestine,[32] but it was very soon annexed by the tribe of Mannasseh—like a number of other Canaanite towns within the area of this tribe—yet without losing its autonomy.[33] Old Testament tradition gives us valuable information about Canaanite worship as it was practised at Shechem. Two sanctuaries are mentioned: the temple of the אל or בעל ברית which was probably situated in the area of the citadel (מגדל

[28] On the 'itineraries', cf. M. Noth, *Überlieferungsgeschichte des Pentateuch* (1948), pp. 237 ff.

[29] According to Joshua xviii. 1 and 1 Sam. ii. 22 the sacred Tent was kept at Shiloh, but 1 Chron. xxi. 29 f. and 2 Chron. i. 3 state that the Tent shrine was at Gibeon.

[30] Cf. Ps. xv. 1; xxvii. 5; lxi. 5; lxxviii. 60.

[31] Cf. G. von Rad, 'Zelt und Lade', *NKZ*, 42 (1931), pp. 476 ff., *Ges. Stud.*, pp. 109 ff.

[32] Cf. A. Alt, 'Die Landnahme der Israeliten in Palästina', *Kleine Schriften*, I, pp 108 ff.

[33] Cf. A. Alt, 'Josua', *Kleine Schriften*, I, p. 191.

Judges ix. 46) and the terebinth outside the gates of the town.[34] Whilst the temple remained a genuine Canaanite sanctuary even after the arrival of the Israelites and its pagan worship cast its spell upon groups of the immigrant community (Judges viii. 33), the terebinth outside the town became a Yahweh sanctuary (מקדש יהוה, Joshua xxiv. 26). It is not entirely clear whether the pillar alongside the terebinth, which is mentioned in both Judges ix. 6 and Joshua xxiv. 26, was a Canaanite object or whether it was a memorial stone just erected by the tribal confederacy. The terminology (מצב in Judges ix. 6 and אבן גדלה in Joshua xxiv. 26) and the account in Joshua xxiv. 26, which seems free from any aetiological purpose, suggest a pillar set up by Israel (Joshua).

Old Testament tradition tells in connection with the story of Abimelech's reign of a Canaanite autumn festival observed by the inhabitants of Shechem: 'And they (the inhabitants of Shechem) went out into the field, and gathered their vineyards, and trod the grapes, and held festival, and went into the house of their god, and did eat and drink, and cursed Abimelech' (Judges ix. 27).[35] At the harvest in autumn the Shechemites went into the vineyards and solemnly gathered and pressed the grapes. Then the הלולים were celebrated. The Hebrew concept is employed in later usage as a description for 'wedding festivities' and seems to have had a special significance in connection with the *hieros gamos* of the nature cult. The הלולים is referred to in another passage in the Old Testament, for in Lev. xix. 23 ff. we find the following regulation recorded:

> 'And when ye shall come into the land, and shall have planted all manner of trees for food, then ye shall count the fruit thereof as their uncircumcision: three years shall they be as uncircumcised unto you; it shall not be eaten. But in the fourth year all the fruit thereof shall be holy, for giving praise (הלולים) unto the Lord. And in the fifth year shall ye eat of the fruit thereof, that it may yield unto you the increase thereof: I am the Lord your God.'

This regulation shows that there was a ritual event in Canaan whereby the fruits of bushes and trees were dedicated to the deity in a solemn act. This dedication of the fruits is influenced by ideas which belong to the world of nature religion. After planting, certain times had to be

[34] Judges ix. 46 speaks of a 'temple of the god of the covenant', and Judges viii. 33 of the 'Baal of the covenant'. Judges ix. 27 also mentions a temple at Shechem. See J. T. Milik, 'Le sanctuaire de *Baᶜal Berit* à Sichem', *RB*, 44 (1959), pp. 560 ff. For the terebinth outside the gates of the city, see Judges ix. 6 and Joshua xxiv. 26.

[35] See J. Wellhausen, *Prolegomena*, p. 94; his view is too sweeping, however, when he states 'this festival must also have taken root among the Israelites at a tolerably early period'.

observed, but in the fourth year הלולים was celebrated. The rite laid down in Lev. xix. 23 ff. coincided, of course, with the festival of the autumn cult, and the dedication of the fruits sometimes took place in the harvest cult. We cannot be sure whether הלולים in Judges ix. 27 should be taken in the special sense which is suggested in Lev. xix. 23 ff. In any case after the gathering and pressing of the grapes at Shechem the fruits of the earth were dedicated to the בעל ברית with resounding jubilation, and a cultic meal was held in the temple of the god. We can clearly recognize here a rite which is called זבח or שלם in the Old Testament. The worshippers entered into a *communio*, a ברית with their covenant god (cf. also Exod. xxiv. 11). The Canaanite festival was marked by the joyful ecstasy of nature religion.

(b) *Joshua xxiv*

The account of the 'assembly at Shechem' in Joshua xxiv is the most important tradition that has come down to us from the time of the emergence of the confederacy of the twelve tribes of Israel. As this account also gives us important information about the early history of Old Testament worship, we shall have to consider the literary and exegetical problems and those concerned with the history of tradition that it presents. In the first place the Deuteronomistic redaction on the basis of which we can attribute certain verses or parts of verses to the period of the Exile is unmistakable.[36] The main part of the chapter, however, is pre-Deuteronomistic and, from the point of view of the history of tradition, points to the earliest period. Joshua xxiv stands in remarkable isolation in the context of the Deuteronomistic history. There are no traditional connections with the pre-Deuteronomistic elements in chapters i–xii,[37] and what we have, therefore, is a separate tradition. The account of the 'assembly at Shechem' shows the 'extension of the covenant relationship established at Sinai to the twelve tribes as a whole, including those tribes which did not take part in the ratification of the covenant at Sinai, in other words, the solemn establishment of the sacral confederacy of the twelve tribes'.[38] We could go so far as to

[36] On the glosses and Deuteronomistic redaction of Joshua xxiv, see M. Noth, *Das Buch Josua*, p. 135. On this chapter see also E. Nielsen, *Shechem. A Traditio-Historical Investigation* (1955), pp. 86 ff.

[37] For the details, see M. Noth, op. cit., pp. 137 ff.

[38] The significance of Joshua xxiv was first recognized by Ben Gorion, *Sinai und Garizim* (1926) and E. Sellin, *Geschichte des israelitisch-jüdischen Volkes*, I (1924), pp. 97 ff. Noth then brought out what part the account in Joshua xxiv played in the development of the confederacy of the twelve tribes (*Das System der Zwölf Stämme Israels*, BWANT IV, 1 (1930), pp. 65 ff.).

call it the 'foundation charter' of the ancient Israelite Yahweh amphictyony. To speak of a single event, however, when the confederacy was established does not give an adequate explanation of the special nature of the tradition. Recent studies have shown that the ברית made in Joshua xxiv. 25 and the promulgation of the divine law were regularly repeated in the tribal confederacy.[39] We have to envisage—as we shall show in greater detail later—an act of worship which was held in the early period at the Yahweh sanctuary at Shechem. For an understanding of the history of the tradition contained in Joshua xxiv this cultic connection is of the greatest importance, as we must allow for the fact that characteristic features of the ceremonial rehearsal of the founding of the confederacy might have influenced the tradition to a large extent. This influence of the cult upon the tradition could have affected the structure of the whole account as well as the individual phrases. If we begin by making a survey of the plan of the whole chapter, the following picture presents itself:

V. 1. *Account* of the summoning of the tribes and their elders to Shechem.

Vv. 2–13. *The word of the Lord* conveyed by Joshua: a survey of redemptive history.

Vv. 14–15. *Joshua speaks* and calls the people to enter the service of Yahweh.

Vv. 16–18. *The people's declaration* and confession of faith in Yahweh.

Vv. 19–20. *Joshua speaks* in exhortation and warning.

V. 21. *The people's declaration* of readiness to serve Yahweh.

V. 22. *Confirmation by oath* of the promise to serve Yahweh.

V. 23. *Joshua's call* to the people to put away all strange gods.

V. 24. *The people's declaration* of faith in Yahweh and of submission to his will.

Vv. 25–26. *Account* of the ratification of the covenant, the promulgation of the divine law, the writing down of the divine commandments and the erection of a memorial stone.

V. 27. *Joshua's declaration* that the stone is a witness to the solemn event that has taken place.

V. 28. *Account* of the dismissal of the people.

The climax of the whole event is the ratification of the covenant described in *vv.* 25–26. The assembled tribes are brought within the

[39] Noth points to a 'sacral tradition concerning a cultic act which was presumably regularly repeated, and which we must think of as being performed at the sanctuary concerned, in this case at Shechem' (*Das Buch Josua*, p. 139).

בּרית, Joshua acting as the mediator of the covenant and proclaiming to the people the commandments of the covenant, the divine law. It is not the establishment of a tribal covenant and the founding of the amphictyonic confederacy that are at the centre, but the בּרית with Yahweh. Or to put it more exactly: it is through the ratification of the Yahweh בּרית that the twelve tribes become an amphictyonic confederacy. The Yahweh covenant and the tribal covenant coincide.

How should we interpret the whole process of the ratification of the covenant in its structure and its phraseology? Recently ancient Eastern parallels have been adduced to help to explain the בּרית rite. G. E. Mendenhall in particular has pointed out that the Hittite ceremony for making a treaty is reflected in the procedure of the Old Testament בּרית.[40] He assumes that there was a strong influence upon the form adopted and holds the view that the Israelites took both the structure and the phraseology of the ratification of the covenant from their ancient Eastern neighbours. The pattern of the Hittite official treaties has been investigated by K. Baltzer,[41] who draws a comparison with Joshua xxiv and arrives at the following results:

The Hittite treaties reveal the following structure:

1. Preamble
2. Past history
3. Declaration of principles governing the future relationship
4. Definition of details
5. Invocation of the gods as witnesses
6. Curse and blessing.

If we compare this pattern with Joshua xxiv we see the following parallels:

1. Preamble (*v.* 2)
2. Past history (*vv.* 2–13)
3. Declaration of principles (*v.* 14)
4. Definition of details (missing in Joshua xxiv)
5. Confirmation of covenant (*vv.* 15 ff.)
6. Appeal to Yahweh as witness (*vv.* 19–22).[42]

Although certain parallels stand out when we make a comparison

[40] G. E. Mendenhall, *Law and Covenant in Israel and the Ancient Near East: The Biblical Colloquium* (1955). Cf. also J. Muilenburg, 'The Form and Structure of the Covenant Formulations', *VT*, 9 (1959), pp. 347 ff.

[41] K. Baltzer, *Das Bundesformular*, WMANT, 4 (1960). Cf. also W. Beyerlin, *Herkunft und Geschichte der ältesten Sinaitraditionen* (1961).

[42] Cf. K. Balzer, op. cit., pp. 20 f., 29 ff.

like this, we must be cautious in suggesting that there is an analogy here, for there is an unmistakable essential difference between the Hittite documents and the tradition in Joshua xxiv. The official treaties belong to the ceremony of ratification which brings together two human partners, whereas the Old Testament ברית establishes fellowship between God and his people. Some of the essential features of this covenant with God are obscured or completely displaced by the introduction of the treaty pattern. Here again we can see the way in which the premiss based on a 'pattern' fails to give adequate attention to the important nuances in the Old Testament tradition. This criticism is not meant to question the fact that certain phrases in the ברית ratified in Joshua xxiv were influenced by a foreign treaty ceremony, but the most urgent task in a comparative study is to start by examining the 'basic element' from the standpoint of form criticism and to bring out the analogies.[43] In investigations of this kind, however, we should not consider only the Hittite texts, for the Amarna letters also provide valuable comparative material as regards the treaty ceremony which has not yet been fully evaluated.

K. Baltzer is correct in pointing out the importance as a basis and an introduction of the 'pre-history' in Joshua xxiv. 2–13 in the act of the ratification of the ברית.[44] But the words of Yahweh do not merely refer to the 'former connections' between the two partners who are entering upon the covenant, for they are of the nature of revelation. By a reminder of the saving events Yahweh makes himself known and confronts a community which used to serve other powers and is still attached to them. The purpose of the proclamation of Yahweh's saving deeds is decision and confession (*v.* 15), and the intention behind it is the knowledge of God and the acknowledgement of Yahweh's saving power. The words of Yahweh and Joshua's exhortation to decision (*vv.* 14–15) are followed by something that has no counterpart in the Hittite records—the acclamation יהוה אלהינו (*vv.* 17 and 24). This acclamation 'authenticated an event, but also had legal validity and confirmed a decision or a choice. It was praise and decision simultaneously'.[45] Directly connected with the acclamation and the decision for Yahweh is the renunciation, which again has no counterpart in the treaty documents (*vv.* 14 and 23). It is a sacral act which acknowledges the sole authority of the one God, into whose service the amphictyony seeks to enter by excluding all strange powers. We can tell how deeply rooted the

[43] This kind of investigation has been made by G. Heinemann, *Untersuchungen zum apodiktischen Recht*, Diss., Hamburg (1958).

[44] K. Baltzer, op. cit., p. 29.

[45] G. van der Leeuw, *Religion in Essence and Manifestation* (1938), p. 431.

rite of renunciation was in Israel's Shechemite cult from the local traditions of the sanctuary which we find also in Gen. xxxv. 2, 4. Alt was the first to draw attention to the significance of this event. He states in his article 'Die Wallfahrt von Sichem nach Bethel': 'The truly ancient act of renunciation was merely what we might call the negative first part of an event which later came to its positive climax in the second part with the solemn promise made by all the people that they would reverence only Yahweh.'[46] Acclamation and renunciation lead to the act of pledging, in which the tribal community solemnly promises to 'fear' (ירא) Yahweh and to 'serve' (עבד, cf. *vv.* 14, 15, 18, 21, 24) him alone. This 'service' does not refer only to the sacral sphere, but to the whole life of the confederacy. There is an account of the actual ratification of the covenant in *v.* 25. Joshua acts as the mediator of the covenant and proclaims the divine law, and when *v.* 26 speaks of writing down the words, we must assume that the fact of the ratification of the covenant and the covenant regulations are sealed by documentary evidence. A memorial stone is then set up as a 'witness' to this event by which the confederacy is established under the terebinth at Shechem, which was formerly a local Canaanite sanctuary. The place is described as a Yahweh sanctuary (מקדש יהוה, *v.* 26).

There are two questions which are of special importance. In the first place it must be considered very remarkable that the Israelites made their ברית with Yahweh in the immediate vicinity of a cult of the אל ברית (Judges ix. 46). Does this mean that there was some connection? Can we assume that the rite of the tribal confederacy was influenced by practices of the inhabitants of Shechem? We can only ask these questions, and cannot give the answers. But if there is some connection, a comparison of Joshua xxiv. 25 with Judges ix. 27 would reveal a fundamental difference. In the worship of the Shechemites the nature element was at the centre, whereas in Israel it was the 'judgement and law' of Yahweh. The Canaanites' covenant with God was based on intimate fellowship with the fertility deity, but the ברית of the tribal confederacy on the redemptive mighty acts by the God of Israel (*vv.* 2–13). The other question concerns the cultic rehearsal of the Yahweh ברית. Alt writes in his essay 'Die Wallfahrt von Sichem nach Bethel': 'We can assume with certainty that this solemn promise by the people was in ancient times one of the ceremonies regularly observed in the worship of the Shechem sanctuary, for it is from this context that are derived the ceremonies that belonged to the place, such as the setting down of the law, and the blessing and the curse in Deut. xxvii. We can see that these

[46] A. Alt, 'Die Wallfahrt von Sichem nach Bethel', *Kleine Schriften,* I, pp. 84 f.

also were meant to be regularly observed at the ceremony of the renewal of the covenant, and that it was this particular sanctuary, which appeared to be the most ancient, that was chosen by all the tribes of Israel together as the place for the worship of Yahweh in Palestine.'[47] This quotation turns our attention to Deut. xxvii, a passage which throws further light on the worship that was celebrated at Shechem.

(c) *Deuteronomy xxvii*

Deuteronomy has come to be seen in a new light as the result of studies in form criticism and the history of tradition. It has been recognized that 'Deuteronomy stands in the tradition of the old Yahweh amphictyony of Shechem. Or rather, it proposes to reintroduce this old cultic tradition in its own advanced period and to set it forth as the form obligatory upon Israel for its life before Yahweh'.[48] The cultic renewal of the Sinai covenant influenced the Deuteronomic tradition in its general structure and in its particular expressions.[49] We may therefore expect to discover that some of the oldest elements which are connected with worship are to be found in that Deuteronomic conception which is aimed at the restoration of the ancient ordinances. The 'Shechemite Dodecalogue' in Deut. xxvii. 15–26 is an element of this kind from the early period of Old Testament worship. This passage could not really have served the movement towards 'centralization' of worship in Jerusalem which has been traced in Deuteronomy. But the Deuteronomists in any case were not the advocates of an 'ideology aimed at making Jerusalem the centre' which sought exclusively to influence the measures of the seventh century; they were witnesses to the institution of the amphictyonic central sanctuary which went back to the earliest period and which was located at Shechem at the beginning of the story of the tribal confederacy.

There are in Deuteronomy in the context of the 'Shechemite Dodecalogue' phrases the cultic significance of which is quite plain. In Deut. xxvi. 16 ff., for example, a passage has come down which reproduces in a remarkable way the procedure of 'mediation' in the act of ratifying the covenant. When we read in Joshua xxiv. 25 that Joshua made the ברית 'for' (לְ) the people, we see the man of God as the 'mediator of the covenant'. But how should we envisage the ceremony? There is no mention in Joshua xxiv. 25 of a sacrificial rite or of the

[47] Ibid., p. 85.

[48] G. von Rad, *Studies in Deuteronomy*, p. 41.

[49] G. von Rad, *Das formgeschichtliche Problem des Hexateuch*, BWANT, IV, 26 (1938), pp. 23 ff., *Ges. Stud.*, pp. 33 ff.

dismemberment of animals (כרת), nor is there any mention of a 'covenant meal' (cf. Exod. xxiv. 11 and Ps. l. 5). We can probably assume that such rites were observed, but what was of outstanding importance was the solemn and mighty word which sealed the pledge. Such a word has come down to us in Deut. xxvi. 16 ff., where the mediator of the covenant is the speaker:

Exhortation:

'This day the Lord thy God commandeth thee to do these statutes and judgements: thou shalt therefore keep and do them with all thine heart, and with all thy soul.'

Statement of Yahweh's declaration (*vv.* 17a and 19a):

'Thou hast avouched the Lord this day to be thy God, and to make thee high above all nations which he hath made, in praise, and in name, and in honour.'

Statement of Israel's declaration (*vv.* 18, 17b and 19b):

'And the Lord hath avouched thee this day to be a peculiar people unto himself, as he hath promised thee, and that thou shouldest keep all his commandments, walk in his ways and keep his statutes, and his commandments, and his judgements, and hearken unto his voice, and that thou mayest be an holy people unto the Lord thy God, as he hath spoken.'

What is remarkable is the cultic actuality of the 'today' that runs through the whole of Deuteronomy and shows the connection that the traditions have with worship. The first statement of the word of the mediator points to Yahweh's covenant promises. The God of Israel declared אני יהוה אלהיך (cf. Exod. xx. 2, etc.) and this formula of revelation and covenant was followed by the promise that Yahweh would exalt His people above all other peoples. Israel's declaration is explicitly set out in the pledges expressed in Joshua xxiv. 16 ff. The particular form of expression of Deuteronomic theology makes a difference of course in Deut. xxvii. 16 ff., but the specific form of the 'word of the mediator' can still be clearly perceived. The act of pledging was followed by the proclamation of the divine law. This consummation of the cultic event can be traced everywhere in the tradition of the festival of the renewal of the covenant. The sequence can be seen most clearly in Deut. xxvii. 9, 10, where we hear first the authoritative declaration of the covenant, 'This day thou art become the people of the Lord thy God', followed immediately by the summons, 'Thou shalt therefore obey the voice of the Lord thy God, and do his commandments and his statutes, which I command thee this day.'

The 'Shechemite Dodecalogue' is proclaimed in a special cultic situation. We can only surmise what the ancient ceremonial was when we are told in Deut. xxvii. 11 ff. that six tribes are to camp on Gerizim, the mount of blessing, and six tribes on Ebal, the mount of the curse.[50] The two groups have evidently brought upon themselves blessing and curse. This event should, however, be clearly distinguished from the proclamations of the apodeictic divine law, which according to Deut. xxvii. 14 is announced by the Levites, but could at one time be promulgated by the mediator of the covenant and the prophet (cf. pp. 108 ff. above). Presumably the ceremony of antiphonal acclamation of 'blessing and curse' comes at the end of the cultic event, that is after the proclamation of the divine law.[51] The Dodecalogue includes with the twelve apodeictic statutes referring to the confederacy of the twelve tribes the word of Yahweh, expressed in the ארור formulae:

'I. Cursed be the man that maketh a graven or molten image, an abomination unto the Lord, the work of the hands of the craftsman, and setteth it up in secret. And all the people shall answer and say, Amen.

II. Cursed be he that setteth light by his father or his mother. And all the people shall say, Amen.

III. Cursed be he that removeth his neighbour's landmark. And all the people shall say, Amen.

IV. Cursed be he that maketh the blind to wander out of the way. And all the people shall say, Amen.

V. Cursed be he that wresteth the judgement of the stranger, fatherless, and widow. And all the people shall say, Amen.

VI. Cursed be he that lieth with his father's wife; because he hath uncovered his father's skirt. And all the people shall say, Amen.

VII. Cursed be he that lieth with any manner of beast. And all the people shall say, Amen.

VIII. Cursed be he that lieth with his sister, the daughter of his father, or the daughter of his mother. And all the people shall say, Amen.

IX. Cursed be he that lieth with his mother in law. And all the people shall say, Amen.

X. Cursed be he that smiteth his neighbour in secret. And all the people shall say, Amen.

XI. Cursed be he that taketh reward to slay an innocent person. And all the people shall say, Amen.

XII. Cursed be he that confirmeth not the words of this law to do them. And all the people shall say, Amen.'

[50] On the background of this description of mount Ebal as a 'mount of the curse', see S. Bülow, 'Der Berg des Fluches', *ZDPV*, 73 (1957), pp. 100 ff.

[51] Cf. G. von Rad, *Das formgeschichtliche Problem des Hexateuch*, p. 24, *Ges. Stud.*, p. 34 and also, on Deut. xxvii, E. Nielsen, *Shechem* (1955), pp. 50 ff.

We cannot go into the question here as to what was the original form of the Dodecalogue, which has certainly been expanded, and what the position is as regards the twelfth clause, which gives the impression of being a later addition. What is essential is the form of the apodeictic clauses which Alt has examined in detail in his form critical studies of Israelite law.[52] In the worship of the tribal confederacy there is a revelation of the unconditionally binding will of Yahweh which penetrates to the innermost parts of man's life. But the apodeictic law can be expressed in different forms. The Decalogue in Exod. xx. 2 ff. begins with the challenging, authoritative 'Thou shalt . . .' or 'Thou shalt not . . .' It has a power that penetrates and governs the life of the whole community. The clauses that are introduced by ארור, on the other hand, have an expulsive force, they exclude from the community the one who transgresses the commandments, place him under an effective curse, and have basically the same significance as the series of apodeictic clauses concluding with the formula מות יומת (Lev. xx. 9–21).[53] In whatever way the apodeictic commandments are formulated, they contain the basic law of the divine covenant and assert the lordship of Yahweh over every realm of life.

Joshua viii. 30–35 contains a Shechem tradition which is not easy to explain.[54] The framework of the cultic ceremony to which the passage refers (*v.* 33) is the same as in Deut. xxvii. 11 ff. The proclamation of the divine law and of the 'blessing and curse' is also mentioned (*v.* 34), but then details are given which indicate the varied history of the Shechemite cult. The setting up of an altar on mount Ebal (or Gerizim?) could point back to early times (*v.* 30; cf. Deut. xxvii. 5, 6) and indicate that sacrifices were offered at the celebrations of worship (*v.* 31). It is hard to tell to which period the custom of writing down the divine commandments on large stones should be ascribed (*v.* 32; cf. Deut. xxvii. 2 f.) We could of course raise the possibility that Joshua xxiv. 27 also should be interpreted to mean that Joshua set up a kind of Torah stele under the terebinth at Shechem, but this can be nothing more than supposition. It may have been the custom at a later period at Shechem to write down the divine law on whitewashed stones on ceremonial occasions (Deut. xxvii. 2 f.). Finally, the mention of the Ark in Joshua viii. 33 raises the question whether this reference is merely an invention of the Deuteronomist, or whether it is based on older traditions. The

[52] A. Alt, 'Die Ursprünge des israelitischen Rechts', *Kleine Schriften*, I, pp. 313 ff.

[53] Cf. G. von Rad, *Studies in Deuteronomy*, pp. 31 ff.

[54] For the details provided by literary criticism and the study of tradition in Joshua viii. 30 ff., see M. Noth, *Das Buch Josua*, pp. 51 ff.

passage Joshua viii. 30–35 has certainly been decisively moulded by the Deuteronomist; it contains 'references back to Deuteronomy'[55] and can be used in a reconstruction of the cultic history of Shechem only with great reservation.

The passages we have considered all support the view that the cultic traditions of Shechem point to a ceremony of proclamation of the divine law which belonged unquestionably to the cultic act of the renewal of the covenant. The cultic regulations in Deut. xxxi. 10 ff., which were explained in a different context (see pp. 74 f. above), suggest that the feast of the renewal of the covenant and of the proclamation of the divine law was part of the ancient שמטה institution. In the early period the cultic community of the twelve tribes assembled 'every seven years' at the central sanctuary of Shechem in order to pledge themselves afresh to the service of Yahweh.

(d) *The Significance of Shechem in Later Times*

In the history of Israel the first central sanctuary of the tribal confederacy never lost its prominent status and its dignity deriving from the early days of the confederacy. When David's kingdom split after the death of Solomon Shechem came immediately to the fore again as the centre for assembly and deliberation for the northern tribes (1 Kings xii. 1, 25). Levitical priests no doubt preserved through the years the cultic traditions and possibly also the rite of the promulgation of the divine law. At times of festivals it was not only the official sanctuaries of the two kingdoms of Judah and Israel that were visited, but pilgrimages were also made to the holy place at Shechem that had been venerated from time immemorial (Hos. vi. 9).[56] The Deuteronomic tradition must have been localized for a long time at the northern Israelite Yahweh sanctuary, and it is possible that it did not reach Judah and Jerusalem until after the collapse of the northern kingdom in 722 B.C. in connection with a migration of the Levitical priesthood. There is a strange reference to Shechem in Ps. lx. 8 (Ps. cviii. 8). It is possible that the Psalm tradition should be linked with the occupation of parts of northern Israel by king Josiah.[57]

After the exile Shechem again experienced a definite revival of its cultic importance.[58] The founding of the Samaritan sanctuary on mount Gerizim was not the outcome merely of a particular religious and political schism, but was at the same time a revival of very ancient

[55] C. Steuernagel, *Das Buch Josua* (2 ed., 1923), p. 240.
[56] A. Alt, 'Die Wallfahrt von Sichem nach Bethel', *Kleine Schriften*, I, pp. 79 ff.
[57] H.-J. Kraus, *Psalmen*, BK 15 (1960), p. 430.
[58] M. Noth, *History of Israel*, pp. 352 ff.

traditions. The newly founded community, basing itself on the authority of the Pentateuch and rejecting as a matter of principle the whole cultic history of Jerusalem, thought of itself as the original Israel. It was a purist tendency that brought about this return to the place of origin of the people of God. At a relatively later period, therefore, the ancient traditions of Shechem are revived and lead to a fateful division of the Jewish community. The fact that it was first and foremost the feast of the Passover that was celebrated on Gerizim is linked with the development in the history of worship which was described earlier (see pp. 54 f.

3. Bethel

(a) *The Ancient Israelite Sanctuary*

The sanctuary of Bethel was not an Israelite foundation but was originally a Canaanite cultic centre.[59] The place was formerly called Luz, then the designation of the sacred place that was situated to the east displaced the place-name Luz, and so Luz became Bethel (Gen. xxviii. 19). Today, however, the site of the cultic centre should probably be sought in the region of *burj betin.* If we reconstruct the most important sacral elements in the Canaanite cultic tradition at Bethel, we find that there are three factors to be noted: (1) the god 'Bethel' who was venerated at the holy place;[60] (2) the מצבה which was set up in the area of the sanctuary (Gen. xxviii. 18); (3) the stairway (סלם) which was certainly not only a visionary element in the *hieros logos* tradition, but an actual object (Gen. xxviii. 12).[61] The Canaanite cultic tradition of Bethel, which gave an account of a theophany and provided the *hieros logos* which gave the sanctuary its authority (Gen. xxviii. 10 ff.) was taken over by 'Jacob and his sons' at the arrival of the Israelite groups.[62]

[59] Cf. O. Eissfeldt, 'Der Gott Bethel', *ARW*, 28 (1930), pp. 1 ff., reprinted in *Kleine Schriften*, I, pp. 206 ff.; J. P. Hyatt, 'The Deity Bethel and the Old Testament', *JAOS*, 51 (1939), pp. 81 ff.; K. Galling, 'Bethel und Gilgal', *ZDPV*, 66 (1943), pp. 140 ff.; 67 (1944/5), pp. 21 ff.; C. A. Keller, 'Über einige alttestamentliche Heiligtumslegenden, I', *ZAW*, 67 (1955), pp. 162 ff.

[60] Cf. O. Eissfeldt, op. cit., and J. B. Hyatt, op. cit.

[61] 'The ladder (or stair) which leads from earth to heaven is not merely an image or symbol, but really is at Bethel . . .' (H. Gunkel, *Genesis*, p. 317). It is possible that the 'stair' which was perhaps cut out of the rock symbolizes the mountain top above which sanctuaries were built in Canaan. Gunkel refers to the six steps of Solomon's throne which very probably 'represent the heavenly throne above the six spheres' (1 Kings x. 18 f.). See ibid., p. 317. It is impossible to answer the question whether the calf image set up at Bethel in the time of Jeroboam (1 Kings xii. 28) had already played a part in the worship of the Canaanite holy place.

[62] If it is a fact that 'Bochim' in Judges ii. 1–5 refers to Bethel, then Galling's suggestion that we have in Judges ii. 1–5 a second *hieros logos* standing over against the Jacob tradition needs to be considered ('Bethel und Gilgal', *ZDPV*, 67 (1944/5), p. 30).

A far-reaching transformation of the tradition of the place occurred first of all as a result of the influence of the cult directed to the 'God of the fathers',[63] then—as a transitional stage—through the assimilation of the tribe that had settled in the area of Bethel, and finally through the confederacy of the twelve tribes of Israel. So Bethel became the central sanctuary of the Israelite amphictyony.[64]

The information which we are given in Judges xx provides clear evidence of the great importance of Bethel as a cultic centre of the tribal confederacy.[65] We are told in this chapter: 'And the children of Israel arose, and went up to Bethel, and asked counsel of God; and they said, who shall go up for us first to battle against the children of Benjamin?' (*v.* 18); and then we read in *vv.* 26 ff.: 'Then all the children of Israel, and all the people, went up, and came unto Bethel, and wept, and sat there before the Lord, and fasted that day until even; and they offered burnt offerings and peace offerings before the Lord. And the children of Israel asked of the Lord (for the ark of the covenant of God was there in those days, and Phinehas, the son of Eleazar, the son of Aaron, stood before it in those days), saying, Shall I yet again go out to battle against the children of Benjamin my brother, or shall I cease? And the Lord said, Go up; for tomorrow I will deliver him into thine hand.' In other words, the tribal confederacy wages war upon the tribe of Benjamin, which has rebelled against the authority of the amphictyony,[66] and this situation leads to the act of seeking Yahweh's guidance at the central sanctuary. At this time Bethel was the amphictyonic cultic centre which derived its status and dignity from the presence of the Ark. The account brings to light three sacral practices at the central sanctuary: a 'fast' which was observed as a solemn lamentation at times of distress,[67] the presentation of burnt offerings and peace offerings and finally the delivery of an oracle, a word from God. We see here one of those cultic events which were celebrated on special occasions (cf. also 1 Sam. vii. 5 f.), but the tradition from the period of the judges in Judges xx clearly shows that the sanctuary at Bethel had a decisive and central importance for the whole amphictyonic cult.

The cultic centre of Bethel did not lose its prominence even when the Ark was set up at a different place and so marked out a new central

[63] Cf. A. Alt, 'Der Gott der Väter', *Kleine Schriften*, I, pp. 19 ff.

[64] See M. Noth, *History of Israel*, pp. 94 f.

[65] Galling assumes that Judges xx. 18, 26 f. have undergone secondary redaction, and that the reference originally was to 'Mizpah', but there is no clear evidence for this (op. cit., p. 31).

[66] See Noth, *History of Israel*, pp. 105 f., for the historical situation.

[67] Cf. H. Gunkel/J. Begrich, *Einleitung in die Psalmen* (1933), pp. 117 ff.

sanctuary. We are told of a pilgrimage to Bethel in 1 Sam. x. 3 and Gen. xxxv. 1–7 Perhaps we even ought to consider the possibility whether there was not a temple building during the early history of this venerable cultic centre. At any rate we can observe that the *hieros logos* in Gen. xxviii. 22 has undergone a secondary expansion and points in an aetiological form to a 'house of God' at Bethel. The מצבה, which was traditionally the sacral centre of the sanctuary, has become a בית אלהים. It is, of course, hard to say when this temple was erected, but there is much to suggest that it was before the monarchy (see p. 149). Perhaps the Ark was accommodated in the בית אלהים at Bethel.

(b) *The Official Sanctuary of the Northern Kingdom*

When David's kingdom split into two after the death of Solomon, at first Shechem won back its old importance. The spokesmen of the northern tribes assembled at the place where the Yahweh amphictyony had been established (1 Kings xii. 1) in order to negotiate with Rehoboam, but these negotiations broke down, David's kingdom was divided and the northern tribes called Jeroboam to be their king and cut themselves off from Judah and Jerusalem. The new king of northern Israel saw as his first and urgent task the provision of a cultic centre equal in status to the official sanctuary at Jerusalem. The annals relate:

> 'Whereupon the king took counsel, and made two calves of gold; and he said unto them, It is too much for you to go up to Jerusalem; behold thy gods, O Israel, which brought thee up out of the land of Egypt.[68] And he set the one in Bethel, and the other put he in Dan. And this thing became a sin: for the people went to worship before the one, even unto Dan. And he made houses of high places and made priests from among all the people, which were not of the sons of Levi. And Jeroboam ordained a feast in the eighth month, on the fifteenth day of the month, like unto the feast that is in Judah, and he went up unto the altar; so did he in Bethel, sacrificing unto the calves that he had made: and he placed in Bethel the priests of the high places which he had made' (1 Kings xii. 28–32).

Jeroboam, in other words, restores Bethel to a place of high honour. The implications of these decisive moves in the history of worship need to be carefully considered. Jerusalem was held in the highest esteem. David had deposited the Ark, the central shrine of the tribal confederacy, on Zion (see pp. 181 ff.), and Solomon had erected the

[68] In the Hebrew text the plural refers of course to the two calves at Bethel and Dan, but the singular form might have been the original one (cf. Exod. xxxii. 4).

mighty structure of the official Temple which went beyond all the cultic conceptions of ancient Israel. What could Jeroboam set up after the division of the kingdom as a counterpart to these sacral institutions that were recognized everywhere? The most obvious thing was the ancient Israelite cultic tradition according to which by the amphictyonic sacral law the Ark changed its resting place and a new central sanctuary was appointed from time to time.[69] When the northern Israelite king declares: 'It is too much for you to go up to Jerusalem', he is repudiating Jerusalem's claim to a permanent retention of the sacral sanctuary rights. On this point Jeroboam could possibly expect some encouragement from some of the ancient Israelite circles, for Jerusalem had usurped the amphictyonic sacral rights as a permanent privilege. But how did it come about that Bethel and Dan were elevated to become official sanctuaries of northern Israel? Why were two places on the southern and northern boundaries of the newly formed kingdom chosen? For what reason was a place as venerable as Shechem not considered? Scholars have been trying to answer these questions for a long time. It has been suggested that Shechem had suffered a 'decline' and that Bethel and Dan were chosen in order to embrace the northern kingdom geographically.[70] But the simplest solution is surely that there were temples in Bethel and in Dan (Gen. xxviii. 22; Judges xvii), and that it was only by granting privileges to these temple sanctuaries that institutions could be set up that could adequately counterbalance Solomon's mighty edifice. Besides, Bethel enjoyed the respect of being an acknowledged cultic centre of the tribal confederacy and was provided with venerable local traditions. Here Jeroboam was able to institute that sacral centre of his kingdom that is called מקדש מלך and בית ממלכה in Amos vii. 13.

The king had calf images set up in Bethel and Dan.[71] The meaning of these cultic objects has been the subject of much scholarly debate. Whilst O. Eissfeldt holds the view that they were standards,[72] more recent studies tend to see in the calf images a base resembling a throne, a pedestal for the deity who is present but unseen.[73] F. Dumermuth, for example, has recently emphasized that Jeroboam evidently meant them

[69] See J. Dus, 'Der Brauch der Ladewanderung im alten Israel', *ThZ Basel*, 17 (1961), pp. 1 ff.

[70] Cf., e.g., K. Galling, 'Bethel und Gilgal', *ZDPV*, 66 (1943), p. 29.

[71] See esp. H. T. Obbink, 'Jahwebilder', *ZAW*, 47 (1929); O. Eissfeldt, 'Lade und Stierbild', *ZAW*, 57 (1940/1), pp. 190 ff., reprinted in *Kleine Schriften*, II, pp. 228 ff.; L. Malten, 'Der Stier in Kult und mythischem Bild', *JDAI*, 43 (1928), pp. 90 ff.; M. Weippert, 'Gott und Stier', *ZDPV*, 77 (1961), pp. 93 ff.

[72] O. Eissfeldt, op. cit., pp. 208 ff., *Kleine Schriften*, II, pp. 288 ff.

[73] Cf. e.g., B. K. Galling, *Biblisches Reallexikon*, HAT, I, 1 (1937), pp. 202 f.; M. Noth, *Exodus*, p. 247.

to be a parallel to the Ark which was thought of as Yahweh's throne.[74] Before we accept this explanation we must bear in mind the point that H. T. Obbink has repeatedly stressed, that popular religion did not distinguish between the pedestal and the invisible God, but linked the calf image with the primitive Canaanite cultic conceptions of fertility religion.[75] But it is by no means certain whether this explanation of the calf image as a pedestal, which has been more and more widely accepted, is really correct. The comparative study of religions brings to light parallels from the Hittite and Syrian sphere which suggest that we should think rather of a representation of God in the shape of a bull.[76] In the Ugaritic texts the deity El is called 'bull' (*ṯr*), and in the myth Baal also appears in the form of a bull.[77] But the statements in the Old Testament itself are more important than these analogies. 'Behold thy gods, O Israel, which brought thee up out of the land of Egypt' (1 Kings xii. 28; Exod. xxxii. 4). It is the calf image itself that is meant in this cultic declaration.[78] Such a statement could never have been made about a pedestal. In addition, it is important to note that an extensive revival of the high places was linked with the setting up of the calf images (1 Kings xii. 31). Although it may have been Jeroboam's aim to keep quite central the tradition of redemptive history concerning the exodus from Egypt, with the setting up of the calf image under the influence of foreign powers and connections the cult inevitably sinks into the sphere of fertility religion, and the forces of Canaan achieve their full effect. But if we interpret the calf image as a representation of God in the form of a bull, we must, of course, not forget that in the religious thought of the ancient world the god and the image were not identical. The image is meant 'to secure and bear witness to the effective presence of the deity in the holy place',[79] and its character is that of an authoritative representation.

[74] F. Dumermuth, 'Zur deuteronomischen Kulttheologie und ihren Voraussetzungen' *ZAW*, 70 (1958), p. 83.

[75] H. T. Obbink, op. cit., p. 269.

[76] M. Weippert, op. cit., pp. 106 f.

[77] On the use of the name *ṯr* for El, cf. C. H. Gordon, *Ugaritic Handbook*, III, Nr. 2148. The mythological narrative IV AB II describes how Baal assumes the form of a bull and meets the cow ᶜAnat. For the text, see Aistleitner, op. cit., pp. 53 f.

[78] Is Noth correct when he states: 'This explanation contains a pejorative exaggeration of the original circumstances which has purposely been introduced with polemical intent'? (*Exodus*, p 247) Is it not more important to see that in 1 Kings xii. 28 ff. as well as Exod. xxxii the calf cult brings out the excesses of an ecstatic Nature worship?

[79] K. H. Bernhardt, *Gott und Bild*, ThA, 2 (1956), pp. 28 ff., 66 ff. Cf. also G. von Rad, *Old Testament Theology*, I, p. 214: 'Ancient peoples felt the divine powers to be very close to them. No doubt these came from below and were incalculable; but in cultic symbols and images they approached men in a way that was helpful. . . .

We can see also from the fact that he rejected the Levitical priesthood (1 Kings xii. 31) how completely Jeroboam broke away from the ancient Israelite traditions, which stood in firm opposition to the cultic institutions of Canaan. The Levites waged constant battle against the vegetation myths and cults of the sanctuaries of the country, and condemned any fusion between the worship of Yahweh and the institutions of the native population (Exod. xxxii. 26 ff.). It was probably for the same reason that Shechem was not considered when the official sanctuary was chosen, because an influential Levitical priesthood was established there which would not have been sympathetic to the efforts of the king.

We certainly cannot overlook the influence of the Deuteronomist in the account given in 1 Kings xii. 28 ff., nevertheless the outline of the annals brings out very clearly how skilfully Jeroboam set about achieving his aims. He appealed to the sacral law of the migration of the Ark (1 Kings xii. 28), upheld the tradition of redemptive history concerning the exodus from Egypt (1 Kings xii. 28b), and at the same time advanced far towards syncretism by introducing Canaanite symbols and institutions. There were probably earlier developments leading up to this cultic assimilation to the world of the native Canaanite inhabitants. It is doubtful whether the tradition in Exod. xxxii was exclusively directed against the calf cult in Bethel,[80] for it seems very possible that even before the setting up of the cults at Bethel and Dan priestly circles in Israel were encouraging a fusion of Yahweh worship and nature worship. The second commandment in the Decalogue—as W. Zimmerli has shown[81]—is mainly directed against Yahweh images which appeared in Israel at a quite early period.

By establishing these sanctuaries Jeroboam laid the foundations for a new autumn cult in northern Israel (1 Kings xii. 32). As we have already shown (see pp. 61 ff.). in the early period of the history of worship in the Old Testament, the autumn festival was the most important of the three annual festivals. In Jerusalem the celebration was held in the month of Etanim, i.e., in the seventh month (1 Kings viii. 2), and this was laid down in the cultic calendar. Jeroboam, however, fixed the eighth month as the time for the autumn cult. This, of course, has nothing to

[80] On the background of the calf worship at Bethel, see O. Eissfeldt, op. cit., pp. 190 ff. Eissfeldt holds the view that the calf image in the form of an ensign was a cultic symbol of the Yahweh faith going back to the pre-Canaanite period (pp. 199 ff.).

[81] W. Zimmerli, 'Das zweite Gebot', *Festschrift A. Bertholet* (1950), pp. 550 ff., reprinted in *Ges. Stud. zum AT* (1963), pp. 234 ff.

Even if the relationship of the deity to the image was complex, and was hardly anywhere a completely clarified concept, still, the crucial thing was that the deity became present in the image.'

do with different times of harvest in the north and the south, for such variations are impossible in the small area of Palestine.[82] On the contrary, the king had a definite goal in view. He could not break Jerusalem's prerogative and had to accept the fact that many groups would still visit the sanctuary at Jerusalem. The claim of the northern Israelite cultic centres could obviously be asserted and in the course of time established only if a new time for the festival made it possible for the people to assemble at the official sanctuaries in the north. The cult at Bethel was thus an outcome of the new political order. The holy place became a royal property (מקדש מלך, Amos vii. 13), and Jeroboam took over the position of cultic leader and offered the sacrifices (1 Kings xii. 32). At the official sanctuary kingship was given a sacral significance and came to stand at the centre of worship.

The official cult at Bethel temporarily forfeited its dominant position in the northern kingdom when the supporters of Omri founded in the king's own city of Samaria a new centre which also made cultic claims. Hos. viii. 6 tells of the setting up of a calf image in Samaria. But after the fall of the sons of Omri, particularly at the time of Jeroboam II, Bethel again shone forth in its old splendour. The official sanctuary (Amos vii. 13) was once again the favoured place of pilgrimage (Amos iv. 4; v. 5) and was able to survive even the catastrophe of 722 B.C. Josiah set about destroying the holy places after he had conquered parts of northern Israelite territory and could sieze the opportunity of vindicating Jerusalem's prerogative by destroying all the rival sanctuaries (2 Kings xxiii. 8, 15). A prophetic legend gave approval to the king of Judah's actions (1 Kings xiii. 2 ff.; 2 Kings xxiii. 16 ff.).

4. Gilgal

(a) *Gilgal and the Tradition of the Conquest*

In his article 'Das byzantinische Gilgal' A. M. Schneider tried to prove the accuracy of the Christian Byzantine tradition concerning the location of Gilgal which persisted right up to the Middle Ages.[83] This tradition located the Gilgal of the Old Testament at *chirbet el-mefjir*, 2 km to the north of *erīḥa*,[84] but against this suggestion

[82] G. Dalman, in opposing R. Kittel's view that the later time of the harvest was an occasion for the fixing of the autumn festival, emphasizes that there was no difference in the time of ripening and harvesting between Jerusalem and Samaria, let alone between Jerusalem and Bethel (*Arbeit und Sitte in Palästina*, I, p. 141).

[83] A. M. Schneider, 'Das byzantinische Gilgal', *ZDPV*, 54 (1931), pp. 50 ff.

[84] Cf. the statements in Josephus, *Antiquities*, V, 1, 11, and Eusebius, *Onomastikon*, 64, 24 ff. The Madeba Map and the accounts by medieval pilgrims also support this position.

had to be reckoned the fact that no traces of a site belonging to the Iron Age or even earlier could be found in the region of *chirbet el-mefjir*. J. Muilenburg was the first to succeed in overcoming the difficulties as the result of a new discovery. To the north of *chirbet el-mefjir* he found pottery fragments from the Iron Age and discovered —in close proximity—two *tulul*.[85] It seems reasonable to locate the Gilgal whose situation is more exactly defined in Joshua iv. 19 at the place suggested by Muilenberg.[86] In earlier Old Testament times this Gilgal was the important sanctuary which we are now going to consider.[87] We must not overlook the fact that the peculiar topography which we find in Deut. xi. 30 has given rise to the assumption that there was another place with the name of Gilgal in the neighbourhood of Shechem,[88] but—as we shall seek to show—this idea is not really in keeping with the facts.

We have to start from the topography we find in Joshua iv. 19, which envisages the Old Testament Gilgal lying 'on the east border of Jericho'. In the early period of Israel's history this Gilgal was a prominent sanctuary which—as we can tell from Joshua iii–v—bore in its local tradition the marks of an amphictyonic cultic centre. On account of the presence of the Ark the place had the status and dignity of one of the most important sanctuaries of the tribal confederacy (Joshua iii. 3 ff.),[89] and the 'twelve stones' set up at Gilgal (Joshua iv. 20) also point unquestionably to the amphictyonic nature of the holy place. It is possible that the pre-Israelite Gilgal was a 'stone-circle sanctuary' which was transformed by the Israelites into a 'twelve-stone sanctuary'. If we examine the Old Testament traditions which enshrine the real significance of Gilgal as a holy place, then we have first to note the tradition of the conquest which was firmly connected with this sanctuary.[90] According to Joshua

[85] J. Muilenburg, 'The Site of Ancient Gilgal', *BASOR*, 140 (1955), pp. 11 ff.

[86] Ibid., p. 21.

[87] Bibliography dealing with Gilgal: K. Galling, 'Bethel und Gilgal', *ZDPV*, 66 (1943), pp. 140 ff.; A. George, 'Les récits de Gilgal en Josué 5, 2–12', *Mémorial Chaine* (Bibliothèque de la Faculté Catholique de Théologie de Lyon, 5 (1950)), pp. 169 ff.; F. M. Abel, 'Galgala qui est aussi le Dodecalithon', ibid., pp. 29 ff.; H. J. Kraus, 'Gilgal—ein Beitrag zur Kultusgeschichte Israels, *VT*, 1 (1951), pp. 181 ff.; F. M. Abel, 'L'apparition du chef de l'armée de Yahweh à Josué, Jos. 5, 13–15', *Miscellanea Biblica et Orientalia R.P.A. Miller oblata* (1951), pp. 109 ff.; J. Muilenburg, 'The Site of Ancient Gilgal', *BASOR*, 140 (1955), pp. 11 ff.; C. A. Keller, 'Über einige alttestamentliche Heiligtumslegenden. II', *ZAW*, 68 (1956), pp. 85 ff.; H. Wildberger, *Jahwes Eigentumsvolk*, ATANT, 37 (1960), pp. 59 ff.

[88] Cf. A. Schlatter, *Zur Topographie und Geschichte Palästinas* (1893), pp. 246 ff. A similar solution is suggested by E. Sellin, *Gilgal* (1917).

[89] Cf. M. Noth, *History of Israel*, pp. 95 f.

[90] See G. von Rad. *Das formgeschichtliche Problem des Hexateuch*, BWANT, IV, 26 (1938), pp. 41 ff., *Ges. Stud.*, pp. 53 ff.

iii–v Gilgal was the first sanctuary in the promised land at which Israel camped,[91] and the expeditions by which the conquest was effected were launched from this sanctuary (Joshua x. 6 ff.; xiv. 6). Scholars have therefore stated quite correctly that the Israelite tradition of the conquest was localized at Gilgal. But it is not easy to answer the question as to what period it was when Gilgal was the central sanctuary of the Yahweh amphictyony, and we shall have to consider this problem later. For the moment we will merely refer to those passages in the Old Testament which presuppose the outstanding importance of Gilgal in the cultic life of the tribal confederacy. The passages in question all point to the period of Samuel and Saul. Samuel judged at Gilgal (1 Sam. vii. 16), and it was at this holy place that Saul was appointed king over Israel by acclamation (1 Sam. x. 8; xi. 14 f.; xiii. 7, 15). Gilgal is mentioned again in the stories about Elijah and Elisha (2 Kings ii. 1 f.; iv. 38) and finally emerges once again in the eighth century as a place of pilgrimage (Hos. iv. 15; ix. 15; xii. 12).

(b) *The Crossing of the Jordan*

The most important and most comprehensive local tradition concerning the ancient Israelite sanctuary of Gilgal is to be found in Joshua iii–v. As this complex of tradition is particularly important for the study of Old Testament worship, it is necessary for us first of all to mention the literary problems and those concerning the history of tradition that this passage presents. The series of chapters Joshua iii–v in which we find Gilgal traditions poses some extremely involved questions, and in chapters iii and iv particularly there are complicated stratifications within the text which so far have not been adequately explained. Attempts have been made to remove the difficulties by means of separating the sources, but the views of the scholars do not only strongly diverge on this point, but the whole range of possibilities from J^1 to P^2 has to be considered in order to be able to explain and understand the numerous stratifications to some extent. But the assumption that there are a considerable number of narrative threads running through the section has not led to any obvious conclusions. Noth in particular has shown convincingly in his commentary on Joshua that a literary criticism that is applied on the basis of Pentateuchal sources is a wrong approach to the Book of Joshua.[92] Gressmann[93] and Alt[94] had recognized previously

[91] The practice of casting lots, of which we read in Joshua xviii. 6, 8, 10, was no doubt carried out here.

[92] M. Noth, *Das Buch Josua*, HAT, I, 7 (2 ed., 1953), pp. 7 ff.

[93] H. Gressmann, *Die Anfänge Israels*, SAT, I, 2 (1922).

[94] A. Alt, 'Josua', *Kleine Schriften*, I, pp. 176 ff.

that there is a complex of aetiological legends in Joshua i–vi. Gilgal and Jericho were the two foci of these legends. In the first volume of his *Überlieferungsgeschichtliche Studien* and his commentary on the Book of Joshua Noth showed that the legends in the first chapters of Joshua were ancient local traditions which—without being affected by Pentateuchal sources—were first taken up by the Deuteronomistic historian, edited to a very slight extent and inserted into the historical framework.[95]

Repeated attempts have been made recently to solve the problem of the history of the tradition in the section Joshua iii–v. K. Möhlenbrink first tried to clarify the complicated text by distinguishing between a Benjaminite and an Israelite stage of tradition; he also took the remarkable fact that 'twelve stones' were set up by the Israelites, once in the Jordan (Joshua iv. 3) and then also at Gilgal (Joshua iv. 20), as the basis for drawing a distinction between the 'Jordan version' and the 'Gilgal version'.[96] Similar attempts to explain the different strata in the text are still being made. C. A. Keller[97] and J. Dus,[98] for example, have continued the literary and the traditio-historical analyses along the lines laid down by Möhlenbrink, and they have drawn more and more distinctions.

In order to provide a basis for tracing the cultic history of this section, we will adopt the position concerning literary criticism and the history of tradition set out by Noth in his commentary on Joshua[99] which assumes that the latest influences affecting the material were the post-Deuteronomistic insertions and glosses as well as the main Deuteronomistic conception. The pre-Deuteronomistic history of the tradition, however, is extremely complicated. The Deuteronomist had before him a whole complex of aetiological legends and separate themes, basic narratives and local traditions.[100] Four main original elements have to be distinguished: (1) the narrative of the miracle of the crossing of the Jordan, (2) the presence of the Ark in the region of Gilgal, (3) the aetiology of the twelve stones on the bed of the Jordan, (4) the aetiology of the twelve stones at Gilgal. But what is the connection between these four elements? The great value in studying the history of tradition is

[95] M. Noth, op. cit., pp. 27 ff.

[96] K. Möhlenbrink, 'Die Landnahmesagen des Buches Josua', *ZAW*, 68 (1938), pp. 238 ff.

[97] C. A. Keller, 'Über einige alttestamentliche Heiligtumslegenden, II—Der *hieros logos* von Gilgal', *ZAW*, 63 (1956), pp. 85 ff.

[98] J. Dus, 'Die Analyse zweier Ladeerzählungen des Josuabuches', *ZAW*, 72 (1960), pp. 107 ff.

[99] Cf. M. Noth, op. cit., pp. 31 ff.

[100] Ibid., pp. 33 f.

that it helps us to grasp and understand the separate elements in a complex of traditions starting from a critical analysis of the traditions, but it still comes up against a limit of explanation when it tries to indicate the inner connection between these separate elements. Thus it is stated, for example, that the separate sections of tradition 'came together' or 'grew together', that they had been 'joined together' or 'linked with one another', but the inner connections or the connecting framework of the traditions can be traced in only a few cases.[101] On this point we must allow a greater importance to the local cult than has been done in the past, for it is in the cult that local traditions are kept alive and continue to exert their influence, but it is also in the cult that the linking of different elements in the tradition takes place.

The first attempt to interpret the tradition present in Joshua iii–v as a 'cultic legend' was made in my essay 'Gilgal—ein Beitrag zur Kultusgeschichte Israels,'[102] since when the suggestions made in this study have been widely discussed. We shall now bring out once again the most important aspects of this approach made from the standpoint of the history of worship by contrasting it with the opposing views that have been expressed. The thesis set out in the article published in 1951 was that we have in Joshua iii and iv the cultic legend of a festival that was celebrated at Gilgal, in the course of which the miraculous crossing of the sea and the entry into the promised land was re-presented and celebrated in a recurring ceremonial. Von Rad's studies in form criticism laid down vital presuppositions for investigating the cult that was observed at Gilgal.[103] Alongside the Sinai tradition von Rad discovered the conquest tradition, which found its expression in a condensed form in the so-called 'short credo of redemptive history' (Deut. vi. 21 ff.; xxvi. 5 ff.). This credo has two main themes—the miraculous exodus from Egypt and the entry into the land promised to the forefathers.[104] The tradition which is contained in the credo existed independently of the Sinai tradition, in Israel's worship. It can hardly be doubted that the cultic representation of the Sinai events took place at the ancient Shechem, the central sanctuary of the ancient Israelite amphictyony (see pp. 136 ff. above), but this gives rise to the question as to where the settlement tradition was localized and how it was actualized in worship.

[101] Cf. H.-J. Kraus, 'Zur Geschichte des Überlieferungsbegriffs in der alttestamentlichen Wissenschaft', *EvTh*, 8/9 (1956), pp. 371 ff.

[102] H.-J. Kraus, 'Gilgal—ein Beitrag zur Kultusgeschichte Israels', *VT*, 1 (1951), pp. 181 ff.

[103] G. von Rad, *Das formgeschichtliche Problem des Hexateuch*, pp. 36 ff., esp. pp. 41 ff., *Ges. Stud.*, pp. 48 ff., 53 ff.

[104] Ibid., pp. 2 ff.

As we have already seen, in the Old Testament Gilgal was the starting point for the conquest. But is it possible that there was a cultic rehearsal of the saving events that were enshrined in the credo? Is it conceivable that there was a cultic celebration corresponding to the cultic realization of the Sinai events in the worship at Shechem? G. von Rad pursued his investigations in form criticism up to this point, but did not carry his inquiry to its logical conclusion, for 'we are faced at this point (on the question of the possibility of a cultic celebration of the events connected with the conquest) with considerable problems, which arise in part from the simple fact that the conquest tradition cannot be a tradition which embraces a cultic celebration *in toto* and cannot provide enough distinctive features which point to historical analogies'.[105] It is true that a little reflection would lead us to conclude that an event as comprehensive as that contained in the conquest tradition and summed up in the 'short credo of redemptive history' could not bring about a cultic celebration *in toto*. And how could the crossing of the sea and the entry into the promised land have been included in one act of worship? The cultic legend in Joshua iii and iv gives us the answer: Israel passed through the Jordan behind the Ark of Yahweh and then entered the promised land. The aetiological explanation in Joshua iv. 22–24 makes it quite clear: 'Then ye shall let your children know, saying, Israel came over this Jordan on dry land. For the Lord your God dried up the waters of Jordan from before you, until ye were passed over, as the Lord your God did to the Red Sea, which he dried up from before us, until we were passed over: that all the peoples of the earth may know the hand of the Lord, that it is mighty; that they may fear the Lord your God for ever.' In this concluding section of the narrative of the crossing of the Jordan the whole event is put in analogy with the event of the exodus from Egypt, an analogy which is attached to the tradition of the place.

We can see here how two of the elements in the tradition isolated by Noth as a result of his critical analysis come together—the crossing of the Jordan and the Ark. In the pre-Deuteronomistic stratum the 'bearers of the Ark' are mentioned,[106] and it seems reasonable to conclude that the cultic act of taking the Ark in procession through the Jordan was the real nucleus of the whole tradition. We shall see later that the Ark appears in Joshua vi also as a cultic and processional shrine. This fact indicates that the local traditions from the region of Gilgal were grouped in the first place around an Ark cult that was rooted in this particular place. Whatever traces we may find of other elements in

[105] Ibid., p. 38. [106] Cf. M. Noth, op. cit., p. 32.

Joshua iii ff. from the standpoint of the history of tradition, the tradition was crystallized in the Ark cult of Gilgal. The aetiologies which are linked with the 'twelve stones' in the Jordan and at Gilgal also have an unmistakable connection with the cultic sphere of the central sanctuary.

If we attempt to reconstruct the Gilgal cult, we must first recognize the focal points of the traditions and try to distinguish them from one another. The traditions in Joshua iii–v are to be ascribed to the sanctuary of Gilgal, but so also probably are the Jericho stories (Joshua ii and vi. 1 ff.).[107] Another focal point which has previously not been taken much into account is the 'altar by Jordan' (Joshua xxii. 10), a sanctuary belonging to those Israelite groups which had settled in the area to the east of the Jordan, across from Jericho. The two complexes of tradition connected with the 'altar by Jordan' and Gilgal become closely associated in Old Testament tradition, and we shall probably not be far from the truth if we assume that there was a 'cultic intercourse' between the two sanctuaries which faced one another. In the cultic legend which tells of the passage of the Ark and the cultic community through the Jordan the marks and forms of expression of a processional act of worship are quite plain. The 'bearers of the Ark' carry the sacred object and lead the way (Joshua iii. 3 ff.) and the Israelites follow at carefully defined distances (Joshua iii. 4). Some features of the account, which serve to emphasize the holiness of the Ark, are certainly later insertions, but they are in keeping with the purpose of the main narrative. The people 'sanctify' themselves for the sacred act (Joshua iii. 6), and then the procession of the Ark reaches its destination at Gilgal.[108] There a circumcision (Joshua v. 1–9), and a feast of the Passover and of Unleavened Bread (Joshua v. 10–12) is held. Certain aetiological and local stories have been attached to and associated with this cultic axis of the Gilgal tradition. Thus, for example, the damming of the Jordan is probably to be traced back to a time when the river bank collapsed, as several reports have been given of such occurrences when the banks of marl were undermined and collapsed.[109] There is also a specific purpose behind the account, for the description of the flooding is obviously meant to heighten the miraculous significance of the crossing.[110]

[107] Ibid., pp. 20 ff.

[108] On the question of the possibility of the crossing of the Jordan, see M. Noth, 'Der Jordan in der Geschichte Palästinas', *ZDPV*, 72 (1956), pp. 123 ff.; H. Wildberger, *Jahwes Eigentumsvolk* (1960), p. 61, note 61.

[109] Cf. J. Garstang, *The Foundations of the Bible in History* (1931).

[110] M. Noth, 'Der Jordan in der Geschichte Palästinas', *ZDPV*, 72 (1956), p. 145: 'The reference in Joshua iii. 15 to the flooding is meant to show that the miracle at the Jordan was a particularly great one.'

The main theme in the tradition, however, is the journey of the Israelites behind the Ark. The presence of the Ark as the central shrine of the tribal confederacy and also the emphatic reference to the 'twelve' stones in the Jordan and at Gilgal show that this cultic event must have been a very significant act of worship for the Yahweh amphictyony. There is a remarkable echo of the cultic rehearsal of the miraculous exodus from Egypt at the Jordan in Ps. cxiv.

> 'When Israel went forth out of Egypt,
> The house of Jacob from a people of strange language;
> Judah became his sanctuary,
> Israel his dominion.
> The sea saw it, and fled;
> Jordan was driven back.
> The mountains skipped like rams,
> The little hills like young sheep.
> What aileth thee, O thou sea, that thou fleest?
> Thou Jordan, that thou turnest back?
> Ye mountains, that ye skip like rams;
> Ye little hills, like young sheep?
> Tremble, thou earth, at the presence of the Lord,
> At the presence of the God of Jacob;
> Which turned the rock into a pool of water,
> The flint into a fountain of waters.'

This cultic hymn mentions 'sea' and 'Jordan' in direct connection with one another. This combination is so unusual that we can assume that the Psalmist is basing his hymn on the cultic tradition of Gilgal.[111]

(c) *Jericho*

The Jericho tradition is also connected with the Ark cult of Gilgal. If the passage of the Ark through the Jordan had as its goal the occupation of the promised land, this cultic event could throw a new light on the story of the conquest of Jericho. Excavations made at the *tell es-sultān* near *erīḥa* have clearly shown that Jericho must have been destroyed before the Israelites entered the land,[112] and the idea that the city was conquered by the invading tribes has therefore to be abandoned. The account of the conquest of Jericho in Joshua vi is consistent in its essentials with these archaeological discoveries. There is no trace of a military undertaking in the tradition, and the whole event is characterized by its cultic and sacral emphasis. The Israelites march round the

[111] Cf. H.-J. Kraus, *Psalmen*, BK, 15 (1960), pp. 778 ff.
[112] M. Noth, *History of Israel*, p. 149, note 2.

city following the Ark day after day until the walls collapse on the seventh day. This account gains a new significance in connection with the Ark cult of Gilgal. It is possible to suppose that at the cultic celebration of the crossing and the settlement Israel chose the ruined city of Jericho which was situated in the neighbourhood of Gilgal as the place for a demonstration in the form of a cultic drama of the occupation. In this case Joshua vi could be taken as the cultic legend for this occasion.[113] We must note that here again the main elements in the cultic traditions have added to themselves other local and aetiological elements from the Jericho sphere, such as, for example, the story of Rahab.

We might wonder whether this cultic interpretation of Joshua ii–vi does not completely undermine the historical value of the traditions. Such an 'undermining' would have to be assumed in any case as far as Joshua vi is concerned, for historical criticism came to the conclusion some time ago that Jericho was not conquered by Israel. But if we assume that there was a cultic event, the emphasis changes from a negative to a highly positive conclusion—that in the act of worship at Jericho the community received 'proclamations' of an imposing and far-reaching kind, and was incorporated into an event in which Yahweh proved his power over all the bastions of the native population. Worship in the early period of the Old Testament was a direct experience of the *actio Dei*, participation in the original Divine act, which became manifest in the cult. The event of the crossing of the Jordan also is to be understood in this sense. It is possible, but cannot be proved, that the crossing of the Jordan once had a historical significance for the tribe of Benjamin and its northern neighbours, but these faint historical outlines disappear completely in the tradition behind the meaning that the event came to have for 'all Israel'. The tribal confederacy entered into the event of the exodus and the conquest. In the cultic realization the worshippers experienced the 'exodus from Egypt' and the 'entry into the promised land'. The Old Testament picture of history emerged in this communal experience of worship, which took place in the presence of Yahweh. This is how it came about that in the Pentateuchal tradition of the 'exodus from Egypt' the tradition of one group was extended to 'all Israel'. To interpret these developments in the light of the history of worship does not destroy the historical value of the narratives, but rather explains the cultic procedures which form the foundation of the Old

[113] The following contain indications of this viewpoint: H. W. Hertzberg, *Die Bücher Josua, Richter, Ruth*, ATD, 9 (1953), pp. 44 f.; J. Dus, 'Die Analyse zweier Ladeerzählungen des Josuabuches', *ZAW*, 72 (1960), p. 109. It should be noted in this connection that in ancient Israel army and congregation were basically identical. See A. Alt, 'Zelte und Hütten', *Kleine Schriften*, III, p. 241.

Testament understanding of history, procedures in which in the presence of Yahweh a sequence of events was compressed into an experience of direct actuality and significance which embraced the whole of Israel.

(d) *The Worship at Gilgal*

We must now try to see the detailed observations we have made concerning Joshua ii–vi in a wider context and clarify the problems that concern the history of worship.[114] In doing so we must first stress the important fact that the cultic community performed the whole Ark cult of Gilgal with its separate stations and various stages in a camp. The starting point was the camp to the east of the Jordan at Shittim (*tell el-hammam*). We are told this in Joshua iii. 1. Camp was then pitched at Gilgal, and this is mentioned in Joshua ix. 6 and x. 6. We must therefore presuppose the camp arrangement which we have already considered in another connection (pp. 128 ff. above) when considering the Gilgal cult.

To what period, however, should the cultic celebrations in the region of Gilgal be attributed? 'Period' here has to be taken in a twofold sense: to what period of the year and to what period in the history of Israel's worship does the Gilgal cult belong? We will consider first the question of the period of the year. As a result of later datings, which are to be traced either to the Priestly Code or to an editor who was dependent on the priestly chronology, the event of the crossing of the Jordan was fixed at the time of the feast of the Passover and of Unleavened Bread. The very fact that this date is fixed by reference to the time of the cult is essential for understanding the traditions. The traditions originating in the Gilgal sphere obviously contained enough indications to suggest a dating made with reference to the cultic calendar. Finally, the descriptions in the cultic legend point to the event described in Joshua v. 10–12:

> 'And the children of Israel encamped in Gilgal; and they kept the passover on the fourteenth day of the month at even in the plains of Jericho. And they did eat of the old corn of the land on the morrow after the passover, unleavened cakes and parched corn, in the self-same day. And the manna ceased on the morrow, after they had eaten of the old corn of the land; neither had the children of Israel manna any more; but they did eat of the fruit of the land of Canaan that year.'

This passage is of great importance for the study of the early history

[114] Cf. also H. Wildberger, *Jahwes Eigentumsvolk* (1960), pp. 55 ff.

of the feast of the Passover and of Unleavened Bread in the Old Testament, for it clarifies questions for which we could find no answer when we were considering the cultic calendar. We must begin, however, by separating two elements: the later dating in *v.* 10 ('on the fourteenth day of the month at even') and the reference in *v.* 12 to the cessation of the manna. Apart from these elements there are three important factors: (1) the reference to a Passover celebrated by the cultic community 'in the plains of Jericho', (2) the mention of the sacral eating of מצות and קלוי, (3) the evidence of a direct connection between the feast of the Passover and of Unleavened Bread in the cult at Gilgal. It would be a hasty and hardly justifiable conclusion to take the whole passage *vv.* 10–12 out of its context and to take it to be a secondary construction in view of the later dating in *v.* 10.[115] Noth has shown very clearly the archaic elements in these verses and pointed out the pre-Deuteronomistic character of the tradition.

Did Israel celebrate a communal Passover in the early period of its worship? In studying the development of the Passover the mistake that is always made is that of starting from the customs that can be found in Deut. xvi. 5 f. According to this evidence the Israelites, before Josiah's reform had led to the centralization of worship, had slain the Passover lamb in their villages and in their families. But is this view of things consistent with the situation in which the tribes of Israel found themselves in the early period? Should we not rather assume that the Israelites as they emerged from the semi-nomadic way of life in the period just after they had entered Palestine observed the Passover rite in the place to which it belonged by origin and by its very nature—i.e. in their tents? This immediately alters the current view of the history of worship—especially if the wider implications of the Gilgal cult and of the feast of the tribal confederacy which was celebrated in tents is taken into consideration. If in the first period after the settlement of the Israelite tribes the semi-nomadic way of life still influenced the amphictyony, it seems reasonable to suppose that in the series of festivals in the springtime the confederacy celebrated the journey out of the desert into Canaan and in the autumn the corresponding entry into the desert. The acts of worship centred upon Gilgal, therefore, are concerned with the entry into Canaan. If they were performed by 'all Israel', as the amphictyonic character of the traditions concerning the Ark and the

[115] This is what E. Kutsch does in his article 'Erwägungen zur Geschichte der Passafeier und des Massotfestes', *ZThK*, 55 (1958), pp. 20 f. Noth rightly points out in his commentary, on the other hand: 'Only the date in *v.* 10 (cf. Ezek. xlv. 20; Lev. xxiii. 5; Exod. xii. 6) and בעצם היום הזה in *v.* 11 come from P' (op. cit., p. 39).

'twelve stones' shows they were, then it is obvious that the feast of the Passover was celebrated in the framework of the tent festival of the families. It is only in this setting that the Passover legend could be given that 'historicizing' interpretation in the context of the cultic realization of the event of the exodus which moulded the traditions in Exod. xii. But we can also see clearly the place the eating of the unleavened bread had in the Gilgal cult. An ancient formula is used in Joshua v. 11 in the account of how the מצות and קלוי are devoutly eaten.[116] This eating of the unleavened bread is 'historicized' by means of the act of worship. The firstfruits of the fields were eaten in the 'promised land' into which they had just entered. Looked at from this angle, the 'historicizing' of the feast of Unleavened Bread in Exod. xxiii. 15 and xxxiv. 18 is not a secondary development but just a faint indication of the effect of the cultic setting. As far as the history of the feast of the Passover is concerned, this confirms the point that was made earlier (p. 51): when it is stated in 2 Kings xxiii. 22 that a feast of the Passover had not been observed for the whole of Israel 'from the days of the judges', this corresponds with the facts. In the early 'period of the judges' Israel had not yet broken with its semi-nomadic tradition, and the encampment at the feast times in spring and autumn was still a reality. In the period of the kings this archaic pattern disintegrated, and with the rise of the Temple worship the Passover rite came to be observed in the villages and families. Only the feast of Unleavened Bread was celebrated at the central sanctuary.

If there are clear indications that the Gilgal cult should be assigned to the springtime, the much more difficult question as to the historical position occupied by this act of worship has now to be faced. As the fact that the worshippers are in camps is mentioned a number of times, we must allow for a very early stage in the pre-monarchical period in Israel in trying to fix a date. On the other hand, the reference to the presence of the Ark at Gilgal raises the question at which period the central sanctuary in the neighbourhood of Jericho could have had the distinction of this presence of the ancient Israelite holy of holies. At the end of the period of the judges the Ark was at Shiloh,[117] and Shechem was evidently the central sanctuary in the early period, so when could Gilgal have been the amphictyonic cultic centre? Before Bethel? C. A. Keller, in his criticism of the cultic theory which concerns the worship at Gilgal, expresses the view that it is 'hardly conceivable that after the transfer of the amphictyonic centre from Shechem to

[116] Cf. M. Noth, op. cit., p. 39.
[117] Cf. 1 Sam. iii. 3; iv. 3 ff.

Gilgal . . . a cult drama of the exodus could have arisen, i.e. a complete rearrangement of the amphictyonic worship . . .'.[118] But what do we know about the origins of the ancient Israelite cult in its various forms? And the assumption that the central sanctuary at Shechem was displaced by Bethel, Gilgal and Shiloh is really only an attempt to reconstruct the development in the history of worship in accordance with the plain statements concerning the stations of the Ark. We shall have to consider later the question whether there were any other amphictyonic sanctuaries. Would it have been possible for different cults of the tribal confederacy to be maintained alongside each other? Is it really conceivable that the tent cult in particular which was observed in camp persisted as an independent institution alongside the worship of the Canaanite sanctuaries—until changed circumstances and the increasing assimilation of the settlers led to its abandonment? These questions simply cannot be answered. All we can do is to point out that in the tradition of 1 Samuel at any rate the high status of the cultic centre at Gilgal is presupposed.

The Ark tradition in the Gilgal narratives deserves special attention in this connection. It is surprising that in Joshua iii–v there is no mention of the 'sacred Tent', which—as we have already seen—elsewhere is part of the camp arrangement. This would suggest that we are really in the sphere of a sacral tradition in Canaan of which we have seen evidence elsewhere in the Old Testament. Joshua iii–v does, in fact, deal with the entrance into the promised land and with a tradition which points to the Gilgal cult. But what part is played by the Ark in this complex of traditions? There are three main aspects which we can pick out: (1) the guiding presence of Yahweh, which is directly connected with the Ark and which precedes the camp after it has broken up (cf. Num. x. 35 f.); (2) the significance of the shrine in the event of the 'holy war' as it is demonstrated in the cult (cf. again Num. x. 35 f.); (3) the character of the sacred Ark as a processional shrine. These three aspects appear time after time with varying emphasis in the Ark tradition.

We must turn finally to the strange passage in Deut. xi. 29 f. The text reads: 'And it shall come to pass, when the Lord thy God shall bring thee into the land whither thou goest to possess it, that thou shalt set the blessing upon mount Gerizim, and the curse upon mount Ebal. Are they not beyond Jordan, behind the way of the going down of the sun, in the land of the Canaanites which dwell in the Arabah, over against Gilgal, beside the oaks of Moreh?' If we examine these place references, one thing is clear—that Gilgal lies in the Jordan plain. But the reference to the mountains Ebal and Gerizim, which are supposed to rise in the

[118] C. A. Keller, *ZAW*, 68 (1956), p. 91.

immediate neighbourhood of Gilgal, is completely unintelligible. In an attempt to avoid the difficulty, it has been assumed that there was another Gilgal in the neighbourhood of Shechem besides the Gilgal situated on the Jordan plain.[119] But Deut. xi. 29 f. does indicate the Jordan plain. Is it therefore a case of a confused place reference which has no claim to credibility? We should not overlook the possibility that Deut. xi. 29 f. might indicate that a cultic transference of the ceremony that was localized in the region of Shechem took place to the district of Gilgal. We could then assume that the festival described in Deut. xxvii was observed in the neighbourhood of Gilgal after Shechem had ceased to be the central sanctuary, and that two mountains near to the new sanctuary took over the rôle of 'Ebal' and 'Gerizim'. However, this is only a supposition.

5. Israelite Cultic Centres in the Early Period

We must now look into the question whether there were any other sanctuaries in the early period which had significance for the whole of Israel alongside or apart from the amphictyonic centres of Shechem, Bethel and Gilgal with which we have already dealt and the centre at Shiloh which we have still to consider. It is only the local traditions of individual centres that can give us information. We shall therefore now turn to local traditions concerning mount Tabor and the cultic centres of Beersheba and Mizpah.

(a) *Mount Tabor*

The impressive dome of mount Tabor, *jebel eṭ-ṭor*, (1850 ft) rises on the southern edge of the lower Galilean range of hills, at the north-east corner of the plain of Jezreel.[120] In the early period of Israel's history this mountain was the meeting-point of several tribal territories. In Joshua xix. 22 Tabor is mentioned as the boundary of the territories of Issachar and Zebulun.[121] This imposing mountain top lent itself to being used as a high place for worship, and so Tabor appears in the

[119] A. Schlatter, *Zur Topographie Palästinas* (1893), pp. 246 ff.; E. Sellin, *Gilgal* (1917).

[120] Bibliography dealing with mount Tabor: O. Eissfeldt, 'Der Gott des Tabor und seine Verbreitung', *ARW*, 31 (1934), pp. 14 ff., reprinted in *Kleine Schriften*, II, pp. 29 ff.; J. Boehmer, 'Der Gottesberg Tabor', *BZ*, 23 (1935/6), pp. 333 ff.; J. Lewy, 'Tabor, Tibar, Atabyros', *HUCA*, 23 (1950/1), pp. 357 ff.; H.-J. Kraus, 'Die Kulttraditionen des Berges Thabor', *BASILEIA—Festschrift W. Freytag* (1959), pp. 177 ff. (The following section is a revised and abbreviated version of this essay.)

[121] Cf. M. Noth, *History of Israel*, pp. 66 f.

M

Old Testament tradition first of all as the border sanctuary for the tribes of Issachar and Zebulun. We read in Deut. xxxiii. 19:

> 'They shall call the peoples unto the mountain;
> There shall they offer sacrifices of righteousness . . .'

The cultic leaders, Zebulun and Naphtali, instituted sacrificial feasts on mount Tabor, to which—as was customary in the ancient world—'peoples', i.e., groups living in the neighbourhood, were invited.[122]

An important rôle was played by the sanctuary on mount Tabor when the tribes of Israel went out against Sisera. Barak, the charismatic leader of the army designated by the prophetess Deborah, was a member of the tribe of Naphtali (Judges iv. 6), and this tribe also bordered on the mountain sanctuary and took part in worship on mount Tabor. Before the military encounter Deborah commissioned Barak to ascend the holy mountain with a militia which had been summoned and assembled in Kedesh (iv. 6), and the expedition against Sisera was to begin from there. On Tabor Barak received the decisive word from God: 'This is the day in which the Lord hath delivered Sisera into thine hand: is not the Lord gone out before thee?' whereupon the army went down into the valley (iv. 14). The song of Deborah, which comes from a different source, also clearly belongs to the same context (v. 13, 14), but the list of the tribes that took part in the battle against Sisera makes it plain that not only Naphtali and Zebulun, but also other groups from the Israelite confederacy, went out from mount Tabor to do battle (v. 13 ff.). We might raise the question at this point, whether the border sanctuary of the tribes of Zebulun, Issachar and Naphtali ceased to be the sanctuary for particular tribes and became for a time an amphictyonic centre for the tribal confederacy.[123]

Of the few passages in which mount Tabor is mentioned in the Old Testament, Ps. lxxxix 13 and Jer. xlvi. 18 are of no significance for the history of worship. The words of the prophet in Hos. v. 1,[124] on the other hand, should be noted, for this passage shows that in the time of Hosea there were priests resident on mount Tabor whose function it was to preserve the law. This is an important piece of information. In Israel the task of transmitting and guarding the divine law was committed to the amphictyonic priesthood in particular. This means, therefore, that mount Tabor was not only a sacrificial sanctuary, but

[122] A fair was probably linked with the sacrificial festival. Cf. C. Steuernagel, *Das Deuteronomium*, pp. 178 ff.

[123] See A. Alt. 'Galiläische Probleme', *Kleine Schriften*, II, p. 404, note 4.

[124] Cf. H. W. Wolff, *Dodekapropheton*, BK, 14, pp. 122 ff.

also a place of the divine law. But the characteristic feature of Hosea's period was the fact that the priests on mount Tabor had reached a decadent stage, for they no longer served the divine law, but their own private interests.[125]

The possibility of discovering anything about the cultic traditions of mount Tabor from the Old Testament would be exhausted if it were not for the fact that there is in the Psalter a psalm of considerable length which—as we shall try to show—had its 'setting in life' on mount Tabor. The psalm concerned is Ps. lxviii, the interpretation of which has for a long time given rise to many problems. The period of historical interpretations, which produced a great variety of hypotheses, recently came to an end with the attempt to interpret the psalm in the light of the cult. This new approach has sometimes led to one-sided views which are often misleading, but in many cases it has not only shed light but has also discovered some surprising connections. Mowinckel in particular has tried to bring out the significance of the cultic festivals which underlie the Psalms,[126] and has devoted a special study to Ps. lxviii in which the idea was first expressed that this psalm might have had its 'setting in life' in the worship on mount Tabor. This line of thought is unfortunately only tentatively expounded, and needs to be pursued more thoroughly.[127] First of all there are two important points which seem to connect Ps. lxviii with the Tabor tradition in the Old Testament: (1) It was already recognized in the period of historical interpretation of Ps. lxviii that there are striking parallels between this psalm and the song of Deborah (Judges v). The ways in which Yahweh manifests Himself in Judges v. 4 f. and Ps. lxviii. 8 ff. correspond, and Ps. lxviii. 11 ff. has also been correctly interpreted by reference to the battle against Sisera. The psalm has therefore been spoken of as a 'song of victory', which breaks out in rejoicing over the destruction of Israel's enemies on the plain of Jezreel. The fact that mount Tabor, as we have already seen, was the starting point for the expedition against Sisera gives strong support to this linking of the two passages. (2) It is noticeable that in the description of a festival procession in Ps. lxviii. 27, of the tribes of Israel only Zebulun and Naphtali are mentioned along with Benjamin and Judah—in other words, the tribes whose border sanctuary was mount Tabor. These connections are significant and throw much

[125] A. Alt suggests that the fact that the northern region was annexed by Tiglath-Pileser III and brought under a new sphere of influence may have had something to do with the decline of the Tabor sanctuary.

[126] S. Mowinckel, *Der achtundsechzigste Psalm*, *ANVAO*, II, Hist.-Filos. Klasse (1953).

[127] Cf. H.-J. Kraus, *Psalmen*, BK, 15 (1960), pp. 464 ff.

light on Ps. lxviii, and it seems indisputable that the 'setting in life' of the psalm is to be sought on mount Tabor. There is one difficulty, however—the fact that Jerusalem is mentioned in Ps. lxviii. 29. We could—as has often been done in the past—ignore all the references to an earlier period and ascribe the whole psalm to the Jerusalem cult, but this would be a hasty conclusion to draw. There are important reasons for not localizing Ps. lxviii in Jerusalem.[128] The description of a solemn procession of the tribes in v. 27 begins with the words:

'There is little Benjamin their ruler'.

Was Benjamin the ruler at the time when Jerusalem was Israel's central sanctuary, and could the prerogatives of Benjamin have been explicitly referred to in a cultic tradition of Zion? This is impossible, for there are traces of the historical circumstances of the period before David. When Saul was king, the small tribe of Benjamin did have the privileges referred to in Ps. xxviii. 27. In addition, the description of the holy mountain, with the cultic tradition of which Ps. lxviii has to be connected, is very strange. There is no mention of Zion in *vv.* 15 f., but instead we read:

'A mountain of God is the mountain of Bashan;
An high mountain is the mountain of Bashan.
Why look ye askance, ye high mountains,
At the mountain which God hath desired for his abode?'

It is certain that in the Old Testament Zion is never called 'Bashan', and therefore the reference must be to some other mountain sanctuary. We do not know the meaning of the term 'Bashan'; it seems likely that it had nothing to do with the district of 'Bashan', but was probably a traditional name for the 'mountain of the gods', mount Olympus. Taken in this sense the term 'Bashan' would correspond to the ancient Syrian name 'Zaphon' used to describe the mountain of the gods.[129] We must note finally, however, that the metre and form of *vv.* 29 ff. provide grounds for believing that these verses are a later interpolation into an older psalm. This helps to explain the reference to Jerusalem in *v.* 30: an older psalm, thoroughly northern Israelite in its traditions and cultic connections, was adopted and expanded in Jerusalem at a later period, after the collapse of the northern kingdom.

If we are correct in our view that Ps. lxviii enshrines the cultic traditions of mount Tabor, we must consider the question whether a

[128] Cf. H.-J. Kraus, *Psalmen*, BK, 15 (1960), pp. 476 f.

[129] Cf. O. Eissfeldt, *Baal Zaphon, Zeus Kasios und der Durchzug der Israeliten durchs Meer* (1932); W. F. Albright, 'Baal Zaphon', *Festschrift A. Bertholet* (1950), p. 1 ff.

psalm as long and rich in content as this one reflects an earlier stratum of religious and sacral traditions. We must first ask whether behind the specifically Israelite traditions (the expedition against Sisera, the sacrificial sanctuary on the tribal border, the description of a theophany) there are any traces of still older, Canaanite cultic traditions which were adopted and subjected to an inner transformation by the tribal confederacy or even by the association of the three neighbouring tribes. Ancient Canaanite and Syrian texts, in particular the cultic remains from Ras Shamra, make it possible for us to trace the pre-Israelite religious elements in Ps. lxviii. There were mountain sanctuaries in Canaan which towered above the smaller high places devoted to sacrifice and worship. Mount Zaphon, situated to the north of Ugarit, was called simply the 'highest mountain', or the 'mountain of the gods'.[130] This predominance of an outstanding cultic mountain is emphasized also in Ps. lxviii. 15 f. The deity of this 'highest mountain' occupied a position of monarchical dominance in the pantheon of the gods, and was שדי (Ps. lxviii. 14). There is an echo here of a primitive Canaanite name for God, which we can see in the one who 'rides upon the clouds' (Ps. lxviii. 4-*rkb ᶜrpt* in Ugaritic).[131] It refers to the 'sky god' who rides on a chariot in the clouds (Ps. lxviii. 17, 33) and sends the fruitful rain (Ps. lxviii. 9). All these statements describe basically the Syrian-Canaanite deity Baal—the 'heavenly Baal' who in the vegetation cult conquered the god of drought and of death (*mōt*, Ps. lxviii. 18) at the beginning of the rainy period, scattered all his enemies (Ps. lxviii. 1) and ascended from the underworld and from the depths to which he had been banished into the height of heaven (Ps. lxviii. 18). This whole action, the victory over the enemies of Baal and over the forces of death was ceremonially celebrated in the cult. Ps. lxviii. 1 f. and also Judges v. 31 recall the rejoicing over Baal which we find in the ancient Ugaritic texts—'Lo, thine enemies, O Baal; lo, thou shalt scatter thine enemies, thou shalt destroy thine adversaries'. This background of cultic myth is also reflected in the late Greek texts, which speak of a 'Baal-Tabor' and so undoubtedly preserve in this name the ancient Canaanite local tradition. But these pre-Israelite traditions are interesting and instructive not only from the point of view of the history of religion, for they also help us to understand the special way in which Israel adopted and transformed existing cultic traditions. We know from numerous

[130] Cf. B. Alfrink, 'Der Versammlungsberg im äussersten Norden', *Biblica*, 14 (1933), pp. 41 ff.

[131] Cf. I AB II, 7; V AB D, 49; II AB III, 11, etc., and see C. H. Gordon, *Ugaritic Handbook*, III (1947), Nr. 1869.

examples that Israel did not simply reject pagan traditions and make a fresh start in sacral matters. By a keen and often very protracted struggle the faith of the people of God penetrated the alien cults, deprived them of their springs of religious life and gave them new forms of expression, which could bear witness to the revelation of Yahweh, the 'God of Israel'. In this process new aspects of Yahweh and his authority and new manifestations of his power were constantly discovered. This leads us to the question as to how this process of radically transforming alien religious traditions was carried out on mount Tabor.

The Canaanite fertility deity, Baal, rose each year from the realm of the dead to the height of heaven and became the 'highest god' who bestowed all blessings. In the cult the fertility myth was brought to dramatic life and activity. But a new force takes over this framework and displaces what was at the heart of the cultic myth. The cultic celebration on mount Tabor is directed to Yahweh, the God of Israel. He ascends to the height of heaven as the 'highest god', and it is his victorious ascent that is celebrated: but Yahweh does not come from the realm of the dead. The psalmist begins with the words:

> 'O God, when thou wentest forth before thy people,
> When thou didst march through the wilderness;
> The earth trembled,
> The heavens also dropped at the presence of God:
> Even yon Sinai trembled at the presence of God, the God of Israel'
> (*vv.* 7 f.).

The event of the revelation on Sinai and the exodus from Egypt is the 'place' from which Yahweh comes. He has performed saving acts, and these events in history take the place of the mythical abyss from which Baal emerges. In this way the whole dualism of Baal and Mot, which is based on the natural cycle, is destroyed. The God who bestows fertility and blessing comes from Sinai. It is very striking to see the way in which the gift of rain on which all life depends is brought about directly by the theophany of the God who approaches from Sinai (*v.* 9). The whole world of mythical spheres, of conflict between the gods in the abyss and of times of renewal experienced by man in fear and trembling disappears before the unique approach and manifestation of Yahweh (*vv.* 17 f.). From the point of view of the history of tradition it is remarkable what significance the Sinai event has in the cultic tradition of mount Tabor. The 'idea of appearing' which we find in the Canaanite cult led to a transformation of the traditional Old Testament view. Other cultic centres in Israel of which we hear in the Old Testament are dominated by the certainty that Yahweh is present: He 'dwells' or 'reigns' in the sanctuary. This idea of Yahweh's dwelling is clearly expressed in Jerusalem especially. The worship at mount Tabor, on the other hand, is dominated by the belief that Yahweh who reigns on Sinai 'comes' from there and 'appears' in his chosen sanctuary (Ps. lxviii. 7 f.; Judges v. 4 f.). In other words, the cultic community celebrates repeatedly the advent and—linked with the 'coming' and 'appearing' of Yahweh—the ascension of its God (Ps. lxviii. 18), who holds all power in his hands. By its attack upon Baal worship and at the same time by its penetration and transformation of the mythical forms of theophany, the worship of Israel proclaims at this pagan centre the true 'king of heaven'. In northern Israel this cultic tradition exercised a great influence. There were times when Yahweh was 'far away', but Elijah went to Horeb because he could be certain there of the *deus praesens* (1 Kings xix).

There is still another element in Israelite worship to be noted in the Tabor tradition. On mount Tabor the traditions of conflict and victory in the battle against Sisera found their permanent deposit. The mighty manifestations of the God who reveals himself became part of the cultic traditions of this mountain sanctuary on the edge of the plain of Jezreel (Judges v. 4 f.). There seems good reason, therefore, for seeing in Ps. lxviii. 11–13 a prophetic message which urged into battle the militia assembled at mount Tabor. This word from God is archaic and mysterious in its proclamation of victory and of the flight of the enemy kings.

We must refer finally to the course followed by the festival. A solemn procession of the worshippers had probably been held on mount Tabor for a long time. In the ancient Canaanite period they climbed up with Baal and in this way accomplished the ascent, the ascension to heaven; but in the Old Testament this ascent is directed entirely to Yahweh and his presence.

> 'They have seen thy goings, O God,
> Even the goings of my God, my King, into the sanctuary.
> The singers went before, the minstrels followed after,
> In the midst of the damsels playing with timbrels.
> Bless ye God in the congregations,
> Even the Lord, ye that are of the fountain of Israel' (*vv.* 24 ff.).

This festival probably corresponded to a large extent to the ancient Baal worship in the external liturgical course that it followed. Thus, for example, the procession no doubt fitted into the traditional pattern, but the heart of it was changed. The appearing of Yahweh drove out the very last remains of mythical elements and forces. All hopes of life and blessings were directed to him alone. The rejoicing was for the God of Israel, and the community sang its songs to him.

It is difficult to fit the cultic traditions of mount Tabor into the history of Old Testament worship. Here again we have to ask whether alongside the great central sanctuaries of the tribal confederacy which were distinguished by the presence of the Ark there were possibly other cultic centres at which Israel gathered. The reference in Ps. lxviii. 27 to the prerogative of the tribe of Benjamin is significant and suggests the time of Saul.

(b) *Beersheba*

In his study *Geschichte und Tradition von Beerseba im Alten Testament* (1932) W. Zimmerli examined the local traditions connected with this sanctuary situated in the south of Palestine, and also touched upon the cultic aspects. We shall mention here just some of these aspects.

Beersheba (*bīr es-seba'*) is mentioned in the Old Testament for the first time in connection with the story of the patriarchs. The Isaac tradition should no doubt be localized at this centre (Gen. xxi. 22 ff.; xxvi. 23 ff.; xlvi. 1 ff.). Although Abraham counts as the actual founder of the cult (Gen. xxi. 33), we have to assume that the pre-Israelite *hieros logos* was claimed primarily by Isaac. The holy place was marked by a tamarisk tree and an altar (Gen. xxi. 33; xxvi. 25), and sacrifices were offered (xlvi. 1). The Beersheba tradition, however, does not only clearly show the way in which the patriarchs of Israel were incorporated into the Canaanite cultic legends, but it also indicates the key position that the sanctuary came to hold in the process of amalgamating the traditions concerning the patriarchs. The sanctuary possessed not only a particular, geographically limited influence, but was a centre of outstanding importance for the whole of Israel.

When we read that the sons of Samuel 'were judges' in Beersheba (1 Sam. viii. 2) we could assume that this does not imply any special position for the southern sanctuary, and that at the time of the Philistine threat holy places were visited which were far enough away to be safe from direct attack and from the surveillance of the foreign power. But we must bear in mind that around the middle of the eighth century the sanctuary of Beersheba was a popular goal of religious pilgrimage, along with Bethel and Gilgal. If these pilgrimages were directed to the ancient cultic centres of the Yahweh amphictyony, which they certainly were in the case of Bethel and Gilgal, then it is possible that Beersheba also played an important part in the period before the monarchy (cf. Amos v. 5; viii. 14).

(c) *Mizpah*

Mizpah (probably: *tell en-naṣbe*) was another place which held an outstanding position in the tribal confederacy in the pre-monarchical period.[132] We are told in Judges xx. 1 ff. that an assembly of the whole confederacy was held at Mizpah on the occasion of a dispute between the Yahweh amphictyony and the recalcitrant tribe of Benjamin. Noth states: 'because Mizpah was nearest to the scene of the crime'.[133] But is this view correct? In the first place, it is noticeable with what emphasis the great tribal gathering at Mizpah is spoken of several times in Judges xxi. 1, 5, 8, but even more significant is the information we are given in 1 Sam. vii. 5–16. Samuel called all the people to assemble at Mizpah and ordered a great cultic fast (1 Sam. vii. 5–7). In accordance with an ancient rite, water was drawn and poured out, as a sign of mourning and repentance.[134] There is merely an indication in the text of the lament: 'We have sinned against the Lord.' But Mizpah appears in tradition not only as a centre of cultic lament, but also as a place where judgement is pronounced (1 Sam. vii. 16). It is quite in keeping with the picture we have outlined when we are told once again in 1 Sam. x. 17 that Samuel brought the people together at Mizpah. It seems reasonable to conclude from all these indications, therefore, that there was a Yahweh sanctuary also at Mizpah, which was of significance for the whole of Israel.[135]

6. Shiloh

(a) *The Worship at Shiloh*

At the end of the period of the judges Shiloh (*chirbet sēlūn*) was the central Israelite sanctuary.[136] The relatively rich traditions concerning this cultic centre which have come down to us are indissolubly connected with the name of Samuel, the man of God, but we receive valuable information about worship at Shiloh also from Judges xxi. 19 ff. and

[132] Bibliography dealing with Mizpah: H. W. Hertzberg, 'Mizpa', *ZAW*, 47 (1929), pp. 161 ff.; C. C. McCown/J. C. Wampler, *Tell en-Nasbeh Excavated Under the Direction of the Late William Frederic Badé*, I/II (1947); A. Alt, 'Studien aus dem Deutschen evangelischen Institut für Altertumswissenschaft 48, Neue Erwägungen über die Lage von Mizpa, Beeroth und Gibeon', *ZDPV*, 69 (1953), pp. 1 ff.

[133] M. Noth, *History of Israel*, p. 105.

[134] H. Gunkel/J. Begrich, *Einleitung in die Psalmen* (1933), pp. 117 ff.

[135] For the significance of Mizpah in later times, see Jer. xl. 1 and 1 Macc. iii. 46.

[136] On the question of the topography, see H. Kjaer, 'The Excavation of Shilo, 1929', *JPOS*, 10 (1930), pp. 87 ff.; ibid., *I det hellige land. De Danske udgravninger i Shilo* (1931).

from the wider context of the Ark narrative.[137] In Judges xxi. 19 ff., for example, there is a description of an autumnal festival that was held annually in the area of the sanctuary: 'Behold, there is a feast of the Lord from year to year in Shiloh, which is on the north of Bethel, on the east side of the high way that goeth up from Bethel to Shechem, and on the south of Lebonah.' חַג־יהוה is the autumnal festival. There is an account in *v.* 21 of the Israelite practices in connection with the feast at Shiloh. The customs were obviously taken over from the Canaanite population (cf. Judges ix. 27). The daughters of Shiloh went out into the fields and danced in the vineyards.[138] In the fertility cult dances were a sacral expression of life; in the words of van der Leeuw, the dance 'is the service of the god, and generates power: the rhythm of movement has a compelling force'.[139] Ecstatic dancing set power in motion, expressed it and brought it into contact with the spirit world. These rites were taken over unaltered into the worship of Yahweh. We can see from this aspect alone how much the worship at Shiloh was affected by nature worship. The autumnal festival was marked by ecstatic celebrations and exultant rejoicing over the harvest. It is, of course, justifiable to wonder whether the customs of which we read in Judges xxi. 19 ff. were not merely a marginal accompaniment to the actual worship of Yahweh. But we should not overlook the fact that such festivals are influenced for the most part by their peripheral elements—as still happens today—whereas the central observances are maintained to a lesser degree. The traditional custom has a power of its own—especially when it has established itself around the central manifestations of the worship of Yahweh and is threatening to undermine what is now at the centre.

For the autumnal festival the tribes of Israel went on pilgrimage every year to the central sanctuary at Shiloh. Although in the earliest period the cultic community was identical with the fighting men, we learn from 1 Sam. i that women had access to the holy place. The pilgrims sought 'to worship and to sacrifice' (1 Sam. i. 3). הִשְׁתַּחֲוֺת refers in the first place to adoration, to obeisance before the *deus praesens*, but also to the requests by which men made their needs known to Yahweh (i. 9 f.). Prayers were offered early in the morning (i. 19), for this time was believed to be the most effective, when one could expect God's answer and God's help (Ps. v. 3; xlvi. 5).[140] Vows were made at the same time

137 On the Ark narrative, cf. L. Rost, *Die Überlieferung von der Thronnachfolge Davids*, BWANT, III, 6 (1926), pp. 4 ff., *Das kleine Credo*, pp. 119 ff.

138 See R. Kittel, *Geschichte des Volkes Israel*, I (5 and 6 ed., 1923), pp. 201 f.

139 G. van der Leeuw, *Religion in Essence and Manifestation* (1938), p. 374.

140 Cf. J. Ziegler, 'Die Hilfe Gottes "am Morgen"', *Festschrift F. Nötscher* (1950), pp. 281 ff.

as the requests (1 Sam. i. 11). 'All the Israelites' sacrificed each year at the holy place (ii. 14) and offered זבח הימים (ii. 19). The father of the family killed the animal (i. 4), which was cooked in cauldrons under the supervision of the priests and then eaten by the worshippers in groups (ii. 12 ff.). As was customary at a זבח the pieces of fat were burned as an offering to Yahweh (ii. 15), with whom the meal was therefore shared, so that the worshippers entered into a *communio* with Him (see pp. 118 ff. above). But gift offerings were also presented to the God of Israel at the holy place. When a request was heard, the votive offering had to be presented to Yahweh (i. 24). As was customary in the earliest times, the gift offering consisted of a bullock, meal and wine (i. 24). A 'full meal offering' was presented and made a burnt offering (Judges vi. 18 ff.; xiii. 19 ff.).

The chief priest Eli supervised with great care all the cultic observances, sitting on a seat 'by the door post of the temple' and watching to see that there was no drunkenness (1 Sam. i. 9, 14). He declared to the supplicants the 'priestly oracle of blessing': 'Go in peace, and the God of Israel grant thy petition that thou hast asked of him' (i. 17).[141] The 'sons of Eli' exercised priestly duties together with the chief priest, and their particular task was to be responsible for the sacrifices (ii. 12 ff.). Youths who had been dedicated served in the temple, wore an 'ephod'[142] and spent nights before the sanctuary of the Ark in expectation of an 'incubation oracle' (ii. 11, 18; iii. 3). The narratives make plain, however, how great a moral decline had taken place at Shiloh. The righteous Eli was too old to put a stop any longer to the undisciplined behaviour of his 'sons', and whilst he himself conscientiously fulfilled his functions as chief priest, they did not care about the sacral order. They disregarded the holiness of what was sacrificed to Yahweh and were only concerned in their greed with their own advantage (ii. 12 ff.). There is an indication in 1 Sam. ii. 22 that the Canaanite practice of temple

141 Cf. F. Küchler, 'Das priesterliche Orakel in Israel und Juda: Abhandlungen zur semitischen Religionskunde und Sprachwissenschaft', *Festschrift Baudissin* (1918), pp. 285 ff.; J. Begrich, 'Das priesterliche Heilsorakel', *ZAW*, 52 (1934), pp. 81 ff., *Ges. Stud.*, pp. 217 ff.

142 O. Proksch states in connection with the meaning of the 'ephod': 'Perhaps it was thought of as the garment of the deity, under the cover of which the priest was endowed with magical power' (*Theologie des Alten Testaments* (1950), p. 109). G. von Rad points out that in Judges viii. 26 f. the 'ephod' is spoken of as something made of metal, but that in Exod. xxviii. 4 ff., 1 Sam. xxii. 18 and 2 Sam. vi. 14 it is made of linen. Perhaps the 'ephod' was originally 'a cuirass-like metal covering put upon a wooden pillar or an image of the deity. . . . But it could also be a woven garment which the priest put on . . . when he gave oracles and acted as the mouthpiece of the deity' (*Old Testament Theology*, I, p. 24).

prostitution had also crept in. The last of the great central sanctuaries of Israel in the pre-monarchical period had thus grown inwardly corrupt and been perverted by nature worship.

There was a temple at Shiloh. Even if we can assume that the holy place at Bethel was marked by a sacral building, it is in the Shiloh traditions that we find the first explicit evidence that the Ark of the Lord was accommodated in a 'house'. We can only surmise what subsequent changes were connected with an institution of this kind. The temple was the highest expression of the worship that was native to Canaan. Its sacral architecture suggested certain conceptions of a spatial kind and imposed tasks and duties upon the cultic officials which were fundamentally alien to the Israelites. The sacrificial cult gained in importance and moulded the religious observances, whilst prophecy and the divine law fell into the background (1 Sam. iii. 1), and therefore the tradition sees in the destruction of the temple sanctuary of Shiloh by the Philistines the well-deserved judgement of Yahweh upon the disastrous deviations in worship (Jer. vii. 12–14; xxvi. 9; Ps. lxxviii. 60).

In a few passages in the Old Testament we are given the strange information that the 'sacred Tent' was at Shiloh (1 Sam. ii. 22; Joshua xviii. 1; xix. 51), but it is not clear how we should interpret these statements. Noth holds the view that in Joshua xviii. 1 there is 'an element of "priestly" revision'[143], and in connection with 1 Sam. ii. 22 H. W. Hertzberg declares: 'This verse—missing in the Codex Vaticanus—which could have been added later from another tradition, is modelled on Exod. xxxviii. 8.'[144] These attempts to clarify these peculiar circumstances are very sound and reasonable, but the question still arises whether the 'sacred Tent', as a venerable relic of Israel's early cultic history, might not have had its place at what was for the time being a fixed local sanctuary. It is still strange, however, that such a widely different conception as that of the sojourn of the 'sacred Tent' could persist alongside the familiar tradition concerning the temple at Shiloh.

No less strange is the fact that mention is made in Joshua xviii. 10 and xix. 51 of the sacral 'lot'. At the cultic act of dividing the land lots were cast and the portions of land were allocated to the tribes, clans and families. A regularly recurring sacral procedure of this kind was only possible at a time when the Israelite groups were emerging from the semi-nomadic way of life and were not yet fully established in the country.[145] The view that the place at which according to Old Testament

[143] M. Noth, *Das Buch Josua*, p. 108.
[144] H. W. Hertzberg, *Die Samuelbücher*, ATD, 10 (1956), p. 23.
[145] Cf. A. Alt. 'Die Ursprünge des israelitischen Rechts', *Kleine Schriften*, I, p. 328.

tradition such procedures took place was Gilgal is therefore correct,[146] for it is hard to envisage it at the historical stage represented by the worship at Shiloh. But how can we explain this phenomenon of 'transference' from Gilgal to Shiloh? Is it a case of deliberate literary interpolation, or should we not rather assume that the traditions concerning the 'sacral lot' associated with Israel's central sanctuary came with the Ark from Gilgal to Shiloh? The lists and documents in which the division of the land was set down no doubt belonged to the amphictyonic cultic centre of the time. Why could not the centre at Shiloh have left its mark upon the tradition? The question we must finally consider is what interest later circles could have had in interpolating into what had been handed down the reference to a sanctuary which had been destroyed and which stood under the curse of Yahweh.

(b) *The Fate of the Ark*

The Ark of the Lord stood in the temple at Shiloh. We learn something of the fact and the significance of this sacred cultic object in a tradition which is to be taken as a *hieros logos* of the Ark sanctuary of Jerusalem.[147] The extensive narrative covers a period of time the beginning of which coincides with the stationing of the Ark at Shiloh, and the end with its removal to Jerusalem. But there are references to the Ark in 1 Sam. iii. 1 ff. as well. The sources provide a very clear and vivid picture. At Shiloh the Ark was the sign of Yahweh's presence, to which worship and petitions were addressed (1 Sam. i. 3, 9 f.), but from the Ark there also came forth the mysterious call and the word that was perceived by those endowed with the prophetic gift (1 Sam. iii. 3 ff.). It was the throne of the יהוה צבאות ישב הכרבים (1 Sam. iv. 4; 2 Sam. vi. 2).[148] The holy God was present above the sacred object, before whose overwhelming majesty and mighty transcendence no man could stand (1 Sam. vi. 20). The כבוד of God was present with the Ark (1 Sam. iv. 21). The sacred object, however, was not only the throne of the *deus praesens* who was revered in worship, but it was also carried out as a palladium into battle when war was being waged for sacral motives (1 Sam. iv. 3). The cultic symbol was welcomed with תרועה, with a resounding shout of joy (1 Sam. iv. 5).[149] Wherever the Ark appeared,

[146] M. Noth, op. cit., p. 108; G. von Rad, *Das formgeschichtliche Problem des Hexateuch*, pp. 41 f., *Ges. Stud.*, pp. 53 f.

[147] Cf. L. Rost, *Die Überlieferung von der Thronnachfolge Davids*, BWANT, III, 6 (1926), pp. 4 ff., *Das kleine Credo . . .*, pp. 122 ff.; also O. Eissfeldt, 'Silo und Jerusalem', *VT*, Supp. 4 (1957), pp. 138 ff.

[148] See esp. M. Dibelius, *Die Lade Jahves* (1906).

[149] Cf. P. Humbert, *TEROU'A—Analyse d'un rite biblique* (1946).

it was received with joy and with fear (1 Sam. vi. 13; 2 Sam. vi. 9), and burnt offerings and peace offerings were presented (1 Sam. vi. 14, 15).

When the Philistines attacked, the holy of holies fell into the hands of the foreign army (1 Sam. iv. 11) and was housed in the temple of Dagon, but even in the country of the Philistines Yahweh demanded His honour (1 Sam. vi. 5). The Ark narrative lays great emphasis on the fact that the God of Israel was always present over His Divine throne and manifested His power even in a foreign land—whilst the tribal confederacy was being defeated as a judgement. The Philistines had to send the Ark back, and it came first to Beth-shemesh (1 Sam. vi. 12) and then to Kiriath-jearim (vi. 21). We can trace in 1 Sam. vi. 7 f., 14 f. and 2 Sam. vi. 3 ff. the ceremony for the transportation of the sacred cultic object,[150] but it is difficult to tell what the meaning of the rite was. It was probably expected that Yahweh would direct the draught animals in the way He chose for them to go and that He would determine the place where His throne should be housed. The 'chosen place' was evidently designated by a Divine choice. It is doubtful whether we can draw from this ceremony any far-reaching conclusions concerning a process of choice which was periodically carried out in pre-monarchical times.[151] We cannot be sure what the regulations and presuppositions were by which a change of place of the Ark sanctuary was brought about.

During the time of the Philistine conflicts and the supremacy of Saul the Ark at Kiriath-Jearim played an insignificant part in the cultic life of Israel. As the Philistines no doubt supervised and imposed restrictions on all the central institutions and procedures of the tribal confederacy, Samuel in person was the ruler of the amphictyony as he went from place to place and was consulted in his home town. It was not until the rise of David that the Ark came back to the centre of Israel's worship.

[150] J. Dus, 'Der Brauch der Ladewanderung im alten Israel', *ThZ Basel*, 17 (1961), pp. 1 ff.

[151] When Dus states (op. cit., p. 3), 'The migration of the Ark takes place every seven years', and supports this view by 'allusions' to the year of release in 2 Sam vi. 6, we can only describe these interpretations as very questionable.

CHAPTER FIVE

THE CULTIC TRADITIONS OF JERUSALEM

1. The Institution of the Official Cult

(a) *The Election of David*

The episode of Saul's reign in Israel had no decisive influence on the worship of the tribal confederacy. The monarchy was on the one hand still strongly attached to the charismatic leadership of the amphictyony, for the presuppositions for the elevation of the ruler lay in the designation, in the 'election' sanctioned by Samuel. On the other hand, the procedure of acclamation, by which the tribes or the elders conferred the monarchy upon Saul, could not yet substitute any other sacral foundation.[1] M. Noth rightly states in connection with the act of choice and appointment of the charismatic leader to be the ruler of Israel: 'Though it took place in the sanctuary and in an atmosphere of religious consecration, the ceremony was not really a sacral rite like the appointment of a charismatic leader, but rather a political act. Israel was acting as a "people", no longer as a racial confederation of tribes.'[2] The spontaneous act of elevation to the monarchy, as a result of political necessity, could not be harmonized with the traditional cultic, sacral institutions which were at the heart of the life of the community in ancient Israel. It was therefore just the logical outcome when Saul made the mistake of not respecting the sacral institutions (1 Sam. xv) and of interpreting the authority of his office to mean, among other things, that he could behave like a despot after the victory over the Amalakites (1 Sam. xv. 12). His presumption was so great that Samuel felt obliged to deprive the ruler once again of the charismatic foundation of his royal status. When the Old Testament tradition tells us that the 'spirit of Yahweh' departed from Saul (1 Sam. xvi. 14), this event is unquestionably based upon the 'rejection' (1 Sam. xvi. 1), i.e., upon the official withdrawal of the charismatic gift by Samuel. The moving stories which tell of the tortured king overwhelmed with melancholy and the delusion of being persecuted show us a man who has lost the charismatic basis of the gift of רוּח and has now lost his bearings by being at the mercy of a royal status that is no longer supported and protected by a sacral order. Israel's first attempts to establish a stable political order failed on account

[1] Cf. A. Alt, 'Die Staatenbildung der Israeliten in Palästina', *Kleine Schriften*, II, pp. 1 ff.; W. Beyerlin, 'Das Königscharisma bei Saul', *ZAW*, 73 (1961), pp. 186 ff.
[2] M. Noth, *History of Israel*, p. 171.

of the lack of a sound cultic and sacral foundation for its kingship. As we consider these events we can see quite clearly that the tribal confederacy had no connections with the basis of cultic myth on which the institution of kingship customarily rested in Canaan. The slender basis of a charismatic endowment was the only contribution that the Yahweh amphictyony could make to this institution governed by new laws and political influences. But this basis collapsed as the monarchy grew and developed. It is almost incredible to see how certain scholars have ignored these historical facts and introduced into Israel the idea of a sacral and mythical kingship, in complete disregard of the Old Testament traditions. We must start from the fact 'that the knowledge of the historical course of the procedure by which the State was formed was preserved in Israel, and also the knowledge that the institution of the monarchy was not originally part of Israel's life, but that it emerged only at a quite advanced stage in Israelite history, and then through the initiative of the "people" or of their "elders".'[3] This shows clearly the limit to which the 'pattern' of the 'Divine Kingship' idea can be applied.[4]

David's royal power rested at first on simple treaties which sought to bring about a new ordering of things in Judah and Israel in times of political decline and complete disorder.[5] It was only at a secondary stage that David's covenant monarchy was given the support of the sacral foundation of the divine election by means of a prophetic utterance. The message of the prophet Nathan promised the ruler and his dynasty an 'eternal kingship'. 2 Sam. vii, which gives an account of the decisive prophetic message, is extraordinarily complex and difficult to analyse.[6] We can probably take *vv.* 11b and 16 as the oldest elements which go back to the time of David. Later traditions have gathered around this core and have expounded and heightened this divine word. But what was the significance of Nathan's message as regards the sacral foundations of the institution? What bearing had the fact that David was the object of Yahweh's 'election' and 'promise' upon Israel's cultic life?[7] In 'David's last words' (2 Sam. xxiii. 1 ff.), a very ancient document

[3] M Noth, 'Gott, König, Volk im Alten Testament', *ZThK*, 47 (1950), p. 178.

[4] It is surprising that the important observations by Noth in *ZThK*, 47 (1950), pp. 157 ff., reprinted in *Ges. Stud. zum AT*, pp. 188 ff., were not taken into account in the Old Testament essays contributed to the volume *Myth, Ritual and Kingship* (1958), edited by S. H. Hooke.

[5] Cf. 2 Sam. ii. 4 and v. 3.

[6] See L. Rost, *Die Überlieferung von der Thronnachfolge Davids*, BWANT, III, (1926), pp. 47 ff., *Das kleine Credo . . .*, pp. 159 ff.

[7] The 'election' of David is stressed in the following passages: 2 Sam. vi. 21; 1 Kings viii. 16 (2 Chron. vi. 5); 1 Kings xi. 34; Ps. lxxviii. 70. The 'promise' is expressed in the typical phrase חסדי דוד: Ps. xxi. 8; lxxxix. 25, 29, 34; Isa. lv. 3.

the essentials of which probably go back to David himself, the relationship between God and the king is described as a ברית (*v.* 5). This phrase brings to light this important fact: David's covenant kingship over Judah and Israel received by means of the prophetic message the sacral basis of a Yahweh ברית (cf. also Ps. cxxxii. 11; Jer. xxxiii. 21). Here we can see the essential difference between David's rule and that of the Benjaminite Saul. The charismatic designation of Saul was valid according to the amphictyonic sacral order only for the time of the emergency. The acclamation of the people then added an alien political institution to this gift of power that could not be bequeathed. But David was appointed to a permanent ברית of royal authority by the prophetic utterance; Nathan's prophecy embraced the whole political institution with the divine promise and transposed it into a relationship of homage and obligation that emanated from Yahweh. Whereas the God of Israel was the ruler of his people in the sacral tribal confederacy, in the royal ברית David now exercised the function of a chosen representative of this Divine rule in the State.

We can tell from the 'royal psalms', in which the 'covenant' with David determines all that is said about the ruler, what a great influence this decisive development in the idea of kingship had in the Jerusalem cult (Ps. lxxxix. 3 ff.; cxxxii. 12). The descendants of David are described as 'kings of Yahweh' (Ps. ii. 6; xviii. 50). The mythical and sacral themes of the ancient Oriental court culture are a secondary addition to the prophetic and historical event of the election of David.[8] Elements of the courtly style and of the royal ideology of their neighbours were certainly adopted in Israel, but they were refashioned in a remarkable way. Thus, for example, in Jerusalem the relationship between God and the king was thought of in terms of adoption (Ps. ii. 7; cx. 3); but the mythical ideas of the *hieros gamos* and of the divine birth of the ruler were excluded. The king was declared to be the 'son of God' by an authoritative word of the prophet. These references to the Psalms give an illustration of the way in which the historical and prophetic election of David became the main basis of the cult in Jerusalem and of the way in which the mythical elements were transformed in the light of these presuppositions.

(b) *The Election of Jerusalem*

After David had conquered the Jebusite city of Jerusalem and the king's own city state had been made the capital of the dual kingdom of Judah and Israel, the task facing the king was that of restoring the central Israelite sanctuary which had collapsed with the fall of Shiloh and to

[8] Cf. H.-J. Kraus *Psalmen*, BK, 15 (1960), pp. lxviii ff.

revive it in the form of a State cult. The *hieros logos* of the Jerusalem Ark narrative depicts the course of events.[9] The king had the ancient Israelite central shrine brought from its long absence at Kiriath-Jearim to Jerusalem. This was an act of the greatest importance. By its installation in the city of David the Ark elevated Jerusalem to the status of an amphictyonic cultic centre and brought the ancient Israelite traditions and institutions of the tribal confederacy to the 'chosen place'.[10] The *hieros logos* evidently intends to make it plain that the cultic history of Jerusalem is linked with the latest station of the Ark, at Shiloh. We can well imagine that the Ark narrative had a great importance as the basic document concerning the election of Jerusalem and was passed on to the pilgrims and expounded by the priests as evidence of the amphictyonic status of the new sanctuary. Difficulties arose over one important point: David had transferred the Ark to the capital on his own authority. This was certainly something absolutely new for the amphictyonic sacral law. We might explain it by saying that the ceremony that is mentioned in 2 Sam. vi. 3 ff. of a free choice of place by the God who is enthroned above the Ark is meant to stress beyond any shadow of doubt that Yahweh, and Yahweh alone, has 'chosen' Jerusalem (cf. 1 Sam. vi. 7 ff., 13 ff.). But, of course, everybody knew that David, who had elevated Jerusalem to be the royal city, had played a major part also in the establishment of the official sanctuary and therefore in the transference of the Ark. But who had authorized David to carry out an act which affected the sacral life of the tribal confederacy so deeply? The reference to the king's achievement in having 'restored the honour' of the Ark probably carried little weight in view of the conservative cultic institutions. Appeal therefore had to be made to the sacral basis of kingship, which was invested with the highest and most embracing authority. This means that in the long run the election of Jerusalem could be explained and justified only by the election of David. We can see clearly from 2 Sam. vi. 21 that the account of the bringing of the Ark to Jerusalem comes to its climax in the reference to the election of the king.

Now that the Ark was present on mount Zion an official cult embracing the whole of the tribal confederacy could be brought into being —a cult which was based on the assumptions and regulations of the amphictyonic central sanctuary. As we know from 2 Sam. vii. 1–7, David conceived the plan of erecting a Temple which, based on models

[9] L. Rost, op. cit., pp. 4 ff.

[10] Cf. M. Noth, 'Jerusalem und die israelitische Tradition', *Gesammelte Studien zum A.T.* (1957), pp. 172 ff.

in neighbouring countries, would be quite suitable for an official cult and for housing the Ark. Through the message of Nathan the king was denied the divine approval, and was told that he should not carry out the plans for building, but that he must keep the Ark in a tent. Although this 'tent' was in all probability not the same as the 'sacred Tent', Nathan's words give valuable evidence about the prophetic traditions that were still alive at David's court. Nathan stood as the witness to and guardian of a tradition that confronted and repudiated the Canaanite institutions (cf. pp. 95 f.). He was an embodiment of the protest of the circles that sought to keep in mind their desert origins. David gave way and during the period of his rule preserved as the sacral sphere a tent cult which was quite inadequate for a whole kingdom. Nothing could make plainer the fact that in its origin the Israelite monarchy had no mythical elements, but was rooted in the historical and prophetic traditions of the tribal confederacy. It was only under Solomon that the basic assumptions changed to any extent.

(c) *The Royal Festival on Mount Zion*

The climax of the *hieros logos* of the Jerusalem Ark tradition was the account of the entrance of the sacred cult object into the city chosen by Yahweh (2 Sam. vi). It tells how David brought the Ark in solemn procession to mount Zion amidst rejoicing, cultic dancing and sacrifices. This record confirmed the election and appointment of Jerusalem as the central sanctuary for all Israel. A *hieros logos*, however, was related and repeatedly told to the pilgrims. When we consider the final act of the transference of the Ark to Zion, as it is related in 2 Sam. vi, it seems very reasonable to assume that there was a cultic repetition of this important event.[11] If we take into account the events described in 1 Kings viii. 3 ff. and Ps. cxxxii, there seems to be no doubt that the ascent of the Ark to mount Zion was an act of worship of fundamental importance. Time after time the original event of the 'election of Jerusalem' was solemnly celebrated and the worshipping community entered into the experience. An event of such basic importance as the establishment of the official cult must have left its marks upon worship. The cultic repetition, however, did not deal only with the 'election of Jerusalem', but also with the 'election of David'. In the early period monarchy and sanctuary were very closely connected. The king was the founder and

[11] Cf. H.-J. Kraus, *Die Königsherrschaft Gottes im Alten Testament*, BHT, 13 (1951), pp. 27 ff.; A. Bentzen, 'The Cultic Use of the Story of the Ark in Samuel', *JBL*, 67 (1948), pp. 37 ff.; R. Porter, 'The Interpretation of 2 Sam. 6 and Psalm 132', *JTS*, 5 (1954), pp. 161 ff.

leader of the cult and had charge of the official worship. But in Jerusalem the question which we have already mentioned presented itself: who had authorized David to bring the Ark to Jerusalem? The answer could be given by reference to Nathan's words or by an actualization of this original message by a cultic prophet. From the standpoint of literary criticism 2 Sam. vi and 2 Sam. vii are two different complexes, but in the cultic actualization of the main facts concerning the official sanctuary in Jerusalem the two basic sacral elements have become intertwined: Yahweh has chosen David, and he has chosen Jerusalem.[12] Ps. cxxxii provides the decisive evidence for a 'royal festival on mount Zion', which actualized in worship the two acts of election.[13]

'A song of Ascents.

Lord, remember for David
All his affliction;
How he swore unto the Lord,
And vowed unto the Mighty One of Jacob:
Surely I will not come into the tabernacle of my home,
Nor go up into my bed;
I will not give sleep to mine eyes,
Or slumber to mine eyelids;
Until I find out a place for the Lord,
A tabernacle for the Mighty One of Jacob.
Lo, we heard of it in Ephrathah:
We found it in the field of the wood.
We will go into his tabernacles;
We will worship at his foot stool.
Arise, O Lord, into thy resting place;
Thou, and the ark of thy strength.
Let thy priests be clothed with righteousness;
And let thy saints shout for joy.
For thy servant David's sake
Turn not away the face of thine anointed.
The Lord hath sworn unto David in truth;
He will not turn from it:
Of the fruit of thy body will I set upon thy throne.
If thy children will keep my covenant
And my testimony that I shall teach them,

[12] In connection with the cultic entrance of the Ark into the Temple of Solomon we should note the key Deuteronomistic verse in 1 Kings viii. 16, which is set out as a word of Yahweh: 'I chose no city out of all the tribes of Israel to build an house, that my name might be there; but I chose David to be over my people Israel.'

[13] Cf. also Ps. lxxviii. 68 ff., where the 'election of Zion' and the 'election of David' are placed directly alongside each other.

Their children also shall sit upon thy throne for evermore.
For the Lord hath chosen Zion;
He hath desired it for his habitation.
This is my resting place for ever:
Here will I dwell; for I have desired it.
I will abundantly bless her provision:
I will satisfy her poor with bread.
Her priests also will I clothe with salvation:
And her saints shall shout aloud for joy.
There will I make the horn of David to bud:
I have ordained a lamp for mine anointed.
His enemies will I clothe with shame:
But upon himself shall his crown flourish.'[14]

This psalm contains a 'selection of the ritual', in which nevertheless the main acts of worship and the exclamations of the cultic prophets are clearly reflected. The two focal points of the psalm are the references to Yahweh's covenant with David (*vv.* 11 f.) and to the election of Zion (*v.* 13). The course of the cultic drama shows very clearly the main stages in the original event: David's desire for a Temple (*vv.* 3–5), the discovery of the lost Ark at Kiriath-Jearim (*v.* 6), the cultic ascent to the sanctuary (*vv.* 7 f.), Yahweh's ברית with David (*vv.* 11 f.), the proclamation of the election of Zion (*vv.* 13 f.) and the blessing of the sanctuary and its king (*vv.* 15 ff.). H. Gunkel pointed out that 'We can deduce from Ps. cxxxii a festival that was dedicated to the remembrance of the founding of the royal dynasty and its sanctuary.'[15] 'On the day celebrating the founding of the sanctuary a liturgy is performed in which there is first a dramatic presentation showing how their forefather David brought the Ark to Zion, and then an oracle of Yahweh resounds in which he promises to bless David and his house in this place. . . . We must assume that there was a festival for the consecration of the sanctuary, perhaps held annually. . . .'[16] But these suggestions made by Gunkel need to be made more precise and seen more clearly in their original context. The real main themes are not 'founding' or 'consecration', but the election of Jerusalem and of David. It is vitally important that we should define the cultic content accurately.

The question we must now consider is at what time and in what manner the cultic repetition of the original events of the establishment of the official sanctuary in Jerusalem took place. Important indications

[14] For a discussion of this passage, see H. J. Kraus, *Psalmen*, p. 877.
[15] H. Gunkel/J. Begrich, *Einleitung in die Psalmen* (1933), p. 142.
[16] H. Gunkel, *Die Psalmen*, HK, II, 2 (4 ed., 1926), p. 568.

are provided by the account that has come down to us in 1 Kings viii. 1 ff. of the introduction of the Ark into the Temple built by Solomon. The Ark was ceremonially brought up to the holy mount in the month of Etanim, i.e., in the seventh month. From this we can assume that the 'royal festival on Zion' was celebrated in Jerusalem on the first day of the feast of Tabernacles.[17] At the beginning of the principal Israelite feast the Ark was brought into the sanctuary, accompanied by a crowd of pilgrims and led by the king who—as David had done before him—sat before the sacred object. Priests had charge of the procession and they accompanied the Ark (Ps. cxxxii. 9). Nathan's message was no doubt actualized from time to time in the exhortations of the cultic prophets. If we turn to those passages in the Old Testament which set down Nathan's words in a particularly striking form, we can see from 2 Sam. vii, Ps. lxxxix and cxxxii what a great variety there is in the ways in which the basic proclamation to David is set down. This variety is a reflection of the periodic cultic realizations and prophetic adaptations of the ancient message. The entry of the Ark came to its climax in the act of adoration before the God enthroned on Zion (Ps. cxxxii. 7).

Yahweh would not allow David to build a Temple, but Solomon was able to carry out the great work.[18] David's son built on the 'threshing-floor of Araunah', which was possibly the sacred area in Jerusalem even in the Jebusite period[19] (2 Sam. xxiv. 16 ff.), an acropolis with the two main buildings—palace and Temple. Like the whole of Jerusalem, the 'threshing-floor of Araunah' was land belonging to the king. The house of God was situated at the holy place of the pre-Israelite cultic centre: it was erected over the 'sacred rock'.[20] Canaanite-Syrian sacral architecture provided the model for the Temple in its three sections. A vestibule

[17] On the designation of the festival, see H.-J. Kraus, *Die Königsherrschaft Gottes im Alten Testament*, loc cit., pp. 27 ff.

[18] Bibliography dealing with the Temple: K. Möhlenbrink, *Der Tempel Salomos*, BWANT, IV, 7 (1932); K. Galling, 'Das Allerheiligste in Salomos Tempel', *JPOS*, 12 (1932), pp. 43 ff.; R. de Vaux, 'Notes sur le Temple de Salomon', *Qedem*, II (1945), pp. 48 ff.; P. L. Garber, 'Reconstruction of Solomon's Temple', *BA*, 14 (1951), pp. 2 ff.; A. Parrot, *Le Temple de Jérusalem* (1954); G. E. Wright, 'The Steven's Reconstruction of the Solomonic Temple', *BA*, 18 (1955), pp. 41 ff.; L. H. Vincent/ A. M. Steve, *Jérusalem de l'Ancien Testament*, II-III (1956), pp. 373 ff.

[19] The legend that has come down to us in 2 Sam. xxiv. 16 ff. may have been the pre-Israelite *hieros logos* of the Jebusite sanctuary; it describes how the 'threshing-floor of Araunah' became a sanctuary. This *hieros logos* was taken over into the cultic tradition of Israel, but it is the Ark narrative that bears witness to the actual foundation of the Yahweh sanctuary. See also G. W. Ahlström, 'Der Prophet Nathan und der Tempelbau', *VT*, 11 (1961), pp. 113 ff.

[20] Cf. H. Schmidt, *Der Heilige Fels in Jerusalem* (1933); H.-J. Kraus, 'Archäologische und topographische Probleme Jerusalems im Lichte der Psalmenexegese', *ZDPV*, 75 (1959), pp. 125 ff.

led into the central holy place, to which the holy of holies, which was completely dark, was adjoined. The 'sacred rock' jutted up into this holy of holies. The structure was built on a plan of about 90 ft long and 30 ft high. The three main rooms were surrounded by the priests' chambers, and an inner and outer courtyard separated the holy place from the outside world. Outside the Temple there was the great altar of burnt offering, and the 'bronze sea', a water-container which rested on twelve bronze oxen.[21] Worship was mainly performed in the courtyards, where sacrifices were offered and solemn feasts held, but on feast days every Israelite would enter the Temple to prostrate himself and pray to Yahweh.

The Temple became the real centre of the official cult. It was—to quote Amos vii. 13—'the king's sanctuary' (מקדש מלך) and 'a royal house' (בית ממלכה). Solomon had the Ark installed in the dark holy of holies and acted—as did all his descendants—as ruler of the Temple and controller of the cult, to whom belonged the right of sacrifice and intercession (cf. 1 Kings viii. 1 ff.).[22] The ruler was not only king of Judah and king of Israel, but also king of his own capital city of Jerusalem. He therefore took upon himself the dignity of the priest-king, which was traced back to Melchizedek (Gen. xiv. 18 f.; Ps. cx). The sanctuary officials were appointed and supported by him, and were dependent on his instructions. During the time of Solomon the Israelite cult in its external manifestations was raised in a relatively short period to the cultural level of the great empires. This development, and particularly the sacral autonomy of the king, brought great dangers in its train. Will the ruler think of himself as 'Yahweh's chosen one', and be obedient to the God of Israel and follow His guidance? Or will he turn his

[21] It is possible that the 'bronze sea' had a cosmic significance and that it symbolized the great deep, which was called *ym* in Ugarit. The bulls were symbols of fertility. Cf. W. F. Albright, *Archaeology and the Religion of Israel* (1942), pp. 149 f. The meaning of the two pillars 'Jachin and Boaz' which stood at the front of the Temple is still disputed. We will merely mention here the possibility that they were symbolical representations of the two original hills. The Temple faced east. See Zech. vi. 1 for the mythological conception. On the theology of the Temple, see: W. F. Albright, *Archaeology and the Religion of Israel* (1942); R. Patai, *Man and Temple in Ancient Jewish Myth and Ritual* (1947); M. Schmidt, *Prophet und Tempel. Eine Studie zum Problem der Gottesnähe im Alten Testament* (1948); M. Simon, 'La prophétie de Nathan et le Temple', *RHPR*, 32 (1952), pp. 41 ff.; J. Daniélou, 'Le symbolisme cosmique du Temple de Jérusalem', *Symbolisme cosmique et Monuments religieux* (1953), pp. 61 ff.; E. L. Ehrlich, *Die Kultsymbolik im Alten Testament und im nachbiblischen Judentum* (1959), pp. 24 ff.

[22] The 'prayer for the dedication of the Temple' in 1 Kings viii. 12 f. shows that the sanctuary at Jerusalem has to be included in the category of 'temples in which the god dwells': 'The Lord hath said that he would dwell in the thick darkness. I have surely built thee an house of habitation, a place for thee to dwell in for ever.'

'election' into the self-assertion of a 'divine kingship'? These were the vital questions.

2. The Ancient Israelite Traditions

(a) *The Divine Law*

However extensive and influential the innovations were which were introduced into the worship of Israel by the institution of the official cult in Jerusalem, the ancient Israelite tradition was kept alive at the Ark sanctuary.[23] In a hymn of pilgrimage from the period of the monarchy it is stressed that it is 'for a testimony unto Israel' (עֵדוּת לְיִשְׂרָאֵל) that the tribes should go on pilgrimage to Jerusalem (Ps. cxxii. 4). The thought of the tribe is, in other words, still linked with the central sanctuary, and it cuts across the official sacral order by virtue of its primitive authority. But Ps. cxxii also indicates other amphictyonic traditions which have been preserved on mount Zion. We read in *v.* 5:

> 'For there are set thrones for judgement,
> The thrones of the house of David.'

This points us first to 1 Kings vii. 7. Solomon had a 'porch of the throne' built on the acropolis in Jerusalem, where stood הכסא אשר ישפט־שם (1 Kings vii. 7). According to this, the king exercised the office of 'judge in Israel' (cf. p. 189). He took over the function which was carried out in the pre-monarchical period by the highest amphictyonic official. There is evidence of these important connections between the official cult in Jerusalem and the ancient Israelite institutions and traditions in several passages in the Old Testament. Absalom, for example, in his rebellion against David, arrogated to himself the right to pronounce judgement, which belonged to the king alone (2 Sam. xv. 6). This authoritative administration applied to all the tribes of Israel (2 Sam. xv. 1 ff.). Although the report in 1 Kings iii. 16 ff. contains legendary features which were widespread, we still cannot mistake the fact that the function of judge was ascribed to Solomon. In Jer. xxi. 12 the 'house of David' is called upon to pronounce 'righteous judgement', and, according to the promise in Isa. xvi. 5, a righteous judge shall always sit in the 'tent of David'. And finally it is said even concerning the Messianic king of the last days, who will come forth from the house of David, that he will be a charismatic judge (Isa. xi. 3 f.). The position is therefore quite plain: on mount Zion the descendants of David

[23] Cf. M. Noth, 'Jerusalem und die israelitische Tradition', *Gesammelte Studien zum A.T.* (1957), pp. 172 ff.

fulfilled the office of the 'judge in Israel'.[24] It is explicitly stated concerning the thrones mentioned in Ps. cxxii. 5 that they are meant for 'judgement' in the 'house of David'. What we have here therefore are not centres of political jurisdiction, but an authority which was applicable to the amphictyonic tribal order (cf. Ps. cxxii. 4). According to this the king was considered as the representative and guardian of the judicial office of Yahweh—in the same way as in the ancient tribal confederacy. In Ps. lxxii. 1 f. we hear the desire and petition of the singer, that the God of Israel will transfer the judicial functions to the ruler.

Wherever the amphictyonic judicial office is in operation, we must assume that the validity of the divine law is basic and determinative. The ancient legal traditions of Israel came to Jerusalem with the Ark, and Isa. ii. 3 (cf. Micah iv. 2) shows that they were set before the people in worship. In the 'eschatological pilgrimage hymn of Zion' which looks to 'the last days' preserved in Isa. ii. 2 ff. (Micah iv. 1 ff.) we have evidence of Jerusalem cultic traditions which give us valuable information.[25] Just as the tribes of Israel came on pilgrimage to Jerusalem in order to receive Yahweh's תורה and דבר, so in the last days all nations will come in order to hear the word of God that guides, judges and brings peace (Isa. ii. 3; Micah iv. 2). The תורה goes out from Zion—divine instruction in the widest sense. Jerusalem is the city of the law of Yahweh, and משפט and צדק dwell here (Isa. i. 21). The chosen city is a עיר הצדק (Isa. i. 26), and here Yahweh reigns as judge (Amos i. 2; Micah i. 2 ff). Ps. l shows most clearly of all that the ancient Israelite traditions of Yahweh as judge and of the proclamation of the apodeictic law came to be associated with Zion (cf. Ps. l. 2). The God of Israel manifested himself in Jerusalem as the judge (Ps. l. 6), and made known to his people the majestic claim of his laws (Ps. l. 7 ff.).[26]

There can therefore be no doubt about the fact that the ancient Israelite traditions of Yahweh's jurisdiction, of the divine law and of the 'judge of Israel' came to Jerusalem along with the Ark. The official sanctuary thus attained the status and dignity of an amphictyonic cultic centre.

(b) *The Davidic Covenant and the Sinaitic Covenant*

As we have already seen, the Davidic covenant was periodically actualized in the festival cult at Jerusalem (cf. pp. 183 ff.). Nathan's message (2 Sam. vii) was proclaimed to David's successors in a solemn

[24] See also F. Horst, 'Recht und Religion im Bereich des Alten Testaments', *EvTh*, 16 (1956), p. 53, reprinted in *Gottes Recht*, p. 265.

[25] For a fuller discussion, see G. von Rad, 'Die Stadt auf dem Berge', *EvTh*, 8 (1948/9), pp. 439 ff., *Ges. Stud.*, pp. 214 ff.

[26] Cf. H.-J. Kraus, *Psalmen*, BK, 15 (1960), pp. 370 ff.

act of worship (Ps. cxxxii). But we must not overlook the fact that the promise expressed by the prophet Nathan points in essence to the future. The cultic realizations of this basic proclamation became more and more marked by this fact, and the promise for the future was always left open. This inconclusiveness and longing for fulfilment became the source of eschatological expectations which looked for a Messianic king of the last days who would come from the house of David. Even the royal psalms are mysteriously permeated with this hope, for they 'reveal the kingdom and office of the anointed one in the light of his divine *doxa*—which is still hidden—which for them is already present and can be made manifest at any moment'.[27] But the Messianic expectations of the prophets are quite openly directed towards the last days when the saving power of the king will be completely revealed. It is significant that these prophetic expectations are set in the context of the whole of Israel (cf. Isa. ix. 1 ff., Micah v. 1 ff.). The rule of the Messianic king covers not only Judah and Jerusalem, but all Israel. This fact proves that the Davidic covenant was not merely based originally upon the cultic and sacral traditions of the tribal confederacy, but that this covenant also looked as regards its fulfilment to Israel as a whole. The Davidic covenant was not meant to be separated from the basic fact of the relationship between God and his people.

We must now consider the question of the relationship between the Davidic and the Sinaitic covenant. In other words, what was the connection between the God-king relationship and the God-people relationship? The Davidic covenant was repeatedly realized in the Jerusalem cult, but what significance did the renewal in worship of the Sinaitic covenant have on mount Zion? Can we assume that the cultic renewal of the Yahweh בְּרִית, which took place in the amphictyonic covenant festival in the pre-monarchical period, still played a part in Jerusalem, or was the Yahweh covenant included along with the people in the Davidic covenant? L. Rost was the first to draw attention to this problem of 'Sinaitic covenant and Davidic covenant'.[28] He came to the conclusion that for a time the two continued alongside each other, and that the Sinaitic covenant was important predominantly in the northern kingdom, and the Davidic covenant in the southern kingdom. Dealing with the foundations of the kingdom of Jeroboam I, Rost states: 'In calling itself officially the kingdom of Israel, the kingdom of Jeroboam I naturally

[27] G. von Rad, 'Erwägungen zu den Königspsalmen', *ZAW*, 85 (1940/1), pp. 219 f.

[28] L. Rost, 'Sinaibund und Davidsbund', *ThLZ*, 72 (1947), pp. 129 ff.; also M. Sekine, 'Davidsbund und Sinaibund bei Jeremia', *VT*, 9 (1959), pp. 47 ff.; A. H. J. Gunneweg, 'Sinaibund und Davidsbund', *VT*, 10 (1960), pp. 335 ff.

assumed all the claims inherent in this name and all the traditions that had gathered around it.'[29] In Judah, on the other hand—according to Rost's view—the idea of the Israelite covenant fell into the background and the Davidic covenant came to the fore.[30] This explanation is unacceptable, as it does not adequately bring out the special principles and manifestations of the Davidic covenant. M. Noth rightly objects to Rost's suggestions. 'In view of the local link between the Ark and the city of David this separation is perhaps too simple; it seems more probable that within the general Israelite tradition the expectations linked with the promises made to the house of David, wherever they were adopted among the Israelite tribes, became part of the ancient traditional relationship of God and people, as a special element and one which pointed more and more to the future.'[31] This view is basically in harmony with what we have already said concerning the way in which the Davidic covenant was linked with the cultic and sacral traditions of Israel.

If we now go on to consider the question whether there is any indication in the Old Testament of the continuing influence of the ancient Israelite covenant traditions in the official sanctuary at Jerusalem, the main evidence we have to examine is that of the Deuteronomic history. There are passages here that we must look at carefully.

We must first remind ourselves that the Israelite cultic tradition rooted at Shechem showed that an important element in the ratification of the divine covenant with the twelve tribes was the purification of the cult. The unconditional requirement for the service of Yahweh that was laid down in the covenant was the renunciation of all heathen gods and their cults.[32] The relationship between God and his people had to be renewed first in the cultic sphere. It is a remarkable fact that in the Deuteronomic history we are told concerning several kings in Jerusalem that after periods of religious aberration they restored the relationship between God and his people by a thorough purification of the cult. In this connection it is plainly emphasized that the rulers concerned have exercised their kingship properly because they sought first and foremost to renew and establish fellowship with God. We shall have to look more closely to those passages which speak of such a purification of the cult, but we must first turn to the question of the royal cult at Jerusalem, in order that we shall be able to grasp the full meaning of those

[29] L. Rost, op. cit., p. 131.

[30] Ibid., p. 130.

[31] M. Noth, 'Gott, König, Volk im Alten Testament', *ZThK*, 47 (1950), p. 188, *Ges. Stud.*, p. 225.

[32] On this act of renunciation, see A. Alt, 'Die Wallfahrt von Sichem nach Bethel', *Kleine Schriften*, I, pp. 79 ff.

passages in which we find the most significant statements about the cleansing of the relationship between God and his people. For this purpose we shall have to retrace our steps once again.

We saw earlier that in the founding of the official cult David's kingship deliberately took its stand on the amphictyonic traditions (cf. pp. 179 f.). David brought the Ark of Yahweh to Jerusalem (2 Sam. vi) and was in the fullest sense 'appointed' by the prophet Nathan (2 Sam. vii).[33] The charismatic gift that had been bestowed by Yahweh upon individual men in earlier times was now promised to a whole dynasty, and the institution of kingship was now stamped with a permanent covenant relationship which, however, pointed first and foremost to the future. In this way a cultic and sacral centre for the state was established, and the human kings were elevated to be representatives of the rule of God. They were supposed to enter into a positive connection with the Ark, the throne of the invisibly present ruler of Israel. In this way David's state, even when it was composed only of Judah, was the sphere of God's sovereignty which, of course, always envisaged the whole of Israel. However, we cannot ignore the fact that David's successors, from the moment they entered office, were faced with an important decision. The king from the 'house of David' was asked whether he would enter upon his rule and fulfil it as the 'chosen one of Yahweh'. The complete devotion of the ruler to Yahweh was accordingly the presupposition for God's unbroken sovereignty over his people. But the Deuteronomist sees even Solomon, the first successor in the Davidic dynasty, faced with a danger fraught with far-reaching consequences—in a fateful situation the significance of which we cannot emphasize too much. The bond that had been established between the cult and the monarchy by the founding of the official sanctuary (1 Kings viii) gave rise to many problems. The question that had to be faced was this: where in the future is the real source of authority to be found—in the cult or in the monarchy? In other words, will the word of election that is actualized in worship (2 Sam. vii; Ps. ii; Ps. cxxxii; Px. lxxxix) control and guide the king?[34] Will the ruler think of himself as 'Yahweh's chosen one' and approach his high office accordingly, or will he abuse the word of promise that confirms his election and so direct the worship of his state Temple independently and according to his own fancy? There was a danger that David's successor might interpret the cultic-sacral basis of his rule for an apotheosis, and then act by virtue of an

[33] Cf. L. Rost, *Die Überlieferung von der Thronnachfolge Davids*, loc. cit., pp. 47 ff., *Das kleine Credo*, pp. 159 ff.

[34] Cf. H.-J. Kraus. *Die Königsherrschaft Gottes im Alten Testament*, pp. 65 ff.

usurped autonomy. The development of an independent policy by the ruler was linked with such a rejection by the kings of Yahweh's claim to sovereignty implicit in the amphictyonic tradition. The Deuteronomistic record declares, however, that the kind of royal supremacy among David's successors that had emancipated itself from Yahweh's sovereign claim had the greatest effect upon the history of Judah. It is therefore all the more striking in the annals of the monarchical period when a ruler adopts the proper attitude towards his election and because of this the sovereignty of God again comes to the fore and a purification of the cult renews the ancient relationship between God and his people. The Deuteronomist must have had at his disposal very reliable traditions about the attitude of the kings to their election. His judgements upon the individual rulers, which seem to follow a set pattern, were a significant attempt to measure the monarchy at any particular time by the yardstick of the sacral foundations of the official Jerusalem cult, which cannot be separated from the amphictyonic traditions. It was only the idea of 'election' that brought the monarchy and the official Temple inescapably into connection with the traditions of Israel as a whole.

In view of the religious dangers facing the monarchy, it is not surprising that the Deuteronomistic record mentions a purification of the cult and a thorough renewal of the relationship between God and his people in only a few places. But these few passages need to be considered carefully. It is possible to interpret the details given of the cultic reforms undertaken by individual kings of Judah as indications of the Sinaitic covenant and its cultic implications attempting a reform by breaking through the usurped Davidic covenant. The first reform of the cult in Judah was undertaken by King Asa (1 Kings xv. 9 ff.). 'And Asa did that which was right in the eyes of the Lord, as did David his father' (*v.* 11). This judgement on the king is followed directly, as though in order to define more precisely and explain the reason for the approval he has earned, by the words: 'And he put away the Sodomites out of the land, and removed all the idols that his fathers had made' (*v.* 12). Although as the judgement proceeds a reservation is made (*v.*14a), the general verdict of the Deuteronomist upon Asa remains a very positive one. Like David, Asa also tried to see his kingship on the basis of a relationship between God and the people cleansed from all foreign cults. But alongside this we must take into account the interpretation of Asa's purification of the cult that is given in the record in Chronicles. The Chronicler states: 'And they entered into the covenant to seek the Lord, the God of their fathers, with all their heart and with all their soul. . . . And they sware unto the Lord with a loud voice, and with shouting, and with trumpets, and with cornets' (2 Chron. xv. 12, 14). The Chronicler clearly believes that a renewal of the covenant took place in connection with the purification of the cult described by the Deuteronomist. The people swear and pledge themselves to serve only Yahweh and remain faithful to him alone. As regards the Chronicler's reading of the events, it is possible to take the view that it was a late interpretation of the cultic purification recorded in 1 Kings xv. 9 ff., which served to express some particular themes of the Chronicler or was based on certain combinations or constructions. But there are three points we must take into account: (1) the Chronicler's view, that the purification of the cult is tantamount to a renewal of the covenant, is in keeping with the oldest traditions that are known to us through the actualization of the Sinaitic covenant such as was practised at Shechem (cf. Joshua xxiv. 23, 25); (2) the Chronicler, who was closely connected with the Deuteronomistic traditions, is familiar with the cultic traditions of the Jerusalem sanctuary and therefore refers to traditions which deserve careful consideration; (3) we can test the interpretation suggested by the Chronicler by reference to the other Deuteronomistic allusions to a purification of the cult during the reign of later kings.

2 Kings xi. 13 ff. contains a second important reference to a cultic reform emanating from Jerusalem.

'And when Athaliah heard the noise of the guard and of the people, she came to the people into the house of the Lord: and she looked, and, behold, the king stood by the pillar, as the manner was, and the captains and the trumpets by the king; and all the people of the land rejoiced, and blew with trumpets. Then Athaliah rent her clothes, and cried, Treason, treason. And Jehoiada the priest commanded the captains of hundreds that were set over the host, and said unto them, Have her forth between the ranks; and him that followeth her slay with the sword: for the priest said, Let her not be slain in the house of the Lord. So they made way for her; and she went by the way of the horses' entry to the king's house: and there was she slain. And Jehoiada made a covenant between the Lord and the king and the people, that they should be the Lord's people. And all the people of the land went to the house of Baal, and brake it down; his altars and his images brake they in pieces thoroughly, and slew Mattan the priest of Baal before the altars. And the priest appointed officers over the house of the Lord.'

This account tells of the elevation of the young Jehoash to be king of Judah.[35] We need not go into the execution of the king's mother Athaliah

[35] In *v.* 17 the text presents certain difficulties. We read at the end of the verse: 'between the king also and the people'. Was this just a repetition, or are we to assume that the ratification of the covenant first mentioned in *v.* 17 was followed by a second ceremony in the course of which the treaty monarchy between the Davidic dynasty and

here. What is important is the information given about the solemn act of enthronement that was performed in Jerusalem, without any doubt at the autumn festival. We must first note as a general fact that there was none of the more important political actions that was not carried out on cultic occasions. An enthronement, in particular, could be held only when the people had gathered in Jerusalem for the autumn festival. *V*. 17 stands out in the account of the enthronement of Jehoash. Jehoiada made 'the covenant' between Yahweh, king and people. In interpreting this passage we must first note that—as in 2 Chron. xv. 12—'the' covenant is spoken of, with the definite article. It is therefore not some agreement between the king and the people, such as is spoken of in *v*. 4. On the contrary, the covenant was made with the clearly defined purpose 'that they should be the Lord's people'. It was therefore without question a ratification of the covenant, to which was significantly joined another purification of the cult (*vv*. 18 ff.). The relationship between God and his people could be what it should be only when all foreign gods had been repudiated. The initiative in the ratification of the covenant came from the high priest Jehoiada. The king was still young, therefore the priesthood of the official sanctuary could make its influence felt. The relationship between God and His people was renewed, and this was meant to make it clear that the real aim behind the tradition of the Davidic covenant, as it was preserved in priestly circles and evidently especially cherished by the 'people of the land', was the renewal of the fellowship between God and his people. At the moment when the autonomous power of the Jerusalem monarchy could not assert itself and therefore could not lay claim to an usurped Davidic covenant, the Sinaitic covenant came to the fore. The measures taken to achieve renewal went back beyond the Davidic covenant to the institutions of the Yahweh amphictyony. Jehoiada appeared as the mediator of the covenant—as Joshua had once done (cf. Joshua xxiv. 25). The Davidic covenant was thus included within the covenant between God and his people. In this passage we can recognize an excerpt from the history of the office of the mediator of the covenant.[36] The high priest

[36] Cf. M. Noth, op. cit., pp. 151 f.

Judah was renewed? It is conceivable that the conservative sections of the population sought a new formulation of the basic covenant in what was for Jerusalem the unusual situation of rule by a woman, murder and the enthronement of a minor. 'The meaning of the ceremony therefore would be that after the reign of the foreigner Athaliah Jerusalem and Judah bind themselves again to the dynasty of David, which had formerly attained sovereignty over Judah by means of a covenant (2 Sam. v. 3)'—cf. M. Noth, 'Das alttestamentliche Bundesschliessen im Lichte eines Mari-Textes', *Ges. Stud.* (1957), p. 152.

ratified the covenant with God and pledged the cultic community to a new obedience.[37]

One fact has emerged more clearly now—that in the official sanctuary at Jerusalem the Sinaitic covenant was not completely obscured by the Davidic covenant. In the historical accounts by the Deuteronomist and the Chronicler situations are described where we can see a renewal of the Sinaitic covenant, in other words a rededication of the people to their amphictyonic origins. These descriptions are all the more significant in view of the fact that at the official Jerusalem sanctuary all the presuppositions for the ratification of a covenant embracing the whole of Israel were lacking. Although the institution of the tribal confederacy was present in the principle of the central sanctuary, it was not present in the actual cultic assembly. And we can hardly assume that deputations came from the north for these acts of ratifying the covenant which were performed so rarely. The separate state of Judah therefore had to stand at the central sanctuary at the festival of the renewal of the covenant as *pars pro toto*—something that is by no means foreign to the Old Testament tradition. L. Koehler rightly stresses in his *Theology of the Old Testament*: 'The people is not the sum of its members, it is not a mathematical quantity. On the contrary, it is represented in any group of members you like, even in individuals; but the individual is never alone where the covenant is concerned. Always, whether by himself or in a number, he is *pars pro toto*.'[38] These fundamental points need to be borne in mind in connection with the renewal of the covenant in Judah.

After referring to the cultic reforms undertaken by Asa and Jehoiada, we must draw particular attention to the purification of the cult by Hezekiah. Hezekiah also first receives from the Deuteronomist the positive verdict: 'And he did that which was right in the eyes of the Lord, according to all that David his father had done' (2 Kings xviii. 3). This verdict is then also followed immediately by an account of the purification of the cult in Judah and Jerusalem. The aim of the Deuteronomist is to make it clear that the only ruler who stands within the Davidic covenant is the one who sees in the Yahweh covenant the basis upon which his office is to be fulfilled. All the other kings have abused their election, for only a few rulers have rightly understood the meaning of the Davidic covenant. If we turn to the Chronicler, we see here again (as in 1 Kings xv. 9 ff.) that the purification of the cult by Hezekiah is interpreted as a cultic renewal of the covenant. The following words are put into the mouth of the king: 'Now it is in mine heart to make a covenant with the

[37] See also G. von Rad, *Studies in Deuteronomy*, pp. 63 f.

[38] L. Koehler, *Theology of the Old Testament* (E.T. 1957), p. 65.

Lord, the God of Israel, that his fierce anger may turn away from us. My sons, be not now negligent: for the Lord hath chosen you to stand before him, and that ye should be his ministers, and burn incense' (2 Chron. xxix. 10, 11). After the investigations we have already made we cannot just describe this as a 'schematizing interpretation' typical of the Chronicler. There are three factors that support his interpretation: (1) the purification of the cult that was customary at Shechem at the renewal of the covenant; (2) the account in 2 Kings xi. 17; (3) the special affinity with the cultic tradition of Jerusalem that is a feature of the Chronicler's historical record.

Having indicated the connection between the renewal of the covenant and the purification of the cult, we must now turn to the question whether the renewal of the relationship between God and his people was accompanied also by a promulgation of the law. There is only indirect evidence of a cultic proclamation of the law on the occasion of the renewal of the covenant. Ideas are expressed in Isa. ii. 2 ff. and Ps. l which are undoubtedly connected with some cultic practice (cf. pp. 188 f.). Instruction in the divine law was given on mount Zion. How otherwise, for example, could the eschatological pilgrimage of the nations to Jerusalem that is spoken of in Isa. ii. 2 ff. be understood than by assuming that some actual cultic event provided the basis for what would happen in the last days?[39]

Only now do we come to the most significant of all the purifications of the cult, to the reformation undertaken by king Josiah. 'And the king sent, and they gathered unto him all the elders of Judah and of Jerusalem. And the king went up to the house of the Lord, and all the men of Judah and all the inhabitants of Jerusalem with him, and the priests, and the prophets, and all the people, both small and great: and he read in their ears all the words of the book of the covenant which was found in the house of the Lord. And the king stood by the pillar, and made a covenant before the Lord, to walk after the Lord, and to keep his commandments, and his testimonies, and his statutes, with all his heart, and all his soul, to confirm the words of this covenant that were written in this book: and all the people stood to the covenant' (2 Kings xxiii. 1–3).

This account of the ratification of the covenant is immediately followed

[39] On this point, cf. G. von Rad, 'Die Stadt auf dem Berge', *EvTh*, 8 (1940/1), p. 441, *Ges. Stud.*, p. 217: 'The event is cultic through and through: Isaiah may have seen the crowds of pilgrims coming to the Temple year by year at the time of the feast of Tabernacles.' If an annual instruction of the pilgrims in the תורה took place, we have to leave open the question whether at the act of renewing the covenant a public proclamation of the divine law as depicted in Deut. xxvii was held.

by a detailed description of the purification of the cult (2 Kings xxiii. 4 ff.), and we can see once again how closely connected the two are. But the account of the renewal of the covenant by Josiah raises a number of special points which we must consider. There are in the first place the literary questions concerning the tradition about Josiah.[40] The description of the period of Josiah naturally receives particular attention in the Deuteronomistic record, because it was then that the Deuteronomic law was found which is the basis of all the historical account drawn up by the Deuteronomist. We can assume that there was a special 'memorandum' dealing with the discovery of the 'book of the law', of which the Deuteronomist made use in this account of the events, and he no doubt obtained further information about the ratification of the covenant and the measures concerned with cultic policy from the annals of the Temple. There can be no doubt, however, that the historian comes to the fore with his own view of the course of events, and it is by no means easy to distinguish in detail between what the Deuteronomist found in the annals and what represents his own views. How are the events of Josiah's period represented? After the description of the discovery of the 'book of the law' in chapter xxii, the section 2 Kings xxiii. 1–3 goes on to the reform of the cult, and in this connection—as we have already seen—an account is given of a renewal of the covenant. We are told: 'and he read in their ears all the words of the book of the covenant' (*v.* 2) and after the reading of the תורה Josiah made a covenant with Yahweh, into which the members of the assembled congregation then entered. These statements give rise to a number of different questions. How does it come about that Josiah himself first enters into the covenant and that it is only afterwards that the assembled people are brought into it? Is there the underlying idea that Josiah is entering into the Davidic covenant? Are we to assume that there was a merging of the Davidic and the Sinaitic covenants, and interpret the event to mean that the covenant made with David or with his successors was extended to include the people in one and the same ceremonial act? This interpretation is hardly feasible, for we cannot combine the Davidic covenant and the Sinaitic covenant in this way. The entering into the covenant which is spoken of in 2 Kings xxiii. 3 concerns the whole congregation, and has to be seen in the light of those passages which—as we have shown earlier—contain an account of the renewal of the covenant. This renewal of the relationship between God and his people in the time of Josiah holds a special place in the history of worship,

[40] See M. Noth, *Überlieferungsgeschichtliche Studien*, I, pp. 86 f.

and cannot be compared with the renewals of the covenant of which we have earlier accounts. What Josiah does belongs to a different setting. A general restoration of the amphictyonic tradition was brought about, and the conditions for this were favourable. After the decline in the power of Assyria Josiah could intervene in the territory of what was formerly the northern kingdom and win back parts of the old Israel.[41] The view held throughout Judah was that the promises of the Davidic covenant were being fulfilled and that the framework of a common life embracing the whole of Israel was being established. The seventh century B.C. was in a special sense a century of restoration. Everywhere men's eyes were turned to the inheritance of their fathers. A new beginning was also made in Judah, in which the Deuteronomic movement played a large part.[42] The Levitical circles which adhered to the traditions of the ancient amphictyony brought the old traditions back into the centre of worship. It is quite possible that it was as part of this great restoration that the old law in Deut. xxxi. 9 ff. was reinstated (cf. pp. 74 ff.). The festival of the renewal of the covenant for all Israel came to be celebrated again as it had been in the past, and the central sanctuary once again attained its dominant significance. Regulations were made requiring the centralization of the whole of worship, and in the sphere of the state ancient Israelite institutions were revived. It would be rewarding to try to discover what areas of political life were affected by this restoration of the ancient Israelite amphictyony during the time of Josiah, and many different aspects could no doubt be brought to light. But we must return to 2 Kings xxiii. 1–3. King Josiah stood forth as the mediator of the covenant; he read aloud the תורה and effected the actual ratification of the covenant. This presents us with a new factor—that of the king as mediator of the covenant. If we consider what we have already seen of the restoration of the amphictyony in the context of the state, we can say without hesitation that the king has now taken over the position in the Israelite cult which was formerly occupied by the mediator of the covenant. In the process of restoration an amphictyonic function falls to the ruler, which was carried out long ago by Joshua (Joshua xxiv. 25; cf. also pp. 196 f.). This office of the king as mediator attained great importance in the cult of the renewal of the covenant, especially as Jeremiah gives expression to an important promise, the significance of which could not be fully grasped previously, which states: 'And their prince shall be of themselves, and their ruler shall proceed from the midst of them; and I will cause him to draw near, and he shall approach unto

[41] M. Noth, *History of Israel*, pp. 272 ff.

[42] Cf. G. von Rad, *Studies in Deuteronomy*, pp. 44 ff.

me: for who is he that hath had boldness to approach unto me? saith the Lord. And ye shall be my people, and I will be your God.' Israel is therefore to be given a mediator who, as ruler and prince (the title 'king' is probably avoided intentionally) can come before Yahweh. According to Exod. xxiv. 1 f., only the mediator of the covenant could 'come near' Yahweh. He alone had access to God, and no other person dared venture to come before Yahweh. The promise in Jer. xxx. 21, 22 declares that the Messianic king of the future will have this final access to Yahweh; then the 'new covenant' will be made, and 'ye shall be my people, and I will be your God'. The prophet Jeremiah—and there are no adequate grounds for questioning the authenticity of this Messianic promise—obviously pictures a royal mediator of the covenant who will seek, like Josiah, to renew the covenant between Yahweh and Israel (cf. Jer. xxxiv. 8 ff.). But first a completely new situation must be created by God: Yahweh himself must grant to the royal mediator of the last days access to his holy majesty. This renewal of Israel that was sought from the days of Josiah onwards failed to bring about a restoration. The reasons given by Jeremiah for the failure of the attempts at renewal cannot be gone into here.

If it is true that Josiah tried to bring about a restoration of the amphictyony within the framework of the state, we can now suggest an interpretation as regards this period of the relationship between the Sinaitic covenant and the Davidic covenant which we refrained from doing in general terms at an earlier stage. Josiah's aim was to bring the Davidic covenant and the Sinaitic covenant finally together. We can therefore now summarize the position as follows: from the time of Solomon the Davidic covenant predominated in the official cult at Jerusalem. All the kings tried to exercise their rule on the basis of the promise expressed by Nathan as it was actualized in worship, but without recourse to the amphictyonic traditions. By this usurpation of the right of election the relationship of God and people was more and more undermined. Pagan gods and cults were introduced to Jerusalem, and only rarely was the Sinaitic covenant preserved on Zion as the basis for the Davidic covenant. But the reforms of the cult indicate a renewal of the Sinaitic covenant. Josiah was the first to include the Sinai traditions in the official Davidic cult as part of a general restoration. Of one thing, however, there can be no doubt: that the Sinai tradition was brought to Jerusalem along with the Ark, and that the cultic institution of the renewal of the covenant was something that was always held before David's successors in that monarchy that was rooted in the amphictyonic sacral order.

3. The Canaanite-Jebusite Cultic Traditions

(a) *The Sacred Mount of God*

In the religion and cult of the Canaanite-Jebusite city of Jerusalem traditions and institutions were developed in the pre-Israelite period which were closely connected with the whole Canaanite-Syrian culture. The texts from Ras Shamra have given us a deep insight into this world, and comparison with Old Testament traditions soon shows, for example, that the cultic traditions of Jerusalem, as they are reflected particularly in the Psalms, contain Canaanite concepts and themes.[43] Two different worlds met on mount Zion: Israel's central sanctuary and the Canaanite cult of the holy city of Jerusalem. The Canaanite-Jebusite traditions were firmly rooted in this holy place. The Ark tradition therefore entered a sphere which immediately exerted its influence upon the amphictyonic sacral language, ideas and institutions. These alien elements had to be taken up into the worship of Israel, transformed and incorporated into the service of Yahweh. Whereas Ps. cxxii is a typical example of a song of Zion based upon the amphictyonic traditions, Ps. xlvi and xlviii are typical expressions of a faith influenced by Canaanite-Jebusite language and ideas. These two psalms contain strange descriptions which are derived from a self-contained mythological tradition from the pre-Israelite period, which had not even originated in Jebusite Jerusalem. Ps. xlviii. 2 declares that mount Zion lies 'in the far north'—a very strange kind of 'topography'. We can find some explanation of this within the Old Testament in Isa. xiv. 13 f., where the presumptuous words of the 'king of Babel' are quoted in a satirical song: 'I will ascend into heaven, I will exalt my throne above the stars of God; and I will sit upon the mount of congregation, in the uttermost parts of the north: I will ascend above the heights of the clouds: I will be like the Most High.' We can see from this passage that the צָפוֹן mountain in the mythological cultic tradition was a seat of the gods near to heaven, a mount Olympus, on which the 'supreme god' had his throne.[44] The

[43] Cf. especially: R. de Vaux, 'Les Textes de Ras Shamra et l'Ancient Testament', *RB*, 46 (1937), pp. 526 ff.; J. Pedersen, 'Canaanite and Israelite Cultus', *AcOr*, 18 (1940), pp. 1 ff.; W. Baumgartner, 'Ras Schamra und das Alte Testament', *ThR* (1940), pp. 163 ff.; (1941), pp. 1 ff., 85 ff., 157 ff.; ibid., 'Ugaritische Probleme und ihre Tragweite für das Alte Testament', *ThZ*, 3 (1947), pp. 81 ff.; G. Fohrer, 'Die wiederentdeckte kanaanäische Religion', *ThLZ*, 78 (1953), pp. 193 ff.

[44] Cf. O. Eissfeldt, 'Zeus Kasios und der Durchzug der Israeliten durchs Meer', *Beiträge zur Religionsgeschichte des Altertums*, I (1932), pp. 14 ff.; A. Lauha, *Zaphon. Der Norden und die Nordvölker im Alten Testament*, Annales Academiae scientarum Fennicae, 49 (1943); W. A. Albright, 'Baal Zaphon', *Festschrift A. Bertholet* (1950), pp. 2 ff.; W. Schmidt, *Königtum Gottes in Ugarit und Israel*, BZAW 80 (1961), pp. 23 ff.

Ras Shamra texts have shown us that the צפון mountain played an important part in the Syro-Phoenician world. It lay to the north of Ugarit and was identical with the *jebel el akra'* on which *b'l ṣpn* (Baal Zaphon) reigned. This mount of the gods, the position of which can be so accurately defined, was the model of the 'mount Olympus' similarly in the Syrian-Canaanite region. The idea and tradition of the 'mount of God' were not fixed, however, and could be transferred to other sacred high places as well. In this way the צפון tradition came to Jerusalem in the pre-Israelite period and surrounded Zion with a mythical splendour. A universal predominance was thus ascribed to the mountain sanctuary (cf. Isa. ii. 2 ff.), and the mount of God came to be thought of as the centre of the earth. It was 'the joy of the whole earth' (Ps. xlviii. 2; Lam. ii. 15), and was thought of as Paradise (cf. Ezek. xxviii. 11 ff., esp. *v.* 15). These ideas were also applied to Jerusalem itself (Ezek. xlvii. 1 ff.).

Equally as strange as the designation צפון is the fact that in Ps. xlvi. 4 the נהר פלגיו is mentioned, by which the holy city is 'made glad'. It is obvious that these 'streams' cannot refer to the small *gīḥōn* spring on the eastern edge of the city of David. Ps. lxv. 9 and Isa. xxxiii. 21 also speak of 'streams' which flow from Jerusalem, and in Joel iii. 18, Ezek. xlvii and Zech. xiv. 8 the streams of water from Zion bring fertility and salvation to the land. H. Gunkel and H. Gressmann were the first to point out that here mythical conceptions of the garden of Paradise or of the mount of God have been applied to Jerusalem.[45] This 'primeval' garden of God is described in Gen. ii and Ezek. xlvii (cf. also Ezek. xxviii. 11 ff.). Further light is thrown on the background of these ideas by the Ras Shamra texts. In ancient Ugarit the god El was pictured seated 'by the courses of the Two Rivers in the midst of the streams of the Two Deeps' (C. H. Gordon, op. cit., p. 44). In other words, El dwells at the place where the subterranean flood bursts forth in streams (*nhrm*) and makes the earth fertile.[46] Whenever a 'Temple spring' is mentioned in the Old Testament, it has to be seen in connection with these mythical conceptions (cf. Joel iii. 18; Ezek. xlvii; Zech. xiv. 8). The tradition was taken over from the Jebusites.

The holy city, the throne of the 'high God' and the heavenly source of all fertility, was thought of in mythology as impregnable. This idea is found in Ps. xlvi. 5 ff. in the Old Testament (cf. also 2 Sam. v. 6; Ps. lxxxvii. 5; cxxv. 1 f.; Isa. xxvi. 1). Mysterious forces rise against this

[45] H. Gunkel, *Das Märchen im Alten Testament,* Religionsgeschichtliche Volksbücher, II, 23/26 (1921), pp. 48 ff.; H. Gressmann, *Der Messias* (1929), pp. 179 ff.

[46] Cf. W. Schmidt, op. cit., pp. 6 f.

place of imperturbable order and salvation (Ps. xlvi. 5 f.; xlviii. 4 ff.; Isa. xvii. 12 f.), but the forces of chaos and the attacks of the nations are repelled with thunder and lightning, and the enemies are destroyed before the holy city (Ps. xlvi. 6 f.; xlviii. 5; lxxvi. 3 ff., etc.).[47]

In all these developments we can trace a threefold process. In the pre-Israelite period a mythological interpretation of the holy mount of God, which belonged primarily to the Syro-Phoenician world but was also widespread in the whole of Canaan, established itself in Jebusite Jerusalem. When the Ark was installed on mount Zion, the cultic traditions even penetrated the Israelite sanctuary, but were applied to Yahweh and refashioned in the light of the faith of the Old Testament. The mythical splendour which radiated from the Syrian-Canaanite traditions served to glorify the place where the God of Israel was present.[48]

(b) *The Kingship of God*

It is particularly in several passages of the Psalms that Yahweh, the God of Israel, is called 'King'. This title has for some considerable time given rise to questions concerning the origin and significance of the designation. In his book *Das Königtum Gottes* Martin Buber could still put forward the view that the title מלך had already been ascribed to Yahweh at Sinai, as the Sinaitic covenant had the meaning of a 'royal covenant' (Deut. xxxiii. 5), and that the royal dignity was connected first and foremost with the directing power of the God of the desert period. Such views are no longer tenable in view of the newly discovered sources from Ras Shamra.[49] In any case it could have been shown by a careful investigation that the title מלך belongs to Canaan and not to the desert. But in recent years Old Testament scholarship has shown 'that the conception of Yahweh's kingship does not appear to have been a basic element in the original content of Israelite religion'.[50] The title

[47] Cf. H.-J. Kraus, *Psalmen*, pp. 344 f.

[48] In his dissertation *Die Bedeutung der Erwählungstradition Israels für die Eschatologie der alttestamentlichen Propheten* (Heidelberg, 1956), pp. 145 ff., E. Rohland puts the cultic traditions that deal with the 'sacred mountain of God' in the category of 'election traditions', which is not correct. The mythological elements in the Canaanite-Jebusite world were taken over by the Jerusalem cult as 'glorification sayings'; they are connected with the election of Zion only in a subordinate sense—by being linked with the *hieros logos* that marks out the elect city.

[49] Cf. O. Eissfeldt, 'Jahwe als König', *ZAW*, 46 (1928), reprinted in *Kleine Schriften*, I, pp. 172 ff., pp. 81 ff.; H. Schmid, 'Jahwe und die Kulttraditionen von Jerusalem', *ZAW*, 68 (1955), pp. 168 ff.; W. Schmidt, *Königtum Gottes in Ugarit und Israel*, BZAW 80 (1961); J. Gray, 'The Kingship of God in the Prophets and Psalms', *VT*, 11 (1961), pp. 1 ff.

[50] A. Alt. 'Gedanken über das Königtum Jahwes', *Kleine Schriften*, I, p. 348.

מלך could not be applied to Yahweh until the Canaanite sanctuary of the temple had become the place where he was present and where he dwelt. W. Schmidt has rightly pointed out that 'according to Canaanite beliefs, as they are revealed in the Ras Shamra texts, the royal status of a god is not firmly established and assured until a temple has been constructed. It is an essential condition that the divine King should possess a temple as his palace. Divine kingship and temple are inseparable'.[51] But this reference to the temple does not go far enough. The conclusions to be drawn from the pre-Israelite cultic traditions need to be pursued further, for the description of God as מלך was part of the cultic veneration of the 'high God'. But where was this 'high God' worshipped? It is here that we see evidence of the *analogia relationis* of monarchical theology. If the king of a city conquered a large area, he triumphed over the princes of the region he had conquered and attained a position of supremacy. The political relationships are directly reflected in the world of the gods. The many local spirits were overthrown by the god of the victorious city king, and this god became the 'high god', the מלך. There was a monarchist view of God corresponding to his position of supremacy. It is hardly conceivable that a theology of God as King was developed at insignificant Canaanite temple sanctuaries, and the idea of the 'high God' seems to be firmly linked with the mount of God where the royal deity is enthroned. All these considerations support the view that the title מלך was first applied to Yahweh in Jerusalem.[52] It was linked with a whole series of other names and titles which were used for the 'high God', among which the epithets (אל) עליון, אדון כל־הארץ and שפט should be particularly noted. In Gen. xiv. 18 the city god of Jerusalem is called אל עליון, a title which is used in the Psalms for Yahweh. He rules over all gods (Ps. xcvii. 9) and is the 'Most High' over all the earth (Ps. lxxxiii. 18; xcvii. 9). All forces and powers are subject to him—not only as subordinate deities, but as a result of their partial dispossession as ministering spirits. Yahweh lays claim to universal power as the Most High God. He is מלך גדול על־כל־הארץ—'a great King over all the earth' (Ps. xlvii. 2) and Judge of the whole universe (Ps. xcvi. 10, 13; xcix. 9). Yahweh is enthroned 'on high' above the peoples (Ps. vii. 7) and judges the nations (Ps. vii. 8; ix. 9, 20; xcvi. 10). But Yahweh as King is not merely 'Most High', 'Lord' and 'Judge', he is also worshipped as 'Creator' of the earth (Ps. xxiv. 1; xciii. 1; xcv. 3 ff.; xcvi. 5, 10; cf. Gen. xiv. 19). This whole complex of titles and concepts entered into the realm of Israelite faith at Jerusalem and opened up new

[51] W. Schmidt, op. cit., p. 57.
[52] Cf. H.-J. Kraus, *Psalmen*, pp. 197 ff.

horizons.[53] But at the centre of worship there still stands Yahweh, the God of Israel, the One who appeared and made himself known at mount Sinai. The foreign titles and concepts did not transpose the God of Israel and the faith of the cultic community at Jerusalem into a different religious sphere, but rather gave it a new vision of the kingly majesty of Yahweh, supreme over all forces and powers.

The prophet Jeremiah sees as the task laid urgently upon the priests, but also applying to the whole of the community of Israel, that of asking insistently in every new sphere and as regards every alien influence the question: איה יהוה (Jer. ii. 6, 8; xxix. 13). Whenever the people of God encountered a flood of religious and cultic forces with which it had not previously been familiar, only one way was open: the cultic community must assure itself afresh of the presence of Yahweh in the alien sphere. In this process the ליהוה which characterized the earliest cultic traditions exerted its influence. What mattered most of all was that the concepts and attitudes, the myths and institutions of Canaan should be applied to Yahweh, interpreted and adopted with reference to him.

(c) *A 'Festival of Yahweh's Enthronement'?*

We have already set out the main theories put forward by Mowinckel (cf. pp. 8 f.).[54] The question we must now consider is whether a 'festival of Yahweh's enthronement' might have been celebrated at Jerusalem. Was a cultic enthronement of God, such as we see in ancient Oriental texts, linked with the application of the title of King to Yahweh? It was not only in Mesopotamia, from where Mowinckel drew his historical parallels, but also in ancient Ugarit that the cult drama of the enthronement of Baal played an important rôle. Should we not expect to find a similar festival in the worship at Jerusalem?

There are a number of Psalms in which Yahweh is worshipped as King (Ps. xxiv. 7 ff.; xlvii; xciii; xcvi; xcvii; xcviii; xcix). The very heart of these Psalms which deal with Yahweh's kingship—and at the same time the evidence on which he based his interpretation—Mowinckel took to be the cry יהוה מלך which we find in Ps. xlvii, xciii, xcvii and xcix, and which was interpreted by him as an acclamation of enthronement ('Yahweh has become king'). Serious objections, however, have

[53] Cf. H. Schmid, 'Jahwe und die Kulttraditionen von Jerusalem', *ZAW*, 68 (1955), pp. 168 ff.

[54] S. Mowinckel, *Psalmenstudien II: Das Thronbesteigungsfest Jahwäs und der Ursprung der Eschatologie* (1922); ibid., *Zum israelitischen Neujahr und zur Deutung der Thronbesteigungspsalmen*, *ANVAO*, II, Hist.-Filos. Klasse (1952).

been raised to this interpretation.[55] The verb with the meaning 'to be king' can certainly be found in many passages in the Old Testament.[56] 2 Sam. xv. 10 (1 Kings i. 11) and 2 Kings ix. 13 suggest the idea of 'becoming king' in the so-called 'enthronement cry'. But the finer points of grammar and syntax require closer attention.[57] We read in 1 Kings i. 11 מלך אדניהו. This verbal construction which in its context is clearly meant to be an exclamation refers to an action that has just been completed. In translating it one has to choose between suggesting the completed action ('Adonijah has become king') or the state brought about by the action ('Adonijah is king'). The syntactical problem is clarified, however, if we read further in the same passage, for in 1 Kings i. 18 the final state is described by the words ועתה הנה אדניהו מלך; the sequence here reads אדניהו מלך. If we see this very significant variation in the word-order in a larger context, it becomes clear that the cry יהוה מלך that we find in the Psalms celebrating Yahweh as king should be translated by the words 'Yahweh is king'.[58] The reference is to a state, not to an act. The word-sequence is different only in Ps. xlvii. 9, a psalm which is definitely influenced by the idea of enthronement.[59]

In addition to the observations concerning grammar and syntax which make the idea of an enthronement appear untenable, there are other important considerations which contradict Mowinckel's theories. In the first place we have to ask how an enthronement of Yahweh could have been carried out at Jerusalem in any case. There is neither a statue of a God which could have been elevated on to a throne, nor do we know of any other symbol which might have been taken to be a representation of Yahweh.[60] We have also to ask in what theological context we should have to consider an 'enthronement of Yahweh'. In connection with Mowinckel's cultic theory H. Schmidt has made it unmistakably clear what the theological context of a 'festival of Yahweh's enthronement' would have to be. Schmidt assumes that the God of Israel—like all other vegetation deities—'actually loses for a period'

[55] See the discussion by J. J. Stamm, 'Ein Vierteljahrhundert Psalmenforschung', *ThR*, N.F. 23 (1951), pp. 45 ff.

[56] Cf. Gen. xxxvi. 31; Joshua xiii. 12, 21; Judges iv. 2; ix. 8; 2 Sam. xvi. 8; 1 Kings xiv. 20, etc.

[57] On the syntactical questions, see L. Koehler, '*Jahwä mālāk*', *VT*, 3 (1953), pp. 188 f.; J. Ridderbos, 'JAHWÄH MALAK', *VT*, 4 (1954), pp. 87 ff.; D. Michel, 'Studien zu den sogenannten Thronbesteigungspsalmen', *VT*, 6 (1956), pp. 40 ff.; ibid., *Tempora und Satzstellung in den Psalmen*, Abhandlungen z. Ev. Theol., 1 (1960).

[58] For the details, see H.-J. Kraus, *Psalmen*, pp. 201 ff. and 647 ff.

[59] It is possible that the ceremony of enthronement for a human king provided the theme of Ps. xlvii. See H.-J. Kraus, op. cit., pp. 203 f. and 348 ff.

[60] Cf. also D. Michel, *VT*, 6 (1956), p. 47.

his supremacy in the natural rhythm of the seasons, and declares that 'This is a myth similar to that of the periodic descent of the gods to the underworld and their resurrection'.[61] Such ideas are taken so much for granted in the dogma of the 'pattern' school of thought that they are accepted as being quite proved. But this is out of the question, as there is no evidence within the Old Testament of this idea of a 'mythicizing' of Yahweh, the Lord of history. It is far more important for us to note the way in which the unchangeable and eternal kingship of Yahweh is emphatically extolled in Ps. xciii. 2. This is the decisive point where the rhythm of nature and its actualization in the cultic drama has not succeeded in asserting itself—in connection with the unchangeable royal supremacy of Yahweh which is subject to no variations.[62]

In discussions concerning a 'festival of Yahweh's enthronement' reference is always made to the Ark, which—as we have already seen—is thought of in some passages in the Old Testament as an empty divine throne. If there had been any kind of cultic festival of enthronement, it would have had to be connected with the Ark; but here we meet considerable difficulties. For one thing, those passages which describe a procession of the Ark and on which Mowinckel confidently bases his case for the reconstruction of the 'festival of Yahweh's enthronement', have no connection with any such cultic act of enthronement. We have already discussed the significance of the solemn bearing of the Ark into the Temple which is described in 2 Sam. vi, 1 Kings viii and Ps. cxxxii (cf. pp. 183 ff.). In any case it must be noted that the suggestion concerning an 'act of enthronement' does not do justice to a passage such as Ps. xxiv. 7 ff., on which the hypothesis of the elevation of Yahweh as king in an act of worship is based. The psalm speaks rather of an introduction of the divine throne into the Temple. There is no mention of Yahweh ascending the throne, but he comes in as the 'King of glory', and is therefore welcomed as the God who is already present above the throne. We could therefore speak of a royal entry by Yahweh above the divine throne of the Ark. The historical background of the Ark narrative as the *hieros logos* of Jerusalem makes it impossible

[61] H. Schmidt, *Die Thronfahrt Jahves am Fest der Jahreswende im alten Israel* (1927) pp. 26 ff.

[62] It is not altogether clear what bearing W. Schmidt's study, *Königtum Gottes in Ugarit und Israel* (1961), has upon the question of Divine Kingship in the Old Testament. The clear distinction made between the distant, unchangeable and creative deity El and the militant deity Baal who is near at hand and who promotes fertility is no doubt correct, but what is the relationship between the two powers? And what bearing would the way we describe this relationship have upon the explanation of the ideas adopted by the New Testament from the sphere of activity of these two deities?

for us to turn the God of Israel as he comes to Zion into a nature deity or to assume that Yahweh forfeited his sovereignty in any way.

4. The Festival Cult at Jerusalem

(a) *The Structure of a Festival*

'And three times in a year did Solomon offer burnt offerings and peace offerings upon the altar which he built unto the Lord . . .' (1 Kings ix. 25). The annals make it clear in these words that the ancient Israelite cultic calendar continued to be observed in Jerusalem. The three main annual festivals were celebrated in the sanctuary as great sacrificial feasts, but it was the feast of Tabernacles that was really the principal festival (1 Kings viii. 2). It was not until the time of Josiah that the feast of the Passover came to the fore (Deut. xvi. 1 ff.; 2 Kings xxiii. 21 f.—see pp. 49 ff.).[63] The division of the autumn festival into three parts must have taken place in the short period of time between the reformation of king Josiah and the Babylonian exile (Lev. xxiii. 23 ff.—see pp. 66 ff.). These few facts give us an outline of the main events in the cultic history of Jerusalem before the Exile. The information that can be gained from the legal and historical traditions in the Old Testament is really very little, and we certainly cannot build up from these sources a picture of the actual course of worship at Jerusalem that is in any way adequate. We can conclude from various passages that sacrifices were offered, but it is difficult to envisage the details of the cult. As there are no extensive descriptions of worship anywhere in the Old Testament, and no full rituals which give details concerning the sacrifices that have to be offered, the most that we can do is to take separate points of detail from the tradition and try to co-ordinate them. The Psalms in particular offer an abundance of material, but it is extremely varied and complicated, and it is not easy to isolate the cultic elements and to see them in their proper relation to one another. The history of research into Old Testament worship teaches us that considerable errors have arisen as a result of adopting a wrong principle for co-ordinating the great variety of details scattered throughout the Old Testament. Mowinckel, for example, included the various details which had a cultic significance altogether in the scheme of 'the festival of Yahweh's enthronement' and so drew up an all-inclusive picture of Old Testament worship that creates a vicious circle.[64] The same is true of the 'pattern' school of

[63] E. Kutsch, 'Erwägungen zur Geschichte der Passafeier und des Massotfestes', *ZThK*, 55 (1958), pp. 10 ff.

[64] The vicious circle arises from the fact that, on the narrow basis of the so-called 'songs of Yahweh's enthronement' and by a chain of associations, Mowinckel puts in

thought, for here again one starts from the usual categories of religious and cultic phenomenology and makes the material of the Psalms fit into them. And now Artur Weiser has found a new category by postulating a 'cult of the Covenant' into which he fits the different elements in the Psalter.[65] The danger, therefore, is that of trying to impose upon the varied cultic traditions scattered throughout the Psalms an order based upon an alien principle.

The only way in which this danger of distorting the cultic traditions in the Psalter can be avoided is by keeping consistently to what the passages really say.[66] We have to be guided by the plain indications in the hymns and poems, and in our desire to trace a pattern we have to take account of the trends within the individual cultic traditions. Even though as a result of this attempt the final picture may appear to lack unity at certain points, and at other points to be drawn too confidently, our aim is to discover the basic structure of worship at Jerusalem and to throw light on certain phases of the cult. It is only with great caution that we can assume that our account can in essence be applied to the principal Israelite feast, the feast of Tabernacles, and it is, of course, quite possible that elements from other cultic contexts should be added to this picture. With this reservation and with the readiness to accept a more accurate interpretation of the arrangement of the separate details, we will attempt to describe the structure of the festival cult at Jerusalem.

The pilgrimage to Zion was the climax of his life for an Israelite. He looked forward to the feast days with yearning and desire:

> 'As the hart panteth after the waterbrooks,
> So panteth my soul after thee, O God.
> My soul thirsteth for God, for the living God:
> When shall I come and appear before God?'

These opening words of Ps. xlii show us how deep and strong this longing for the place of God's presence was (cf. Ps. lxxxiv. 2). It was like a ray of light when the routine of everyday life was interrupted by the 'invitation to pilgrimage'[67] and the journey to Jerusalem was begun:

[65] A. Weiser, *The Psalms* (E.T. 1962), Introduction.

[66] Cf. G. Quell, *Das kultische Problem der Psalmen*, BWANT, 11 (1926).

[67] This 'call to pilgrimage' has been taken over even into the 'eschatological hymn of Zion' (Isa. ii. 2 ff.).

---

the same category as the particular themes in these 'enthronement psalms' similar statements in other psalms. This method soon sets in motion an extremely questionable 'demonstration', and the forms and outlines of the types become confused. The 'festival of Yahweh's enthronement' becomes a magnet which attracts the most varied elements, so long as they contain even a trace of the relevant material.

'I was glad when they said unto me,
Let us go unto the house of the Lord' (Ps. cxxii. 1).

The pilgrims gladly faced the trials of the journey. They had to cross dry regions (Ps. lxxxiv. 6), laden with the sacrificial animals and the offerings (Jer. xli. 5), but their strength revived as they drew near to the place of the holy and saving presence of the God of Israel (Ps. lxxxiv. 8). The worshipper in Ps. cxxii remembers the wonderful moment of arrival in the sanctuary:

'Our feet are standing
Within thy gates, O Jerusalem.'

The journey was accompanied by songs of pilgrimage and even on the journey, particularly immediately outside the gates of the city of God, the 'songs of Zion' were sung.[68] In Ps. cxxxvii. 3 this category of psalm is specifically mentioned, and we can well imagine that Ps. xlvi, xlviii, lxxvi (lxxxiv), lxxxvii and cxxii had their 'setting in life' in these same circumstances. But the jubilation of the songs praising the sanctuary subsided when the pilgrims entered Jerusalem. Requests and prayers for Zion were brought before Yahweh (Ps. cxxii. 6 ff.), and a prayer of intercession for the king as the ruler of the Temple was uttered (Ps. lxxxiv. 9 f.).

The actual festival cult began with the solemn ascent of the Ark to the Temple mount.[69] We can only make suggestions as regards the place where the congregation gathered for this preliminary act of worship, and suggest that it was probably in the area to the south of the city of David.[70] The procession began with an act of adoration 'at his holy hill' (Ps. xcix. 9), and the first hymns were no doubt struck up here, coming to their climax in the 'summons to enter the Temple':

'O come, let us sing unto the Lord:
Let us make a joyful noise to the rock of our salvation.
Let us come before his presence with thanksgiving,
Let us make a joyful noise unto him with psalms.
For the Lord is a great God,
And a great King above all gods.
In his hand are the deep places of the earth;
The heights of the mountains are his also.
The sea is his, and he made it;

[68] Cf. H. Gunkel/J. Begrich, *Einleitung in die Psalmen* (1933), pp. 309 ff.

[69] See H.-J. Kraus, *Die Königsherrschaft Gottes im Alten Testament*, loc. cit., pp. 27 ff.

[70] It is impossible to say to what extent the cult legend in 2 Sam. vi. 10 f. gives any concrete evidence concerning the topography, which is so significant for the cultic festival.

And his hands formed the dry land.
O come, let us worship and bow down;
Let us kneel before the Lord our Maker' (Ps. xcv. 1–6).

The solemn ascent could now begin. The exhortations of the cultic prophets and the teachings of the priests recalled the original event by which Jerusalem was established as a 'chosen' Kingdom.[71] By means of the action of the cultic drama the congregation was transported into the time of David, and caught up into the events connected with the discovery of the Ark at Kiriath-Jearim (Ps. cxxxii. 6). When the cry rang out:

'We will go into his tabernacles;
We will worship at his footstool'

the people knew that they had been transported back to the time of David. Priests accompanied and directed the ceremony. As was the custom in early times, the תרועה was carried out at this solemn ascent of the Ark.[72] The congregation burst out in loud jubilation and shouts of joy (*v.* 9; Ps. xlii. 5). The 'election of David' was celebrated along with the 'election of Zion' (*v.* 13). The basic ברית was remembered, by which supremacy in Jerusalem had been promised to the Davidic dynasty (*vv.* 11 f.). The whole official cult was built on these two pillars, and the welfare of the people depended on the securing of these foundations. So the congregation heard through the mouth of the cultic prophet Yahweh's message:

'This is my resting place for ever:
Here will I dwell; for I have desired it.
I will abundantly bless her provision:
I will satisfy her poor with bread.
Her priests also will I clothe with salvation:
And her saints shall shout aloud for joy.
There will I make the horn of David to bud:
I have ordained a lamp for mine anointed.
His enemies will I clothe with shame:
But upon himself shall his crown flourish' (Ps. cxxxii. 14–18).

When the solemn procession was approaching the sanctuary and had reached the gates which opened into the courtyards the priests intoned the 'Entrance Torah' (Ps. xv; xxivA).[73] At the שערי־צדק through which

[71] For the details, see the discussion on pp. 183 ff.
[72] Cf. P. Humbert, *TEROU'A. Analyse d'un rite biblique* (1946).
[73] Cf. H.-J. Kraus, *Psalmen*, pp. 110 ff., 193 ff.

only the צדיקים could enter into the holy place (Ps. cxviii. 19 f.), there was first heard a voice which set out the 'Entrance Torah' in question form:

> 'Lord, who shall sojourn in thy tabernacle?
> Who shall dwell in thy holy hill?'

Priests gave the answer, which was held up before each individual for the purpose of self-examination as he entered Yahweh's sanctuary:

> 'He that walketh uprightly, and worketh righteousness,
> And speaketh truth in his heart.
> He that slandereth not with his tongue,
> Nor doeth evil to his friend,
> Nor taketh up a reproach against his neighbour.
> In whose eyes a reprobate is despised;
> But he honoureth them that fear the Lord.
> He that sweareth to his own hurt, and changeth not.
> He that putteth not out his money to usury,
> Nor taketh reward against the innocent.
> He that doeth these things shall never be moved' (Ps. xv).

In Israel worship was not considered as an 'exceptional activity'. Those who came to Jerusalem did not enter a sphere of religious enthusiasm and exaltation, of overwrought emotion and ecstasy. The worshippers were asked about how they worshipped God in their everyday lives. In the Old Testament עבד refers not only to the sacral sphere, but to the whole of life, which is subject to the commandments of Yahweh (cf. Joshua xxiv). Only the צדיק may come before Yahweh—the man who lives a life in keeping with the covenant under the regulations of the ברית. The priestly words of the 'Entrance Torah' are reminiscent of the apodeictic divine law, for they penetrate to the deepest motives and call upon the worshippers to examine themselves in penitence concerning their innermost thoughts and feelings (Ps. xv. 1; xxiv. 3).[74] In other words, at every entry into the Temple sanctuary the joy of the congregation was abruptly interrupted by the holy severity of the divine law. We can probably assume that at the שערי־צדק great individual prophets appeared along with the priests, in order to take the people to task as they approach and call upon them to return to the Lord (Ps. xcv. 8–11; Jer. vii. 2).

After the 'Entrance Torah' was completed the 'Entrance Liturgy'

[74] Mowinckel's assumption that the Decalogue arose from the 'Entrance Torah' is based on inadequate form analysis. A. Alt was the first to clarify the form critical basis in *Die Ursprünge des israelitischen Rechts* (1934), (*Kleine Schriften*, I, pp. 278 ff.) Cf. S. Mowinckel, *Le Décalogue* (1927).

proper could begin. We can see the connections between the two very clearly in Ps. xxiv. In *vv.* 3–6 there is a direct parallel to Ps. xv, and then a solemn entrance is celebrated as follows:

The priests accompanying the Ark procession exclaim:

> Lift up your heads, O ye gates;
> And be ye lift up, ye everlasting doors:
> And the King of glory shall come in.'

The priests awaiting the Ark in the sanctuary call for the confession to be made upon entering:

> 'Who is the King of glory?'

The reply from outside:

> 'The Lord strong and mighty,
> The Lord mighty in battle.'

The cry once again from outside:

> 'Lift up your heads, O ye gates;
> Yea, lift them up, ye everlasting doors:
> And the King of glory shall come in.'

The question about the confession of faith to be made upon entering is repeated:

> 'Who is the King of glory?'

The reply from outside:

> 'The Lord of hosts,
> He is the King of glory.'

The climax of the ceremony was the mighty official proclamation of the sacred cultic name of Yahweh. The exclamation of the name was an important act of worship. Yahweh is to be known and addressed as יהוה צבאות (*v.* 10).[75] 'Yahweh Sabaoth' is the name of the God who is present at Jerusalem. When we examine Ps. xxiv carefully we cannot fail to see that the connections with the Ark tradition of the Jerusalem *hieros logos* come out in a quite unambiguous way. The traditions which point back to Shiloh come to the fore (cf. 1 Sam. iv. 4; xvii. 45). The God who appears on mount Zion is the 'God of Israel', the יהוה צבאות of the

[75] On the significance of the divine name, cf. B. N. Wambacq, *L'épithète divine Jahvé Sebaoth* (1947); O. Eissfeldt, 'Jahwe Zebaoth', *Miscellanea academica Berolinensia* (1950), pp. 128 ff.; G. von Rad, *Old Testament Theology*, I, pp. 18 f.

sanctuary of Shiloh. The מלך הכבוד which was venerated at Jerusalem—under the influence of Canaanite-Jebusite cultic traditions—is still the יהוה צבאות that has come from Shiloh to Jerusalem. This festival of the installation of the Ark—which has no connection with an 'enthronement', but could rather be described, in the light of the title מלך הכבוד, as an 'installation of the throne'—is therefore to be thought of exclusively as an act of confession of the God of Israel and his first act of election (*v.* 10). Yahweh does not become King, but he comes as King. The title מלך is therefore merely the garment of the יהוה צבאות, merely a title of honour, not something that affects the person or that influences the cult.

The procession into the sanctuary came to its conclusion and its climax in the solemn act of adoration before Yahweh:

> 'We will go into his tabernacle;
> We will worship at his footstool' (Ps. cxxxii. 7).

A number of psalms are linked by a summons of this kind with the act of adoration (cf. Ps. xcv. 6; xcvi. 9; xcix. 5). By means of glorifying titles and themes (derived partly from the Jebusite cultic traditions) Yahweh was praised as the 'high God', as 'King', 'Creator', 'Judge' and Lord of all gods and men.[76] We are familiar with the 'Trisagion' from the literature of the Temple:

> 'Holy, holy, holy,
> is the Lord of hosts:
> the whole earth is full of his glory' (Isa. vi. 3).

This liturgical passage is perhaps the most concise expression of the hymns and prayers that were uttered in this act of adoration (cf. also Ps. xcix). Many of the hymns in the Psalter probably had their 'setting in life' here, and the Temple music[77] no doubt also played its part in this solemn act of worship:

> 'Praise ye the Lord.
> Praise God in his sanctuary:
> Praise him in the firmament of his power.
> Praise him for his mighty acts:
> Praise him according to his excellent greatness.
> Praise him with the sound of the trumpet:

[76] The psalms that speak of Yahweh as King and a large part of the hymns are probably to be attributed to this cultic act of adoration. Cf. H.-J. Kraus, *Psalmen*, pp. xli ff.

[77] See H. Gressmann, *Musik und Musikinstrumente im Alten Testament* (1903); H. Sachsse, 'Palästinische Musikinstrumente', *ZDPV*, 50 (1927), pp. 19 ff.

Praise him with the psaltery and harp.
Praise him with the timbrel and dance:
Praise him with stringed instruments and the pipe.
Praise him upon the loud cymbals:
Praise him upon the high sounding cymbals.
Let everything that hath breath praise the Lord.
Praise ye the Lord' (Ps. cl).

The deeds and perfections of the God of Israel were extolled in the praise that was offered. Although the Jebusite cultic tradition had given the Israelite faith a wider vision of Yahweh's glory in creation and of his universal sovereignty, there still stood at the heart of the hymns of the people of God grateful praise for the mighty saving acts of God (cf. Ps. cxxxvi). These acts of worship were, of course, accompanied by sacrifices and offerings.

In the cultic theology of Jerusalem the idea of the 'dwelling' of Yahweh in the sanctuary came to be linked with the entrance into the Temple (cf. 1 Kings viii. 12 f.; Ps. cxxxii. 13 f.). The Temple, considered from the standpoint of its sacral architecture, was of the type of a Temple where the god dwelt, but a 'theophany expectation' was closely linked with the presence of Yahweh above the Ark. The fact that the God of Israel was not immanently present in the Ark or permanently connected with it in a magical sense, but could freely appear, 'rise up' (Num. x. 35), or 'cause his face to shine' (Ps. lxxx. 3), made it possible for the cultic community to hope for a theophany.[78] Ps. lxxx opens with the words:

'Give ear, O Shepherd of Israel,
Thou that leadest Joseph like a flock;
Thou that sittest upon the cherubim, shine forth'

and Ps. l. 2 f. speaks of the theophany on mount Zion:

'Out of Zion, the perfection of beauty,
God hath shined forth.
Our God shall come, and shall not keep silence:
A fire shall devour before him,
And it shall be very tempestuous round about him.
He shall call to the heavens above,
And to the earth, that he may judge his people.'

[78] On the question of 'theophanies', cf. A. Weiser, 'Zur Frage nach den Beziehungen der Psalmen zum Kult. Die Darstellung der Theophanie in den Psalmen und im Festkult', *Festschrift A. Bertholet* (1950), pp. 513 ff., reprinted in *Glaube und Geschichte im AT* (1961), pp. 303 ff.; H. Bückers, 'Zur Verwertung der Sinaitraditionen in den Psalmen', *Biblica,* 32 (1951), pp. 401 ff.; E. Beaucamp, 'La Théophanie du Ps. 50 (49)', *NRT*, 61 (1959), pp. 897 ff.

There is a considerable number of such descriptions of theophanies in the Old Testament, and the question is how we should understand and interpret these descriptions of divine manifestations. As far as the content of these accounts is concerned, we can recognize three strata, which have become closely linked with each other: elements from the Sinai tradition,[79] concepts connected with the כבוד theology,[80] and Canaanite religious traditions[81] which speak of the appearing of the storm god. But this concerns only the content of the descriptions—what can we say about what actually happened? The views of scholars vary between the extremes. On the one hand, since Mowinckel expounded his theories, it has become customary to allow the possibility that a 'dramatic representation' of the theophany took place in the cult; and on the other hand, the theophanies which transcend all bounds are interpreted 'eschatologically'. Both hypotheses, however, give rise to serious reservations. Is it really conceivable that scenic and dramatic means were used in Israel's worship to command a divine revelation? If this was so, how are we to understand the imploring and expectant prayers and requests that look for a free and gracious self-revelation by Yahweh? The evidence of the Psalms is overwhelmingly unanimous that revelation is not cultically 'manipulated' but belongs to the sovereign freedom of the God of Israel. However, the theophany was not merely eschatological, but was an event that had an immediate cultic connection. When we try to decide how to picture this event to ourselves, and how and when a divine manifestation was perceived, if we are not to let our imagination run away with us we must restrict ourselves to those passages in which an actual theophany is described. In this connection the traditions in 1 Kings xxii. 19 f. and Isa. vi. 1 ff. are of particular importance. These accounts depict the divine manifestation as a prophetic, visionary event, and in Ps. l also the theophany is directly linked with the prophetic proclamation.[82] It seems reasonable, therefore, to conclude that in the accounts of the appearance of Yahweh we have the evidence of prophetic visionary perception. We must distinguish, therefore, between the faith in the presence of God in the sanctuary, which is basic to all worship, and the expectation of his manifestation in the theophany as proclaimed in prophecy.

We can discover only in part the many different rites and observances

[79] G. von Rad, *Das formgeschichtliche Problem des Hexateuch*, p. 18 ff., *Ges. Stud.*, pp. 28 ff.

[80] G. von Rad, *Studies in Deuteronomy*, pp. 41 ff.

[81] H.-J. Kraus, *Psalmen*, pp. 233 ff.

[82] Cf. E. Beaucamp, op. cit., pp. 897 ff.

that had to be carried out by the congregation during the festival week. The peace offerings were presented in groups, gift offerings were dedicated to Yahweh and dues paid to the sanctuary and its priesthood (cf. pp. 118 ff.). The harvest thanksgiving, in particular, could be offered to the God of Israel, as had been the custom from the earliest times. A hymn such as Ps. lxv. 9–13 was probably used at these thanksgivings:

'Thou visitest the earth, and waterest it,
Thou greatly enrichest it;
The river of God is full of water:
Thou providest them corn, when thou hast so prepared the earth.
Thou waterest her furrows abundantly;
Thou settlest the ridges thereof:
Thou makest it soft with showers;
Thou blessest the springing thereof.
Thou crownest the year with thy goodness;
And thy paths drop fatness.
They drop upon the pastures of the wilderness;
And the hills are girded with joy.
The pastures are clothed with flocks;
The valleys also are covered over with corn;
They shout for joy, they also sing.'

In these hymns of thanksgiving there was the deep conviction that the abundance of gifts came forth from the sanctuary. The 'river of God' springs from the cultic centre, and here is the 'fountain of life' (Ps. xxxvi. 9).[83] But the decisive thing about the city of God was not that it was a sphere where magical powers were at work, but the fact that 'God is in the midst of her' (Ps. xlvi. 5). The greatest blessing, therefore, was to be able to stay at the place where Yahweh was present:

'For a day in thy courts is better than a thousand.
I had rather be a doorkeeper in the house of my God,
Than to dwell in the tents of wickedness' (Ps. lxxxiv. 10).

This basic experience of joy and peace in the presence of the אל חי (Ps. lxxxiv. 3) made the worshippers wish time after time that the priestly privilege of living always at the holy place might be granted to them too (Ps. lxxxiv. 4; xxiii. 6).[84]

[83] See the discussion on p. 202.

[84] For a discussion of this problem, see G. von Rad, ' "Gerechtigkeit" und "Leben" in der Kultsprache der Psalmen', *Festschrift A. Bertholet* (1950), pp. 418 ff., *Ges. Stud.*, pp. 225 ff.

The fact that the cultic community gathered on mount Zion even for nocturnal festivals shows how completely and deeply the presence of Yahweh was experienced in the sanctuary (Ps. cxxxiv; Isa. xxx. 29). Ps. viii, for example, was probably sung on such occasions (cf. esp. *v.* 4). Processions were held around the holy mountain to the accompaniment of 'songs of Zion' (Ps. xlviii. 12 f.).

When the day came when the pilgrim had to leave the sanctuary, he did so with a 'ceremony of departure' such as has come down to us in Ps. cxxi.[85] The priest commends the pilgrim to the help of the God of Israel, as he looks anxiously at the threatening mountains that surround Jerusalem (*v.* 1) but at the same time trusts God come what may (*v.* 2):

> 'He will not suffer thy foot to be moved:
> He that keepeth thee will not slumber.
> Behold, he that keepeth Israel
> Shall neither slumber nor sleep.
> The Lord is thy keeper:
> The Lord is thy shade upon thy right hand.
> The sun shall not smite thee by day,
> Nor the moon by night.
> The Lord shall keep thee from all evil;
> He shall keep thy soul,
> The Lord shall keep thy going out and thy coming in,
> From this time forth and for evermore.'

With this word of blessing the pilgrim returned to his everyday life.

(b) *The Individual in the Festival Cult*

In the great congregation, whose acts of worship we have been describing, there were individual people with their need and suffering. The 'personal songs of lamentation'[86] in the Psalter are an eloquent witness to the fact that the individual was not submerged in the crowd, but on the contrary had his clear and definite place in the worship of Israel. Scholars veer between two extremes in interpreting these individual psalms. On the one hand the connection of these 'personal songs of lamentation and thanksgiving' with the ritual and the common cult is emphasized, whilst on the other hand some speak of a 'private piety' and of the 'outpourings of the heart' by individual people. Ps. xxii shows very clearly what the attitude is in these personal songs. With his

[85] Cf. H.-J. Kraus, *Psalmen*, pp. 833 ff.

[86] H. Gunkel/J. Begrich, *Einleitung in die Psalmen* (1933), pp. 172 ff.; C. Barth, *Einführung in die Psalmen*, Biblische Studien 32 (1961), pp. 22 ff.

petitions and expectations the individual worshipper has his place in the community of Israel. His cultic expressions are based on the fact

'But thou art holy,
O thou that inhabitest the praises of Israel.
Our fathers trusted in thee:
They trusted, and thou didst deliver them.
They cried unto thee, and were delivered:
They trusted in thee, and were not ashamed' (Ps. xxii. 3–5).

There is no private piety in the Psalms. Every expression has its roots and its presuppositions, its basis of faith and its assurance of fulfilment in the community of Israel. If it so happened that the suppliant received Yahweh's help and was saved from some great distress, then his grateful praise and his confession of faith recounting what God had done was declared to the קהל רב the 'great congregation', which was the basis of religious life.

'. . . thou hast answered me.
I will declare thy name unto my brethren:
In the midst of the congregation will I praise thee . . .
Of thee cometh my praise in the great congregation'
(Ps. xxii. 21b, 22, 25a).

Suppliants came before Yahweh in the sanctuary in distress of different kinds: injustice, illness and guilt. The man who had been wrongly accused uttered the cry: 'Judge me, O Lord' (Ps. vii. 8; xxvi. 1; xliii. 1, etc.).[87] The sick man who was not allowed to enter the holy place in certain ritual-medical circumstances prayed: 'O Lord, heal me' (Ps. vi. 2; xli. 4, etc.). The man who had fallen into guilt and sin finally implored: 'Blot out all mine iniquities' (Ps. li. 8). These various needs were closely linked with one another. The magical idea of causality thought of the sick man as having 'attracted' to himself his infirmity through some definite offence, and he had therefore to prove his innocence. The links between sufferings which we often find in the Psalter cannot be broken and only occasionally does the pattern emerge more distinctly. Every suffering meant a diminution of life, being attacked by the sphere of שׁאול.[88] The man in great distress believed that he had been abandoned by God (Ps. xxii. 1).

But what took place in the cult? The sufferer poured out his heart before Yahweh in the sanctuary, and sang his lamentation whilst the

[87] Cf. H. Schmidt, *Das Gebet der Angeklagten im Alten Testament*, *BZAW* 49 (1928).

[88] See especially C. Barth, *Die Errettung vom Tode in den individuellen Klage- und Dankliedern des Alten Testaments* (1947), pp. 53 ff.

burnt offerings were being presented (Ps. iv. 6). Only in the rarest cases probably were these songs composed by the worshipper himself. They were either derived from materials of worship already in existence, from forms influenced by the cultic traditions, or they were conceived by the priestly circles—formal prayers repeated by the individual. We can see clearly from the 'individual songs of lamentation' that the sufferings described follow one basic pattern and set out an 'archetypal suffering' which covers the actual need of each individual sufferer. All the statements conform to one dominant type. The suppliants were simply the 'poor',[89] and described themselves as עני or אביון, דל or ענו. They were the needy in the fullest sense. In their laments they could take comfort from the fact that the sufferers enjoy a special privilege in the sanctuary. The ענוים piety outlined in the psalms of lamentation is based on this prerogative of Yahweh's mercy towards the 'poor' (cf. Isa. xiv. 32).

How do the suppliants make their requests, and what do they hope for? The Psalms show that the sufferers made their requests known to Yahweh ceaselessly by day and night. Their hopes and longings were set upon a דבר, a mighty word of God communicated by the priest or the cultic prophet (Ps. cxxx. 5).[90] If this came, it could 'heal' them and 'deliver them from their destructions' (Ps. cvii. 20). God's word gave the suppliant the assurance: עניתני—'thou hast answered me' (Ps. xxii. 21). The much-discussed 'change of mood' in certain psalms, the sudden change from lamentation to joyful gratitude, could be the result in most cases of a 'divine oracle' whereby the suppliant has received assurance that he has been heard (cf. Ps. vi; xxviii; lvi; lxix). Together with the expectation of a divine utterance we sometimes find also the request for a theophany. That the God who was present above the Ark would come forth, and that he would prove his willingness to help by an act of self-revelation—this was the wish of the worshipper. The Ark saying in Num. x. 35 f. obviously exerted a strong influence on such wishes and requests (Ps. iii. 7; vii. 6; ix. 19; xvii. 13, etc.). In Ps. xviii. 8 ff. a theophany of this kind is described; under the influence of prophetic, visionary ideas it turns into a hymn of thanksgiving. He who has experienced Yahweh's saving intervention can express it in no other way then that Yahweh has 'arisen' and proved his might. Among the 'individual songs of lament' the petitionary psalms of those who have

[89] See A. Rahlfs, *'Anī und 'Anāw in den Psalmen* (1892); A. Causse, *Les 'pauvres' d'Israel* (1922); H. Birkeland, *'Anī und 'Anāw in den Psalmen* (1933); cf. also J. J. Stamm, 'Ein Vierteljahrhundert Psalmenforschung', loc. cit., pp. 55 ff.

[90] J. Begrich, 'Das priesterliche Heilsorakel', *ZAW*, 52 (1934), pp. 81 ff., *Ges Stud.*, pp. 217 ff.

been wrongfully accused occupy a special place. It was an ancient sacral law that all those whose case could not be handled by the local jurisdiction because it was too difficult had to come to the central sanctuary, in order to receive there the verdict of Yahweh (Deut. xvii. 8–13).[91] This sacral judgement required that the accused should adhere to a very strict ritual. Along with a variety of purification rites which we need not go into here, there were two observances that had to be carried out: the *abiuratio*[92] and the night spent in self-examination. The procedure followed in the *abiuratio* can be seen from Ps. vii. 3–5:

> 'O Lord my God, if I have done this;
> If there be iniquity in my hands;
> If I have rewarded evil unto him that was at peace with me;
> (Yea, I have delivered him that without cause was mine adversary:)
> Let the enemy pursue my soul, and overtake it;
> Yea, let him tread my life down to the earth,
> And lay my glory in the dust.'

The accused proclaims his innocence in an act of ritual renunciation and execration of himself in case he were declared guilty. We can understand Ps. vii more clearly if we see it against the background of 1 Kings viii. 31 f.: 'If a man sin against his neighbour, and an oath be laid upon him to cause him to swear, and he come and swear before thine altar in this house; then hear thou in heaven, and do, and judge thy servants, condemning the wicked, to bring his way upon his own head; and justifying the righteous, to give him according to his righteousness.' In order to prove his innocence before Yahweh, the accused submitted to the night of testing which is mentioned in Ps. xvii. 3:

> 'Thou hast proved mine heart; thou hast visited me in the night:
> Thou hast tried me, and findest nothing.'

Ps. cxxxix provides an example of the prayers used during the testing, coming to its climax with the petition in *v.* 23:

> 'Search me, O God, and know my heart:
> Try me, and know my thoughts.'

The accused looked expectantly for Yahweh's judgement, which was pronounced in the holy place.

If a suppliant experienced a change in his fortunes, if he received an oracle or enjoyed the miracle of divine grace, he then took part in the ceremony of thanksgiving (תודה). We can trace in Ps. cvii a liturgy for a

[91] Cf. H. Schmidt, *Das Gebet der Angeklagten im Alten Testament*, loc. cit., pp. 2 ff.

[92] See F. Horst, 'Der Eid im Alten Testament', *EvTh* (1957), pp. 366 ff., *Ges. Stud., Gottes Recht*, pp. 292 ff.

solemn thanksgiving, in which the priests recall the different vows and all those who have to offer thanks are called upon to offer תודה and sacrifices were offered (Ps. l. 14; cvii. 22; cxvi. 17). The man who had been delivered held a feast with his relatives and friends at which, having earlier been abandoned in his suffering, he now celebrates the *communio* with Yahweh and with his family (Ps. xxii. 26; xxiii. 5). The ceremonial anointing with oil was very important in this connection (Ps. xxiii. 5; xcii. 10; Isa. lxi. 3). In gratitude the 'cup of salvation' was raised (Ps. cxvi. 13), which was probably used for a libation (cf. Exod. xxix. 40 f.; Num. xxviii. 7).[93] Most important, however, were the praise and proclamation. In a hymn of thanksgiving the man who had been delivered praised Yahweh for his help (Ps. xxxv. 18; xl. 3; lxix. 30; cvii. 31; cix. 30, etc.). Before the assembled congregation he related and confessed the mighty acts of the God of Israel that he had experienced in his own life (Ps. xxii. 22; xl. 10). This kind of proclamation which was expressed in praise, confession of faith and personal narrative developed a more didactic emphasis in the course of time, and under the influence of the חכמה it adopted the form of helpful instruction (Ps. xxxiv).

There can be no doubt that in the worship of Israel the individual had ample opportunity to express his petitions and lamentations, but above all his praise, his confession of faith and his proclamation.

5. Festivals for Special Occasions

(a) *The Enthronement of a King*

When a king died in Jerusalem, the accession of his successor took place on the occasion of the next autumn festival. The solemn event was celebrated in the presence of the whole cultic community, for it was a sacral act.[94] Unfortunately we have no complete ritual to show us what course the ceremony followed. In Ps. ii and cx only isolated parts of the ceremony of accession have come down to us, and it is not even

[93] Cf. H. Gressmann, 'Der Festbecher', *Festschrift E. Sellin* (1927), pp. 55 ff.; H. L. Ginsberg, *Psalms and Inscriptions of Petition and Acknowledgement* (1945), pp. 159 ff.; S. B. Frost, 'Asseveration by Thanksgiving', *VT*, 8 (1958), pp. 380 ff.

[94] Cf. C. R. North, 'The Religious Aspects of Hebrew Kingship', *ZAW*, 50 (1932), pp. 8 ff.; A. R. Johnson, 'Divine Kingship and the Old Testament', *Expos. Times*, 62 (1950), pp. 36 ff.; ibid., *Sacral Kingship in Ancient Israel* (1955); J. De Fraine, *L'aspect religieuex de la royauté israélite. L'Institution monarchique dans L'Ancien Testament et dans les textes mésopotamiens* (1954); S. Mowinckel, *He That Cometh* (1956); R. de Vaux, *Ancient Israel: Its Life and Institutions*, pp. 108 ff.; S. H. Hooke (ed.), *Myth, Ritual and Kingship* (1958), pp. 204 ff.

certain whether Ps. ii had its 'setting in life' in the act of enthronement.[95] Although the tradition is relatively scanty, repeated attempts have been made to reconstruct the course of the ceremony of accession, particularly in the light of Ps. cx. L. Dürr, for example, suggests the following stages: (1) enthronement (*v.* 1), (2) investiture (*v.* 2), (3) homage (*v.* 3), (4) institution as priest (*v.* 4), (5) victory over his enemies (*vv.* 5 f.), (6) sacramental drink from the sacred spring (*v.* 7).[96] G. Widengren suggests a different picture, and sees the structure of the ceremony as follows: (1) divine oracle with proclamation of the divine sonship of the king, (2) enthronement, (3) bestowal of the sceptre, (4) offering of gifts to the king, (5) investiture with the sacred garments, (6) presentation of the king, (7) drinking of the water.[97]

These reconstructions not only ignore for the most part the question of 'types', but they also overlook the basic complexity of the event of enthronement on mount Zion. The king of Jerusalem was not only the successor to the Davidic dynasty (2 Sam. vii; Ps. cxxxii) and the covenant monarch of Judah (2 Sam. ii. 4) or Israel (2 Sam. v. 3), but also heir to the Jebusite city kingdom, which as the possession of the crown had become the 'city of David' (2 Sam. v. 9; Ps. cx; Gen. xiv. 18 f.). There must have been, therefore, several acts of institution, which means that Ps. cx contains only part of the ceremony of enthronement—oracles, requests and descriptions of the situation. We can only recognize the outline of the following stages:

1. A ceremony of anointing which took place at the spring *giḥon*; this is also referred to in 1 Kings i. 38–40, and it was accompanied by a sacramental drink (Ps. cx. 7).

2. The proclamation of enthronement conveyed by the prophets:

> 'The Lord saith unto my lord, sit thou at my right hand,
> Until I make thine enemies thy footstool' (Ps. cx. 1).

We cannot tell clearly from this proclamation what the place 'on the right hand' of Yahweh signifies. Does it mean the throne-room or palace, which lay 'on the right' of the Temple, or was the ruler who was now exalted as priest-king given—according to Jebusite tradition—access to the holy of holies on the day of his accession to the throne (cf. Jer. xxx. 21)?

[95] Cf. H.-J. Kraus, *Psalmen*, pp. 11 ff.

[96] L. Dürr, *Psalm 110 im Lichte der neueren altorientalischen Forschung* (1929).

[97] G. Widengren, *Sakrales Königtum im Alten Testament und im Judentum* (1955), p. 49.

3. A prophetic acclamation called the king to close fellowship with Yahweh as the 'son of God' (Ps. cx. 3; ii. 7).

4. The sacral acts of enthronement were naturally strongly influenced by the Jebusite ritual. Although the Nathan prophecy in 2 Sam. vii may have played a certain part,[98] we can hardly assume that a confirmation or even a renewal of the covenant kingship was regularly made. The event recorded in 2 Kings xi. 17 seems to describe an exceptional instance.[99]

5. In the ceremonies of enthronement the king was lifted on to a עמוד (2 Kings xi. 14), where he received the homage of the congregation.

6. The institution to the office of a priest-king and to the dignities of the first (Jebusite) king Melchizedek are at the heart of Ps. cx. The sacral functions of the ruler in the Temple are based upon this investiture.

7. Demonstrations in the form of cultic drama of the victorious might of the newly enthroned king over all his enemies were of great importance (Ps. cx. 1, 5, 6; ii. 8 f.).[100]

The enthronement of the king was a special occasion of cultic activity in Jerusalem, and it naturally had a great influence and affected the contents of the 'royal psalms'. On the other hand, it cannot be proved that the ruler played a part in the cultic drama of the annual rhythm of nature. A few echoes of the fertility cult are not enough to provide evidence of a 'pattern' which could be the basis of an all-embracing interpretation. So, for example, the much-discussed Ps. xlv, which clearly bears the marks of some particular historical connection, has nothing to do with a *hieros gamos*. It is rather a 'marriage song', which has a sacral connection only in the sense that the king in his office as cultic leader touches upon all spheres of life as he fulfils his functions at the holy place.[101]

[98] See pp. 183 ff.

[99] After the death of Queen Athaliah and the extraordinary confusion brought about in the monarchy in Jerusalem, an excellent opportunity presented itself for renewing the foundations of the covenant monarchy. See M. Noth, 'Das alttestamentliche Bundesschliessen im Lichte eines Mari-Textes', *Gesammelte Studien zum A.T.* (1957), pp. 151 f.

[100] We do not know what these demonstrations were like in detail, but we can perhaps find certain clues in Egyptian ceremonies. For example, the 'breaking in pieces of a potter's vessel' in Ps. ii. 9 recalls the custom at Egyptian coronation or jubilee festivals of symbolically destroying pots inscribed with the names of foreign nations. Cf. the texts referring to a proscription: K. Sethe, 'Die Ächtung feindlicher Fürsten, Völker und Dinge auf altägyptischen Tongefässcherben des Mittleren Reiches', *Abhandlungen der Preuss. Akad. der Wiss.* (1926) and G. Posener, *Princes et pays d'Asie et de Nubie. Textes hiératiques sur des figurines d'envoûtement du Moyen Empire* (1940).

[101] Cf. H.-J. Kraus, *Psalmen*, pp. 330 ff.

(b) *Lamentation and Thanksgiving by the People*

Situations where the people found themselves in great need presented occasions for special cultic observance.[102] If the land was threatened by hostile invasion, or if there was drought or famine or plagues broke out, a 'fast' (צום) was instituted. The festival for the purpose of lamentation and repentance first had to be 'proclaimed' throughout the country (Isa. xxii. 12; Joel i. 14). Priests and elders led the assembly at the holy place. The קהל came together in the sanctuary (Joel ii. 16; Jer. xxxvi. 6, 9; 1 Kings viii. 33, 35), and this was the custom even in the earliest period (Judges xx. 23 ff.; xxi. 2 ff.; 1 Sam. vii. 5 f.). The 'fast' was 'sanctified' (Joel i. 14; ii. 15 f.). The community assembled at Jerusalem strictly abstained from all food and all pleasures (Isa. lviii. 3 ff.), clothes were stripped off or torn (Isa. xxxii. 11; Mic. i. 8; Joel ii. 13), and a coarse sackcloth was put on (Isa. xxii. 12; lviii. 5; Jer. iv. 8, etc.). All the beauty of the human form was destroyed, by cutting off the hair (Isa. xv. 2; xxii. 12; Mic. i. 16) and by disfiguring the skin (Hosea vii. 14; Mic. iv. 14). The suppliants threw themselves to the ground, rolled in the dust (Ps. xliv. 25; Mic. i. 10; Jer. vi. 26) and scattered ashes on their head (Neh. ix. 1). Under the direction of the priests, who were similarly clothed in sackcloth, the assembled congregation spent day and night in the sanctuary (Joel i. 13). Moans and wails, howls and cries came up from the dust (Isa. xxix. 4; Mic. i. 8; Jer. xiv. 12; Joel i. 5, 8; ii. 1). 1 Sam. vii. 6 and Lam. ii. 19 refer to the rite of pouring out water, which accompanied the tears and laments.

The many 'songs of lamentation of the people' that have come down to us in the Old Testament had their 'setting in life' in this act of lamentation.[103] It was the priests who uttered the requests and the prayers (Joel i. 9, 13; ii. 17), and they called the congregation to join in a common lamentation (Joel i; Zech. xii. 12 ff.). Their distress was described and held up before Yahweh, and the suppliants reminded him of his faithfulness; they proclaimed their willingness to return and repent, asked the God of Israel to intervene and pledged themselves to fresh obedience. Sacrifices were offered in connection with the songs of lamentation (Jer. xiv. 12; cf. also 1 Sam. vii. 9). We can take Joel ii. 17 as an example of the prayers that were offered:

'Spare thy people, O Lord, and give not thine heritage to reproach, that the nations should rule over them: wherefore should they say among the peoples, where is their God?'

[102] On the following, see H. Gunkel/J. Begrich, *Einleitung in die Psalmen* (1933), section 4.

[103] Cf. the passages assembled by Gunkel, op. cit., pp. 117 ff.

The congregation waited for a priestly oracle, which confirmed that its requests had been heard.[104] Proclamations by the cultic prophets no doubt also had a great importance in this connection.

When Yahweh had heard their requests, averted the danger that threatened and helped his people, then the people's songs of thanksgiving were sung in the sanctuary on mount Zion.[105] These psalms are characterized by joy and gladness at Yahweh's intervention, and they were no doubt accompanied by sacrifices, burnt offerings and peace offerings. One special custom was that of drawing water from the wells of salvation (Isa. xii. 3).

(c) *The Lament for the Destruction of Jerusalem*

The festivals of lamentation that we have just been considering were held on special occasions in particular situations of need, but the destruction of Jerusalem by the Babylonians gave rise to a regular lamentation cult which was celebrated at the ruined sanctuary.[106] The Lamentations, and also certain of the Psalms, give us an idea of the hymns and prayers that were used at these celebrations. Ancient Oriental parallels show very clearly that it was customary in the ancient world to sing songs of mourning among the ruins of a holy place that had been destroyed by one's enemies. A few passages from the lament for the destroyed sanctuary at Ur provide a good illustration of what took place:[107]

'The Lord of all the lands has abandoned (his stable), his sheepfold (*has been delivered*) *to* the wind,
Enlil has abandoned . . . Nippur, his sheepfold (*has been delivered*) *to* the wind . . .
Bau has abandoned Urukug, her sheepfold (*has been delivered*) *to* the wind;
The holy Bagara, her chamber, she has abandoned, her sheepfold (*has been delivered*) *to* the wind . . .
His sheepfold *has been delivered to* the wind, he makes [grie]vous its wail . . .
O city, a bitter lament set up as thy lament;
Thy lament which is bitter—O city, set up thy lament.
His righteous city which has been destroyed—bitter is its lament . . .
O city thy rites *unto inimical dread and awe*,
Thy ordinances—unto inimical ordinances, have been transformed . . .
The woman, *after* her . . . *had set the lamentation down upon the ground*,
Herself utters *softly* the wail *of the smitten house*.

[104] J. Begrich, 'Das priesterliche Heilsorakel', *ZAW*, 52 (1934), pp. 81 ff., *Ges. Stud.*, pp. 217 ff.

[105] Cf. H. Gunkel/J. Begrich, op. cit., section 8, p. iv.

[106] See H.-J. Kraus, *Threni*, BK, 20 (2 ed., 1960), pp. 8 ff.

[107] J. B. Pritchard, *Ancient Near Eastern Texts*, pp. 455 ff.

"The storm *ever breaking forth*—its wail has filled me full.
Raging about because of the storm . . .
At night a bitter lament having been *raised unto me*,
I, *although*, for that night I tremble,
Fled not before that night's violence . . ."
Like a tent, the house where the crops have been . . . ,
Like the house where the crops have been . . . , to wind and rain verily has been exposed . . .
Ur—its weak and (its) strong perished through hunger;
Mothers and fathers who did not leave their houses, were overcome by fire;
The young lying on their mothers' laps, like fish were carried off by the waters . . .
Verily my (precious) metal, stone and lapis lazuli have been scattered about—"O my possessions" I will say.
My treasure verily *has been dissipated*—"O my possessions" I will say . . .
O my righteous house, my city which has been made into ruins,
In the *debris* of thy righteous house which has been destroyed, I lay me down alongside of thee.'

The last line of this passage shows where this 'lament for the ruined sanctuary' took place. The elegy was sung among the ruins of the Temple, where the dreadful event of the conquest was once again set before the congregation.

A similar situation is indicated by the laments for the destruction of the sanctuary on Zion that have come down to us in the Old Testament (Lam. ii. 1 ff.):

'How hath the Lord covered the daughter of Zion with a cloud in his anger!
He hath cast down from heaven unto the earth the beauty of Israel,
And hath not remembered his footstool in the day of his anger.
The Lord hath swallowed up all the habitations of Jacob, and hath not pitied;
He hath thrown down in his wrath the strongholds of the daughter of Judah;
He hath brought them down to the ground:
He hath profaned the kingdom and the princes thereof.
He hath cut off in fierce anger all the horn of Israel;
He hath drawn back his right hand from before the enemy:
And he hath burned up Jacob like a flaming fire, which devoureth round about.
He hath bent his bow like an enemy, he hath stood with his right hand as an adversary,
And hath slain all that were pleasant to the eye:
In the tent of the daughter of Zion he hath poured out his fury like fire.
The Lord is become as an enemy, he hath swallowed up Israel;
He hath swallowed up all her palaces, he hath destroyed his strongholds:
And he hath multiplied in the daughter of Judah mourning and lamentation.

And he hath violently taken away his tabernacle as if it were of a garden;
He hath destroyed his place of assembly:
The Lord hath caused solemn assembly and sabbath to be forgotten in Zion,
And hath despised in the indignation of his anger the king and the priest.
The Lord hath cast off his altar, he hath abhorred his sanctuary,
He hath given up into the hand of the enemy the walls of her palaces:
They have made a noise in the house of the Lord, as in the day of a solemn assembly.
The Lord hath proposed to destroy the wall of the daughter of Zion;
He hath stretched out the line, he hath not withdrawn his hand from destroying:
But he hath made the rampart and wall to lament; they languish together.
Her gates are sunk into the ground; he hath destroyed and broken her bars:
Her king and her princes are among the nations where the law is not;
Yea, her prophets find no vision from the Lord.
The elders of the daughter of Zion sit upon the ground, they keep silence;
They have cast up dust upon their heads; they have girded themselves with sackcloth.'

Mourning for the collapse of Israel was, of course, linked with the lament for the destruction of Jerusalem, for Jerusalem was the central sanctuary of the ancient amphictyony, and never lost this primary significance.

We can see from Zech. vii. 5 that the lament for the destruction of Jerusalem was performed not only in the fifth month, in remembrance of the time of the great catastrophe, but also in the seventh month, at the time of the autumn festival (cf. also Zech. viii. 19, where a lament in the tenth month also is mentioned). As part of the 'fast' people went on pilgrimage to Zion (Jer. xli. 5), and remembered the great disaster as they made penance and offered their petitions. Similar feasts of lamentation were no doubt observed by the exiles as well.

Did the congregation in its fasting and lamentation expect any answer from Yahweh or any sign of his gracious intervention? There is an indication in Lam. ii. 9 that neither a priestly oracle nor a prophetic message was received, and the only place where there are traces of an oracle is Lam. iv. 22a:

> The punishment of their iniquity is accomplished,
> O daughter of Zion;
> He will no more carry thee away into captivity.'

But these words promise merely an ending of judgement, not a complete change of fortune. The prophetic message of salvation was first proclaimed by that unknown prophet of the exile whom we usually call

'Second Isaiah'. His message of salvation probably had its 'setting in life' in the feasts of lamentation held by the exiles.[108] It was only on the initiative of Zechariah that the cult of mourning was instituted (Zech. vii. 1 ff.), because a new sanctuary had been conceived and the worship of Israel could be started once again at the holy place.

6. The Post-exilic Cultic Community

(a) *Worship during the Exile*

The exiles in a foreign land were faced by the tremendous difficulty that the sacral presuppositions for any cultic activity were lacking. None of the acts of worship they had celebrated in their homeland could be simply transferred and adopted to an alien environment. The congregation could assemble only where Yahweh was present, and where he had given unmistakable signs of his presence. Hitherto the place of the *praesentia Dei* had been the sanctuary of Jerusalem, for there the Ark was to be found, which marked out the chosen place. How could they be sure of Yahweh's presence in a foreign land, and on what basis could assemblies for worship be authorized in Babylonia? The saving word from God—a word of basic importance for the exiles—was received by the prophet Ezekiel in the vision he received at his call (Ezek. i).[109] Yahweh appeared on a throne chariot in the foreign land; 'the heavens were opened' (Ezek. i. 1) by the river Chebar, and the God of Israel came down to the exiles in the radiant splendour of His כבוד. In other words, he was present in Babylonia. This event provided the justification for the performance of worship on foreign soil. The opening verses of Ps. cxxxvii are probably not only a lyrical description, but they also give an actual indication of the place where assemblies for worship were held during the exile. If Yahweh had manifested his presence in a field by the river Chebar, then it seems reasonable to assume that the cultic assemblies of the exiles who were settled in village communities were held at the same place. These gatherings 'by the rivers of Babylon' were marked by lamentations for Zion (Ps. cxxxvii—cf. pp. 226 f.). We are also told in the Book of Ezekiel of gatherings of elders in the house of Ezekiel (Ezek. viii. 1; xiv. 1; xx. 1), and it is here that new ways of cultic expression were no doubt explored. But all the presuppositions were lacking, for the exiles had neither cultic objects nor insignia. As no sacrificial feasts could be held in the foreign land—except at the place

[108] Cf. H. E. von Waldow, *Anlass und Hintergrund der Verkündigung Deuterojesias*, Diss., Bonn (1953).

[109] See W. Zimmerli, *Ezechiel*, BK, 13, pp. 1 ff.

where Yahweh had appeared—the cult had to renounce more and more every material and sacramental support, and greater attention had to be given to the spiritual and the intangible. The sabbath came to have a dominant importance in the various groups and families, as the time of the assembly for worship.[110] As far as the content of worship was concerned, the sacred traditions and writings became central, and the life of the community was concentrated upon the Word. Prayers, especially prayers of repentance and petition, accompanied the insistent concern with the ancient traditions. We can therefore probably assume that there were two spheres of cultic activity: communal feasts of lamentation 'by the rivers of Babylon', at the place where Yahweh had appeared, and sabbath assemblies in the village and family communities. The view that there were already synagogues during the Babylonian exile is not really tenable,[111] but it is true that important preparatory steps towards the establishment of this institution, which was later to be so important for Judaism, were taken during this sojourn abroad.

Along with the sabbath, circumcision also came to the fore during the exile as a sign of the covenant and of the confession of faith. The 'fasting' during the feasts of lamentation also increased in importance. In certain circles a rite became customary when uttering prayers which probably already played a part in the homeland—that of turning to the direction in which Jerusalem lay (1 Kings viii. 48; Dan. vi. 10).[112] Worship gave the exiles strength to overcome the misery of being in a foreign land and to serve Yahweh faithfully in the 'unclean land', and it was above all the saving bulwark against the influences of Babylonian religion, which was always a dangerous temptation to the exiles, with its impressive Marduk cult and its magical incantatory rites.

The great transformation was brought about by the message of salvation proclaimed by the unknown prophet of the exile (Isa. xl–lv),[113] which promised the end of captivity and judgement (Isa. xl. 1 ff.). Once again it was a vision connected with the prophet's call that powerfully brought to light the activity of the God of Israel in these days. The prophet saw in his vision a processional highway exceeding all human dimensions, which was built through the (Syrian-Arabian) desert by heavenly forces (xl. 3 ff.). Along this highway the exiles, surrounded by the holy presence of Yahweh, were to travel to freedom (xl. 10 ff.). This 'second exodus' meant in the visionary message the return home of the

[110] See the discussion on pp. 87 ff.

[111] Cf. K. Galling, 'Erwägungen zur antiken Synagoge', *ZDPV*, 72 (1956), pp. 163 ff.

[112] Cf. H. E. von Waldow, op. cit., pp. 119 ff.

[113] On the message of Second Isaiah, see G. von Rad, *Theologie des Alten Testaments*, II (1960), pp. 252 ff.

community of Zion to Jerusalem (li. 11), the return of Yahweh to the ancient central sanctuary (lii. 8), and the renewal of God's sovereignty on the holy mountain (lii. 7).[114] In this eschatological event the ברית with the people of God would be confirmed (liv. 10). But the final theophany will be for all peoples (lii. 10), for all the nations will be included in God's saving activity at the last. This 'second exodus' goes beyond the compass of the history of Israel, and the 'new Moses', the עבד יהוה, fulfils in an eschatological sense the functions of the 'Mosaic office' (cf. pp. 108 ff.). He will deliver the divine law to the peoples (xlii. 1 ff.), act as the 'mediator of the covenant' for the heathen (xlii. 6; xlix. 8) and make the sacrificial offering of his life as an intercessor (Exod. xxxii. 32 ff.) by dying the atoning death of a substitute (Isa. liii). The radiance of a universal message shines forth in the proclamation of Second Isaiah, and the new cult at Jerusalem has the splendour of an eschatological fulfilment. The whole world is included in the events of the last days.

The outline of a cultic constitution in Ezek. xl–xlviii[115] is parallel to the eschatological message of Second Isaiah, for in this complex, too, an eschatological order is foreshadowed, down to the minute details of the sacral institutions. The Temple will become the redemptive centre of the world in the last days.

(b) *The Restoration of the Sanctuary*

The victorious king Cyrus gave his subject peoples permission to restore their local cults. In the 'Cyrus Cylinder'[116] we find the highly significant proclamation: '(As to the region) from . . . as far as Ashur and Susa, Agade, Eshnunna, the towns Zamban, Me-Turnu, Der as well as the region of the Gutians, I returned to (these) sacred cities on the other side of the Tigris, the sanctuaries of which have been ruins for a long time, the images which (used) to live therein and established for them permanent sanctuaries. I (also) gathered all their (former) inhabitants and returned (to them) their habitations. Furthermore, I resettled upon the command of Marduk, the great lord, all the gods of Sumer and Akkad whom Nabonidus has brought into Babylon to the anger of the lord of the gods, unharmed, in their (former) chapels, the places which make them happy.' The Persian king's policy of tolerance and appeasement also benefited Jerusalem. The Old Testament quotes

[114] Cf. H.-J. Kraus, 'Die Königsherrschaft Gottes im Alten Testament', loc. cit., pp. 102 ff.

[115] Cf. H. Gese, *Der Verfassungsentwurf des Ezechiel* (1957)

[116] D. Winton Thomas, *Documents from Old Testament Times* (1958), p. 316.

the text of a decree issued by Cyrus in the year 538 B.C.: 'Concerning the house of God at Jerusalem, let the house be builded, the place where they offer sacrifices, and let the foundations thereof be strongly laid; the height thereof of threescore cubits, and the breadth thereof threescore cubits; with three rows of great stones, and a row of new timber: and let the expenses be given out of the king's house: and also let the gold and silver vessels of the house of God, which Nebuchadnezzar took forth out of the temple which is at Jerusalem, and brought into Babylon, be restored . . .' (Ezra vi. 3–5).

Sheshbazzar came to Jerusalem as the special envoy of the Persian king and laid the foundations of the new Temple (Ezra v. 14–16). But the work soon came to a standstill, and the problems in Jerusalem proved insuperable. The Judaeans who had been left behind at the deportation had neither the initiative nor the ability to undertake the rebuilding of the Temple sanctuary. The leaders among the exiles could not make their influence felt as Cyrus' decree did not order any repatriation and it was almost impossible at first to exert any influence upon circumstances in Jerusalem. The message of Second Isaiah, which was set down by one of his disciples (Isa. lvi. ff.) was utterly incongruous with the actual measures to rebuild the sanctuary. Fervid expectations saw the Temple as a place of prayer for all nations (Isa. lvi. 7), and a vision was caught of the heathen going on pilgrimage to the place of Yahweh's epiphany (Isa. lx).[117] The appearance of the 'eschatological mediator of the covenant' was already being proclaimed (Isa. lxii. 1 ff.). But despair at the 'delay of the Parousia' seized men's hearts:

> 'Therefore is judgement far from us, neither doth righteousness overtake us: we look for light, but behold darkness; for brightness, but we walk in obscurity.
>
> We grope for the wall like the blind, yea, we grope as they that have no eyes: we stumble at noonday as in the twilight; among them that are lusty we are as dead men.
>
> We roar all like bears and mourn sore like doves: we look for judgement, but there is none; for salvation, but it is far off from us.'

These laments in Isa. lix 9 ff. show us the atmosphere of disenchantment and disillusionment in which men awaited in Jerusalem the final renewal of the cult announced in the eschatological message of Second Isaiah and his disciple.

About the year 520 B.C. the building of the Temple was given a new impetus by the prophets Haggai and Zechariah. These two prophets

[117] On the history of tradition in Isa. lx, see G. von Rad, 'Die Stadt auf dem Berge', *EvTh*, 8 (1948/9), pp. 439 ff., *Ges. Stud.*, pp. 214 ff.

stood in the tradition of the Jerusalem cultic and שלום prophets. Their message revolved around the theme of the election or re-election of Zion (Zech. ii. 16; iii. 2; viii. 3) and the dignity of the elect king of David's house (Hag. ii. 23; Zech. iv. 9 ff.). Zerubbabel was thought of as the new founder of the Temple (Zech. iv. 9) and as the one authorized to appear before Yahweh (Zech. iv. 14). Alongside Zerubbabel, the 'royal' descendant, there emerged the high priest, and with him an office which was to assume direction of the whole cult at Jerusalem in post-exilic times (Hag. ii. 2; Zech. iii. 1 ff.; iv. 14). Haggai proclaimed his message on the occasion of a feast of Tabernacles (Hag. ii. 1). Both he and Zechariah were sanctuary prophets. The measures taken to renew the cult were still dominated by the eschatological expectation (Hag. ii. 6 ff.; Zech. ii. 8; vi. 15).

How was the cultic community to be made aware of the re-election of Zion? There was no longer any central cultic object that could have been set up in the sanctuary. The Ark had not been heard of for a long time; after the destruction of Jerusalem it was no longer in existence, nor was it among the objects which Nebuchadnezzar had taken off to Babylonia. The question that was raised repeatedly was, what sacral object could be preserved in the holy of holies in the newly built Temple? The Old Testament traditions are silent on this point, and give no clear information. The only possible hint is to be found in Zech. iv. 1–14, where the 'golden candlestick' has a unique and outstanding importance as representing the presence of Yahweh (*v.* 10). The two anointed men who stand before the candlestick have the privilege of ministering 'before the Lord of the whole earth' (Zech. iv. 14). This suggests the possibility that the golden candlestick was one of the sacred objects of special significance which Nebuchadnezzar had taken to Babylonia which later—as a result of Cyrus' decree—were handed back to the cultic community of Jerusalem. Is it not conceivable that the post-exilic community installed this venerable sacral object in the holy of holies as a symbol of the presence of Yahweh, at the same time preserving the continuity with Solomon's Temple? In any case it is worth noting that the golden candlestick (in its later altered form) appears on the Arch of Titus as a trophy of the conqueror of Jerusalem. Here, however, we are in the realm of supposition. The Old Testament passages which mention the 'seven-branched candlestick' certainly reveal the great importance of this cultic object, but they contain no evidence that it was set up in the holy of holies.[118]

[118] Cf. Exod. xxv. 31 ff.; xxvi. 35; xxx. 27; xxxv. 14; xxxvii. 17 ff.; xxxix. 37; xl. 4, 24; Lev. xxiv. 4, etc.; 1 Kings vii. 49; 2 Chron. v. 20; xiii. 11.

(c) *The Life of the Post-exilic Cultic Community*

The newly built Temple of Jerusalem was not only the sanctuary for those living in the area, but was also the cultic centre for the whole Diaspora. As far as possible, the Jews of the Dispersion came on pilgrimage to the holy place and paid their dues. But in the first decades after its rebuilding the Temple stood on insecure sacral foundations, and an atmosphere of disorder and confusion prevailed. The eschatological expectations faded and there were no obvious institutions which might have given stability to the worship of the post-exilic community. Corruption within the priesthood spread (Mal. i. 6 ff.), the sabbath was not observed (Neh. xiii. 15 ff.), dishonesty in connection with the dues became the rule (Mal. iii. 6 ff.), and disorder as regards marriage had a disturbing effect (Mal. ii. 10 ff.). The political status of Jerusalem as a district of the Persian imperial governor in charge of Samaria was extremely unstable and subject to very great dangers. In this difficult situation some of the exiles living in Babylonia seized the initiative. Nehemiah's deputation gave Jerusalem, with the erection of the city walls and the establishment of a government independent of Samaria, the possibility of internal consolidation,[119] but Nehemiah did not intervene in matters of worship. The reordering of this central realm was left to Ezra, a priest and a highly placed official adviser on the religious affairs of the Israelites at the Persian court.

The sacral order of the Temple sanctuary at Jerusalem was laid down on the occasion of an autumn festival. In accordance with the regulation in Deut. xxxi. 9 ff., Ezra read aloud the תורה (Neh. viii. 3, 18) and pledged the congregation to the service of Yahweh and to obedience to the תורה along the lines of the ancient renewals of the covenant. 'This making of a covenant committed the whole of "Israel" to the new law.'[120] The expressions of assent by the assembly which are described in Neh. viii. 6 are reminiscent of Deut. xxvii. 15 ff. The adoration before Yahweh (Neh. viii. 6—cf. p. 214) corresponded to an ancient rite, and the feast celebrated in booths was marked by joy (Neh. viii. 10, 12, 17; cf. Deut. xvi. 15), but also by the solemnity of making vows and promises. It is disputed which 'law' Ezra gave to the cultic community at Jerusalem, but it is certain that the 'canon' of the regulations became the basis of the sanctuary and of its worship.[121] The central position of

[119] Cf. M. Noth, *History of Israel*, pp. 321 ff.

[120] Ibid., p. 334.

[121] There are two main possibilities to be considered as regards the question of the 'law' that Ezra proclaimed in Jerusalem, the one envisaging the Priestly Code and the other the whole Pentateuch. It is a problem that is very difficult to solve, but it is at any rate necessary to see it in a wider context. Is it not a fact that the great 'source

the תורה soon affected the Diaspora as well. Scribal learning and devotion to the law developed, and last of all there emerged in the Hellenistic period the synagogue, the place of instruction, in which the purposes of the cult based on the תורה were continued.

The fact that the Jerusalem sanctuary was re-established cultically on the basis of obedience to the law and renewal of the covenant as the result of Ezra's work apparently had no great influence upon the worship offered at the autumn festival. As far as we can tell, this achievement was not repeatedly celebrated in the autumn cult. On the other hand, the feast of the renewal of the covenant soon seems to have become an essential part of the feast of Weeks (cf. pp. 59 f.). The most important feast in the post-exilic community was the Passover (cf. 2 Chron. xxx). The effects of king Josiah's reformation can be clearly seen (cf. pp. 49 ff.).

A priestly hierarchy ruled in Jerusalem, with the high priest at its head, to whom were applied the royal dignity and the rôle of the 'prince' in Ezekiel's eschatological vision (cf. Ezek. xlv. 7 ff.). The Zadokites were the privileged priesthood which was traced back to Aaron (cf. Lev. viii and ix; 1 Chron. v. 27 ff.), whilst the Levites functioned as a *clerus minor* (cf. pp. 99 f.). This world of the Jerusalem cult which was so self-contained and so secure as a result of Ezra's reforms was faced by a severe crisis and violent controversies by the Samaritan schism (cf. pp. 54 f.). Even more far-reaching in effect were the political interventions of the Seleucid empire and the constant struggles for the office of high priest under the Hasmonaeans. At this point the history of worship and political history are interlocked.[122] And outside the Temple groups

[122] Cf. M. Noth, *History of Israel*, pp. 349 ff.

---

documents' of the Pentateuch had a basic connection with this founding of the cult in the Temple sanctuary? And is it not possible that the views of the Yahwist were connected with the building of Solomon's Temple, and that in the so-called 'Elohist' there are fragments of a sanctuary document from the pre-monarchical period? In this case, Ezra's law could be either a new basis for the post-exilic cult, perhaps the Priestly Code drawn up during the period of the Exile in Babylon or a 'canon' which included the two older documents in this Priestly Code. Deuteronomy also is to be understood as the basis of the restored 'amphictyonic cult' in the time of Josiah, and was probably similarly included in the 'canon'—although it appeared as the 'basic document' in the Deuteronomistic history (cf. M. Noth, *Überlieferungsgeschichtliche Studien*, II). There is a tendency to consider the 'sources' of the Pentateuch from the standpoint of modern literary criticism and to overlook the requirements of the cult, which rests on the basis of historical and legal documents. The fact that the Deuteronomists connected their תורה with the Ark and spoke of something discovered in the holy of holies suggests important clues concerning a document that was deposited in the Temple sanctuary and can be considered as the basis of the cult—just as at Ugarit the mythical texts in the Temple provided the norm for the practice of worship.

and sects sprang up, some of which cherished the eschatological and apocalyptic expectations set out by Second Isaiah and in the Book of Daniel, and others which placed the תורה in the centre of their life and thought.

With the destruction of the Temple in A.D. 70 the history of Israel's worship came to an end. The central sanctuary was destroyed, the priestly ministry abolished and the cultic community dispersed. The Jewish leaders who gathered at the Synod of Jamnia finally placed the emphasis in worship upon the 'Diaspora institution' of the synagogue.

The New Testament, on the other hand, proclaims the fulfilment of the worship of the last days which was prophesied by Second Isaiah in the 'kingly rule of God' that was made manifest in Jesus Christ. The Letter to the Hebrews, in particular, proclaims that the cultic institutions of the Old Covenant have reached their climax and their conclusion. The 'first' is taken away, in order that the 'second' may be established. 'By which will we have been sanctified through the offering of the body of Jesus Christ once for all' (Heb. x. 9 f.). We have now come to the point where we have reached the limit of our account of Old Testament worship. It is the task of the New Testament scholar to depict the worship of the early Church on the basis of its Old Testament foundations.

INDEX OF OLD TESTAMENT REFERENCES

PAGE

GENESIS
i. 14 . . . 44
ii. 1 ff. . . 202
ii. 2 f.. . . 88
iv. 4 f. . . 113
viii. 20 f. . . 115
viii. 22 . . 44
xiv. 18 ff. 98, 187, 204, 223
xv. 9 ff. . . 119
xx. 7 . . . 104
xxi. 22 f. . . 172
xxi. 33 . . 172
xxii. 1 ff. . . 118
xxii. 13 . . 118
xxvi. 23 ff. . . 172
xxviii. 10 ff. . 146
xxviii. 18 f. . . 146
xxviii. 22 . . 148 f.
xxix. 34 . . 94
xxx. 14 . . 44
xxxiv. 25 . . 94
xxxv. 1 ff. . . 148
xxxv. 2 . . 140
xxxv. 4 . . 140
xli. 1 ff. . . 42
xlvi. 1 ff. . . 172
xlix. 5 ff. . . 94
l. 26 . . . 126

EXODUS
xii. 1 ff. . . 163
xii. 2 . . . 44, 54
xii. 6 . . . 54
xii. 14 . . 45
xii. 21 ff. . . 45
xii. 23 . . 46
xii. 34 . . 47
xii. 39 . . 47
xix. 1 ff. 13 f., 47, 58 ff.
xx. 1 ff. . . 108
xx. 2 . . . 142 ff.
xx. 8 ff. . . 79, 88
xx. 10. . . 80, 87
xx. 18 ff. . 107 f., 111
xx. 22 ff. . . 11
xx. 23. . . 27
xxii. 19 . . 27
xxiii. 10 ff. 26 ff., 70 ff., 80
xxiii. 12 . 32, 79 ff.
xxiii. 14 ff. . 5, 36, 48
xxiii. 15 47, 49, 56, 163
xxiii. 16 . 56, 61 f.
xxiii. 17 . . 29, 49
xxiii. 18 . . 45, 47
xxiii. 19 . . 46, 49
xxiii. 20 ff. . . 14
xxiv. 1 f. . . 14, 200
xxiv. 6 . . 120
xxiv. 9 ff. . . 120
xxiv. 11 . 136, 142
xxv. 21 . . 125
xxv. 31 . . 233
xxvi. 35 . . 233
xxix. 15 . . 121
xxix. 18 . . 115
xxix. 26 f. . . 121
xxix. 40 f. . . 222
xxx. 1 ff. . . 121
xxx. 27 . . 233
xxxi. 12 ff. . . 88
xxxii. 1 ff. . . 12, 96
xxxii. 4 . . 150
xxxii. 6 . . 120
xxxii. 8 . . 120
xxxii. 26 ff. . .96, 151
xxxii. 32 ff. . . 231
xxxiii. 7 ff. . . 128
xxxiv. 18 ff. 5, 28 ff., 47, 49, 163
xxxiv. 19 . . 117 f.
xxxiv. 21 . . 79 f.
xxxiv. 22 56 f., 61 f., 67
xxxiv. 23 . . 29
xxxiv. 24 . . 49
xxxiv. 25 . . 45 f.
xxxiv. 26 . . 46
xxxv. 14 . . 233
xxxvii. 6 . . 125
xxxvii. 17 ff. . 233
xxxviii. 8 . . 176
xl. 3 . . . 126
xl. 4 . . . 233
xl. 24 . . . 233

LEVITICUS
i. 1 ff. . . 116
ii. 1 ff. . . 115
ii. 11 ff. . . 121
iv. 25 ff. . . 121
v. 14 ff. . . 122
vi. 7 ff. . . 115
viii. 1 ff. . . 235
viii. 18 ff. . . 116
ix. 1 ff. . . 235
x. 12 . . . 115
xiv. 10 ff. . . 116
xiv. 14 ff. . . 122
xvi. 2 ff. . 68, 132 f.
xvi. 10 69, 122, 133
xvi. 11 ff. . . 68
xvi. 16 . . 121
xvi. 21 f. . . 68
xvi. 26 . .69, 133
xix. 20 ff. . . 122
xix. 23 ff. . . 135 f.
xx. 9 ff. . . 144
xxiii. 1 ff. . 5 f., 32, 63, 68, 93
xxiii. 3 . 79 f., 87
xxiii. 4 ff. 32 ff., 45, 53 ff., 83 ff.
xxiii. 15 f. . . 56 f.
xxiii. 23 ff. . 66 f., 208
xxiii. 26 ff. . . 69
xxiii. 27 . . 66, 68
xxiii. 33 ff. . . 66, 83
xxiii. 34 . . 63

	PAGE
xxiii. 39	62 f.
xxiii. 40 ff.	62 ff., 69, 90, 132
xxiii. 42 f.	63
xxiii. 43	53, 64 f.
xxiv. 4	233
xxv. 1 ff.	71 f.
xxv. 4.	71
xxv. 6 f.	72
xxv. 8 ff.	73 ff.
xxvi. 34 ff.	76

NUMBERS

ii. 17	129
iii. 1 ff.	99
iii. 38	129
vi. 10 f.	121
vi. 12	122
viii. 7	94
ix. 9 ff.	55
x. 10	77 f.
x. 35 f.	125 ff., 164, 215
xii. 6 ff.	105 ff.
xv. 27 ff.	121
xxiv. 1 f.	133
xxv. 10 ff.	94
xxvi. 55	72
xxviii. 1 ff.	5 f., 35 ff.
xxviii. 7	222
xxviii. 11 ff.	77 f.
xxviii. 16 ff.	45
xxviii. 24	56
xxviii. 26	56 f.
xxix. 1 ff.	5 f., 35 ff., 66
xxix. 7 ff.	68, 70
xxix. 12	63
xxxv. 54	72
xxxvi. 2	72

DEUTERONOMY

i. 1 ff.	14
v. 12 ff.	79
vi. 21 ff.	156
x. 1 ff.	125
x. 8	94, 97
xi. 29 f.	164 f.
xi. 30	119, 153
xii. 1 ff.	14
xii. 4 ff.	121
xii. 7	120
xv. 1 ff.	72, 75
xvi. 1 ff.	5, 30 ff., 45, 50, 63, 208
xvi. 3	83, 87

	PAGE
xvi. 5 f.	162
xvi. 9 f.	56 f.
xvi. 12	57
xvi. 13	61, 87
xvi. 14	62
xvi. 15	62, 83, 234
xvi. 16 ff.	49, 56
xvii. 8 ff.	97, 221
xvii. 18	97
xviii. 7	94
xviii. 15 ff.	106 ff.
xviii. 20 ff.	110
xxi. 5	97
xxiii. 1	97
xxvi. 1 ff.	117
xxvi. 5 ff.	156
xxvi. 16 ff.	14, 141 f.
xxvii. 1 ff.	14
xxvii. 2 ff.	144
xxvii. 7	120
xxvii. 9	97, 142
xxvii. 11 ff.	12, 143 ff.
xxvii. 12 ff.	95
xxvii. 14	94 f., 97
xxvii. 15 ff.	141 f., 234
xxxi. 9 ff.	12, 22, 74 ff., 97, 199, 234
xxxi. 10 ff.	63, 83, 145
xxxiii. 5	203
xxxiii. 8 ff.	96, 110, 112
xxxiii. 19	166
xxxiv. 9	111

JOSHUA

i. 1	111
iii. 1 ff.	125 ff., 153 ff., 161
iii. 3 ff.	94, 153 f., 158
iii. 6	158
iii. 15	44
iv. 3	155
iv. 19	153
iv. 20	153 f.
iv. 22 ff.	157
v. 1 ff.	158
v. 10 ff.	51, 158, 161
v. 11	47 ff., 163
vi. 1 ff.	157, 159 ff.
vi. 6 ff.	86
viii. 30 ff.	144 ff.
viii. 33	94, 127, 144
ix. 6	135, 161
x. 6 ff.	154, 161
xiv. 2	72

	PAGE
xiv. 6	154
xviii. 1	134, 159, 176
xviii. 10	176
xix. 22	165
xix. 51	176
xxii. 10	158
xxiv. 1 ff.	126, 136 ff.
xxiv. 16 ff.	142
xxiv. 23	194
xxiv. 25	137 f., 140 f., 194 f., 199
xxiv. 26	135 ff.

JUDGES

i. 22	44
ii. 1 ff.	146
iv. 6	166
iv. 14	166
v. 1 ff.	167 ff.
v. 13 f.	166
vi. 18 ff.	115, 175
vi. 19	93, 115
viii. 33	135
ix. 27	5, 135 f., 140, 174
ix. 46	135, 140
xi. 30	115
xi. 31	116
xiii. 19 ff.	93, 115, 175
xv. 1	44
xvii. 1 ff.	149
xvii. 5	93
xvii. 7 ff.	95
xvii. 10	94
xviii. 30	93
xx. 1 ff.	173
xx. 18	147
xx. 23 ff.	225
xx. 26 f.	127, 147 f.
xxi. 1 ff.	173
xxi. 2 ff.	225
xxi. 19 ff.	5, 62, 173 f.

RUTH

i. 22	44

I SAMUEL

i. 2 ff.	93
i. 3	174
i. 4	118, 175
i. 9 f.	174 ff.
i. 11	175
i. 17	104
i. 21	118
i. 24	175

PAGE

i. 28 . . . 109
ii. 12 . . . 93, 175
ii. 13 f. . . . 93, 118
ii. 14 . . . 175
ii. 15 . . . 118
ii. 19 . . . 175
ii. 22 . . . 134, 159, 176 f.
ii. 28 . . . 94
ii. 35 . . . 98
iii. 1 ff. . . . 109 ff., 176 ff.
iii. 3 . . . 109, 127, 175
iii. 14 . . . 118
iii. 19 . . . 110
iii. 20 . . . 105, 109
iv. 3 . . . 177
iv. 4 . . . 125 f., 177, 213
iv. 11 . . . 178
iv. 21 . . . 177
v. 5 . . . 96
vi. 1 ff. . . . 8
vi. 2 . . . 96
vi. 5 . . . 178
vi. 7 ff. . . . 182
vi. 12 . . . 178
vi. 13 ff. . . . 178, 182
vi. 14 f. . . . 116, 178
vi. 20 f. . . . 177 f.
vii. 5 f. . . . 105 110, 147, 173, 225 f.
vii. 9 . . . 115
vii. 15 f. . . . 105, 154
viii. 2 . . . 172
ix. 13 . . . 93
x. 3 . . . 148
x. 5 ff. . . . 101
x. 8 . . . 120, 154
x. 17 . . . 173
xi. 7 . . . 119
xi. 13 ff. . . . 120
xi. 14 f. . . . 154
xii. 17 . . . 44
xii. 23 . . . 105
xiii. 7 . . . 154
xiii. 9 . . . 120
xiii. 15 . . . 154
xiv. 34 . . . 93
xv. 1 ff. . . . 179
xvi. 1 . . . 179
xvi. 14 . . . 179
xvii. 45 . . . 213
xix. 19 ff. . . . 101
xx. 5 ff. . . . 76 f.
xx. 18 ff. . . . 76 f.
xxii. 11 . . . 93

PAGE

2. SAMUEL

ii. 1 . . . 103
ii. 4 . . . 223
v. 3 . . . 223
v. 6 . . . 202
v. 9 . . . 223
v. 19 . . . 103
v. 23 . . . 103
vi. 1 ff. . . . 183 ff., 192, 207
vi. 2 . . . 125, 177
vi. 3 ff. . . . 178, 182 ff.
vi. 9 . . . 178
vi. 17 . . . 120
vi. 21 . . . 182
vii. 1 ff. . . . 180, 182 ff., 189, 192, 223 f.
vii. 4 ff. . . . 103
vii. 9 . . . 225
viii. 17 . . . 98
xii. 1 ff. . . . 103
xv. 1 ff. . . . 188
xv. 7 ff. . . . 155
xv. 10 . . . 206
xv. 24 . . . 94, 97
xx. 25 . . . 98
xxi. 9 . . . 44
xxiii. 1 ff. . . . 180
xxiv. 16 ff. . . . 186

1 KINGS

i. 8 . . . 103
i. 11 . . . 206
i. 18 . . . 206
i. 38 ff. . . . 223
ii. 26 . . . 98
iii. 4 . . . 116
iii. 16 ff. . . . 188
vii. 7 . . . 188
viii. 1 ff. . . . 8, 65, 151, 183 f., 187, 207 f.
viii. 9 . . . 125
viii. 12 f. . . . 215
viii. 31 f. . . . 221
viii. 33 . . . 225
viii. 35 . . . 225
viii. 48 f. . . . 230, 233
viii. 63 ff. . . . 120
ix. 25 . . . 49, 57, 65, 116, 120, 208
xi. 29 . . . 102
xii. 1 . . . 145, 148
xii. 11 ff. . . . 105
xii. 25 . . . 145
xii. 28 ff. . . . 148, 150 f.

PAGE

xii. 31 . . . 98, 150 f.
xii. 32 f. . . . 55, 65, 96, 152
xiii. 2 ff. . . . 152
xiii. 11 ff. . . . 102, 105
xv. 9 ff. . . . 193 ff., 196
xv. 12 . . . 59
xviii. 21 . . . 45, 102
xix. 1 ff. . . . 171
xx. 13 ff. . . . 105
xxii. 5 ff. . . . 103 f., 105 ff.
xxii. 19 . . . 106, 216

2 KINGS

ii. 1 ff. . . . 102, 154
ii. 3 ff. . . . 102
ii. 9 ff. . . . 110
iv. 23 . . . 77, 79
iv. 38 . . . 154
vi. 1 ff. . . . 103
ix. 13 . . . 206
xi. 5 ff. . . . 81
xi. 13 ff. . . . 194, 224
xi. 17 . . . 197, 224
xviii. 3 . . . 196
xix. 15 . . . 125 f.
xxii. 1 ff. . . . 50
xxiii. 1 ff. . . . 59, 197 ff.
xxiii. 4 ff. . . . 198
xxiii. 8 . . . 99, 152
xxiii. 9 . . . 96, 99
xxiii. 15 . . . 152
xxiii. 16 ff. . . . 152
xxiii. 21 ff. . . . 54, 208
xxiii. 22 . . . 51 f., 65, 163

1 CHRONICLES

v. 27 ff. . . . 235
xxi. 29 f. . . . 134
xxiii. 31 . . . 78
xxv. 1 ff. . . . 99
xxvi. 1 ff. . . . 99

2 CHRONICLES

i. 3 . . . 134
ii. 3 . . . 78
v. 20 . . . 233
vii. 7 ff. . . . 70, 90
viii. 13 . . . 49, 57, 63
xiii. 11 . . . 233
xv. 10 ff. . . . 58 ff., 194 f.
xv. 12 ff. . . . 194 f.
xxix. 10 f. . . . 197
xxx. 1 ff. . . . 51 f., 235
xxx. 2 . . . 55

	PAGE
xxx. 10 f.	52
xxxvi. 21 f.	76

EZRA

	PAGE
iii. 4	63
v. 14 ff.	232
vi. 3 ff.	232
vi. 19 ff.	54 f.

NEHEMIAH

	PAGE
viii. 1 ff.	61 f., 70
viii. 2	66
viii. 3	234
viii. 6	234
viii. 14 f.	63 ff.
viii. 15 ff.	63, 65, 90
viii. 17	234
viii. 18	67, 234
ix. 1	225
x. 34	78
xiii. 15 ff.	234

ESTHER

	PAGE
iii. 7	91
ix. 19	92

JOB

	PAGE
i. 6 ff.	106
ii. 1 ff.	106
ii. 13	86

PSALMS

	PAGE
ii. 1 ff.	192, 222 ff.
ii. 6	181
ii. 7	181, 224
ii. 8 f.	224
iii. 7	220
iv. 6	220
v. 3	124, 174
vi. 2	219 f.
vii. 3 ff.	221
vii. 7 f.	204
vii. 8	219
viii. 1 ff.	218
ix. 9 ff.	204
ix. 19 f.	204, 220
xv. 1 ff.	13, 211 f.
xv. 1	134
xvii. 3	221
xvii. 13	220
xviii. 8 ff.	220
xviii. 50	181
xx. 3 f.	115 f.
xxii. 1 f.	219
xxii. 3 ff.	219
xxii. 21 f.	219 f., 222
xxii. 26	121, 222
xxiii. 5	121, 222
xxiii. 6	217
xxiv. 1 ff.	13, 204, 211 ff.
xxiv. 7 ff.	205, 207, 213
xxvi. 1	219
xxvii. 5	134
xxvii. 6	124
xxviii. 1 ff.	220
xxx. 1	90
xxxiv. 1 ff.	222
xxxv. 18	222
xxxvi. 9	217
xl. 3	222
xl. 10	222
xli. 4	219
xlii. 1 ff.	209
xlii. 5	211
xliii. 1	219
xliv. 25	225
xlv. 1 ff.	224 f.
xlvi. 1 ff.	201 ff., 210
xlvi. 4	174, 202
xlvi. 5 ff.	202, 217
xlvii. 1 ff.	8, 17, 205
xlvii. 2	204
xlvii. 9	206
xlviii. 1 ff.	201 ff., 210
xlviii. 4 ff.	203
xlviii. 12 f.	208
l. 1 ff.	14, 189, 197, 215 f.
l. 5	120, 142
l. 7 ff.	111, 189
l. 9 ff.	114 f.
l. 14	222
li. 8	219
liv. 8	124
lvi. 1 ff.	220
lvi. 13	124
lx. 8	145
lxi. 5	134
lxv. 9 ff.	202, 217
lxviii. 1 ff.	167 ff.
lxix. 1 ff.	220
lxix. 30	222
lxxii. 1 f.	189
lxxviii. 60	134
lxxx. 1 ff.	215
lxxxi. 1 ff.	14
lxxxi. 3	68, 78
lxxxi. 5	111
lxxxi. 10	111
lxxxiii. 18	204
lxxxiv. 2 ff.	209, 217
lxxxiv. 6 ff.	210
lxxxiv. 10	217
lxxxvii. 1 ff.	210
lxxxvii. 5	202
lxxxix. 1 ff.	186, 192
lxxxix. 3 ff.	181
lxxxix. 13	166
xcii. 10	222
xciii. 1 ff.	8, 17, 204 f.
xciii. 2	207
xcv. 3 ff.	204
xcv. 6	214
xcv. 8 ff.	111, 212
xcvi. 1 ff.	8, 17, 205
xcvi. 9 f.	204, 214
xcvii. 1 ff.	8, 17, 205
xcvii. 9	204
xcviii. 1 ff.	205
xcix. 1 ff.	8, 17, 205, 214
xcix. 9	204, 210
civ. 19	44, 77
cv. 26	94
cvii. 20	220
cvii. 22	120, 222
cvii. 31	222
cviii. 8	145
cix. 30	222
cx. 1 ff.	187, 223 ff.
cx. 3	81, 224
cxiv. 1 ff.	159 f.
cxvi. 13	222
cxvi. 17	222
cxviii. 19	212
cxxi. 1 ff.	218
cxxii. 1 ff.	201, 210 ff.
cxxii. 4 ff.	188 f.
cxxv. 1 ff.	202
cxxvi. 3 ff.	203
cxxx. 5	220
cxxxii. 1 ff.	8, 183 ff., 190, 192, 207, 223
cxxxii. 6	211
cxxxii. 7	214
cxxxvii. 11 f.	181
cxxxvii. 13 f.	215
cxxxvii. 14 ff.	211
cxxxiv. 1 ff.	218
cxxxvi. 1 ff.	215
cxxxvii. 1 ff.	229
cxxxvii. 3	210
cxxxix. 23	221
cl. 1 ff.	215

PAGE

ISAIAH
i. 13 . . . 77, 81
i. 21 . . . 189
i. 26 . . . 189
ii. 2 ff. 189, 197, 202
vi. 1 ff. . . 216
vi. 3 . . . 214
ix. 1 ff. . . 190
xi. 3 f. . . 188
xii. 3 . . . 226
xiv. 13 f. . . 201
xiv. 32 . . 220
xv. 2 . . . 225
xvi. 5 . . . 188
xvii. 12 f. . . 203
xxii. 12 . . 225 f.
xxvi. 1 . . 202
xxviii. 7 f. . . 104
xxix. 1 . . 66
xxix. 4 . . 225
xxix. 10 . . 104
xxx. 29 . . 66, 218
xxxii. 11 . . 225
xxxiii. 20 . . 134
xxxiii. 21 . . 202
xl. 1 ff. . . 230
xlii. 1 ff. . . 231
xlii. 6 . . 231
xlix. 8 . . 231
li. 11 . . . 231
lii. 7 f. . . 231
lii. 10 . . 231
liii. 1 ff. . . 231
liv. 10 . . 231
lvi. 1 ff. . . 232 ff.
lvi. 2 ff. . . 88
lvi. 7 . . . 232
lviii. 3 ff. . . 225
lviii. 13 . . 88
lix. 9 ff. . . 232
lx. 1 ff. . . 232
lxi. 1 . . . 74
lxi. 3 . . . 222
lxii. 1 ff. . . 232
lxvi. 23 . 77 f., 88

JEREMIAH
ii. 6 ff. . . 205
iii. 16 f. . . 126
iv. 8 . . . 225
vi. 14 . . . 104
vi. 26 . . . 225
vii. 2 . . 12 ff., 176
vii. 22 . . 112
xiv. 12 . 115 f., 225 f.
xiv. 13 . . 104
xvii. 4 . . 76
xxi. 12 . . 188
xxiii. 18 . . 106
xxiii. 26 ff. . . 106
xxv. 11 . . 76
xxvi. 7 ff. . . 104
xxvi. 9 . . 176
xxviii. 1 ff. . . 104
xxix. 13 . . 205
xxx. 21 f. . 200, 223
xxxiii. 21 94, 119, 181
xxxiv. 8 f. . 74, 200
xxxiv. 15 ff. . . 74
xxxiv. 18 . . 119
xxxvi. 6 ff. . . 225
xli. 5 . . 210, 228
xlvi. 18 . . 166

LAMENTATIONS
ii. 1 ff. . . 227
ii. 15 . . . 202
ii. 19 . . . 225
iv. 22 . . . 228

EZEKIEL
i. 1 ff. . . 229
viii. 1 . . 229
xiv. 1 . . . 229
xx. 1 . . . 229
xx. 12 ff. . . 87 f.
xxii. 8 . . 88
xxiii. 38 . . 88
xxviii. 11 ff. . 202
xl. 1 . . . 67, 84
xl. 46 . . . 98
xliii. 19 . . 99
xliv. 15 ff. . . 93, 99
xlv. 7 ff. . . 235
xlv. 17 . . 78
xlv. 20 ff. 66 ff., 68 ff.
xlv. 21 ff. . . 45, 58
xlv. 25 . . 66
xlvi. 1 ff. . . 77, 88
xlvi. 6 f. . . 77 f.
xlvi. 17 . . 74
xlvii. 1 ff. . . 202

DANIEL
vi. 10 . . . 230

HOSEA
ii. 7 . . . 131
ii. 10 . . . 39
ii. 13 . . 77 f., 79
ii. 16 . . . 131 f.
iv. 15 . . . 154
v. 1 . . . 166
vi. 9 . . . 145
vii. 14 . . 225
viii. 6 . . 152
ix. 5 . . 63, 132
ix. 7 . . . 102
ix. 10 . . . 131
ix. 15 . . . 154
xi. 1 . . . 131
xii. 9 . . 64, 131
xii. 12 . . 154

JOEL
i. 5 . . . 225
i. 8 f. . . . 225
i. 13 f. . . 225
ii. 1 . . . 225
ii. 13 . . . 225
ii. 15 f. . . 225
ii. 17 . . . 225
iii. 18 . . 202

AMOS
i. 2 . . . 189
iv. 4 . . 120, 152
iv. 5 . . . 121
v. 5 . . 152, 173
v. 25 . . . 112
vii. 13 149, 152, 187
viii. 1 ff. . . 62
viii. 5 . . 77, 79
viii. 14 . . 173

MICAH
i. 2 ff. . . 189
i. 8 . . . 225 f.
i. 10 . . . 225
i. 16 . . . 225
iii. 5 f. . . 103
iv. 1 ff. . . 189
iv. 14 . . . 225
v. 1 ff. . . 190
vi. 6 ff. . . 116 f.

HAGGAI
ii. 1 . . . 233
ii. 6 ff. . . 233
ii. 23 . . . 233

PAGE

ZECHARIAH
ii. 8 . . . 233
ii. 16 . . . 233
iii. 1 ff. . . . 233
iv. 1 ff. . . . 233
iv. 9 ff. . . . 233
vi. 15 . . . 233
vii. 1 ff. . . . 229
vii. 5 . . . 263
viii. 3 . . . 233
viii. 19 . . . 263
xii. 12 ff. . . . 225
xiv. 8 . . . 202
xiv. 16 . . . 63, 66
xiv. 18 f. . . . 63

MALACHI
i. 6 ff. . . . 234
ii. 10 ff. . . . 234
iii. 6 ff. . . . 234

INDEX OF SUBJECTS

Aaron, 99, 120, 129, 132 f., 147, 235
Abib, 26 ff., 44, 50
Abimelech, 135
abiuratio, 221
Acclamation, 139 f., 154, 179
Adoption, 181
Adoration, 8, 43 f., 158, 183, 186, 210 f.
Agriculture, 5, 36 ff., 43, 46 f., 63, 71
Akkadian, 91
Altar, 7, 69, 90, 93, 98, 115, 121, 158, 172
Amarna letters, 119, 139
Amphictyony, *see* Confederacy of Twelve Tribes
Animism, 24
Apotropaic rite, 46
Archaeology, 6 ff., 159 f.
Architecture, sacral, 186 f.
Ark, 69, 94 ff., 109, 120, 125 ff., 147 ff., 153 ff., 163 f., 173 ff., 177 ff., 192, 201, 203, 207, 211 ff., 220
—— stations of, 127, 151
Astral mythology, 42
Astronomy, 44
Atonement, 116 f., 121 f., 231
—— feast of, 6, 68 ff., 132

Baal, 39 ff., 48, 85 ff., 114, 117, 131, 150, 169 f., 201 f., 207
Babylonia, 6 ff., 17, 21, 46, 54, 79, 81 ff., 202, 226 f.
Beersheba, 172 ff.
Bethel, 55, 65, 102, 127, 134, 146 ff., 164, 172
Blessing, 5, 14, 39, 48, 94, 104, 138, 143, 218
Booths, 63 f., 132, 234
'Bronze Sea', 187

Calendars, 5 f., 11, 26 ff., 38 ff., 43 ff., 52 f., 58, 67 f., 82 ff.
Calf image, 98, 149 f.
Canaan, 5 f., 36 ff., 44, 47 f., 57, 63 f., 71 f. 78 f., 85 ff., 95, 111, 113, 123, 134 f., 146 f., 150 f., 169, 174, 201 ff., 204, 214
Candlestick, golden, 233
Canon, 234 f.
Central sanctuary, 49, 55, 77, 81, 94, 97 ff., 110, 127, 156, 164, 168, 173 ff., 201 ff.
'Centralization', 8, 31, 49 f., 57, 78, 121, 127, 141, 199
Charisma, 103 ff., 109 ff., 166, 180 f.
communio, 114 ff., 118 ff., 136, 175, 222
Comparative religion, 1, 21, 150, 205
Confederacy of Twelve Tribes, 24, 36, 94, 125 ff., 133, 136 ff., 147 ff., 153 f., 162 f., 166, 178, 181, 190, 195 f., 199
Confession of faith, 87, 222, 230
Covenant, 13 f., 50, 60, 86, 137 ff., 189 ff., 195 f.
—— ideology, 23, 209
—— mediator, 108 ff., 137 f., 141 f., 195, 200, 231, 232
—— renewal, 13 ff., 23, 60, 108 f., 111, 141 ff., 196 ff., 234 f.
—— sign, 88, 230
—— with David, 180 f., 189 ff., 195 f.
—— with Levi, 84 f.
Cyrus cylinder, 231

Dance, 45, 174
Debts, release from, 72, 75
Decalogue, 9, 12 ff., 29 f., 78 ff., 108 f., 111, 151
Demonic, 46 f., 133
'Denaturalization', 5 f., 9
Desert, 24, 36, 46, 69, 71, 96, 112, 125 ff., 130 ff., 203
Designation, 179 ff., 192
Deuteronomistic history, 51 f., 59 f., 136, 191 ff.
Diaspora, 91 f., 236
Dodecalogue, 141 ff.
Drama, 9 ff., 14, 39 f.

Ebal, 143 f., 164 f.
Ecstasy, 101 ff., 212
Egypt, 9, 21, 40, 42, 47, 53, 132, 160
Elamite, 91

Encampment, 69, 128 ff., 161 f.
Enthronement, Davidic dynasty, 195, 222 ff.
—— *see also* Yahweh.
Entrance liturgy, 13, 211 f.
Entrance Torah, 211 f.
Eschatology, 8 ff., 17, 197, 230 f.
Etanim, 44, 186
Exile, 24, 34 f., 74, 76, 87, 229 ff.

Fallow, 70 ff., 79 f.
Fasts, 68 f., 115, 147 f., 173, 225 f., 230
First-fruits, firstlings, 6, 27, 117 f.
Form criticism, 10 ff., 22 ff., 74, 107, 124, 138, 141 f., 156

Gerizim, 54 f., 143 f., 164 f.
Gezer calendar, 38
Gift offering, 113 ff.
Gilgal, 51, 94, 102, 127, 134, 152 ff., 172

Hammurabi dynasty, 81
Hands, filling, 93 ff.
—— laying on, 111
Hanukkah, feast of, 88 ff.
Harvest, festival of, 5 f., 8, 38 f., 43 f., 48 ff., 56 ff., 70, 73, 134 f., 151, 217
Hasmoneans, 235
Hebron, 129
'High places', 99, 150
'Historicizing', 45 ff., 49, 57, 64, 163
History, 4, 21, 76, 89, 180 ff.
—— redemptive, 5 f., 47, 53, 122, 139
Hittite treaties, 138 ff.
Holiness Code, 34 ff., 52 f., 69, 73, 76
Holy of Holies, 187
Homage, 115 f., 125, 224
Human sacrifice, 117 f.
Hymns, 210 ff., 214

Institutions, 23 ff., 70 ff., 75 f., 101, 129, 133, 150 f., 188, 192, 201, 205
Intercalation, 43 ff., 76 f., 84
Intercession, 105 f., 109 f., 231
Itineraries, 134

Jebusites, 126, 181, 201 ff., 214, 223
Jericho, 86, 153, 158, 159 ff.
Jerusalem, 17, 24, 28, 50 ff., 54 f., 89, 94, 98, 126, 134, 141, 148 f., 168, 177, 179 ff., 201 ff., 208 f., 222 ff.
Jezreel, 165 ff.
Jordan, 154 ff.
Josiah's reform, 50 f., 59, 76, 198
Joy, 77, 92, 118, 136, 177 f., 217, 226, 234
Jubilee, year of, 73 f.
Judah, 45, 52, 145, 190, 196

Kadesh, 96
Kingdom of Israel, 179 ff., 189 ff., 211 ff.

Lamentation, 48, 218 ff., 225 ff., 230, 232
Law, 4 f., 13 f., 27 ff., 50, 59, 66 f., 112, 125 f., 140, 188 f., 197, 234 f.
Levites, 94 ff., 112, 129, 151, 199, 235
Libation, 222
Lights, feast of, 7, 90
Lot, sacred, 72, 130, 176 f.
—— oracle, 91, 97, 100, 110
lustrum, 41

Maccabees, Books of, 1 and 2, 89 ff.
Magic, 22, 117, 119, 123, 217
Marduk, 7 f., 91, 231
Mari texts, 119
Markets, 82 f.
Melchizedek, 98, 187, 224
Mesopotamia, 40, 43 ff., 205
Messiah, 107, 190, 200
Migration, 24, 46 f., 130 f.
Minoan scripts, 95
Mishnah, 7, 67, 84
Mizpah, 147, 173
Month, lunar, 43 ff., 67 f., 76 ff., 79 ff.
Mot, 39 f., 85
Mountain of gods, 168 ff., 201 ff.
Mourning, 86
Music, 102, 214 f.
Myth, 2, 9, 15 ff., 18, 21, 85 f., 92, 117, 150, 180, 201, 203, 207
Mythology, 39, 202

Nature cult, 2, 4 f., 38 f., 44, 79, 131, 150, 175, 207
New year festival, 6, 7 ff., 15 ff., 43 f., 62, 67
New moon, 68, 76 ff.
Nomadic way of life, 24, 45 ff., 71, 112, 130 f., 162
Northern Kingdom, 24, 52, 54, 65, 98, 103, 145, 148 ff., 169
'Number saying', 85 ff.
nundinae, 82

Oaths, 174, 234

Passover, feast of, 4, 27 ff., 45 ff., 73, 83, 93, 113, 161 ff., 208, 235
Peace offering, 118 ff., 147, 226
Pentateuch, 4 ff., 26 ff., 74, 128

Pentateuch sources, 4 ff., 20, 26, 154 f.
Periods, 41 f., 56 ff., 76, 82
Phenomenology, 14 ff., 19 ff., 209
Pilgrimage, 7, 45, 47, 50, 57, 62, 140, 148, 174 f., 183, 209 f., 218, 232
—— hymn, 188 f.
Pleiades, 57, 86
Priests, 6, 43 ff., 93 ff., 133, 166 f., 217, 234
—— priestly knowledge, 43 ff., 100
—— priest king, 223 f.
Prophets, 101 ff., 180 f., 190, 220, 223, 230, 233
—— court prophets, 103 ff.,
—— cultic prophets, 101 ff., 183 f., 187, 211, 226, 233
Proscription texts, 224
Purim, feast of, 91 ff.

Ras Shamra texts, *see* Ugarit
Rain, 38 ff., 169
Release, year of, 12, 22, 70 ff., 145
Religion, 3, 5 f., 9, 15 f., 36 ff., 79, 85 ff., 149 f., 201
Renunciation, 139 f., 191 ff.
Revelation, 3 f., 105 f., 108, 123, 139, 170
Rhythm, seasonal, 38 f., 207
Rites, 7, 10, 15, 21, 27, 34 f., 36, 45 ff., 55, 68 f., 70, 79, 86, 99, 115 f., 123, 129, 173, 208, 221, 224

Sabbath, 27, 56, 66, 68, 70 f., 78 ff., 87 f., 230
Sabbatical year, 27 ff., 70 ff., 145
Sacrament, 9
Sacrifice, 5, 34 ff., 43, 46, 53, 66, 77 f., 88, 93 ff., 97, 110, 112 ff., 144, 147, 172, 208, 225 f.
—— sacrificial meal, 77 f., 114 ff., 118 ff., 135 f.
—— sacrificial omen, 119
—— sacrificial Torah, 101, 116 ff., 124
saeculum, 41
Salvation, oracle, 104 f., 175, 220, 223
—— message 104 ff., 119, 131, 230
Samaria, 152, 234
—— Samaritans, 51 f., 54, 145
Sanctuary, 8, 36 ff., 47, 63, 66, 93 ff., 102 f., 125, 134 ff., 153 f., 179 ff., 210, 225 ff., 231 f.
Second Isaiah, 17, 228 f., 230, 232, 236
Sed festival, 41
Seers, 95 f.
Seleucids, 89, 235
Self-examination, 212
'Setting in life', 11 ff., 22, 167, 223, 225
Seven, number, 42, 85 ff.
Shechem, 94, 127, 134 ff., 149, 153, 163, 174
Shiloh, 102, 105, 109, 125, 127, 163, 173 ff., 213
Sinai pericope, 9, 12 ff., 23, 58, 107 f., 120, 156, 170 f., 189 ff., 200
Sirius 43
Sociology, 46, 72 f., 130
Solar year, 43 ff., 77
Sowing, 38 f., 44, 73
Spirits, 36 f.
State, 24, 44
—— cult, 55, 65, 103, 105, 148 ff., 182, 187, 211
Succession, 109 ff.
Symbolism, 1 ff., 9, 42, 151, 177
Synagogue, 230

Tabernacles, feast of, 7 ff., 12 f., 55, 61 ff., 82 f., 87, 90, 134 ff., 173 ff., 186 ff., 208 f., 228, 234
Tabor, 165 ff.
Temple, 28, 57, 69, 77, 78, 88, 90, 98 f., 104, 116, 126, 134, 148 ff., 175 f., 186 f., 204, 207, 223, 227, 232 ff.
—— dedication of, 88 f., 185
Tent, 46, 54, 128 ff., 162 f.
—— festival, 54, 131 ff.
—— sanctuary, 68, 129 ff., 164, 176
Terebinth, 135, 140
Thanksgiving, hymn, 221 f., 225 ff.,
—— sacrifice, 121, 222
Theophany, 13 f., 115, 119, 146, 170 f., 220, 229 f.
Titus, Arch of, 233
Torah, 34, 74, 125
—— stele, 144
Tradition, history of, 8, 10, 20 f., 29 f., 58, 66, 68 f., 109, 129, 136, 155 ff., 170
Trumpets, 66 ff.
Turn of year, 7 ff., 43 ff., 67, 206 f.
Types, literary, 10 ff., 34 f., 91, 222 f.

Ugarit, 16, 21, 39 ff., 105 ff., 113 ff., 150, 201 ff., 204 ff.
Unleavened Bread, feast of, 27 ff., 47 ff., 73, 83, 87, 162 f.

Victory, song of, 167
Visions, 105, 220

War, holy, 8, 120, 147 f., 166

Weeks, feast of, 27, 55 ff.
Wen Amun, 102

Yahweh; anger of, 22
—— council of, 106
—— enthronement of, 8 ff., 13 f., 23, 58, 205 ff.
—— glory of, 128 f., 133
—— judgement of, 100 f.
—— kingship of, 8 ff., 16 ff., 203 ff., 213
—— law of, 10 ff., 74 f., 95, 97, 108, 110, 117, 123, 140 f., 166 f., 176, 188 ff., 212
Yahweh, messenger of, 103 ff.
—— Spirit of, 179 ff.
—— throne of, 149 f., 177, 192, 202, 207
Yam, 40

Zadokites, 98 ff., 235
Zaphon, 168 f., 202 f.
Zeus Olympius, 89
Zion, 8, 168, 179 ff., 201 ff., 209 ff., 222 ff.